Women of the Celts

Jean Markale

Translated by
A. Mygind, C. Hauch and P. Henry

Inner Traditions International, Ltd.
Rochester, Vermont

Inner Traditions International, Ltd.
Park Street
Rochester, Vermont 05767

First U.S. edition 1986 by Inner Traditions
First published in French under the title *La Femme Celte* by
Editions Payot in 1972.
Copyright © 1972 by Editions Payot
English Translation copyright © 1975 by A. Mygind,
C. Hauch and P. Henry.

**LIBRARY OF CONGRESS CATALOGING IN
PUBLICATION DATA**

Markale, Jean.
　Women of the Celts.

　Translation of: La femme celte.
　Includes bibliographical references and index.
　1. Women, Celtic—History. 2. Civilization, Celtic.
3. Women in literature. I. Title.
HQ1137.C45M313　　1986　　305.4′2′094　　86-20128
ISBN 0-89281-150-1 (pbk.)
ISBN 0-89281-201-X (cloth)

10　9　8　7　6　5　4　3　2

Printed and bound in the United States of America

Distributed to the book trade in the United States by Harper &
Row Publishers, Inc.

Distributed to the book trade in Canada by Book Center, Inc.,
Montreal, Quebec

Dounoc'h eo kaloun ar merc'hed 'vit ar mor douna euz ar bed
(The heart of woman is deeper than the deepest sea in the world)

Breton proverb from the Île de Batz

To Heather Gordon Cremonesi

Contents

Introduction

Twentieth century "Western" society has become so evidently discontented that everyone is doing his utmost to find some kind of solution, whether by "revolutionary" or "reformist" means. We can dispose of the reformist solutions immediately as they stand little chance of leading to positive results; superficial repairs never amount to more than plastering over holes while waiting for further cracks to appear. The replacement of worn-out parts does not make a new engine; at best it may make it start up a few more times and so prolong hope; but the final breakdown will be all the more spectacular, proscribing any options. Revolutionary solutions, on the other hand, have no real value unless they primarily relate, not to a change of social structure, but to a change of mental attitudes. In fact, it is sheer hoodwinking to put forward scintillating new schemes which, on analysis, turn out to be the same old shabby principles under a different name. Besides, social structures are abstractions that attain reality only through men's activities; their value depends on mankind itself, especially on its aims.

As shown by its cultural past, contemporary society is based on a gigantic swindle. This swindle, now being challenged timidly, is inherent in all political, religious, social, economic and cultural problems. Essentially it consists of the relationship between men and women. This relationship conditions the married couple and therefore the family, the basic unit of society. It is much more important to challenge the preposterous relationship that has existed between men and women for centuries, even thousands of years, than it is to burble on about "class war", because, if we are successful in demonstrating the swindle (basically the aim of this book), the whole of Western society (including the so-called Marxist societies, which are mere heresies of the West) stands to lose its basic assumption that "man is biologically superior to woman".

There is no need to go into details of customs and habits: they develop with the rhythm of history. Much more solid realities exist. They have persisted from the dawn of what we call "civilisation", until the present day. These realities are the "mental attitudes" handed down from generation to generation. Sometimes they appear in shimmering new colours, but they nevertheless remain constant. Without them — and, above all, without their permanence — our society could not exist. These mental attitudes are the self-evident first principles of society, the product of a great synthesis of Judaic, Roman, and Christian traditions. In fact, society is but an essential biological *modus vivendi*; without it mankind would lose a vital element of its humanity, namely its sociability. But a *modus vivendi* is created by the human spirit and is adapted to the needs of the human race, to its limitations and aspirations. We forget the latter far too often.

Every *modus vivendi* depends on conventions and basic assumptions. Mathematics, a key factor in technical progress, is no exception to this rule. For centuries mathematics has been based on Euclid's famous assumption: "Through a point outside a straight line one may draw a parallel to this straight line, and only one." This assumption could not be proved, of course, but it was beyond dispute. No one could cast any doubt on the validity of such a proposition; and from it a perfectly logical and coherent system, which gave undeniable practical results, was gradually built up. Thus Euclid's basic assumption became a mental attitude which was handed on unchallenged.

However, not only is this assumption unprovable, but it is also out of touch with reality, because there is no such thing as a straight line. This fact allowed Rieman to put forward another proposition: "Through a point outside a straight line, no parallel to this straight line may be drawn." On this, as on Lobatchevsky's assumption ("An infinity of parallels may be drawn"), a perfectly coherent system could be built. The domination of Euclidean mathematics was at an end; the door was opened to the boldest explorations of reality. Reality had been hidden behind the mists of established and inherited mental attitudes, not unlike the "deceptive illusions" that the genius of Pascal could discern in the depths of every human being.

The assumption that man is superior to woman is fundamental in our society. Few people doubt this, least of all women themselves, and we must examine its basis. It might seem obvious that women are incapable of heavy work, which is therefore reserved for members of the so-called stronger sex. But people who claim this as basic truth have certainly never seen an old peasant woman working in the fields; nor can they have given much thought to the fact that women live longer than men, even allowing for the mortality rate from maternity (in which lies the real weakness of the female constitution). Women have not always been considered weak in relation to men. Just as the division of labour requires some people to be dependent on others, as Jean-Jacques Rousseau showed in his excellent *Discours sur l'origine de l'inégalité*, so it has brought about inequality between men and women, men keeping the *noble* tasks to themselves, thus retaining their freedom and safeguarding their authority, while the humbler chores were foisted onto the women.

Because civilisation depended on output for its survival, it was necessary to eliminate from productive life anything that might reduce this output. Women, with their power of diverting men sexually, had to be removed from the system and confined to the role (indispensable, of course) of child-bearing. This is not to suggest that humanity experienced happy periods in the beginning of time with a perfect state of harmony between men and women, nor to praise the ancient so-called matriarchal societies by contrasting them with existing patriarchal ones. We have to go back beyond history and examine every aspect of the ancient myths, and so bring to light again what history has forgotten. Then we may be able to demystify an assumption that is perhaps no longer valid now that the concept of work is changing and society is passing from the stage of unadulterated profit motive to one of consumer orientation.

The idea of male superiority, which is an attitude of mind, is so powerful, so general and so normal that we must acquire it in some way at birth. The whole of a child's upbringing is based on this sexual inequality. A boy is conditioned to behave differently from a girl: he must not cry or be soft like her; he must assume responsibilities for himself and her as well; he must protect her (which means reducing her to a state of inferiority); and he must work for his future and play only boys' games. The girl is given to understand that some things are not for her. She must play with dolls, be self-effacing and reserved (if not actually timid), be content to take second place, be aware of her frailness (she is told this constantly, so she believes it in the end). She must prepare for her future role as a good housewife and mother of a family: an inferior role, being deprived of freedom.

Mothers pass this mental attitude on to their children, just as their own mothers did to them. There has been no change in thousands of years. The attitude has been sustained by the essentially masculine morality which has governed us since Moses, and by every religion, particularly Christianity (although at first Christianity made itself out to be a doctrine for the liberation of women, which explains why they received it so favourably). There is no apparent reason why it should change. This acceptance led Freud to formulate the most ridiculous, reactionary and anti-feminist of all his theories: woman is inferior because she lacks something, and "penis-envy" conditions all her behaviour! This idea was immediately taken up by all the other psychoanalysts. There is no doubt that women do lack something, but that "something" is entirely psychological. Man stole it from her at some vague point in history, and women, at first in resignation, later through mental conditioning, made themselves unwitting accomplices of this masculine fraud. Now its effects rebound on our society, which is incapable of finding an equilibrium precisely because this mental attitude no longer corresponds to the needs of the species.

Realities must be faced. That is why the basic assumption of this work will be distinctly Marxist, without extending into theories of historical materialism. In the beginning there was little to distinguish the human species from rival animals all over the world. From the moment *Homo faber* became *Homo sapiens* and slowly became aware of his intelligence, we can see the elements of a rudimentary dialectic: material conditions engendered mental attitudes; these reacted back on material conditions, which evolved and even transcended themselves. This was the beginning of human progress. In practical terms, man found himself prey to the basic threefold preoccupation of the primitive creature: food, shelter (from weather, illness or enemies), and reproduction. He was forced to find answers to these problems: he organised his life. This organisation became essential and, just like mental attitudes, imposed itself on the real world to which it tried to adapt. Conditions of life are changed in this way.

It is almost certain that there were several human races, even species. One of these must eventually have outstripped the others, probably because of its superior mental outlook. So we come to the later Palaeolithic period, about 40,000 B.C., when, as far as we know, man became artist, philosopher and *Homo religiosus* for the first time. His way of life was that of nomadic hunters: large groups followed the wild herds, which provided most of their subsistence, the rest coming from fruit gathering. The ice age descended, so the need for shelter was added to the need to hunt; hence the importance of caves. But, as game became ever more scarce, man developed the idea of breeding animals himself, and this was the beginning of nomadic, pastoral peoples, whose earliest records are in the Jewish Bible.

Mental attitudes must have changed considerably to meet the demands of circumstance. The inability to adapt probably led to the disappearance of some groups. However, we can evaluate these attitudes only in so far as they have been expressed in artistic form. On the cave walls and in the tombs of late Palaeolithic man we mainly find hunting scenes and female representations, such as the Venus of Lespugue or the Venus of Willendorff, statuettes with greatly exaggerated sexual characteristics, showing that woman's sexuality was a major preoccupation of these peoples.

Woman is the most mysterious phenomenon in nature. We know from ethnological studies that, among people usually classed as "primitive" (a description valid only in the chronological sense), the reproductive function of woman has always aroused a mixed reaction of wonder and fear. Perhaps this is one of the reasons for misogyny, even gynaephobia, which we find in all our so-called "developed" societies. This awe was the more genuine and frightening since man, i.e. the male, did not have a clear picture of how conception took place. He almost certainly questioned his own function.[1] As Gustave Welter said, "Primitive people had difficulty in realising that an act so swift and in their eyes so common and natural could result in the birth of a human being. Such an extraordinary event could have no ordinary cause."[2] Did a spirit introduce a seed into the woman's body? This belief is elaborated in the Rabbinical texts about Eve, into whom the snake thrust its defilement. It would give some justification for assuming that primitive people believed the male had no part in conception.

All this relates to very early and almost unknown times, prior to the cult of the phallus, or Priapism, which probably marked a reversal of values and an understanding of the precise role of the male in copulation. Before this "phallic" stage woman was a magical creature, in touch with the divinities and uniquely indispensable for the survival of the species; a creature precious enough to be both protected (already!) and carried off from a neighbouring tribe when the chance arose. But fertility was not associated with sexuality.[3] It is just probable (for there is no proof)[4] that these ancient societies had a sexual freedom infinitely greater than any we know, a kind of promiscuity comparable with the contemporary practice of group marriage.[5]

These beliefs must have given woman a predominant social role and resulted in the worship of a goddess, or at least a divinity with female characteristics. This is found at the beginning of all civilisations.[6] They must also have had some matriarchal characteristics.[7] Little exists to confirm or deny the extent of the purely matriarchal society, but it may be claimed, in contradiction of Freud, who takes great pains in *Totem and Taboo* to prove the existence of a primitive father figure, that this was the Golden Age for women. (All his life Freud was burdened by the memory of the scene when his own mother tried to throw herself and him in the path of a train.) The oldest myths match the observations of the ethnologists. In the beginning, humanity was convinced that woman was mainly responsible for procreation, and the first divine being worshipped was the mother goddess.

When the male began to assert that he was essential to fertilisation, the old mental attitudes suddenly collapsed. This was a very important revolution in man's history, and it is astonishing that it is not rated equally with the wheel, agriculture and the use of metals. The male, who had been inferior or equal to the woman, now became superior. This was expressed in myths by the appearance of god-husbands to the original mother goddess. As the male had, in a way, been cheated for centuries, he was going to take his revenge. Equality was no longer enough: he now understood the full implications of his power, and was going to dominate.

This revolution coincided with a basic development for humanity, that of agriculture, which took place during the Neolithic period, around 8,000 B.C. in the East and 4,000 B.C. in the West, and was of great importance because it enabled humanity to settle down. But this radical change of life-style must also have changed attitudes. Neolithic culture is basic to all our modern societies, even the industrial. The male, strengthened by his new-found confidence, seized the opportunity of assuming all rights for himself. He did the agricultural work — admittedly heavy — by himself and foisted the purely domestic chores onto the female. The typical married couple of the twentieth century still lives in this way The "little woman at home" was invented by Neolithic people and became an attitude of mind impossible to eradicate without tearing off the mask that hides society's shortcomings.

Along with agriculture came the division of labour. Some tilled the soil and others guarded the flocks; some were hunters, while others made tools. We know Jean-Jacques Rousseau's arguments showing the origins of inequality: each person depended on someone else, with the exception of one whose activity was so crucial that he could make all the others conform to him. He did not necessarily have to be the strongest, but he was certainly the cleverest. A well-known example was the caste of blacksmiths, who were later to become outcasts on the fringes of society. This was a clear reminder of the original revolt against the Father, and symbolised by the lame Hephaistos, banished to the bowels of the earth. He was replaced in heaven by Zeus, who castrated his own father Chronos, and became the purified, righteous and forgiving version of Hephaistos.

All this happened to the detriment of woman. From then on all societies were to become patriarchal. New legends and myths proliferated to match the new mental outlook. This was the time when the sun hero, also called the "hero of physical strength", appeared. His most perfect example in the Mediterranean was

Heracles. The most enigmatic was Apollo, worshipped at Delphi; he conquered the snake Python, who was a female version of the Earth divinity. Himself a sun god, it seems that he was a masculine version of the original sun goddess, who, under the name Artemis, was demoted, becoming associated with the moon.

Just as Christianity was unable to stamp out pagan ideas and had to give its blessing to beliefs and customs of Celtic Druidism and other religions, the new myths never quite superseded the old. Artemis was still there, Aphrodite increased in importance, Hera stood up to Zeus in argument, Demeter went on changing the seasons. The beautiful Apollo, although he was the champion of the new outlook, needed a woman to make himself understood by humans: the whole Mediterranean constantly lent an ear to the Oracle of Delphi. When an old feminine myth became troublesome, it was either ridiculed or inverted and given a male image. Great pains were taken to show women in the worst possible light. The myth of Pandora unleashing evil on the world resembles that of Eve, and especially the story of the disturbing Lilith, who, being the most dangerous and subversive threat to the established male order, was buried in the furthest depths of the Hebrew unconscious.

There are innumerable reasons for this "eclipse" of woman and what she originally represented. It seems to have reached its zenith in Greek classical society, with the semi-official functions of the courtesans and hetairai, and, above all, with the introduction of paederasty as a system of education; in early Rome, where it was exemplified by Cato the Elder; in France at the beginning of feudalism; and, finally, in Western Europe at the end of the nineteenth and the beginning of the twentieth centuries, with the triumph of puritanism, misogyny and hypocrisy.

When Rome spread its empire over the whole Mediterranean and into part of Western Europe, care was taken to eliminate anything that might harm its socio-political organisation. This is very evident in Celtic countries: the Romans pursued the Druids until they disappeared into Gaul and later into Britain. The Druids represented an absolute threat to the Roman State, because their science and philosophy dangerously contradicted Roman orthodoxy. The Romans were materialist, the Druids spiritual. For the Romans the State was a monolithic structure spread over territories deliberately organised into a hierarchy. With the Druids it was a freely consented moral order with an entirely mythical central idea. The Romans based their law on the private ownership of land, with property rights entirely vested in the head of the family, whereas the Druids always considered ownership collective. The Romans looked upon women as bearers of children and objects of pleasure, while the Druids included women in their political and religious life. We can thus understand how seriously the subversive thought of the Celts threatened the Roman order, even though it was never openly expressed. The talent of the Romans in ridding themselves of the Gallic and British élites is always considered astonishing, but this leaves out of account the fact that it was a matter of life or death to Roman society.

Christianity inherited all the structures of the Roman State and continued to destroy Celtic values systematically when it launched itself upon Western Europe. They represented the same danger to the temporal institutions of the Church. This is shown in the struggle of the Papacy against the Celtic Churches of Ireland, Britain and Brittany, who clung to their own doctrines; in the preference shown the Saxon Church over the British Church, which eventually enabled the Saxons to conquer Britain; and, finally, in the treachery of the Pope in the twelfth century in handing Ireland over to Henry Plantagenet and the Anglo-Normans, with consequences we all know. Societies that are determinedly patriarchal have at all times been suspicious of everything Celtic (official Christianity is a notable example), because Celtic thought is not consistent with the patriarchal ideal. So Celtic culture almost disappeared completely, choked by Graeco-Roman culture, aided to some extent by the Germanic, which was no threat to their order. It is interesting to note that when the role of women has blossomed to some extent, it has been, if only in a limited way, in periods marked by a certain renaissance of Celtic thought: the Courtly Period in the twelfth and thirteenth centuries coincided with the reappearance of old Celtic legends in European literature. The present day, when we shall no doubt see women genuinely reinstated to their proper role, is also a time for rediscovering Celtic culture in all its aspects. Another interesting fact is that the great sanctuaries dedicated to the worship of the Virgin Mary (for example, the cathedral at Puy-en-Velay, or Notre Dame at Chartres) are mostly sited in places consecrated to a female Celtic divinity.[8]

It is not a matter of eulogising Celtic societies, whether Breton, Welsh, Irish or even Gallic. We must not delude ourselves: they were and still are patriarchal societies. The Celts were Indo-Europeans, who were all ardent advocates of the patriarchal idea. Though the Celts imposed their social customs, language and a single religion on the indigenous populations that they subdued, they were only a small intellectual and warrior élite, who assimilated systems that were not their own. Among the people they conquered and ruled were all the survivors of previous civilisations gathered around the Atlantic fringe and retaining their own ways of thought. Archaisms that show a more pronounced non-Indo-European influence are more numerous in Wales and Ireland than on the continent itself.

Here it is necessary to observe that the Celts, as inheritors of non-patriarchal societies, stood halfway between these and the patriarchal Indo-European societies other than their own. This fundamental observation is based on the well-documented knowledge we have of Celtic law, where women enjoyed privileges that would have made the Roman women of the same period green with envy. Here was a harmony between the roles of men and women that was not dependent on the superiority of one sex over the other, but on an equality in which each could feel comfortable. For we must avoid the opposite error: men should not allow themselves to be dominated by women (even when they deserve it) or society would again be out of balance.[9]

Then there are the myths. Not everything was perfect in Celtic society, and, as the Celts were particularly noted for their anti-historical attitude, and aspired to a history rather than living it, we have no alternative but to refer to the Celtic legends about women. They will be revealing on two different levels: first, because legends hand down the realities of the past in a symbolic fashion; second, because they transcend reality and become the purest expression of a people's ideals. We may go even further: the Celts were a people who had always dreamed their history, so we shall not discover the basis of their thought in historical events, but in their myths, which are a faithful reflection of that thought.[10]

These legends are open to interpretation and they are meant to be -- otherwise they would only be pretty stories for children; but it should be borne in mind that the Celtic system of logic has little in common with the one generally dispensed by our Graeco-Roman education. It is generally claimed that we are reviving the ancient legends, bringing them up to date and living them again, because human beings need to identify with a myth that transcends and connects them to higher values, whether political, religious or artistic. But surely an identification is an interpretation. Myths are keys to the imagination; otherwise they would not exist, or would have been forgotten. There is nothing more tenacious than a myth: it is a channelling of thought. As Mircea Éliade says, it is a "a true story because it always refers to reality" (*Aspects of the Myth*).

To return to a Marxist line of argument: man should know and interpret his history, and, allowing for a few modifications, project it into the future. In the Celtic sphere, history is the myth; that is to say, a knowledge of history is already to be found on a mythical level, and at this point the thought provoked by the myth takes on an active power because it influences real life. Perhaps Evhémére was right when he said that myths were historical events with a bias and that the gods were deified heroes. But he saw only one side of the problem, as the dialectic process history-into-myth is ambivalent and may easily become reversed as myth-into-history. Without trying to find out which came first, which would be like the story of the chicken and the egg, let us confine ourselves to stating that the myth has always had an effect upon history; otherwise many powerful figures in history would not have behaved as they did and, above all, would not have had the motivation. There are numerous examples.

After examining the authentic records of Celtic law, we shall interpret, in detail, the Celtic myths relating to women. This will lead us to two kinds of observation: the first purely factual — to study the role and position of women in the civilisations that had not yet developed a fully patriarchal structure; the second theoretical – with the myths representing an ideal situation, how will they help us to throw light on the problem of women in the twentieth century? Besides illuminating a much-neglected historical period, we may help prepare the way for a more broadly human outlook in future society, when men and women will no longer indulge in the devious sex war that they have allowed to undermine them for centuries.

Bieuzy-Lanvaux
1971—1972

Part I

Women in Celtic Societies

Chapter 1

The Historical Context

Before studying the behaviour, position and effective role of women in various Celtic societies, it is important to define and describe these in relation to their contemporaries, as well as to later societies that have preserved demonstrable Celtic elements.

Countries that are definitely Celtic are those in which a Celtic language is spoken, albeit by only part of the population. Into this category come Ireland, Wales, Brittany and, to a lesser extent, the Isle of Man and Scotland. But to confine our study to these countries would mean ignoring an important part of our sources. In the Iron Age the Celts occupied half of Western Europe and left their mark in many ways: through place-names, folklore, and even customs adapted into common law and perhaps influencing modern legislation.

Thus a vast field of exploration opens, from the Rhine to the Atlantic, with occasional unexpected forays into Central and Eastern Europe. Ancient Gaul originally consisted of France, Belgium, the Rhineland, Switzerland and the Po valley; the Celtiberians in northwest Spain showed some recognisable Celtic features; and then there is the whole of the British Isles to be taken into consideration. The Alpine complex and its bordering regions, where Celts settled, even though sporadically, should also be included.

We know that the Celts, like all other Indo-Europeans, came from the great plains of Central Asia. A very long time ago, some tribes from this original Indo-European race made their way towards the valleys of the Indus and Ganges and the high plateaux of Iran. In Neolithic times a body of Indo-Europeans migrated westwards, following the loess of the Asiatic plain, which extended into Northern Europe — a logical enough route for a population beginning to live from agriculture and livestock breeding.

This settlement was the result of many waves of migration, as the conditions of life gradually improved and the population increased. In this way, the first influx of Hellenes arrived on the shores of the Aegean Sea from a base probably on the periphery of the Carpathians. They were the famous Achaeans celebrated in Homeric poems. At the same time another group migrated west and south, passing through the Harz mountain region. The groups continuing west were the Goidels, or Gaels, whom we find very early in Ireland, without knowing where else they settled on the way. Those going south were the Italiots, amongst whom were the Osques, Umbrians and Latins, who merged with the existing Etruscan population on the Italian peninsula.

These migrations took place in the middle and late Bronze Age, i.e. from 1500 to 900 B.C. Archaeologically this corresponds to the culture known as "Urnfield", because of the custom of cremating the dead and placing their ashes in funeral urns. Among these wandering Indo-European tribes the Celts were represented by the mysterious Gaels, who settled on the extreme west of Europe. But the question arises as to whether this first Celtic wave did not settle in other places as well. Common-sense would suggest that they did, but there is no way of proving this. However, the study of Indo-European languages leads me to some very odd facts, which might cast doubt on accepted views of Europe's prehistory.

As regards place-names, the Gauls left indelible traces of their passage and settlement. Such names were scarcely affected by Romanisation, except in the regions closest to the Mediterranean, though there are pre-Indo-European words and subsequent German influence to take into account. The Latin names generally describe owners of villas who were Romanised Gauls, and often Latin and Gallic words were joined together, as in the famous example of Autun (Augustidunum, the citadel of Augustus). The names of principal French towns are the names of Gallic people who inhabited the region at the time of the conquest: Paris, the Parisii; Nantes, the Namnetes; Rheims, the Remi; Rennes, the Redones; Vannes, the Veneti; Limoges, the Lemovices; Arras, the Atrebates; Sens, the Senones; and so on. Others still carry the old name from before the conquest: Rouen (Rotomagos), Lyon and Laon (Lugdunum), Vienne (Vindobona), Toulouse (Tolosa), Bordeaux (Burdigala), Boulogne (Bononia). Strasbourg is the Germanic translation of the Gallic "Argentorate" ("silver fortress"); Châteaudun is a tautology (*dun* means *château*). The names of a great many small towns, boroughs and other places still carry the Gallic mark. The names of rivers and mountains are very ancient, mostly Celtic, but sometimes dating from much earlier.

The study of place-names (toponymy) shows us the area occupied by the Gauls. This extended throughout Western Europe, well beyond the actual frontiers of France. In fact, "The purpose of toponymy is not only to rediscover the roots, etymology and original meaning of place-names, but also to give a helping hand to human geography, assisting the reconstruction of the history of settlement and the development of the land. In the absence or poverty of historical proof, the names of places, when they can be interpreted, constitute the authentic and unimpeachable testimonies which, short of actually dating, at least point to the time of the founding of human settlements. Besides which, they often give information about the appearance of places at the time when they were first occupied."[1] In this way, it can be proved that Gaul was a territory dedicated to agriculture, whereas Ireland and Britain were devoted to livestock. This distinction is largely based on toponymy and is of major importance in the study of Celtic society in general, and the study of the position of women in that society in particular.

These linguistic and toponymic considerations have a purpose. The exact framework in which the Celts evolved and their spirit developed has to be defined. All myths of Celtic origin can be studied only in a solid context, or else we run the risk of not understanding their deepest implications.

These considerations illuminate the fact that while the Celts occupied Western Europe in the Iron Age, they were not the only ones to live there. Not only did the Britons mix with Gaelic populations who had settled there earlier, but in addition the two waves of migration met peoples who had already been there since prehistory and had been neither dislodged nor killed. The Celts were not very numerous: they were hardly more than an intellectual, warrior élite possessed of certain techniques that enabled them to dominate the earlier non-Celtic population, imposing their own way of life and assimilating their predecessors. However, this assimilation was not a one-way process. Just as the Greeks contributed to the radical transformation of early Roman society when conquered by the Romans and brought under Roman discipline, the ancient populations of Gaul, Britain and Ireland deeply influenced early Celtic civilisation. This explains the important differences between Mediterranean or Germanic Indo-European societies and Celtic societies, especially in matters of religion, political and judicial organisation, as well as family structures and consequently the role of women.

To summarise the landmarks of Celtic history: the Britons of the Tene civilisation were firmly settled in Gaul, in the British Isles and

north-west Spain from the fourth century B.C. They even pushed
further south, forming Cisalpine Gaul in the Po valley and on the
shores of the Adriatic, where they presented a serious threat to the
Latins. They took Rome in 387 B.C., after the victory at Allia, when
the Senone Brennus routed the Roman troops.[2] The Romans
reacted gradually, first containing the Gauls successfully and then
eliminating them from northern Italy. According to some writers of
antiquity, Gaul became overpopulated in this period, and other Gauls
set off to the Hercynian forest and the Balkans. In the Balkans
expedition, at the beginning of the third century B.C., another
Brennus swept across Greece, even pillaging the sanctuary at Delphi
in about 290 B.C.[3] The remains of his army passed into Asia and
became the foundation of the famous kingdom of Galatia, where the
Celtic language was still spoken at the time of St Jerome.

The period of greatest expansion for the Celts was the third
century B.C., when they were to be found not only in the western
regions, but also almost everywhere else in Europe: on the right bank
of the Rhine, where they influenced the Germanic people considerably (these were very likely non-Aryan but Indo-Europeanised);
along the Danube and in the Carpathian regions, where the Boiins
were to leave their name (Bohemia); in Illyria, which is now
Yugoslavia; in Asia Minor, where, having served as mercenaries to
different Eastern kings, they were to found Galatia; and, in all
probability, on the Black Sea coast as far as the Crimea, where they
would have been in touch with the northern Slavs and the famous
Scythians of the Steppes. This has given rise to vague theories of a
Celto-Scythian community, and would explain a certain relationship
between Celtic art and the art of the Steppes.[4]

The second century B.C. saw the beginning of the decline of the
Celtic empire, to use the word in a very loose sense, for the ties
between those immense territories were linguistic and religious rather
than political. The Germanic people had profited from lessons given
to them by the Gauls, and increasingly made their presence felt when
driven from their homeland by Baltic or Slavonic peoples. They
occupied the whole right bank of the Rhine, and some of their tribes
even settled in the north of Belgium.[5] It is worth noting that all
the big invasions followed the east—west axis, and that eventually all
the peoples driven back found themselves on the western fringe of
Europe; this proves yet again the futility of searching for a pure
Celtic race, even in countries where Celtic languages are still spoken.

But the Germanic people were not yet an immediate danger to the
Gauls. The Romans had not forgotten the outrage that the Senone
Brennus had inflicted on them when negotiating the departure of the
Gauls from Rome in 387 B.C. They agreed the sum of a thousand
pounds of gold. The Gauls used false weights and the Romans
refused indignantly. Brennus added his sword to the scales and cried

out "Woe to the conquered!" (*Vae victis*). From then on the Romans spared no effort in seeking vengeance and the elimination of the dangerous noisy Gallic troops, whose mere approach to a Latin town unleashed the famous *tumultus gallicus*; this was a mass rising against a formidable enemy and was how the Romans assured their domination of the whole of Cisalpine Gaul from 241 B.C. to 202 B.C.

The Gauls began to realise that Roman power presented some inconvenience. This explains why they allied themselves with the Carthaginians during the Punic wars. Not only did they help Hannibal and his troops along the Rhone and across the Alps, but numerous Gallic contingents took part in the triumphant march of the Carthaginians into northern Italy, as well as in the victory at Cannae. But after the fatal indecision of Hannibal at Capua, the fate of Western Europe and the Mediterranean basin was settled: there was nothing left to stop Roman military expansion, "that enormous machine for suppressing people". In 197 B.C. the Celtiberians fell under the Roman fist, and, although they revolted in 153 B.C., their capital Numance was finally taken by Scipio Aemilianus in 133 B.C. A Romano-Gallic war flared up in 121 B.C. in the Celtic region; this ended in the defeat of the Averne chief Bituitos.

A diversion occurred in the rather cool relations between Romans and Gauls. It arose from the common danger from the Cimbri and the Teutons. These people, who are generally classed as Germanic, were very probably pre-Indo-European and deeply Celticised, as their principal chiefs' and generic names show. Coming from Jutland, they hurled themselves upon Gaul, northern Italy, Pannonia and the Iberian peninsula, looting everything on their way. They were eventually beaten in 102 B.C. and 101 B.C. by Roman legions under the command of Marius, at Fos-sur-Mer and at Pourrières, near Aix-en-Provence (following the latter battle, the neighbouring mountain took the name of a war goddess, later Christianised into "St Victoire").[6] Meanwhile, the whole of southern Gaul had been occupied by the Romans, who made it the *Provincia Romana*, known as Narbonnaise and again as *Gallia Togata*, the Gauls benefiting from the right to Roman citizenship.

During the first century B.C., Gallic civilisation became particularly splendid. Towns grew everywhere. The land was improved, thanks to manuring, which consisted, as Pliny the Elder said, "of enriching the earth with earth; this is known as marl". The wheel plough fitted with a mobile coulter was used, and was greatly superior to the Roman swing plough of the same period. The harrow was already known, and above all there was harvesting machinery, pictured in bas-reliefs in Belgium, and described by Pliny as "A big box, the edges armed with teeth and supported by two wheels, moved through the cornfield, pushed by an ox; the ears of corn were uprooted by the teeth and fell into the box." So Gallic corn was abundant and could be bought by Roman merchants, but it also drew covetous eyes to this rich agricultural land. Metallurgy developed, iron being worked as well as bronze, tin and silver. New methods for making glass were discovered, an enamelling technique invented, coopering and the building of sea and river craft perfected. Art did not lag behind: witness the decorated pottery, the many stone and the still greater number of wooden statues, the work of goldsmiths, the engraved cauldrons and decorated utility objects. Even coins became works of art, such was the delicacy of engraving and the extent of the discoveries made regarding it.

Two increasingly imminent dangers now arose: the Germans and the Romans. The Belgae, driven from their homeland by German pressure, came to settle in southern Britain. The Helveti, fleeing from Ariovistus's Suebi, collided with the Aedui. Rivalries between the Gallic peoples flared up openly.

Julius Caesar profited from this situation. He had waited for just such a chance to advance his political and military career and so re-establish his fortunes, and he intervened as mediator and protector. Having restored order to Gallic affairs, he kept his troops in Gaul. The Gauls did not challenge this, choosing what they considered to be the lesser of the two dangers; unfortunately for them, they realised the proconsul's intentions a little too late. The same thing happened in 56 B.C. with the outbreak of the revolt of the Bretons, who were lured on by the Veneti; this ended in the annihilation of the Veneti fleet at the entrance to the gulf of Morbihan. Caesar twice tried to pursue his conquest of Britain, but without success. In 52 B.C. there was a general uprising against the Roman occupation of Gaul. After much hesitation, it was led by the Arverne Vercingetorix, around whom, for good or ill, the majority of Gallic chiefs rallied, including those who, like Commios Atrebate, had initially believed in the possibility of collaboration with the Romans. The result is well known: the defeat at Alesia, due mainly to a tactical error by Vercingetorix, and that despite the vigorous action of of Commios, the last Gallic resister, who afterwards withdrew to Britain.[7]

This was the end of Gallic independence. The Gauls were to lead a new life, deprived of their own organisations, their religion soon to be forbidden, their language belittled. The territory was divided into provinces and became the prey of bureaucrats of the Empire, who were nearly all Gauls on the make. The worship of imperial gods, of Rome and the Emperor was to supplant, at least officially, the metaphysical beliefs of the Druids. Triumphant Christianity later established itself within this imperial edifice. Nothing Celtic survived except a popular oral tradition of stories and narratives as well as resilient superstitions which the Christian religion could not completely stamp out, preferring to integrate them as far as possible into its worship. The Christianisation of fountains, the recognition of some highly suspect saints and some peculiar forms of devotion, still in use in the twentieth century, are a few examples.

Britain had escaped Romanisation for the time being, but fell victim to the Romans in 51 A.D., despite the heroic resistance of certain Britons like the famous Caratacus. Ten years later, after the horrible massacre of the Druids on the Isle of Mon (Anglesey), the Britons revolted, under the leadership of Boudicca (Boadicea), Queen of the Iceni, but to no avail. In 83 A.D. the Romans reached the Clyde and the Forth. There, in order to protect the new *provincia* against the Picts of north-east Scotland and the last independent Britons of the north-west coast, the Emperor Antoninus built the famous wall that bears his name.

Unlike Gaul, Britain was never truly Romanised. The British preserved their language and their culture. These still exist in Wales today and have never ceased to exist.

But though the British were to emerge relatively well from the rather irregular Roman occupation, this was not the case with the Germanic invasions that followed. From the third to the sixth centuries A.D., the British were incapable of settling their domestic quarrels and, under pressure from the Angles, Jutes and Saxons, had to retreat to the west of the island; although there were, of course, periods of victorious resistance, such as those attributed to King Arthur in the legend. Britain became three-quarters Anglo-Saxon and, as there was not room for all the British in Wales and Cornwall, some survived by crossing the sea and settling in Gallic Armorica, which thus became Brittany. Cornwall very quickly fell into the Saxon orbit. Only Wales was able to keep its unity and ethnic purity, but lost its independence in 1282, when Edward I gave the title of "Prince of Wales" to his son.[8]

Ireland avoided Romanisation, but experienced no more political unity than had either Gaul or Britain. At the beginning of the Christian era a rather astonishing ethnic mixture may be distinguished: prehistoric and megalithic populations (the Fomors and the Tuatha Dé Danann of mythology); Gaels, who still bore their generic name of "Scots"; and Gallic, British and Belgian tribes (Fir Gailcoin, Fir Domnann and Fir Bolg), who settled there from the middle of the first century B.C. Numerous tribes were grouped, in varying degrees of harmony, in five provinces: Ulster, Connaught, North Leinster, South Leinster and Munster. These provinces were always at war, above all Ulster and Connaught, who fought for the control of the island. In the middle of the second century, the King of Connaught, Conn of the Hundred Battles, founded on the ruins of North Leinster a new kingdom called Mide or Meath (middle). It was based on Tara, an ancient sanctuary dating back to the beginning of time, the seat of supreme royalty, with power over all the other kings of Ireland. He appointed himself *Ard-Ri*, which means High King. This institution of supreme royalty (most of the time a purely theoretical power) was to last until Ireland lost her independence.

Meanwhile, Christianity came over from Britain, propagated in particular by St Patrick (who died in 461). It overwhelmed Ireland, putting an end to the Druidic worship. But, in contrast with the case in Gaul, Christianity did not destroy the Gaelic language or the Celtic traditions. It could even be argued that the Irish Church saved all there was to be saved of Celticism: it was the monks who transcribed the precious literary manuscripts with their typically Celtic and pagan inspiration into the Gaelic language. Irish Christianity had very unusual features, showing a Druidic influence, and epitomised in St Columcill. These spread to Britain and Brittany, and gave birth to a prodigiously enthusiastic and active Celtic Church which contributed to the evangelisation of the continent, though it soon became very suspect to Roman orthodoxy.[9]

Despite internal difficulties and the Scandinavian invasions, Ireland became not only a centre of spirituality during the early Middle Ages, but also, like Wales, a veritable conservatory of language, literature and Celtic art. Meanwhile, after complex intrigues in the twelfth century, in which the papacy seems to have played a far from admirable role, the title of High King of Ireland was given to the Plantagenet Henry II. Following the death of his son Geoffrey, he also administered Brittany, during the minority of his grandson Arthur. The Anglo-Norman dynasty kept Ireland, which for several centuries suffered the worst plundering and oppression at the hands of the English and the Scots. In 1921, Ireland regained part of her freedom thanks to the establishment of *Saorstat Eireann*: the main essential was saved, but what has become of the Gaelic language, which, despite the fact that it is the official language, is now spoken only in some western counties and by the intellectuals?[10]

Brittany carried on until the sixteenth century as the only independent Celtic state. After the British had settled there, the *plous* were established and counties substituted for the Gallo-Roman *pagi*, and Brittany tried as best it could to preserve both its unity and integrity in the face of two lots of very covetous neighbours, the Franks and the Saxons. For ten centuries, in fact, the history of Brittany was a continual balancing act between the English and French influences. On 13th August 1532, the King of France signed a treaty that proclaimed the unity of Brittany and France.

Thus the Celtic nations disappeared. But, despite the systematic suppression of all Celtic tradition, this still exists, and has been passed on to us by valuable Irish and Welsh manuscripts. There is also a complete oral tradition, not only in Ireland and Wales, but also in Scotland, a country Celticised by the Gaels and which still preserves its Gaelic language today.[11] The Isle of Man has relearned it. Brittany, the most important contemporary Celtic-speaking country, does not, unfortunately, possess any ancient written literature, though it has an incredible wealth of stories, poems and customs. Finally, there are, throughout Western Europe, many direct links with Celtic periods, particularly in France, Walloon Belgium, and England.

The tradition has not disappeared. It intermingled with other important influences and produced a synthesis that was often fruitful. Celtic Christianity proves this; French writers like Chateaubriand drew inspiration from Brittany; there are the Anglo-Irish authors, Yeats, Synge and others, who revived the Celtic tradition in a language available to a wider public. "The invasions in Ireland's history effectively prevented the development of an integrated Gaelic civilisation in Celtic Ireland. On the other hand, these invasions have never been absolute . . . consequently we have two traditions in Ireland, two civilisations, two languages, two sets of laws. It is the aim of our policy to try to reintegrate and reunify the two traditions of the past."[12]

This is also true for Wales, that synthesis of British and Saxon cultures, and for Brittany, the crucible in which Celtic Breton and French Latin cultures were melted down. Brittany is a bilingual country where neither of the two traditions need harm the other; on the contrary, they can open up the way to a greater intellectual development.[13] This could also apply to all other countries that still bear the Celtic mark, for there is nothing more tenacious than tradition, nothing more firmly rooted than the ancient beliefs and systems of thought when they are concealed within new forms. The myths never die. They are constantly being revived in new and varied shapes, and sometimes surprise us in unexpected places.

This is our area of investigation, and in order to explain the role of women in the Western world since the dawn of history and even prehistory, we must neglect nothing. That is why it was so important to be precise about the area we designate as "Celtic". It is almost unexplored and great surprises await us.

Chapter 2

The Judicial Framework

f one's reading on Celtic society is
limited to Greek and Latin authors' work on the Gallic family, it
seems that the Celtic did not differ from other contemporary
Indo-European societies. But it so happens that Celtic law — Irish,
Welsh and Breton — is extremely well documented, much more so
than their history and mythology. We possess codes and compilations
of Welsh and Irish laws going back to the early Middle Ages, and
these, even in a Christian context, show great originality when
compared with institutions of countries with Roman law.[1]

Gaul has to be considered separately from other Celtic countries
for two reasons: first, because the Gauls were Romanised very early
on and Gallo-Roman institutions and customs were closer to Roman
law; secondly, because Gallic agriculture had already evolved the
early Gallic law, nearer to the Roman type based on ownership of
land. It is this early law about which we know least: a few remarks
by Caesar — however well-informed — by Dio Cassius, Strabo and
Diodorus of Sicily are not enough to draw a complete picture. It is
therefore essential to start with the collections of Irish and Welsh
laws, which express the original Celtic spirit best.

The basis of Celtic society is the family in the wider sense of the
word, i.e. the Indo-European *gens*, comparable to its counterpart in
Greek cities and Rome. Among the ancient Britons, this consisted of
all relatives as far as the ninth remove, under an authority equivalent
to that of the Latin *paterfamilias*. This family was called the *fine* by
the ancient Gaels. The word comes from the same root as *Gwynedd*

(north-west Wales), *Veneti* (the name of the Gallic people who inhabited the country around Vannes), and *Gwened* in Breton.[2] In Ireland, when this family reached a certain size it took the name of *deirbhfine*, and consisted of four generations, from the father, called *cenn-fine* (head or chief of a family), to the great-grandchildren. Beyond this point another family would be formed, with a compulsory sharing of the communal goods.[3]

Several *fine* made up a tribe, the *tuath*, which was the basic political unit in Ireland. The *tuath* was self-sufficient: it possessed a well-defined social hierarchy, from the chief, or king (*ri*), down to slaves, with goods owned in common, its own rules and regulations and its own gods. The quasi-autocracy of a *tuath* had quite remarkable consequences in the history of the Celts, and explains the impossibility of political unification, characteristic of Gauls, Britons, and Irish and, of course, the Scots, traditionally attached to their clans.

Ireland is a poor country compared with Gaul or even Britain, and it is tempting to say that Gaelic society was pastoral. But the term is not entirely accurate, for to say "pastoral" means "nomadic", and this was not the case. The Gaels were a settled people, solidly planted in the different regions of Ireland. Only the frontiers between the different *tuatha* were movable, and this did not occur without unleashing relentless wars. However, this also suggests a certain reluctance in assigning fixed limits to an area that depended more on the king's moral power than on his actual physical power.[5]

Unlike Roman society, which was based on the ownership of land through one or several title-holders, Celtic society, especially the Gaelic, was based on the communal ownership of land, which indicates a complete orientation towards the breeding of livestock. As with the Germanic people and the Latins, the oldest money was cattle, and hence considered the only basic wealth.

The feudal type of contract was for the leasing of cattle, as we shall see in the case of Ireland. Theoretically the land was the property of the kingdom, therefore communal and indivisible. The king was elected by the community and therefore in charge of the administration, and he could authorise any member of the *tuath* to take over a piece of land. This could be as reward for services, to allow him to work for the public good, or to make his home there and develop the land. However, in direct contrast to the practice on the continent in the same period, he imposed no rent, no other particular service upon the individual he had settled, and did not concede him a fief in the proper sense. He made him a kind of privileged tenant, with the aim of furthering the common property of the *tuath*.[6]

Most of the time the privileged individual did not receive land, or rather the right to settle on it, but heads of cattle. The Celtic feudal system was based on this. The lessee received several head of cattle and so contracted obligations towards the lessor. These were precisely stipulated in a contract agreed in the presence of the Druid (or, in the Christian era, the priest).[7] All who received cattle were therefore, *ipso facto*, drawn into the social hierarchy, in varying degrees according to their personal importance. Such people were of two kinds: serfs and free men. The serfs owned no more than those on the continent in the same period. The free men ranged from the king down to the humblest peasant. In the cattle-leasing contract, serfs and free men were known as the *ambactoi*, a Gallic term used by Caesar and meaning "servants" or, more appropriately, "vassals", from the Gallic word *vassos*, which also means "servant" (Welsh *gwas*, "servant"; Breton *gwaz*, "of servant origin", nowadays "man" in the wider sense, and also "varlet"). This cattle-leasing contract was retained very late in Ireland, and it explains why women, who could own herds, were not excluded and therefore enjoyed a different position from women in societies based entirely on the tilling of the soil.

The system in these Celtic societies is evidently patriarchal, and suggests an earlier organisation compared with other Indo-European societies of the same period. Although his role is more often moral than actual, the ruler of a *tuath* is a man. Nevertheless there are historical examples of women ruling: the Queen of the Iceni, Boudicca, unleashed the great British revolt of 61 B.C. She had been birched by the Romans and seen her daughters raped by those leaders of civilisation, the legionaries. This revolt united all the people of the island after the slaughter of the Druids on Anglesey by the army of Suetonius Paulinus. Then there was Cartimandua, Queen of the Brigantes, who, traitor to her people, delivered up Caratacus, chief of the British resistance, to the Romans.[8]

But, although royalty was masculine, the queen still played an important role. The Gaelic laws specified that the queen must receive, for her personal account, a third of the booty from war and a third of the fines imposed through the penal code and exacted in the form of money or the equivalent in jewels or heads of cattle. In legendary tradition, there was Queen Medb, who held the real power in Connaught; the numerous female figures of supreme authority who appear in Irish and Welsh epic texts; and the ideal queens of the Next World, symbols of an attitude of mind that the patriarchy could not uproot from the ancient Celtic spirit.

There is much evidence, particularly in the writings of Latin and Greek authors, that a woman had the theoretical right to choose her husband. Better still, she could not be married without her own consent, which was a very enviable situation compared with that of the Roman woman. "When there was a daughter to be married, a great feast was organised to which all young people were invited. The girl herself would choose, offering water to the man of her choice to wash his hands" (Fulgose, book II). In Irish legendary tradition, as we shall see, this choice of the man loved by the woman is an almost magical act, which has a rather surprising implication. According to the oldest Welsh laws, those of Gwynedd, girls could be married at the age of twelve.[9]

But the choice made by the girl did not mean that the relatives had no hand in the marriage contract. The family was the basic unit. Leaving a family to set up another was too serious a matter for the community not to be concerned. Therefore the two families would come to an arrangement which led to a marriage based exclusively on the dowry system, whatever the social class of the bride and groom. Caesar tells us (*De Bello Gallico*, I, 3), "When a man wishes to marry a woman, he must pay a certain sum; the woman for her part must give the same amount. Every year the fortune of the two parties is counted. The profits accrued are retained, and a surviving partner will enjoy the part that was his, augmented by all the previous joint profit." The text is very clear: each of the two partners must bring their share. But in the event of the husband's death, the wife does not inherit his share: she takes her share only, along with the yield of the joint property. It is the same for the man on becoming a widower. This property system therefore in no way presupposes a joint estate in the judicial sense, for no judicial system in which the dowry co-exists with the marital donation allows joint estate.

There is a second way in which the Gallic woman enjoyed a position equal to her husband's, though this did not prevent Caesar from asserting that she remained obedient to him. The third century jurist Ulpien stated that on top of her dowry, the woman owned "what the Greeks called paraphenalia, and the Gauls *peculium*". The Irish and British women were even better off.

In Ireland, a man wishing to marry a woman had to deposit a right of purchase, the *coibche*. This *coibche* was intended for the father of the fiancée if she were marrying for the first time. If his daughter were marrying for the second time, the father received only two-thirds of the sum, the remaining third going to the girl. If she were marrying for the third time, the father took no more than half, and so on. Even the daughter's twenty-first marriage was allowed for, by which time the father's right had disappeared. When the father died, the brother, as a rule the eldest, had a right to half of what the father would have received. In republican Rome the purchase of the fiancée by the future husband was purely symbolic. This means that the Celtic custom reflects very ancient institutions.

In spite of this purchase, this *coibche*, the Irish woman did not enter the husband's family. This is the opposite of the case in Roman law. The Roman woman fell *in manu mariti*, through coemption, and belonged to the husband's family; she could no longer own property. In the same way the Germanic woman could not inherit, because of the well-known masculine privilege that later resulted in the law of primogeniture and the Salic law. The Irish woman continued to own her own property, but, if her husband were killed, it was not she who received compensation for the murder, but the husband's family. If she remarried, she shared the new *coibche* with her own family. So the married woman was assured a fairly complete independence in law.

In fact, the only right that the husband acquired through the *coibche* was to the body of the woman and the children born during the marriage. The woman could not confer to her husband any more rights over her goods than she had herself, because the basic principle of the feudal contract, which we have already seen in Irish law and the establishment of a fief, was that the real owner was the family, *fine*, or the tribe, *tuath*. This is the basic principle that separates Celtic from Roman and Germanic law and explains the position characteristically held by women in all Celtic societies.

The Irish woman brought her personal dowry, *tinnscra*, to her marriage. This was a collection of presents received from relatives. It was her personal property, for, in the event of dissolution of the marriage by divorce or death, she took it back in full, along with her own freedom and any acquisitions, or the proportion of them laid down by law.

The same method was followed in Wales. The man deposited the purchase price of the woman, the *gobyr*, which was the exact equivalent of the *coibche*. The woman brought her marriage settlement, *argweddy*, also a personal possession. But, in addition, the husband or his family had to pay the *cowyll*, which means the price of virginity. Significantly, this *cowyll* was paid *before* the first night, whereas in Rome and with the Germanic peoples it was given only on the *morrow* following the night of nuptials, from which comes its technical name of *morgengabe*. It is a simple difference, but expresses the respect that the Celts had for women; they always considered woman as morally superior, whereas the Germanic peoples and the Romans — and the Christians in their turn — made her into a hypocritical and false creature.

There is actually a curious concept behind this custom and its name. The current Breton word meaning "settlement", the equivalent of the original *cowyll*, is *enebarz*. We find it in the Cartulary of Redon, in its ninth-century form *enep-uuerth (enep-werth)*, comparable to the modern Welsh *wyneb-werth*. This is a judicial term meaning "compensation", "price of honour" (compensation due for an outrage suffered), in the literal sense of "price of face", like its Irish equivalent *log-enech*. Therefore it was originally a matter of a price of honour in general, this honour being centred on the face, which can blush or turn pale under insult. So we may assume that with the early Celts the face was held to be the very place of honour and consequently shame. Taken in conjunction with our knowledge of their lack of sexual prejudice, this calls to mind the Moslem custom of women wearing veils, their shame and honour being located solely in the face.[10]

In Wales, the woman would receive paraphenalia from her family, the *argyfreu*, as well as her dowry, the *argweddy*, which she brought with her. These goods, Ulpien said, were called *peculium* by the Gauls. They were chattels in the judicial sense: precious objects, ornaments and jewels, utensils for cooking and other domestic uses, furniture, and animals other than cattle. According to the Laws of Hywel Dda, they were handed over in their entirety to the woman when the marriage dissolved before the seventh year; but she lost them if she sued for divorce without valid motive, and they were shared equally with the rest of the patrimony if the marriage were dissolved after the seventh year.

Then there is the question of divorce. Surprisingly enough, even in the Christian era it was an incredibly easy matter for the Celts.[11] This was due mainly to the fact that marriage did not have the inviolable and compulsive character that it has acquired in so-called modern societies. It was never more than a contract with certain conditions. When the conditions were not respected the contract became void. There were no great marriage ceremonies. Welsh and Irish literature mention only a feast at the end of which the marriage was consummated. Welsh laws drawn up in the Christian era do not mention any religious marriage. Celtic marriage was essentially contractual, social, not at all religious, but based on the freedom of the husband and wife; it would therefore appear to have been a kind of free union protected by laws, which could always be broken. Celtic divorce was not a repudiation, as it was in ancient Rome or in good Christian society, where powerful men could divorce for the highest moral motives, such as the inability to have male children, or the discovery — by pure chance — of a blood relationship. Repudiation, a triumph of sophistry, has always worked against the woman and to the man's advantage. This never occurred in Celtic divorce, where the man and woman were treated with absolute equality.[12]

In Ireland, when the woman did not give her husband legitimate grounds for divorce but he nonetheless acquired another bride, the price of purchase automatically went back to the first wife, to the detriment of the second and her relations. The famous "price of honour", received by the second wife, had to be transferred to the first. This is a fairly uncommon example of protecting the legitimate wife. Furthermore, if the husband were reconciled with his old wife, he had to give her a new *coibche*. There are many grounds for divorce foreseen by these laws. If a Welsh woman flung the supreme insult, "Shame on your beard", at her husband, he automatically had the right to divorce. If the husband were guilty of adultery, the wife could immediately obtain dissolution of the marriage. In short, divorce by mutual consent was perfectly legal with both the Irish and the Welsh.

Another reason for the ease with which divorce could be obtained, and hence for the relative fragility of marriage, was that the Celts always wavered between monogamy and polygamy, and even polyandry. Caesar referred to certain British tribes that practised a kind of polyandry,[13] but his information is rather nebulous and relates to the Picts in the north and not to the British.

Nevertheless, we may be sure that polygamy existed in Celtic countries, for in historical times we find unmistakable traces of the institution of legal concubinage. Every man, even husbands, could have one or several concubines. A proper contract was drawn up by which the man bought the concubine, the *ben urnadna* (contracted wife). But what was important, and very original, was that he bought her for only one year, to the day, the contract being renewable for the following year. This condition again shows the anxiety of the Celtic legislators to safeguard the liberty of the woman: the doctrine of *habeas corpus*, peculiar to Anglo-Saxon law, seems to apply particularly in this case. In fact, if the contract were for a year and a day, the concubine belonged to the man, after the end of the time allowed, through usucapion: the man would have the right to sell back the concubine and pocket the money, to her relations' and her own cost. Thus the concubine was forced to take back her freedom.

In Ireland this concubinage, or annual marriage, expired at a date roughly corresponding with a pagan festival. D'Arbois de Jubainville compares this custom with one surviving in some parts of France, where servants are hired by the year, and the year ends, for example, on the day of St John or St Martin, which are relics of the feasts of Beltaine and Samain. At the beginning of the Christian era the old custom of annual hiring of the concubine could well have been replaced by the annual hiring of servants, male servants as well.

In any case, the legal status of concubinage prejudiced none of the rights of the legal wife, who was the only rightful spouse; she could obtain help in her domestic work from her husband's concubines. Furthermore, the wife could refuse the presence of any concubine in the family home. If the husband overruled this, she could always divorce him. In the legend of St Bridget of Kildare, the Druid Dubhthach had bought a concubine and made her pregnant. The legitimate wife, who refused to recognise this fact, threatened divorce if Dubhthach did not separate from the concubine. For, through divorce, she would take not only her *coibche*, the price of purchase, with her, but also her savings and her *tinnscra*. This threat made the Druid think again and he ended up separating from his concubine in order to keep his legitimate wife — and the property she owned.

So, although the man was apparently head of the family, he was not always the dominant marriage partner. Irish laws deal with three very different situations in marriage where the role of the woman — or the man — could change round completely. When the wife, the *cetmunter*, had a fortune equal to her husband's and was of the same birth, she was on a completely equal footing. She could settle all contracts deemed advantageous on her own authority. The husband's consent was necessary only when a contract was deemed unfavourable. Equally, the wife had the right to demand the cancellation of all disadvantageous contracts made by her husband relating to his own fortune.

When the wife was inferior in rank, and especially when her fortune was less than her husband's, these rights were severely reduced. This was the reason for the famous quarrel between Queen Medb and King Ailill related at the beginning of the great narrative of the *Tain Bo Cualnge*; their disagreement over the valuation of their joint fortunes resulted in a relentless war started by Medb in order to gain possession of a bull that was worth more than her husband's bull.

On the other hand, when the woman had a greater fortune than her husband, she was the unchallenged head of the family. The husband's authority was almost nil. This was called *fer fognama*, meaning "man of service", or even *fer for ban thincur*, "man under the power of woman". In many of the epic narratives, it was King Ailill who had absolutely no say against the decisions of Queen Medb. This was obviously a privileged position for the married woman, who was not only mistress of her own destiny, but also of the man's. This no doubt derived from an earlier social state, not unlike a certain kind of matriarchy (though we should not assume that the word includes all the features that it might suggest), in which the woman had enjoyed a more important role in family and political life.

There was almost the same arrangement in Wales and Brittany. The Cartulary of Redon, dating from the ninth century, gives examples of married women who owned property and could dispose of it as they wished, without their husband's consent. Breton women could rule, if they belonged to a royal line and were elected to do so.[14] They could take their husbands into the royal house, and it was possible for them to inherit the reign if they did not have sons. Breton country women still retain a very great moral authority and are often head of the family.

Traces of an earlier matriarchy (again we use the word with caution) also appear in the preference given to the wife's family concerning inheritance when the husband disappeared; above all in the old custom in Irish and Welsh literature of naming heroes *after their mother and not their father*: King Conchobar was known as "son of Ness"; Gwyddyon and Arianrod were son and daughter of

Don; Setanta-Cú Chulainn was the son of Dechtire. Definite traces of matrilineal descent were still remembered by the story-tellers.[15]

Women, whether, married or not, could assume many different functions. Although no proof exists that they could have been Druidesses, they were nevertheless sorceresses and prophetesses. Christianity in the British Isles even allowed women access to certain forms of religious worship. There is positive evidence[16] that they took part in the celebration of Mass, a practice denounced by the strictly Roman bishops on the continent. There existed monasteries for men and women together, such as the one founded by the celebrated St Bridget on the site of a pagan temple at Kildare, where the women kept vigil over a fire that was on no account to go out. This recalls the Roman Vestals, or the perpetual fire kept going at Bath in honour of the goddess Sul.[17]

It is very likely that women did not confine themselves to these semi-priestly functions, and had a more important role to play in the education, not only of children, but also of young people. There was the rather unusual custom of fostering, in which children were sent away from their natural family to a foster-parent, who was in charge of their feeding and upbringing. Often the bonds between the foster-father and adopted child were stronger than between the true father and child; and not only between the child and its adopted parents, but also between the children brought up together. There are many examples of this in Irish literature. Fostering was probably of pre-Celtic Nordic origin; but it was not enough for the education of a young warrior. One fine day he would have to leave his foster-parents and be initiated into the profession of arms. This was done by some extremely mysterious warrior women, half witches, half amazons, generally living in the north of Britain in the land of the Picts. In Ireland, the accounts in *The Education of Cú Chulainn* and *The Childhoods of Finn* are the most telling in this respect.[18] In Wales, the narrative of Peredur, archetype of the *Quête du Saint Graal*, is full of archaic details of this custom.[19]

This literary tradition matches the vision that authors of classical antiquity had of robust Gallic women always ready to help their husbands in wars or quarrels, even provoking these quarrels themselves. According to Diodorus of Sicily (V, 32), "Among the Gauls the women are nearly as tall as the men, whom they rival in courage." The same observation, with pithy details, is found in Ammiamus Marcellinus (XV, 12): "The mood of the Gauls is quarrelsome and arrogant in the extreme. In a fight any one of them can resist several strangers at a time, with no other help than his wife's, who is even more formidable. You should see these viragos, neck veins swollen with rage, swinging their robust and snow-white arms, using their feet and their fists and landing blows that seem triggered off by a catapult." A flattering description, proving beyond doubt that Celtic women knew how to instil respect! In the Irish narrative *The Festival of Bricriu*, the wives of three Ulster champions quarrelled over the heroes' relative capacities; none would give in and all were prepared to tear each other's hair out to settle the matter.[20]

Another function of these women warriors, educators, officers and witches was that of sexual initiator. Later we shall study the connections between the myth of the woman as mother and woman as lover, but it is important to point it out in a historical context. For this curious warrior institution also served as a more or less sacred kind of prostitution, once more revealing a widespread sexual freedom among the Celts. There are hardly any sexual taboos, at all events no prudery, in the legal codes or literary texts untouched by Christianity — not that Christianity succeeded in eradicating these attitudes.

The instability of marriage and the practice of concubinage prove the point. Besides which, anyone could contract one of the famous annual marriages. The wife who accepted such a situation was by no means pilloried by society; on the contrary. Before Christianity, Celtic society had no conception of sin: least of all in sexuality. Like all other peoples, the Celts knew homosexuality: "The men are inclined to let themselves be dominated by the women; this is not an unusual tendency amongst energetic warrior races", declared Aristotle solemnly. "Apart, of course, from the Celts, who respect manly love quite openly, so to speak" (*Politics*, II, 6). This reflection — along with remarks by several other Greek authors — is not without its humour, coming as it does from a disciple of Socrates and citizen of a country that was scarcely shocked by such things. Nonetheless, it would appear that the Greek authors were right. There are discreet references in some of the epic narratives, notably in connection with Cú Chulainn. There are also signs of clandestine homosexuality in the institution of women warriors, corresponding to the ones found in associations of Lesbians which flourish all over the world.

This sexual freedom to a large extent explains the importance of women in Celtic society. As they were not objects of sin, nor weak creatures in a preponderantly pastoral and warrior society, all they had to do was to protect the role that they should have fulfilled in later periods. It is generally agreed that the laborious work entailed by agriculture resulted in women being removed from public life and relegated to domestic work. Clearly this is only one of the reasons, and, though we shall come to others, psychological, religious and metaphysical, it is a perfectly logical and valid one. Celtic society was full of archaisms largely gathered and integrated from the original inhabitants of Western Europe. It was halfway between the patriarchal type of society, which was agricultural and based on the ownership of land by the father of the family, and matriarchal societies, in which the mother, or women in general, remained the basic link in the family and a symbol of fertility.

We have seen how the Celtic woman, Irish, Breton or British, enjoyed freedom and rights according to her social rank or personal fortune. She could become head of the family, rule, be a prophetess, enchantress or educator, could marry or remain a virgin (which meant refraining from marriage), and could inherit part of her father's or mother's property.[21]

Part II

Exploring the Myth

Chapter 3

The Submerged Princess

"In the beginning God created the heaven and earth. And the earth was without form, and void; and darkness was upon the face of the deep. And the spirit of God moved upon the face of the waters." In the Hebrew Bible, the last sentence reads, "And the *Elohim* moved upon the face of the waters." This word occurs hundreds of times in the Hebrew version and is sometimes translated as "*spirits* controlling the world". Whatever inversions, additions and cuts the original biblical texts may have undergone, this sentence would appear to be the key to all explanations of the beginning of the world and of life.

The ancient Finnish epic, the *Kalevala*, which may be more complete because it was handed down over the centuries by word of mouth, tells how the Virgin of the Air descended from the sky onto the boundless, spuming sea; "then the sea and the wind blowing on her breathed life in her". So she became Ilmatar, Mother of the Waters, and after seven centuries of swimming the oceans she gave birth to the first human being, the bard Väinämöinen. This recalls the birth of Aphrodite from the foam and, again, the name of the divine creature Morgan (Muirgen), which probably means "born of the sea".

All traditions confirm the role of water in the genesis of life. Macrobius says in *Saturnalia* (I, 20), "the Seraph's head is the sky and his belly the sea". Seneca, in his *Physical Investigations* (III, 13), asserts that "the earth is upheld by water on which it floats like a ship". A Japanese legend tells how a god, wishing to leave the sky,

43

said to his companion one day, "there must be a world somewhere on which we can settle; let us look for it *under the waters* seething far below" (Dubois de Jancigny, *L'Asie*, p. 44).

So there is a god or spirit who fertilises the sea, which is seen as the primeval mother, both in a scientific sense and metaphorically as the Virgin of the Waters, the Siren or the invisible being in its depths. But, on reflection, it seems justifiable to wonder whether this "divine" interference is really indispensable. Contemporary science may have established that all life originated in the great oceans, which almost covered the earth millions of years ago, but the catalyst that set off the evolutionary process must have been cosmic radiation. The *Kalevala's* account of the fertilising wind is consistent with other ancient ideas dating from the time when the male was still unsure about his own role in fertilisation and frightened of parturition as an exclusively female process, with only the very vague intervention of a spirit or god. Since the Neolithic period, all societies have tried to give the individual male a more decisive role, but the traditions that have kept alive the memories of earliest times for longest still emphasise the essential and virtually single-handed role of the female.

The belief in the sea as mother of all life has survived into our own times. Its mystery and depth made it the supreme feminine symbol, and as patriarchal ideas gained predominance its secret and forbidden aspects were increasingly stressed. It contained strange creatures, hidden palaces and hoarded treasures; only exceptional, divine beings were able to live in it. But endless taboos came between the sea and man. It was dangerous to probe its depths, and only in particular cases were faultless heroes allowed to travel through the marvellous universe of that lost paradise.

For it really was a question of paradise lost. All the myths of Eden, the Golden Age, the Age of Innocence, focused on the sea as they were later to focus on its symbolic substitutes, the cave and the abyss. Psychoanalysis has indicated that these images of seas, caves and dark forests are linked with the archaic concept of woman as mother and lover. Human imagination elaborated the theme to such effect that it crops up everywhere in a variety of guises, proof that is is one of the most basic preoccupations of mankind.

The myth of the submerged town, the basic myth of creation for the Celts[1] was embodied in the legend of the town of Ys, known throughout Britanny, and recurring with significant variations in other Celtic countries, notably Ireland and Wales. Thus, by examining this legend and its two chief variants, we shall be able to probe the myth of the submerged woman.

Britanny, *Legend of Ker-Ys*
    Gradlon, King of Cornwall, had a magnificent city, Ker-Ys ("the City of the Depths") built for his daughter Dahud, or

Ahes. It was protected from the sea by a dyke and lock-gates, the key to which he jealously guarded.

A rebel against Christianity, and something of a nympho-maniac, the king's daughter joined the inhabitants of the town in their life of debauchery. "So the surrounding seas engulfed the city for the sins of its inhabitants. King Gradlon, who was in the city, miraculously escaped the flood with the help of St Gwennole" (Pierre le Baud, *Chronique*, 1638, pp. 45—6).

Warned by St Gwennole, founder of the abbey of Lande-vennes, of his impending doom, King Gradlon fled on his horse. But his daughter, who had stolen the key to the lock-gates to give to her lover, threw herself at him and jumped on his horse, which began to sink, so that "Princess Dahud, the shameless daughter of a worthy king . . . almost caused his death" (Albert Le Grand, *Vie des saints de Bretagne armorique*, 1636, p. 63).

But St Gwennole touched Dahud with his cross and she disappeared beneath the water. Since then, fishermen have sometimes seen her swimming among shoals of huge fish, and in calm weather they may catch a glimpse of the city of Ys, with its ramparts, palaces and churches, and hear the mournful toll of its bells. To this day the city still opens its gates to men on occasion, and if anyone were able to buy something directly from one of its inhabitants, Ys would be restored to life. But "when the day of resurrection comes for Ker-Ys, the first man to catch sight of the church spire or hear the sound of the bells will become king of the city and all its domains" (A. Le Braz, *Légende de la mort en Basse-Bretagne*, vol. 2, p. 41).

Wales, *Legend of Maes Gwyddneu*

"Seithynin Veddw ['the Drunkard'] in his drunkenness unleashed the sea onto Cantre'r Gwaelod ['the Land of the Underworld']; all the land and houses were lost. Before there had been sixteen important towns. . . . Cantre'r Gwaelod had been part of the land of Gwyddneu Garanhir" (Triad 126, J. Loth, *Mabinogion*, vol. 2, pp. 309—10).

"For Seithynin had violated a young girl who guarded a magic fountain. This had then overflowed and flooded the lands of Gwyddneu" (*Black Book of Carmarthen*, poem 38, translated in *Cahiers du Sud*, no. 319, p. 383).

Ireland, *The Flooding of Lough Neagh*

King Ecca had erected a fortress and dwellings in a low plain where there was a magic well surrounded by thick walls. "And he chose a woman to watch over the fountain, ordering her to keep the door closed except when the people of the fortress came to fetch water" (*Leabhar na hUidre*, eleventh-century MS., extracts and analysis in J.M., *L'Épopée celtique d'Irlande* pp. 39—43).

Following prophecies of flooding, "on one occasion the woman in charge of the fountain forgot to close the door. The water flooded the plain, immediately forming a large lake. Ecca, his family and all his people drowned, except his daughter, Libane." She was probably the woman in charge of the fountain and "lived for a whole year in her room under the lake with her little dog". In the end she grew bored and wanted to be turned into a fish. "On these words she took the form of a salmon, keeping only her own face and breasts." She lived like this for three hundred years before being rescued by St Congall, who baptised her Muirgen, "born of the sea".

The dominant feature of these three versions of the legend is the part played by the woman. She is the guardian of the water, and her thoughtlessness or shortcomings incur the flood, which engulfs the town and the surrounding country. The Breton version has obviously been adapted to Christian tastes, but there are clearly definable traces of the conflict between Christianity and paganism at the end of the fifth century, when the submersion was supposed to have taken place. Since Dahud-Ahes had rejected the Christianity adopted by her father, she was a shameless sinner doomed to the abyss of hell, whereas Gradlon was rescued by a saintly symbol of the new religious order. But heathen traditions endure; both Dahud-Ahes and the town of Ys continue to exist in the depths of the sea. One day they will be restored to life along with the ancient pagan gods, which are the Celtic ways of thought eclipsed and stifled by the new doctrines of Christianity. Already, in this sense, the legend is very expressive.

Who, then, is Dahud-Ahes? It is necessary to establish her identity since she is the main character in the drama. The name Dahud comes from the ancient *dago-soitis*, which means "good witch", a derivation perfectly consistent with her fierce, pagan opposition to Christianity. She also possesses the magical powers of the true witch, which in popular traditions are often a debased form of the powers attributed to divinities. This would make Dahud an ancient Breton goddess honoured in the region of the Pointe du Raz and invariably remembered as the "good witch".

Apart from representing paganism in opposition to Christianity, however, she also symbolises the rebellion against masculine authority, since she stole the key from her father. The full significance of this act becomes clear when one considers her dissolute life as contrary to the teachings of the Christian Church, here represented by St Gwennole, himself the very symbol of masculine authority. Similarly, in the Welsh tale, the girl who relaxed her guard on the fountain while resisting the drunken Seithynin was in fact rebelling against the excessive authority of the king, thereby incurring the flood, which we must assume to have been disastrous. Indeed the poem of Gwyddneu Garanhir says, "Cursed is the young girl, guardian of the fountain, who struggled and then let loose the devastating sea." Libane, daughter of King Ecca, also disobeyed the royal orders, and her rebellion led to the submersion of the town. But like Dahud-Ahes, she continues to live under the water.

This underwater survival is of the greatest importance in understanding the myth and all its implications. From a strictly psychoanalytic point of view, it is a case of inhibited thought. Having proved abortive, the rebellion against masculine authority is repressed into the subconscious. But *it will rise again*, and the first person to take advantage of this resurrection will succeed in taking control of the land, though only on specific occasions, at certain festivals for example, when distant memories can be released from the unconscious and the heart of the citadel is open to the intrepid.

If the rebellion is repressed, however, it is automatically forbidden and becomes the province of the Devil. Since, etymologically, hell is everything that is hidden, Ys is bound to be hell. Its female ruler, who has dared to pit her strength against the king's authority (for which read "God"), and whom the king has punished, is necessarily a bad and lewd woman. She is a *Mala Lucina*, a goddess of darkness, like Hecate who rules the crossroads at night, and even the Devil's own wife, Lilith. Yet, surely she is a reflection of the goddess of ancient, pre-patriarchal societies, the *Magna Mater*, who haunts every corner of life, but reveals herself only very reluctantly, sometimes even as a Black Virgin, that is, the Virgin Mary.

The divine woman is not always submerged under water. Celtic legends abound with stories of princesses shut away in castles and caves, and on islands. Indeed, such stories can be found all over the world, though we shall confine ourselves to the Celtic tradition. In general, they have been taken as simple fairy tales and adventure stories, but if they are related to the legend of Ys and its variants, their dynamic implications become only too evident. Let us look at some of them.

Brittany, *The Story of Guengualc'h*

Some young people returning from their studies were walking along the river bank in the valley of Tregurier. One of them, nicknamed Guengualc'h ("White Falcon") because he was so handsome, fell silent. When his friends tried to ask him a question there was no reply, and turning to look at him, they realised he had disappeared. They searched the river-bank in vain and, finally, in despair, called upon St Tugdual for help.

"Immediately the young man rose to the surface of the river, with a silk sash tied to his right foot." He told how the "ladies of the sea" had taken him away and lured him under the rocks.

He had been rescued by a venerable old man (St Tugdual). "At the sight of the prelate, the nymphs had fled, but one of them forgot to untie her sash." They all offered up thanks to St Tugdual for having rescued Guengualc'h, who had been "temporarily deluded by the Devil". Guengualc'h "went to confession, took Communion, and, exactly a year to the very day after the Devil had led him astray, he left this world" (*Vita Sancti Tutguali Episcopi*, 33, twelfth-century MS. in the Bibliothèque Nationale).

The pious hagiographer who set down this piece of folklore cannot have realised how unedifying the story really was, since Guengualc'h left this world after a year in order to meet the "lady of the sea" who had tied her sash to his right foot. But the legend must have been well known in Celtic countries in the eleventh and twelfth centuries, because it appears in an almost identical Gaelic version, in an Irish manuscript from 1200 A.D., this time in a Druidic context.

Ireland, *The Story of Condle the Red*
　　A woman dressed in the most beautiful clothes appeared to Condle, son of King Conn of the Hundred Battles. He alone could see her, though everyone else could hear her. When the King's Druid cast a spell that drove her away, Condle remained sad and silent for a month, eating nothing but an apple the woman had left him. Then she appeared to him again and invited him to come with her to the "Land of Promise inhabited only by women", in the strange world of the *sidh*, which is underground or over the sea. Despite the Druid's efforts, Condle left his father and family and sailed away in the fairy's "glass boat" never to be seen again.

In every version of the legend there is a distinct conflict between the established religion, whether Christian or Druidic, and the marvellous woman who comes to fetch the man of her choice. But her choice is binding, since she stands as a reminder of an earlier age when women had powers lost to them even in Celtic societies. She is rebelling against masculine authority, as in the legend of Ys, and is equally damned for it in the Christian version of Guengualc'h and the Druidic version of Condle, being banished in both cases to regions farthest removed from acute consciousness, the depths of the waters or a remote island in the middle of the sea, beyond the horizon. And yet she retains her wonderful beauty and her power to attract men even as she alarms them. In this way, the fiction of the beloved witch, the *femme fatale*, begins to take shape, and develops through the witch burnings of the Middle Ages and Renaissance to the commercial exploitation of the vamp in modern cinema and its fantasy world.

The story of Condle is not unique, for there are many songs in Ireland and the Hebrides about the fairy who tries to lure the man of her choice away to magic lands. There is the Greek legend of the Sirens, in which Odysseus, who blocked his men's ears and lashed himself to the ship's mast, typifies the Indo-European patriarchal society. Although man, the male, is instinctively attracted by the female, he knows from experience that, whatever his pride and potency, he will be conquered in the act of love. For him orgasm is almost death, the temporary sapping of his strength, whereas woman is triumphant, regenerated by the act. "The almost universal, male fear of succumbing to women's fascination, even though they are attracted by such subservience, explains why women's effect on men is often satanic. The disparaging attitude many men adopt towards women is symptomatic of an unconscious attempt to dominate a situation which they feel to be to their own disadvantage."[2]

This process of debasing women and banishing them, with a great show of morality, into prohibited areas is particularly apparent in the successive changes made to old legends that retain no more of the original myth than its outline dressed up with circumstantial detail. And within these stories, the polarity is inverted. What was good becomes evil, what was feminine becomes masculine, what was broad daylight fades into darkness, and what was on the surface of the earth disappears under the waters or down into subterranean labyrinths. So, in a popular song from the Tregurier region, in Brittany, revived at the time of the French Revolution, the theme of the story of Guengualc'h and Condle reappears in another form, but in a tone suggesting a puritanical development.

Brittany, *The Girls of Tregurier*

The girls of Tregurier are all pretty, but there has never been any more lovely than the Stoubinenn ("oakum-spinner", meaning loose-living girl). She had a house by the sea and rowdy orgies used to take place there. It was when the churches were closed and the "Blues" (republican soldiers) occupied the country. After that period, people went to look inside the house and there found a tunnel that went under the sea. (Collected in 1898 by Narcisse Quellien.)

The Stoubinenn belonged to a category of women rejected by society, but necessary for its survival. As the Fathers of the Church said, sewers are necessary to ensure the wholesomeness of palaces; or in the words of Simone de Beauvoir, "A caste of 'shameless women' allows the 'honest woman' to be treated with the most chivalrous respect. The prostitute is a scape-goat; man vents his turpitude upon her and he rejects her" (*The Second Sex*, Cape, 1953, p. 529). That is why literature that manifests this masculine attitude makes such a point of the immoral side of the prostitute's life. Indeed, research shows that the clients of such women are the first to deplore their way of life. And, though these opinions are obviously expressed only to salve the conscience, they are significant all the same. "She [woman] knows that masculine morality, as it concerns her, is a vast hoax" (Simone de Beauvoir again). "Man pompously thunders forth his code of virtue and honour; but in secret he invites her to disobey it and he even counts on this disobedience; without it, all that splended façade behind which he takes cover would collapse." The prostitute is therefore the two-fold woman, both rejected and desired. Dreams may adorn her with the most seductive colours, but the preachers of morality proclaim that she breathes only the odour of sin and that men who associate with her are condemned not only to eternal damnation but also to experiencing the misery and degradation of this vile world as acutely as she does, to gradual annihilation, transfixion and death.

But the prostitute is not rejected and forbidden for moral reasons; rather because she is dangerous to the society that tolerates her even as it condemns. As man recalls his subconscious, ancestral obsessions, woman becomes enigmatic, mysterious, dangerous and destructive. His vague memories of life as a carefree foetus in his mother's womb, the scars he still bears of his birth, a brutal uprooting from that warm, damp environment, are both marvellous and terrifying; for they bring back a time of absolute well-being, of paradise, but also the hypnotic nothingness of an earlier non-existence to which he is afraid to return.

Every woman possesses and projects the power of a mother. Every woman is both life and void. "Thus the Woman—Mother has a face of shadows: she is the chaos whence all have come and whither all must one day return; she is nothingness. The multiple aspects of the world which daylight reveals are confused together in the night: night of spirit confined in the generality and opacity of matter, night of sleep and of nothingness. In the deeps of the sea it is night: woman is the *Mare Tenebrarum* dreaded by navigators of old; it is night in the entrails of the earth. Man is frightened of this night, the reverse of fecundity, which threatens to swallow him up" (Simone de Beauvoir, *The Second Sex*, p. 166). So it follows that those who go to explore the house of the Stoubinenn *in the light of day*, simply to know and certainly not to profit from her favours, should descend to the very bottom of the sea and there find nothing, non-existence, the negation of everything. But, since everything exists only through its negation, we return to the dialectic cycle in which there has to be a Stoubinenn to attract men to the bottom of the sea, or there would be no earth above it, no light and no life.

This ambivalent attitude towards women, discernible in the traditional writings of the past or in old folk-songs, is, behind the wealth of legends, about sirens, fairies and enchantresses. Being both everything and nothing, woman becomes the absolute mistress of riches which are, however, hidden, difficult to reach, and dangerous. All traditions alike speak of treasures to be found at the bottom of the sea. According to Hesiod's *Theogonie*, the sea nymphs live in caves under the sea near Triton's golden palace. A Scandinavian legend tells of a divine couple owning the sea bed. The woman, Ran, prepares sky-blue cushions on the sand at the bottom to receive ship-wrecked sailors. In Greenland, the daughter of Tangarsuk lives under the sea and rules over all marine animals. Her lamp overflows with whale oil and the vase below it is full of swimming birds. Marine dogs in front of the door bite those trying to enter the forbidden palace. According to the *Kalevala*, the virgins of Wellamo made their home at the far end of the "cloudy cape under the deep waves". The ruler of the seas rises from the depths to listen to the voice of the bard Väinämöinen. In the Indian epic *Mahabhararta*, when the *Daityas* (demons) were conquered by Indra, symbol of the patriarchal culture, they took refuge under the sea. Similarly, in Irish mythology, when the Tuatha Dé Danann, the people of the goddess Dana, were conquered by the sons of Mile, the Gaels, they had to withdraw into the hills and down into the earth, or to mysterious islands beyond the horizon. They were aquatic creatures who rode seahorses on the green meadows of the sea.

Ireland, *The Voyage of Bran, Son of Febal*

A marvellous woman appeared to Bran, gave him an apple-tree branch and invited him to come and regraft it at Emain, the Island of Women. Bran went there with his companions, travelling over the sea. He met a horseman riding on the surf who introduced himself as Mananann, son of Lir ("the waves") and guided him to Emain. There Bran and his fellows lived an enchanted life among the women, and when, one day, in a fit of homesickness they returned to Ireland, they realised that centuries had flown by. One of the sailors leapt ashore and instantly turned into ashes. Bran and the rest put back to sea without landing. (G. Dottin, *L'Épopée irlandaise*, pp. 55—63.)

Ireland, *The Voyage of Maelduin*

After many adventures and extraordinary encounters at sea, Maelduin and his companions reached an island where they were welcomed by the queen and her seventeen daughters. "So the seventeen men slept with the seventeen daughters and Maelduin with the queen." In the morning the queen said to Maelduin, "Stay here and old age will never overtake you. You will always be as young as you are now and what happened for you last night will happen every night." Tempted by this delightful prospect, "they stayed for three months of that winter and it seemed to them that those three months lasted three years". Even so, they became homesick and tried to leave secretly. But the queen "threw a ball of thread at the boat, Maelduin caught it, and it stuck to his hand. All the queen had to do was reel in the thread and the boat returned to port." So then they stayed three times three months on the island and finally set off again. The queen threw her ball and a seaman caught it. But someone cut off his hand and it fell into the sea with the ball. "Then the queen set up such a lamenting and shrieking that the whole earth was nothing but cries, screaming and despair." (Analysed in J.M., *L'Épopée celtique d'Irlande*, pp. 196—202.)

The older of these two legends, *The Voyage of Bran*, has the heroes succumbing to the charms of the Island of Women, and taking care, except for one impetuous wretch, not to disembark on the homeland to which they have nostalgically returned. But the marvellous country to which they prefer to return is, as Chrétien says of Meleagant's kingdom of Gorre, "the land whence no one comes back". The second version, *The Voyage of Maelduin*, celebrates the successful escape from woman's charms of the man who has fully and consciously succumbed to them. In this we can see the imprint of Christianity, or, at the very least, of a growing mistrust of all the feminine activities formerly considered perfectly beneficent. There exists a further development of the myth in *The Voyage of St Brendan*, a common story in a mediaeval Latin and French literature, in which the Bran—Maelduin hero has become confused with a hypothetical Brendan, Abbot of Clonfert. But, far from denouncing the malice of women and revealing the secret means of escape, the myth has, in this case, been completely restyled by Christian scholars, just as crosses were added to menhirs, churches built over pagan sanctuaries, and some of the divinities of the Celtic pantheon "beatified". Amazingly enough, however, this process has made the myth very easy to understand, for St Brendan sets out quite simply in search of *paradise*, showing that the Land of Women is the Celtic conception of heaven.

The same theme recurs in the myths of Circe and Calypso, though the caution Odysseus displays in Circe's house says a great deal about the Greeks' distrust of female divinities, if not their outright misogyny. Invited to share Circe's couch, Odysseus replies, "You want me to be naked to make me weak and unmanly, but I will not consent to enter your bed unless you, goddess, solemnly promise not to lay another trap for me"; nor will he touch the food and drink prepared by Circe until she has restored to their original shape all the men she changed into animals. When Zeus orders Calypso to free Odysseus and provide him with a boat, the hero demands from her a pledge not to deceive him, to which the nymph replies, "You really are a scoundrel, and a crafty one at that." These words are rather appropriate for a divinity, for basically Odysseus is a sly and deceitful scoundrel, reflecting the men of masculine, Mediterranean societies, who excelled in equivocal legislation and accorded women spurious honours to ensure that real power never fell into their hands. Yet Calypso did love him, and says to Zeus' messenger, Hermes, "I meant to make him immortal and give him eternal youth." As the denying, rational model of patriarchal society, Odysseus is afraid of what happens in the depths of the unconscious, fears woman's power to "make him weak and unmanly", to send him back to the marvellous, timeless world of infancy.

The Celtic hero is less cautious. Once set on a course, he has no misgivings. But then he has no fear of being "emasculated" by women. Even the Christian Celtic hero is ready to face the possibility of submersion. So St Brendan returns to the world of the living a disappointed man, for, according to the harsh laws of God, he had to pass through death before reaching the true paradise. Since the *Odyssey* represents the dawn of Achaean Hellas and is full of references to a bygone era when woman was accorded more honour and power, and the Celts, settled at the other end of Europe, had inherited traditions dating from earliest prehistory, we can take these disparities in attitude as a measure of the difference between the two societies.

For though both Calypso and Circe are distinctly alarming, the queen of the Island of Women is not. She appears as the Divine Horsewoman in *The Voyage of Maelduin*, as Macha in Ireland, Rhiannon in Wales, Epona in Gaul and Roman Gaul. And the horse, being the ceremonial animal that drew the chariot of the sun into the night and led it out again in the morning, was always credited with the ability to enter the Other World. The oldest objects of worship from the Bronze Age are chariots drawn by horses. Some of the animal's qualities passed on to the mediaeval knight, who was himself mysterious, itinerant, sometimes entering strange castles, which were also openings into the Other World. Gradually, however, in more developed traditions, the horse came to take on a satanic aspect, and eventually the mark of Satan became the print of a horse's hoof.

Although man longed to find the beautiful woman of his dreams, he seems to have been deliberately deflected from his search. There were always arduous ordeals and menacing creatures to overcome. Without delving fully, as yet, into the reasons for the quest for woman, let us just examine some traditional images of the submerged woman guarded by repulsive monsters, which in the Christian tradition obviously become tools of Satan or creatures conjured up by the ingenious Prince of Darkness.

Ireland, *The Adventures of Art, Son of Conn*
    Art was bound by a *geis* ("taboo" or "magic and religious constraint"; see Chapter 8 for a full discussion) to procure in

marriage Delbchaen, daughter of Morgan, who lived on an island somewhere in the sea. To reach her, he had to face terrible dangers, cruel stags, "butcher-dogs", hideous toads and thick-maned lions. He had to cross a river of ice and fight a giant. Then he had to choose between two cups, one of which contained poison. Finally, when he had fought and killed the girl's parents, he was able to take her away with him, though not before looting all the treasures of the Marvellous Country as well. (Analysed in J.M., *L'Épopée celtique d'Irlande*, pp. 184—91.)

Brittany, *The Princess Marcassa*

A puny young man, Luduenn ("Drudge"), had to go and search for the bird Dredaine, which was to be found in a golden cage in an inaccessible castle, for it alone could cure the king. Luduenn had to cross three courtyards, one full of venomous reptiles, the second of tigers and the third of giants. But they all slept from eleven to noon, and advantage had to be taken of this. Then he had to pass through three rooms. In the first he grabbed a loaf of bread that stayed the same size no matter how much was eaten, in the second a jug of wine that never emptied, no matter how much was drunk. In the third room he saw a "princess beautiful as the dawn, lying on a purple bed and sleeping deeply. The wine had emboldened him and made the blood rush to his head, and he stripped off his shoes and kissed the princess without rousing her." Finally, in a fourth room he found the bird Dredaine. After a series of adventures, Luduenn returned and was able to improve the king's health but not cure him; for that the monarch had to sleep with the Princess Marcassa, whom Luduenn had "known" in the castle. Meanwhile, the princess, who had given birth to a son, set off in search of Luduenn. She found him, cured the king and married Luduenn. (Told in 1875 by Marie Manac'h de Plougasnou in North Finistère. Luzel, *Contes*, vol. 2, pp. 176—94.)

Brittany, *The Princess of the Enchanted Palace*

Young Efflam was sent by the king to find out why the sun was light red in the morning. He arrived at the palace of the Mother of the Sun, who prevented the sun from destroying him and told him that the sun was light red in the morning because of the radiance of the Enchanted Princess, who stood at the window of her palace. As the king had now fallen in love with the princess, he sent Efflam to look for her. The young man crossed the kingdom of lions, the kingdom of ogres, and the kingdom of ants. He came to the Enchanted Palace and was received by a girl of great beauty, who set him three tasks: to spend one night in a lion's cage, a second in an ogre's den, and on the third night to sort out a great pile of wheat. He succeeded and the girl led him into the presence of the Enchanted Princess, who agreed to follow him home to the king. The king wanted to marry her immediately, but she, objecting that he was too old, suggested that she kill him and then restore him to life as a twenty-year old. He agreed, so she killed him, then coldly declared, "Since he is dead, let him remain so, and the man who took all the trouble can receive the reward." So she married Efflam. (Told by Marc'harid Fulup at Pluzunet, Côtes-du-Nord, in 1869. Luzel, *Contes*, vol. 1, pp. 258-88.)

The hero of these three legends sets out in search of the woman not of his own free will, but because he has been forced to go, and his success does not make sense in a patriarchal context. All three stories are connected with the concept of feminine supremacy; though, while Art has to kill Delbchaen's parents to get her and the Enchanted Princess kills the king to marry Efflam, it is only by chance that Luduenn discovers the Princess Marcassa, while looking for the healing bird. Significantly, the story-teller emphasises that he succumbed to the charm of the princess because of the wine he had drunk. In all three cases the obstacles to be overcome are super-natural and so terrifying that only a valiant warrior like Art, or "innocents" like Luduenn and Efflam, could confront them.

For these monsters keeping their protective vigil over the sub-merged woman are as much materialisations of social prohibitions as they are hallucinations engendered by male psychology. Social taboos began very simply, and the chief of them was the taboo on incest, which Freud has shown to be fundamental in all so-called primitive societies. He pointed out that this taboo is not itself innate and instinctive; on the contrary, incest itself is innate. But Freud thought that the first societies were masculine, patterned on the tribe ruled by the father, i.e. the strongest man, and he explains the act of incest as rebellion against the father by the sons in league with their mother. He had therefore to resort to the Oedipus complex to explain the incestuous instinct in man.

While the Oedipus complex is irrefutable, though overworked, Freud never admitted the possibility of matriarchal societies pre-dating the patriarchal, in which case the initial repression of incest would become a necessity. For all close contact between men and women, whether brothers and sisters or mothers and sons, must be prevented, to save men from female domination. The incestuous instinct derives directly from the promiscuity practised by members of a community that permits free sexual relationships within the same family.

While all supposedly well-ordered societies made incest illegal, they nevertheless tolerated it in special cases and for exceptional people. Such a breaking of taboos echoes through Greek mythology: Hera is both sister and wife of Zeus. For the Egyptians also, the goddess Isis was both sister and wife of Osiris, and the early Pharaohs had to marry their own sisters. If we take Genesis to the letter and accept that Eve gave birth only to boys, we might assume that the human race sprang from incestuous relations between Eve and her sons. Celtic mythology contains similar allusions: Mordred, who rebelled against King Arthur, is the incestuous son of Arthur and his sister; Cú Chulainn is the son of Conchobar and his sister Dechtire; Cormac Conloinges, disputed successor to Conchobar, is the son of Conchobar and his mother Ness; Lleu Llaw Gyffes is the son of Gwyddyon and his sister Arianrod. Finally, Merlin and his sister Gwendydd maintained ambiguous relations so apparent to mediaeval authors that they replaced Gwendydd with Vivienne, who was unrelated to the prophet-wizard.

Such social taboos, directed against incest in particular, served to regulate sexual life throughout a community. But however much constraint they exerted in societies that established absolute monogamy, they were quite useless in circumstances where sexual relationships were free. Consequently, any breaking of sexual taboos to be found in the mythology of monogamous societies suggests the memory of an earlier social state. Simone de Beauvoir says, "these remote ages have bequeathed to us no literature. But the great patriarchal epochs preserved in their mythology, their monuments and their traditions, the memory of the times when women occupied a very high position."

But there are also individual taboos, apparitions that the human being himself shapes from the depths of his subconscious only to repress them again. They are propagated from one generation to the next through social customs, moral or religious prohibitions, and, above all, through deliberate silence. These taboos furnish a fascinating field of study, since they are the clearest expression of the evolution of human thought from the distant past, when woman was gifted, actually or theoretically, with omnipotence, up to modern times, when man, while conceding some secondary rights to woman, himself controls social, economic and religious life.[3] So successful is he that women themselves, conditioned by their education, approve and support this state of affairs, notably by their vote.

Except within specialised works, we seem to be ashamed of discussing individual taboos, though it must be admitted that frankness tends to crush the artificial and romantic delusions fed us about women and love. If women themselves knew the incredible fantasies that haunt the imagination of their bed-fellows they would doubtless be horrified. But Simone de Beauvoir seems to have fathomed the origin of these male obsessions. In *The Second Sex* (p. 165) she writes, "but more often man is in revolt against his carnal state; he sees himself as a fallen god: his curse is to be fallen from a bright and ordered heaven into the chaotic shadows of his mother's womb." This explains the Allegory of the Cave, found in Plato's writings, though attributed to the anti-feminist Socrates. This portrays men as prisoners chained up in a cave, their backs turned towards the entrance so that they cannot see the reality of the outside world except as shadows on the opposite wall. Leaving aside any metaphysical interpretations, it is easy to identify the cave with the uterus, for, as we shall see, it is one of the most common symbols for the womb. And this allegory constitutes one of the pillars of Western philosophy, having influenced the whole system of thought inherited from Greeks, Romans, and Judaic Christians.

Yet Simone de Beauvoir insists on the *macabre* aspect of the maternal womb. "This quivering jelly which is elaborated in the womb (the womb sealed like the grave) evokes too clearly the soft viscosity of carrion for him not to turn shuddering away. . . . The slimy embryo begins the cycle that is completed in the putrefaction of death" (*The Second Sex*, p. 165). In view of this, the amount of suspicion of pregnant women and of procreation itself is hardly surprising. Leviticus says that if a woman bears a male child, she is impure for seven days and must afterwards purify herself for thirty-three days. If the child is a girl, the mother will be impure for two weeks, and must purify herself for seventy days. Sometimes this suspicion can change, for various reasons, into real hatred; witness the many, regrettably true, accounts of pregnant women disembowelled by bloodthirsty maniacs, who are simply labelled "sadists" without much thought being given to the frightening fantasies that consume their sick imaginations. Two Celtic legends clearly illustrate this hatred of pregnant women.

Brittany, *The Legend of Conomor and Tryphina*

King Conomor (or Kynvawr), a historical monarch who reigned in the sixth century A.D. over both the Domnonée Islands and Breton Domnonée and had been widowed several times, married Tryphina, daughter of Waroc'h (or Eric), King of Vannes. According to public rumour, Conomor had maltreated all his former wives from the moment they were with child. When Tryphina became pregnant, she too noticed her husband's hostility and fled. But, at the end of an eventful chase, Conomor overtook her and cut off her head.

Then St Gildas (or Weltas) replaced the head on her shoulders and brought her back to life so that she was able to give birth to a boy, Tremeur, who was unfortunately to be beheaded by Conomor in his turn. After this, by a kind of magic more

Druidic than Christian, St Gildas destroyed Conomor's castle and all its occupants. (Florian le Roy, *Bretagne des saints*, Paris 1959, pp. 211—14.)

Ireland, *The Illness of the Ulstermen*

The goddess Macha, daughter of Etrange, came to live in the house of the peasant Crunniuc, a widower. Macha became pregnant. Then Crunniuc went to the assembly of the Ulstermen, and, as a result of his boasting, the king had Macha brought to him and forced her to take part in a race against his horses. Macha, arguing her advanced state of pregnancy, asked for a delay, but the king was unmoved. She won the race and gave birth to twins. However, she put a curse on the Ulstermen and their descendants. who at certain times would have to suffer the pangs of childbirth for four days and five nights. Only the hero Cú Chulainn was to escape this curse. (D'Arbois de Jubainville, *L'Épopee celtique en Irlande*, Paris 1892, pp. 320—5.)

This fear of pregnant women is related to the mystery surrounding the act of procreation. As we have already mentioned, early man had little idea of his own role in conception, or did not attach much importance to it in view of the prevailing sexual promiscuity. So all the men of the tribe were, in a sense, the fathers of all the children. But if the female privilege of childbearing was awesome it was also ambiguous, since, within the balance of nature, to give life to one being means taking the life of another. The reason why Conomor set upon his wives and on the son born to him by a miracle was because of their implied threat to his own life.

Macha, though the victim of a male conspiracy, was also a goddess and heiress of ancient feminine civilisations. So in revenge she inflicted her own suffering upon her tormentors, as Uranian Venus punished the Scythians for pillaging her temple in Ascalon (Herodotus, *Histories*, IV, 67). The illness of the Ulstermen may be one aspect of the custom of couvade (still practised in some parts of the world), in which the father takes to his bed and simulates the pains of childbirth while his wife is in labour.

This fear of parturition has given rise, throughout the world, to certain traditions in which man's desire to bear children without competition from woman is only too clear. Athene, for example, came out of the skull of Zeus, and Dionysus from his hip. The Hittite god Koumarbu gave birth to two children through two different parts of his body. Bandicoot, ancestor of the American Aranda people, gave birth to a son through his armpits. And the Indian *Mahabharata* (I, 67) tells how Bharadvaja, when about to be anointed king and therefore bound to the strictest chastity, suddenly caught sight of the young Ghritaci naked. He was unable to resist his desire and his sperm spurted to the ground. As it was not decent to leave it there, he collected it up in a jar (*drona*) from which a child was to be born and called Drona, an *ayonija* (who has not come from a *yoni*, or from relations with a female). An almost identical legend from the *Commentary on Sarvanukramani* tells how the celestial nymph Urvaci was banished to earth by the curse of Mithras and Varuna. Then the two gods, travelling on the earth, caught sight of the naked nymph, were no more able to resist, and collected in a pitcher the sperm that flowed from them. From this vessel was born the infant Skanda, and the unfortunate Urvaci was banished from the earth as well.

Given the symbolic importance of the jar or pitcher as the image of and substitute for the womb, it is easier to understand why the people of the first Iron Age cremated their dead and then shut away their ashes in urns, a custom retained in the majority of Indo-European societies. The Greek festival of Anthisteries was the feast of the dead, celebrated in the spring with fantastic drinking bouts, which began with the "Day of Open Jars" in memory of the jars containing the dead of long ago. Similarly, at Samain, the Irish feast of the dead, celebrated on the night of 1st November, the mounds where the gods and the dead resided were opened, to permit interchange between the living and the dead.

The jar, the pitcher, then the hole in the ground, the cave, the underwater grotto, the island in the middle of the sea — all symbols of woman — are also symbols of death. Indeed, death personified is nearly always a woman, except in Brittany where there is a masculine character, the Ankou. In his *Gynophobia ou la peur des femmes*, Wolfgang Lederer draws attention to those mediaeval statues that from the front look like a beautiful woman, adored by a knight, but from the back appear to be rotted away or resemble the back of a skeleton. In the arts, as in literature, witches were deliberately represented as horrible, grimacing hags, whereas accounts of mediaeval and Renaissance trials indicate that women accused of withcraft were often young and beautiful. Celtic literature also contains examples of this kind, in which the hero grapples with hideous women who can only have risen from the world of the dead.

Wales, *Peredur ab Evrawc*

One day at the court of Arthur at Caerleon-on-Usk, a young girl with black hair came before the king, Gwalchmai, Owein and Peredur mounted on a decrepit mule. "She was coarse and fat, her face and hands blacker than the blackest iron steeped in pitch . . . she had bulging cheeks, an elongated jaw, a little nose with distended nostrils, one gleaming eye greenish-grey, the other black as jet and deep set, and long yellow teeth, yellower than gorse flowers. Her belly stuck up from her abdomen as

high as her chin and she had a hunched back." She saluted all
those present, but cursed Peredur because, although he had
been to the Castle of Marvels and there witnessed a strange
spectacle, he had not put the question that would have restored
health to the wounded king and prosperity to his lands. She
added that in her own home there was imprisoned a beautiful
girl, and that "he who freed her would acquire the greatest
renown in the world". Then Gwalchmai decided to go and
attempt the adventure that later led him to discovering the
mysteries of the Castle of Marvels. (J. Loth, *Mabinogion*, vol. 2,
pp. 103–6).

In Chrétien's *Perceval* there is an episode that is almost identical,
even down to the description of the hideous damsel, while in
Wolfram von Eschenbach's *Parzival* there is Kundry the Witch, an
equally ugly woman.

Kundry is a female divinity highly typical of the Celtic tradition.
She may be disguised as a repulsive virago, as the need arises, but
may also bring happiness or misery in her amorous relationships with
mortals. It was she who drove the Fisher-King Amfortas to his
wretched state, but she also made Parzifal (who is the equivalent of
the Welsh Peredur, and Chrétien's Perceval) King of the Grail.
Though her dangerous aspect is brought out and symbolised by her
ugliness, she never for an instant loses her fundamental ambiguity,
which is why she attracts men. Obviously very few men will succeed
in possessing her. Access to forbidden domains is restricted to the
privileged. Since the submerged woman represents knowledge, wealth
and power all at the same time, logically she cannot belong to
everybody, or so aristocratic patriarchal societies would have men
believe. It is therefore necessary to divert the desires of ordinary
mortals away from her by means of taboos or fear, which is really
just another form of taboo. The breaking of taboos is then a magical
act accomplished by the man who loves, who has overcome his
repugnance and is resigned to annihilation in order to win all. For,
just as there is no spark of new life without death and putrefaction,
so the new man of whom the myths dream can be born only after
total annihilation in the woman's embrace.

Ireland, *The Sons of Eochaid Muigmedon*

The five sons of Eochaid, King of Ireland, suffered from
thirst while out hunting, and each in turn tried to find water.
They met a horrible-looking old woman whose "whole body
was black as coal from top to toe. Her bristly grey hair stood up
like a wild horse's tail. Her teeth were green and reached to her
ears; they could have been used to cut green oak branches. She

had dark and bleary eyes, a hooked nose with cavernous nostrils. Her body was stringy, sickly and covered with boils. Her legs were twisted in all directions, her ankles thick, her shoulders wide, her knees fat, her nails green." This woman refused to give anyone water from her well unless they gave her a kiss. The four eldest sons of Eochaid refused, but the youngest, Niall, agreed and kissed her. She then turned into the most beautiful and marvellous girl in all the world and announced that her name was Flaithius, which means "royalty". That is how Niall became King of Ireland. (J. M., *Les Celtes*, pp. 176–8.)

Scotland and Ireland, *The Daughter of the King under the Waves*
The Fiana had gathered around Finn one evening when a horrible, repulsive woman asked leave to come in. Finn and his son Oisin both refused. but Diarmaid alone took pity on her, brought her in close to the fire and, despite the revulsion she aroused in him, went as far as allowing her to share his bed. There he realised that she had become a very beautiful girl. By means of magic she built Diarmaid a castle on Ben Endain hill, and agreed to live with him on condition that he would not upbraid her three times with the kindnesses he had shown her. Naturally he broke this taboo and the girl and the castle disappeared. Then Diarmaid set off to look for her, borrowing a boat that took him way under the sea. There he learnt that the king's daughter had returned after seven years' absence, but that she was very ill and nobody could cure her. After many adventures, Diarmaid obtained a magic goblet that restored her to health, but he could then feel only disgust for her, and so abandoned her and returned to Ireland. (A story collected by Campbell in the Highlands. Loys Bruyere, *Contes populaires de la Grande-Bretagne*, 1875, pp. 175–83.)

In most such stories it was the youngest and weakest who dared overcome his aversion. Niall was the youngest son of Eochaid, Diarmaid the youngest of the Fiana. This seems to endorse the psychoanalytic claim of an important social revolution in the dim and distant past, when the youngest son in league with the mother seized power from an all-powerful father, the other brothers later following his example. In some stories his brothers, jealous of his success, disabled him and appropriated his gains, as in the biblical story of Joseph and his brothers.

However, although Niall was happy with the kingship he had won by his ritual gesture, Diarmaid had doubts about his fate. The first time he lost the daughter of the King under the Waves was because, by breaking the taboo, he unconsciously wanted to be rid of her, possibly because he regretted having given himself body and soul to a mysterious woman of unknown origins. But when he realised she had gone, he was torn, and his conscious mind bade him search for her and bring her back, as Orpheus descended to Hades to reclaim Eurydice from the God of the Underworld, because he still knew so little about her. Then, once he had found and cured her, he rejected her again, this time of his own conscious free will, because, like Orpheus turning to look at Eurydice, he had seen her as she really was, the ugly and repulsive woman who had entered the house of the Fiana. Everything else was merely an illusion.

The story of Diarmaid seems to be entirely patriarchal and Christian in context. By accepting the woman's proposition, he betrayed his own people and his social background, and was so infatuated that he took a long time to return to the straight and narrow path of patriarchal law, which he should never have left.

The same idea appears, even more heavily imbued with Christian notions, in the *Quête du Saint Graal,* a composite work constructed from pagan Celtic legends and thirteenth-century Christian mysticism.

Two Adventures of Perceval

In search of the mysterious Castle of the Grail, Perceval, after many adventures, found himself without a horse in an unknown place. A woman offered him a magnificent charger, which he accepted only to be given a hair-raising ride. Suspicious, he crossed himself, and the horse tossed him to the ground and dashed headlong into the river, which it set on fire. (*Quête du Saint Graal,* trans. A. Béguin, pp. 90—1.)

Soon after, Perceval saw a magnificent ship approaching over the sea, and on board a damsel adorned in the most sumptuous clothes. She invited Perceval aboard and told him what had happened to Galahad and the other knights. Perceval followed her and was received with all honour and the greatest respect. After an enormous meal of meat and drinks, the damsel had a pavilion erected on the river-bank, so that Perceval could rest from the heat of the sun. Then she came to join him and made him promise to stay with her. Overcome with drink, Perceval gave way to all her wishes, but, just as he was about to perform the act, he caught sight of the cross on the hilt of his sword. He immediately made the sign of the cross and "the pavilion turned upside down, smoke and cloud enveloping it so thickly that he could see nothing and such a stench all around that he thought himself in hell." Naturally, when he opened his eyes again there was no trace of the pavilion and the ship was sailing away, with the damsel on board crying, "Perceval, you have betrayed me!" Later a hermit, to whom he told his story, explained that the damsel, a creature of "the enemy" had wanted to shut him in the round pavilion, which is the world tainted by sin, and to screen him from the great sun, which is the fire of the Holy Ghost. (Ibid., pp. 93—101).

In Perceval's second adventure, the whole pattern of the myth of the submerged woman is clearly delineated, as is its subsequent development from an interpretative point of view. Like Dahud-Ahes, who still rules over the city of Ys beneath the waves and invites her lovers to follow her, the damsel of the ship, robed in beautiful clothes which symbolise the spiritual or material riches found *below*, asked Perceval to come and share the feast of immortality she had prepared for him. Then, through the sexual act, which would be a kind of death for Perceval, she would restore him to the pre-natal paradise where there was only the innocent bliss of original existence. In a last surge of male pride, as well as fear of submersion, Perceval freed himself from her clutches.

The story of Merlin and Vivienne contains the same idea. Vivienne used the magic powers taught her by Merlin to enclose him in a castle of air, outside the world. But Merlin, who was entirely aware of his impending fate, accepted the return to an earlier state and submerged himself voluntarily. Perceval was not mature enough for such an experience and was to come to it later through his discovery of the Grail, which has exactly the same significance but with mystical overtones. For the Grail, like the round pavilion and Merlin's castle of air, is an image of the maternal womb. It contains blood, and nobody can look inside it without risking his life. Seeing the bottom of the Grail led Galahad to his death.

Meanwhile the hermit's Christian interpretation of Perceval's adventure as an attempt of the maiden to separate him from the great sun, which is the Holy Ghost, is extremely significant. It revives the pagan myth of the black sun, the spiritual sun that shines only for the initiated, who can see in the dark, and which would have shone for Perceval once he had left the visible and material world of ordinary sunlight. But the Christian adaptors of the legend found this idea dangerous. Everything black is suspect because uncontrollable, and must therefore be forbidden. That is why the damsel of the ship is a creature of "the enemy" and why one shrinks even from calling her by name, for the real names of dangerous things should never be uttered.

In the Middle Ages everything female was more or less in league with "the enemy". It is only surprising that Satan himself was not feminised. But, be that as it may, "the enemy" was believed to rule over women and operate through them, to preside at the witches' Sabbath. Having first incited Eve to sin, to make Adam sin, he supposedly continues trying to make man sin through the wiles, seductiveness and sexuality of woman. "The iniquity of man comes from woman, and the iniquity of woman comes from herself", says the Bible. Every day in their morning prayers, the Jews recite, "Blessed be thou, Lord our God, King of the Universe, for not having made me a woman." From then on Christianity did nothing but stress, to the point of frenzy, this hatred of woman, seizing upon minor physiological details and using them to construct prohibitive and insurmountable barriers. With the exception of St Jerome, the Fathers of the Church exemplified to perfection the type of person we now call "sex-obsessed". Having said that woman was "the gateway to the Devil", Tertullien then redefined her as "a temple built over a sewer", and St Augustine solemnly pronounced, "*inter faeces et urinam nascimur*".

We have reached the crux of the problem. Woman really is a temple, as Tertullien said, but to reach it one must travel by paths that, in the words of Simone de Beauvoir, are ' hidden, tormented, mucous, damp, full of blood and sullied with secretions". That is why the roads leading to the Castle of the Sun, a symbol of femininity because the sun was originally feminine, are so secret, dangerous, bristling with monsters, and full of swamps, quagmires and infernal torrents. "Woman as body vessel is the natural expression of the human experience of woman bearing the child 'within' her and of man entering 'into' her in the sexual act . . . woman is the life vessel as such in which life forms, and which bears all living things and discharges them out of itself and into the world. . . . All the basic functions occur in this vessel-body schema, whose 'inside' is an unknown. Its entrance and exit zones are of special significance. Food and drink are put into this unknown vessel, while in all creative functions, from the elimination of waste and the emission of seed to the giving forth of breath and the word, something is 'born' out of it. *All* body openings — eyes, ears, nose, mouth, rectum, genital zone, as well as the skin — have, as places of exchange between inside and outside, a numinous accent for early man."[4] As the memory of man is extremely retentive, this fascination becomes confused and tainted with shame in the various practices of love. In fact, all kinds of embraces, the normal penetration of the vagina, and even those acts usually classed as "perversions", however repugnant they may seem, are no more in the final analysis than a normal impulse to discover the way to the inside, the *open door into the closed castle of the king*, of which the alchemists wrote.

Man's simultaneous attraction and aversion towards woman is an indisputable biological fact. All ancient myths bear evidence of this, the Celtic as much as others. We have examined some examples, particularly those emphasising the external ugliness of woman. There are others which concern the woman herself.

The ambivalence of male feelings towards woman has persisted in the literature of every country. It finds violent expression in a short and little-known tale by Georges Bataille. *Dirty*, the name of the eponymous heroine, says a great deal in itself. But the remarkable thing about the Celtic tradition is that it painted a far less monstrous or ignoble portrait of woman than, say, Greek, Latin or modern literature. Presumably the Celts were willing to respect this mysterious creature, whom they certainly feared, but who nevertheless retained a certain image of purity and perfection, as is clear from a detailed analysis of twelfth- and thirteenth-century courtly romances, which were all Celtic in inspiration.

Masculine fantasies are more evident in the quests for the submerged woman, who is always in a castle, or a cave, on an island, or in a palace deep under the sea, somewhere where there is "nothing but luxury, calm and sensual pleasure", as Baudelaire put it. But the way to this Holy of Holies must first be found, and the mythological paraphernalia used by storytellers to describe the passage of the bold man in his attempts to reach the woman reveal all the repulsions that served both as a barrier and a stimulus to desire in the man. Naturally, the patriarchal structures of pagan Celtic society, followed by the moral imperatives of Christianity, stressed these repulsions, choosing evocative images to endow them with a formidable power over the imagination. The submerged woman is well protected, the prohibitions insurmountable for ordinary mortals.

Take the myth of the cave, for example. It is hardly necessary to emphasise the uterine or vaginal significance of the grottos held sacred by religions throughout the world, including Christianity. It is no accident that the Virgin Mary manifests herself in caves, such as at Lourdes, nor that tradition places the birth of Christ in a cave serving as a stable. The legacy of the Palaeolithic era, when human beings actually lived and slept, prayed to their gods, died and buried their dead in caves, is evident in Romanesque churches, especially their crypts. But the Celtic inheritance came in an even more direct line from the Neolithic era, with its natural or engineered caves (such as those in the valley of Petit Morin, near Coizard (Marne), where the submerged woman, portrayed on the chalk walls as a funeral goddess, waited for her zealots), and its megalithic monuments, dolmens with a single chamber, and, most importantly, strange covered walks, consisting of a long corridor, sometimes in an L-shape, leading to the sanctuary chamber deep in the earth. The corridor is very low at the entrance and grows higher as one approaches the cavern, which is where the Gaels believed their gods and goddesses lived, the divinities whom folklore was to transform into fairies and good women, the memory of whom still lives in the countryside, even in our technocratic age.

The Caves of the Fairies

"In the bay of Yaudet in Ploulec'h, on the edge of the English Channel, everyone once talked about a very deep cave which held, not a fairy, but a princess who had been enchanted there along with vast treasures. And there she had to remain asleep until the day when a bachelor, impervious to fear, came to release her." (Paul Sébillot, *Le Folklore de la France*, Guilmoto, Paris 1904—7, vol. 2, p. 121.)

There is a fairy cave in Guernsey which can be entered only at low tide, by clambering over great masses of rocks heaped around the entrance. (Ibid., vol. 2, p. 116.)

A hunchbacked hunter entered a cave near Lourbières (Ardèche), saw that the moss was changed to gold and there were lights lit, and in the middle a well-stocked table. So he ate. Then he saw golden skittles falling and a golden ball, but it was the body of a fairy, who began to sing. (Ibid., vol. 1, p. 437.)

"Black fairies of the Pyrenees carried off young cowherds who had left their cattle to look for the nests of white partridge. The Margot fairies also kept men in their caves, but without compulsion. The men were so pleased to be there that the time seemed to pass more than twice as quickly as normal." (Ibid., vol. 1, p. 442.) "Fairies had an underground home near Giromagny, not far from Belfort, and often farmers at the plough heard them scraping at their troughs." (Ibid., vol. 1, p. 451.)

At St Aignan in the Ardennes, deep faults let out steam, which is sometimes very dense. People believed that fairies lived there and the steam came from their cooking. (Ibid., vol. 1, p. 452.)

"A cave in the valley of the Vienne, near St Victurien, was once inhabited by supernatural beings, half woman, half animal, known as *fanettes*, which means 'bad fairies'." (Ibid., vol. 1, p. 453.)

On the Channel coast, at St Brieuc near Dinard, fairies known as *houles* inhabited caves that "extended a long way into the earth, as far as the outskirts of small towns, from whence the crowing of the fairies' cockerels could be heard. One of the caves stretched as far as Notre Dame de Lamballe, twenty-five miles from its entrance. According to some accounts, one could, after passing through a kind of tunnel, see a world like ours, with its own sky, sun, earth, trees and even beautiful castles at the end of long avenues." (Ibid., vol. 2, p. 108).

This last superstition has a strange affinity with the Irish belief that after crossing the borders of the fairy hill, the *sidh*, one discovered a universe like our own. It was there that the Tuatha Dé Danann lived, the gods of ancient times and champions of a civilisation that, according to mythology, was so organised as to allow women greater participation in communal life. Thus it is hardly surprising that people believed there to be fairies in such caves and in the artificial hills formed by megalithic monuments.

The way into this universe, however, is difficult, dangerous and cruel. Countless legends are based on the fantasy of the *toothed vagina*. For the myth of perilous penetration into the cave where the submerged woman is secluded is just symbolic imagery for the act of defloration. The fear of unforeseen hazards in the darkened cave is the fear that something might befall the "noble parts" of the man. In India, many stories tell of women whose vagina is full of teeth which cut the man's penis.[5] In other places, particularly the fabulous kingdom of Prester John, which was renowned throughout the Middle Ages, there are snakes in the vagina and wild beasts guarding the entrance, ready to devour all lovers caught in the vital act. According to accounts of the trials of witches, they too were reputed to mutilate the penis during copulation.

This strongly held and almost universal belief is obviously connected with the fear of blood. Apart from imposing an incredible number of taboos on menstrual blood, which was considered alarming and *unhealthy* (as the Bible shows all too clearly), men believed that the blood of defloration brought misfortune. Their fears may have been increased by difficulties encountered in the act itself, whether as the result of male weakness or of tightness or deformity in the woman; which would explain why, in certain countries, defloration was practised with the aid of a cutting instrument, or just a stick or stone. More importantly, it explains the curious custom inaccurately called *droit de siegneur*, a privilege not necessarily accorded to or monopolised by a lord. On the contrary, if defloration is dangerous, then it must be performed by a physically and *spiritually* powerful person, whether priest, king or prince, who can ward off the curse that would otherwise afflict the unfortunate husband. There is proof of this in the fact that they who succeed in penetrating the cave are always exceptional beings, gifted with extraordinary physical and spiritual strength. The hero has to overcome the wild beasts that guard the entrance, and then his own hallucinations, those spells he believes to be inflicted on him, before at last gaining the sanctuary, the temple. His mission is therefore sacred. Several Celtic tales illustrate this theme.

Wales, *Peredur and the Addanc*

The sons of the King of Sufferings were killed each day by an *addanc* (giant beaver), which lived in a cave. And each day they were brought back to life with the aid of a resurrection cauldron. Peredur had promised to kill the monster, and a woman of marvellous beauty appeared to him, saying, "I know the object of your journey: you are going to fight the *addanc*. It will kill you not by courage, but by cunning. On the threshold of its cave stands a pillar of stone. There it hides so that it can see all comers without being seen, and kills them with a poisoned dart. If you give your word that you love me more than any other woman in the world, I will give you a stone which will enable you to see it as you go in, without its seeing you." That is how Peredur managed to enter the cave and kill the *addanc*, whose head he bore away. (J. Loth, *Mabinogion*, vol. 2, pp. 94—6.)

Ireland, *The Raid on Fraech's Cattle*

Fraech's wife and his herd were carried off to a mysterious fortress guarded by a snake, which stood in the way of all access by the unwary. Fraech arrived at the fortress accompanied by Conall Cernach, foster brother of Cú Chulainn and one of the three best warriors in Ulster. Conall fought so well that the snake fell back in coils and Fraech was able to recover his wife and cattle. (G. Dottin, *L'Épopée irlandaise*, p. 100.)

Ireland and Cornwall, *Tristan and the Great Crested Snake*

Sent by his uncle, King Mark, to obtain the hand of Iseult the Fair, daughter of the King of Ireland, Tristan disembarked in disguise, because there was a price on his head in Ireland. A great crested snake was devastating the island and the king issued a proclamation that he would give his daughter to whoever killed it. Tristan entered the snake's cave and managed to kill it after a fierce battle. But, poisoned by the foul breath of the monster, he fell down in a faint. A cowardly knight cut off the snake's head and went to claim the reward, but Iseult was suspicious and came to the cave, where she found Tristan. The impostor was punished and Tristan sailed away with Iseult. (André Mary, *Tristan*, pp. 49—52.)

Courtly romance, *The Bridge of the Sword*

Queen Guinevere had been abducted and imprisoned by Meleagant in his kingdom of Gorre (or Verre), "whence no one returns". Launcelot set out in search of her. There were two ways into the kingdom of Gorre, by the Bridge of the Sword or by the Bridge under the Water. Launcelot chose the first, and had to crawl laboriously along a great sword thrown across a river of boiling water. "His hands, feet and knees were bleeding." And he could see two lions lying in wait for him at the other side. But when he reached the far bank "he cast his eyes about him and saw nothing, not even a lizard, no animal at all that could cause him harm . . . so he had proof that, as neither of the lions was to be seen, he had been deluded by a magic spell." And yet it was Gawain who, entering with great difficulty by the Bridge under the Water, managed, after complicated adventures, to rescue Queen Guinevere. (Chrétien de Troyes, *Le Chevalier à la charrette*.)

Courtly romance, *The Castle of the Grail*

After an enchanged voyage, Launcelot reached the foot of a mysterious fortress. "At the back of the castle was a doorway facing over the water, and open night and day. There was no sentry at this side, because two lions guarded it and no one could reach the gate without passing between them." Launcelot stepped out of his boat and prepared to tackle the lions. But a flaming hand hit him violently on the arm, knocking the sword out of his hand, while a voice bade him listen, reproaching him for his lack of faith. Indeed, when he approached the lions, they let him pass without a murmur. Launcelot went up into the castle and came upon a sealed door. He asked God to allow him to see something of the mysteries hidden behind this door. Then "Launcelot saw the door to the room swing open and such brightness shone out that the sun might have made its home there. . . . At this sight Launcelot felt such joy and such longing to see whence the light came, that he forgot everything else." But he was not allowed to enter the room of the Holy Grail. (*Quête du Saint-Graal*, trans. A. Béguin, Editions du Seuil, Paris 1965, pp. 222—4.)

All these tails emphasise the strange and sacred character of the place that the hero must enter. And in every case it is to win a woman or a substitute for her (the Grail being a feminine symbol, as its solar brightness proves, since the Celts saw the sun, if not as a goddess, then at least as a feminine power; Iseult the Fair is herself the sun personified). All the animals that stand in the hero's way, whether snakes or lions or the fantastical *addanc*, are illusions or apparitions projected by the imagination. The details in the *Quête du Saint-Graal*, despite its Christian overtones, may well be even more ancient, if we take the trouble to interpret them. Once he has overcome his *ante portam* repulsions, the man enters the woman. So the description of Launcelot's happiness and oblivion is simply the sublimation of a physical orgasm; but incomplete because Launcelot was disqualified from total and ultimate possession of the Grail by his sin, his unbroken attachment to the patriarchal system of his education. This whole passage is reminiscent of a hymn recited by the initiates into the cult of Cybele, the goddess of Asia Minor, and written down by Clement of Alexandria:

I have eaten on the tambourine,
I have drunk from the cymbal,
I have carried the Sacred Cup,
I have entered the Bridal Chamber.[6]

The way in which the myth of the cave (or castle) guarded by monsters was developed can be illustrated by two tales taken from Christian hagiography. The first was recorded in a twelfth-century Anglo-Norman work; the second occurs, with a remarkable number of variations, in the Breton oral tradition.

Ireland, *St Patrick's Purgatory*

The knight Owen, reputed to be a man of piety and courage, braved the well of St Patrick in Ireland, a place of darkness from which nauseating smoke and terrible cries emerged. There he saw all kinds of atrocity, for it was in fact purgatory, a kind of small, temporary hell. He left purified by the ordeal and lived a devout life for the rest of his days. (J. Marchand, *L'Autre monde au Moyen Age*, Paris 1940, pp. 81—115.)

King Arthur, who had vowed to destroy superstition in Ireland, arrived at the cave that led to the place of the dead and from where, after purification, souls flew up joyfully towards heaven. Gawain stopped Arthur from exploring the depths of this cave, where they could hear the boom of a waterfall that gave off the smell of sulphur and echoed with mournful voices. (After a sixteenth-century Latin work quoted by G. Dottin in *Annales de Bretagne*, vol. 26, p. 792.)

Brittany, *St Efflam and King Arthur*

Young Efflam, son of the king of Ireland, did not consummate his marriage with the British princess, Enora; for during the wedding night he ran away and sailed to Brittany. Hardly had he set foot ashore when he saw a monstrous dragon going into its cave. He met King Arthur, who was pursuing the monster but could not catch up with it. Efflam guided Arthur to the cave and the king fought the dragon but had to give up the struggle. Then the next day, by dint of prayer, Efflam forced the monster to submerge itself in the sea, where it disappeared. (Albert le Grand.)

These two Christian adaptations of a pagan legend are rather curious. The Purgatory of St Patrick is a kind of inferno, a god-forsaken cave entered only by those who are already sinners. But, paradoxically, it is also the way to heaven. The knight Owen purified himself in the bowels of the earth, meaning the inside of woman. The story of St Efflam is quite clear-cut. Whatever the hagiographers may have said, it was not fear of losing his virginity that made him run away on his wedding night, but his inability to perform the act. He was inhibited psychologically, and could not overcome his obsessions until encouraged by the king's example. This is reminiscent of the *droit de seigneur*, which eventually became a simple ceremony in which the lord ritually placed one leg in the marriage bed. Once Efflam had managed to make the dragon sink into the sea, access to the cave became free, as if by chance.

Efflam's inhibitions were the result of an anti-feminist education, from which men have suffered for many centuries. In her book *Female Sexuality* (University of Michigan Press, 1970), Janine Chasseguet Smirgel quotes the case of a young man of twenty-two, who suffered from premature ejaculation and was unaware of the existence of the vagina as a purely sexual organ. For him it was a place of terror and atrocities, requiring it to be abused and kept locked up. Eventually his obsessions reached the point of anal sadism, which can obviously be regarded as abnormal, but which proves that everything he had been told about women involved exaggerated horror and prohibition. The flight of St Efflam, which was skilfully exploited by the preachers of conjugal chastity, was a flight from the terrors of the slimy cave containing the dragon, which he had to conquer to regain his potency and sanity. Peredur, as we shall see in a later chapter, was faced with the same predicament during his quest for the Grail.

As we have seen, the cave had an equivalent in the fortress, usually surrounded by water or buried in the earth. But apart from their similarity in shape and origin (early man must have taken refuge in natural caves), the analogy between the fortress and the woman is evident in the word *ark*, usually taken to mean "vessel" or "shelter". The Latin word *arca* means "chest," "coffin" and "womb," and derives from a root, probably of Etruscan origin, that also became *arcanum* ("mystery," "secret," "arcane") and *arx* (genitive *arcis*), meaning "citadel," the most central point of the fortress, or the "keep," its mediaeval equivalent. Moreover, as Otto Rank observed, towns are captured and treated like women, and sometimes women are treated like towns, both to be conquered. Historical study suggests that the violation of women after the capture of a town may have been more than just an act of brutality, and in fact a symbolic gesture, unconsciously recalling ancient ritual.

The hero who manages to enter the cave or fortress is re-enacting his own birth, though in reverse, for the Submerged Princess is his mother, welcoming and protecting the child, who gives her an intense new life. For this, however, he must overcome all taboos and prohibitions. "The difficulties and dangers lying in wait for the newborn child on his emergence (from the maternal womb) are replaced by the difficulties and dangers obstructing Price Charming's approach to Sleeping Beauty (thorny plants, slippery paths, crags strewn with pitfalls), while the final liberation of the beloved is represented by the destruction of the armour, the opening of the coffin and the tearing of the bodice, all coverings that make the virgin inaccessible."[7]

This emphasises the dual nature of the act, its pleasure and its pain, and shows that "the anguish caused by the trauma of birth can be overcome by redeeming love. Consequently, the liberation of the Sleeping Beauty depends on a negation of the anguish following birth. This is particularly evident in stories where the hero, after having killed the dragon, himself falls into a death-like sleep."[7]

One interesting point worth noting is that the cave or fortress is almost always surrounded by water or marshland, in some wasteland covered with moors and damp forests, either wrapped in mist or explicitly in the sea or a lake. Human imagination has always made marshes places of trouble and devilry, for they are an intermediate zone, neither earth nor water, where all life is both made and destroyed. We are made from water and clay, to which we shall return in decomposition, so marshland becomes the alarming region of exchange between the living and the dead. In Brittany, in the Arrée hills close to St Michael's Mount of Braspart, there is a large marshy hollow called Yeun Elez, which is supposed to be one of the gates to hell. Close by, at Brennilis, there is a statue to Our Lady of Breach-Ilis or Breach-Ellez, which means "Our Lady of the Ellez Marshes". The word Ellez, also found in the river Ellé or the Forest of Brocéliande (Breach-Elliant), derives from the same Indo-European root as has given us "hell" in English. So the submerged woman is more than ever the "empress of the salt-marshes" to whom François Villon refers in his *Ballade pour prier Notre Dame*.

But the connection between woman and water has further implications, for, as Sandor Ferenczi observes,[8] the sex act represents both birth in reverse and an unconscious enactment of the desire to return to dampness. This in fact means a negation of the disaster of drainage, which expelled the distant ancestors of man from their watery environment millions of years ago. It explains why the fish is used to symbolise the penis and the unborn child, and through it the unconscious memory of an earlier aquatic existence experienced by every human being during the process of foetal maturation in an enclosed and damp environment. So the desire of the hero who rushes into the quest for the Submerged Princess is related "to the endeavour to re-establish the lost way of life in a watery environment which also contains nourishing substances, in other words, the damp and well-fed aquatic existence inside the mother."[9]

Hence the specific significance of the fish in certain traditions. According to the Life of St Korentin, first Bishop of Quimper, he would feed for several months from one fish, cutting a slice from it in the evening only to find it had become whole again during the night. Among the Chaldeans, the fish Oannes was supposed to be the first living thing and was therefore regarded as the primordial god and provider. The early Christians used the image of the fish not only as a badge of recognition, but also because Christ represented the eternal food that his message had come to promise, namely a return to the life of paradise preceding the disaster.

Through the affinity between the watery worlds of the fish and of woman, the fish eventually came to symbolise woman herself, as is borne out by the myth of the Sirens or mermaids, marine women with a fish's tail. The Indian divinity Satyavati, whose name means "truth", was also named "Stinking Fish". Woman is ruled by a lunar cycle of twenty-eight days, which matches the influence of the moon on the tides. The vaginal liquid secreted as a result of sexual stimulation has a characteristic smell of fish, due to the presence of trimetylamine, a substance found in fish when it begins to decompose. All these facts explain why the approaches to the cave or the swamps exhale a smell that makes the fastidious recoil while paradoxically attracting them. Myths are never gratuitous fictions, but convey in imaginary form the fundamental truths of being and of life.

Once he has overcome all repulsions, however, and surmounted the threshold, the hero finds the delights of paradise.

Vosges, *Lyon and the Austrian Princess*
Young Lyon entered a marvellous castle, after overcoming many obstacles and killing three giants. He crossed a first room of silver, a second of gold, and a third which contained precious stones. In a fourth room he discovered the Austrian Princess asleep, and above her a sign bearing the words "he who releases me after killing the three giant guards of the castle will win me and remove the ring I have on my finger". (L. F. Sauvé, *Le Folklore des Hautes-Vosges*, Paris 1889, pp. 326—40.)

Brittany, *The Night of Pentecost*
There is a city submerged under the sands of St Efflam (Côtes-du-Nord), and every year on the night of Pentecost, during the twelve strokes of midnight, it rises up and is accessible. Perik Skoarn found his way in to fetch a hazel-wand that gave absolute power. He crossed through rooms full of silver, gold and precious stones and reached the room where the wand lay. But there he saw "a hundred girls beautiful enough to deprave the souls of saints. Each of them held in one hand a crown of oak and in the other a cup of fiery wine." Perik Skoarn fell down in ecstasy and stayed until the twelfth stroke of midnight had sounded. So he disappeared along with the town. (E. Souvestre, *Le Foyer Breton*, W. Coquebert, Paris 1845).

Ireland and Scotland, *Diarmaid and Grainne*
Grainne ("the Sun") wife of King Finn, fled with young

Diarmaid, compelling him with a *geis*. They both took refuge in
a cave until daylight, when they were betrayed by the wood
shavings swept along by the stream that flowed out of the cave.
(J.M., *L'Épopée celtique d'Irlande*, pp. 153—64.)

German version, *Tristan*

When Tristan and Iseult were caught in the act of love by
King Mark and managed to escape execution, they took refuge,
not in the Forest of Morrois, as other versions have it, but in a
cave built by giants, where the keystone of the arch was made
from precious stones. In the middle was enthroned a bed of
crystal, and there the two lovers performed the liturgy of love,
using the bed as an altar. (Cf. Denis de Rougemont, *Passion and
Society*, Faber and Faber, 1940.)

These tales show how paradise is made real again, when the
"sanctuary", the very heart of the castle, is reached. The citadel may
be in the centre of a submerged town, as in *The Night of Pentecost*,
or set in the depths of a natural or artificial cave, which in *Diarmaid
and Grainne* retains obvious female sexual characteristics, even down
to the flowing stream, which symbolises mentrual flow. In Gottfried
von Strassburg's *Tristan*, however, the cave actually becomes a
well-appointed temple, *super cloacam*, as Tertullien called it. And the
fact that this German version has a cave, rather than the more usual
forest, leads us quite naturally to see a symbolic equivalence between
the two.

The mysterious forest, which becomes "virgin" forest when
impenetrable, is one of the universal images of femininity. This goes
for the sanctuary in the middle of the forest; the *nemeton* (a lighted
clearing within the trees) of the ancient Druids; the pretty "little
garden" of Francois Villon and the Renaissance poets; and, at a later
date, the "bushes" and "thickets" of pornographic writers. It is in
the mediaeval orchard, that secret, enclosed and perfumed microcosm of an image, that the Submerged Princess awaits her lover.
Courtly literature contains many illustrations of this theme, which
were carried right across Europe by the troubadours.

Provence, *Roman de Jaufré*

After a series of adventures in the Forest of Brocéliande,
Jaufré came to a house of lepers, where he found a beautiful
young girl. He had to fight the lepers, but could not leave the
house until he shattered the statue of a child. The house
collapsed and Jaufré found himself in an orchard "surrounded
by a marble wall", with trees, flowers and birds found nowhere
else in the world, which made him think of paradise. The
orchard belonged to Brunissen, a young orphan who had been

mourning for the last seven years and showed her grief by weeping three times every night and four times during the day. Only the songs of the birds could lessen her sorrow. After admiring the orchard, the hero lay down and fell into heavy sleep, where Brunissen found him and fell in love. (*Roman de Jaufré*, lines 3040 ff.)

This text is of particular interest, first of all because of the character of Brunissen, the "Brown Queen" (who is, however, fair-haired in the romance, as was fashionable in the thirteenth century). She is one of the faces of the Queen of the Darkness, and therefore an equivalent of Hecate, the Greek goddess of the cross-roads. As we shall see later, her fondness for the song of the birds suggests comparisons with Rhiannon, the Great Queen of the Welsh pantheon, whose birds "awaken the dead and put the living to sleep". Secondly, Brunissen, confined to her castle and orchard, is clearly in mourning for some unknown reason, very much as the occupants of the Castle of Marvels are in the Welsh *Peredur*,[10] the original setting for the Procession of the Grail. Lastly, the theme of the story is only too apparent. After losing his way in the *forest*, Jaufré found the beautiful young girl (Brunissen), but had to fight the lepers (his fantasies and disgust) and shatter the *statue of a child* — that is, shatter his own childhood, deny his birth. Then everything collapsed (slipping away from consciousness at the moment of orgasm) and he found himself in the middle of a marvellous orchard (annihilation *post coitum*), having regained the original state of paradise.

For this orchard is surely the paradise garden of all versions of Genesis, the paradise, lost in the depths of the subconscious, that every human being tries in some way to realise in himself. The troubadours always set their lovers' meetings in an enclosed orchard during the night. The coming of dawn brings the rift, the disaster, a re-enactment of birth with all its attendant trauma.

"In an orchard, under the leaves of a hawthorn, the lady drew close to her friend, until the watchman cried out that dawn had come. Oh God! The dawn comes so quickly. I wish to God that the night never ended, that my friend never had to leave me, that the watchman never saw the light of dawn. Oh God! How soon the dawn comes." (G. Picot, *La Poésie lyrique du Moyen-Age*, Classiques Larousse, Paris 1963, vol. 1, pp. 69—71.)

"Watch well, watchman of the castle, when I have the best and loveliest man here with me till dawn, day comes without fail. The dawn robs us of new games, yes, the dawn. Watch, friend, keep awake, cry out, howl, I am rich, I have what I desire most, but I am the enemy of dawn. The sadness that day brings us hurts me more than the dawn, yes the dawn." (Ibid., vol. 1, pp. 79—81.)

The supreme example of the orchard theme is that exceptional work, the *Roman de la Rose*. Of its two authors, Guillaume de Lorris stressed the courtly considerations inherited both from Celtic customs and from the thinking of the Provençal troubadours; while Jean de Meung was haunted by the agonising problems posed by questions of femininity. The lover catches sight of a marvellous rose in the midst of an orchard, and can no longer bear to live without plucking it. But there are so many difficulties to overcome, dangers to avoid, thorns to bypass, before he is able to perform this act of regeneration. The sense of Jean de Meung's poem is very clear. Behind his allegories lie the human obsessions that must be removed from his path. In many cases these are not portrayed as monsters guarding the entrance to the home of the Submerged Princess; for the troubadours usually saw them as the *gelos* and *losengiers*, the jealous and slanderous, sometimes in the form of the father himself, sometimes the husband.

Usually the husband is old and despotic, locking his wife away and killing all potential lovers. Just as Yspaddaden Penkawr (in Welsh tale of *Culhwch and Olwen*) imposed impossible tasks upon his daughter's suitor and even tried to kill him, so the husband in courtly romance brings to bear a wealth of cunning and perversity in order to keep his wife safe.

"The lord who governed the city was a very old man whose wife was a lady of high birth, honesty, courtesy and beauty. But he was excessively jealous and the way he watched over her was no laughing matter. By the keep a totally enclosed orchard led down to the water. The high surrounding wall was of thick green marble, with only one entrance where guards kept vigil night and day. At the other end stretched the sea, and the only access on that side was by boat. There the lord had built an apartment as a safe place for his wife, and there was never a more beautiful room under the sun. At the entrance a chapel, and all round the walls of the room beautiful portraits of Venus, Goddess of Love. So there her lord locked his lady, giving her a damsel to serve her and ... an old, florid, white-haired priest to keep the keys to the door. (Marie de France, *Lai de Guigemar*.)

The Lays of Marie de France are adaptations of Celtic legends from Britain and Brittany, as her use of Breton sources for proper names makes clear. There is an obvious militancy in her writing, a protest against marriages imposed on women without regard for their wishes, and an even stronger attack on monogamous marriage, which supposes *ipso facto* adultery, a fact corroborated by a study of all twelfth- and thirteenth-century courtly romances. Courtly love, an essentially extra-marital activity, whether platonic or sexual, was a rather disconcerting concept for mediaeval Christian society, and, though allegedly Provençal in origin, it is closely related to the Celtic socio-judicial system and Celtic ideas. But apart from this claim to free love for women, the Lays also present the typical outline of the myth of the Submerged Princess. In *Guigemar*, we have a fortress by the sea, and in the fortress the orchard and the sanctuary of a room full of paintings portraying Venus. Then, as the narrative continues, the lover arrives *by sea*.

For ultimately it is water that remains the essential element of the myth. In Chrétien's *Lancelot*, the hero, Queen Guinevere's lover, attempts to rescue her from imprisonment by Meleagant in his kingdom of glass. Faced with a choice between the Bridge of the Sword and the Bridge under the Water, the only two means of entry to the kingdom (themselves reminiscent of the "Immediate" or "Dry" Way and the "Long" or "Damp" Way open to alchemists in search of the Philosopher's Stone), Launcelot opts for the former. For the sword is a phallic symbol and Launcelot is the lover. But the sword also symbolises fire, and, though Launcelot manages to enter the kingdom, he fails to release Guinevere because he has come by the dry and igneous route. Gawain, on the other hand, after narrowly escaping death by drowning in his passage over the Bridge under the Water, succeeds in bringing her back, because as Guinevere's nephew, or substitute son, he instinctively recognises the natural way to his goal.

For woman is obviously the mother, a role that may be expressed in a wide variety of ways. What Gawain accomplished, and Launcelot did not, was a *regressus ad uterum*, during which he had to overcome the water of the amniotic fluid separating the foetus from the outside world and recalling the first ocean, which embraced all living things before the disastrous drying up forced them to adapt to a new, dry and laborious life on the land. In his choice of the Bridge of the Sword, Launcelot picked the way natural to him as a lover, for the sword is an extension of him, as the penis is the extension of the man. But the union of lover with the mother–woman is inevitably incomplete, because "in both sexes, the working out of desire passes through a longing impossible to satisfy".[10] If, on the other hand, sexual union is a kind of return to the mother's womb, "intercourse achieves this temporary regression in three ways: the whole body enacts it but in a solely hallucinatory way, in the manner of a dream; the penis, with which the entire body identifies, is already successful in part, that is to say *symbolically*; but only the sperm has the privilege, as the representative of the self and its narcissistic *alter-ego* the genital organ, of actually reaching into the depths of the womb".[12]

That Gawain succeeded through real submersion in the depths of the maternal waters emphasises the importance of water as a theme. As the frontier between the two worlds, any passage through it is an exchange between the two, as is evident in an episode of the Welsh *Peredur*, in which the hero sees white sheep turn black as they land on one bank, and black sheep turn white on reaching the other (J. Loth, *Mabinogion*, vol. 2, p. 95). A curious Latin work by the fourteenth-century writer Pierre Bercheur contains a significant adventure of Gawain, who, diving under the waters of a lake, enters a fortress where he finds a fully prepared meal, to which he does justice. Then he witnesses a sight strangely reminiscent of the original procession of the Grail described in *Peredur*. There is also a rather painstaking Irish account of an adventure in the underwater world.

Ireland, *The Expedition of Loegaire, son of Crimthann*
The men of Connaught assembled near the Lake of Birds, when out of the mist arose a mysterious warrior who claimed to be "of the fairy race" and who asked some of the heroes to help him rescue his wife, who had been abducted by an enemy. Loegaire, son of Crimthann, agreed to help Fiachna, which was the name of the fairy warrior, and, taking with him "fifty warriors, he plunged into the lake with his men behind him. They saw a fortress in front of them and a battle ensued." Loegaire and his men carried the day and released the woman. In reward Loegaire received Fiachna's daughter, Der Greine, and lived for a year in the fairy land.
When Loegaire and his companions evinced a desire to go and seek news of their country, Fiachna told them to take horses and on no account ever dismount. So they reached the world above, arriving in the assembly of the men of Connaught, said a brief farewell to their relatives and returned once more to the Marvellous Country. (G. Dottin, *L'Épopée irlandaise*, pp. 53—5.)

The variations on the original theme are important. This account concerns the reconquest of a woman, but also the conquest of another woman, a fairy woman of the other world, by a person from the real world. Her name, Der Greine, is revealing, since it is reminiscent of Grainne, Finn's wife, who fled with Diarmaid and hid in a cave. As *Greine* or *Grainne* means "sun", she is also one aspect of the female sun goddess, who seems to have been common to all early Indo-Europeans. So, in this respect, the myth of the Submerged Princess coincides with the main myth of the sun, in that the sun disappears for a length of time on the other side of the vast ocean encircling the earth. There are definite archaeological traces of this sun myth in the Bronze Age; for instance, in the famous sun chariots of Baltic civilisations.

Indeed, the solar theme may well be of Nordic (even Arctic) origin. It has certainly been more thoroughly exploited by the peoples of Northern Europe, and of the Great Plains of Asia, as far east as the shores of the Pacific. It has an equivalent in the Japanese legend of the sun goddess Amaterasu, who, annoyed by her brother's behaviour, hid in a cave and refused to come out (a reminder of man's ancestral anxiety that the sun might not rise in the morning). All the gods gathered before the cave with a mirror to reflect the goddess, who finally emerged to light up the world out of curiosity, because another goddess, Ama-no-uzume, had performed an obscene dance that made the gods laugh.

Once we are aware of the Celtic habit of giving feminine qualities to the sun, the image of the sun hidden in a cave or under water makes it easier to understand the nature of all legends related to the Submerged Princess, who has treasures and secrets in her keeping, and who waits for the coming of the bold man who will wake and free her. The round reflection of the sun on water leads us to examine another aspect of the same myth, the island where the princess reigns. This was of special importance for the Celts. We have already seen it in *The Voyage of Maelduin* and *The Voyage of Bran*. We can also recognise it in its most developed and, equally, most celebrated form in the legend of Morgan and the Isle of Avalon, which the *Romans de la Table Ronde* spread throughout the world.

The Isle of Avalon

When King Arthur, mortally wounded at the battle of Camlann, arrived on the seashore, accompanied by the knight Girfleet, he asked to be left alone. A violent storm broke out, then "a ship full of ladies" appeared, one of whom, the fairy Morgan, the king's sister, called to him. He went into the ship, which sailed away and, so it was said, "went straight to the Isle of Avalon, where King Arthur still lives, lying on a golden bed." (*La Mort du roi Arthur.*)

"The Isle of Apples was also called Fortunate Isle, because all the vegetation there grew naturally with no need of cultivation . . . the harvests were rich and the forests thick with apples and grapes . . . nine sisters ruled over it . . . and one of them surpassed all the others in beauty and power. Her name was Morgan and she taught how plants could be used to cure illness. She knew the art of changing her outward form and could fly through the air like Daedalus, with the aid of feathers . . . that was where we took Arthur, wounded after the battle of Camlann. . . . Morgan received us with all suitable honours and

had the king carried into her room and onto a golden couch. . . .
She watched over him a long time, and at last said he would
regain his health through her, if he stayed on the island and
accepted her cures." (Geoffrey of Monmouth, *Vita Merlini*. J.M.,
L'Épopée celtique en Bretagne, p. 120.)

"This island in the midst of the ocean was not affected by
any sickness. There were no thieves or criminals, no snow, fog
or extreme heat. Eternal peace reigned. There were always
flowers and fruits under their foliage. The inhabitants were
without fault and always young. A royal virgin, fairer than the
fairest, governed that island." (Guillaume de Rennes, *Gesta
Regum Britanniae*.)

The island in the ocean, which has all the outward appearances of
paradise, is a straightforward symbol, projected into space and
removed from the vaguely remembered past to a timeless future, of
life inside the womb. Death, illness and old age are unknown. Fruits,
particularly apples, grow naturally and abundantly there. In fact, this
is the Golden Age that has haunted man's imagination for millenia,
the calm and peaceful condition of the foetus protected by the
warmth of the mother and fed by her in a secluded world, whether
orchard, cave, impregnable fortress or island, where there is as yet no
moral life, no distinction made between good and evil, no conscious
psychic life, and no distinction between self and non-self.

It is the island of apple-trees, as Eden was the apple orchard and
the Garden of the Hesperides contained the golden apples. The name
Avalon became the Celtic word for apple (Breton and Welsh *aval*,
compared with English "apple" and Latin *malum*). In Irish
legend the Island of Women, towards which the hero Bran sailed, was
known as Emain *Ablach*, and poets praised the apple-trees that grew
there and the beauty of their fruit. According to Pliny the Elder
(*Natural History*, XXXVIII, 35), the Teutons, a Celtic people, used
to trade amber with the inhabitants of the Isle of Abalum (now
known as Oesel) on the east side of the Baltic. There was a village on
the island called Aboul, which name, like that of Abalum and the
Italian island Abbella Malifera, derives from the same root as Avalon.
We should also point out that British tradition makes Morgan the
daughter of Evallach, the name given in the *Quête du Saint Graal* to
King Mordred before his baptism. And he was a double of Pelles, the
rich Fisher-King, keeper of the sacred cauldron or Grail, an object
shaped as a vessel and unquestionably a feminine symbol.

The remarkable thing about the Celtic paradise was that it
remained outside the sphere of influence of the patriarchal structure
that, with just a few exceptions, shaped Celtic society. The Isle of
Avalon, or its Gaelic equivalent Emain Ablach, was ruled by women
in matriarchal organisations. Whether this is a relic of an earlier
epoch, either Celtic or pre-Celtic, when woman ruled society, or

whether it is the projection of an unconscious desire for *regressus ad uterum* remains an unanswerable question. It is probably both together. In any case, the myth of the Island of Women was not created by mediaeval writers, nor by the French authors of the *Romans de la Table Ronde*. It existed long before, as the authors of Greek and Latin antiquity show.

"Facing the Celtic coasts lie a group of islands which takes the collective name Cassiterides because they are very rich in tin. Sena in the British Sea [the Channel], facing the coast of Osimi [North Finistère] was renowned for its Gallic oracle, whose priestesses, sacred for their everlasting virginity, were said to be nine in number. They were called 'gallicians' and were reputed to have the power to unleash the winds and storms by their spells, to metamorphose any animal according to their whim, to cure all disease said to be incurable, and, finally, to know and predict the future. But they reserved their remedies and predictions exclusively for those who had travelled over the sea expressly to consult them." (Pomponius Mela, III, 6.)

"In the ocean, not right out in the open sea, but just facing the mouth of the Loire, Posidonius pointed out to us a rather narrow island inhabited by the so-called Namnetes women, who were possessed by Bacchic passion. They tried by means of mysteries and other religious ceremonies to appease and disarm the god who tormented them. No man ever set foot on their island: it was they who crossed to the mainland every time they wished to do business with their husbands." (Strabo, IV, 4.)

Note that the picture drawn by Pomponius Mela, the Romanised Iberian writer and geographer, tallies on all points with Geoffrey of Monmouth's twelfth-century account. Pomponius Mela seemed to regard the women of his island as Vestal virgins (though we shall have to define later what ancient writers understood by "virgins"); whereas Strabo, on the evidence of Posidonius, regarded them as bacchantes who had relations with men. Judging from the various accounts of King Arthur's sister, "the hottest and most lustful woman in all Great Britain", as the author of *Lancelot en prose* described her, Morgan and her sisters were more like bacchantes. But, be that as it may, the island paradise belongs to a very ancient tradition, of which there are traces even in folklore.

Despite the fact that Pomponius Mela places it in the Channel, the island of Sena may well be the Île de Sein, believed to be the Other World, on the far side of the Bay of the Dead and the Hell of Plogoff.[12] There have also been attempts to locate Avalon, both in Brittany, as the Isle of Aval, not far from Trebeurden (Côtes-du-

Nord), and in Great Britain, as the Isle of Mon (Anglesey), though chiefly as the ancient abbey of Glastonbury, *in the centre of marshland.*[13] But such attempts have little point, because the island in question is outside the time and space of the living world.

Plutarch says as much in *De Defectu Oraculorum* (XVII): "Demetrios said that, of the islands round Britain, . . . some took the names of demons or of heroes . . . and he landed on the nearest of the deserted islands. . . . On his arrival there was a great disturbance in the air, accompanied by a number of celestial signs. The winds blew noisily and lightning struck in several places. When calm had returned the inhabitants told him there had been an eclipse of some superior being. . . . There, he added, was Chronos asleep and guarded by Briareos. Sleep had been hit upon as the bonds to keep him prisoner. All around him there were a great number of demons, who acted as his servants." According to Irish texts, the Tuatha Dé Danann came from such an island in the Northern world, and had learned "science, magic, Druidism, wisdom and art" there.

Plutarch's reference to Chronos sleeping on this island is an interesting one, for Chronos was the ancient father of the gods, who was deposed and castrated by his son Zeus, as Arthur was wounded by his own incestuous son. For a king, any wound counts as a degrading wound that disqualifies from rule, and thus as a wound causing sexual impotence, as in the case of the Fisher-King. The fact that Chronos sleeps, just as Arthur lay dormant while waiting to return, suggests that sleep and death are equated in a wider and clearly psychological sense. Sleep follows orgasm, or, to put it another way, a state of unconscious bliss marks the return to life in the womb. In this context, the dividing line between life and death is inevitably hazy. Sandor Ferenczi commented in *Thalassa* that "absolute death may not even exist; the germs of life and retrogressive tendencies may be present but concealed in the inorganic self. In that case we would have to abandon the question of the beginning and end of life once and for all, and see the whole universe, organic and inorganic, as an endless see-saw between tendencies of life and death where neither ever becomes sole ruler."

At all events, this is the idea that arises from a perceptive reading of the different versions of the myth of the Submerged Princess. Ferenczi's endless see-saw between the life and death instincts is very much in evidence in the episode of the sheep in *Peredur* and in the Gaelic narrative of *The Voyage of Maelduin*. Indeed, both in the epics found in the old manuscripts, and, equally, in the more recent oral traditions collected in Celtic countries, there are continual exchanges between the two worlds. When the burial mounds are open on the night of Samain, it is enough just to cross the threshold or stand by the entrance to see the mysterious girls of the *sidh* glide out from behind their ramparts of earth or water. But the night of

Samain is itself outside time: it endures every evening in the life of the stars. Every man is Oedipus in the ruins of the dead city meeting the Sphinx, a dark and secret female let out of her cave as a privilege on the night of Samain. She asks us stupid questions, but we are even more stupid because we cannot reply; we are blind, or, rather, we do not want to see the obvious answers. We court disaster, for the Sphinx will tear us apart — quite rightly, because her questions are about ourselves. It is to be hoped that somebody (male or female) will one day condescend to open his eyes and sincerely seek to discover what is inside him and what disturbs him.

We began with the myth of the town of Ys for good reason. In the beginning everything was water, and in the end it will be water again. We have tried to follow Dahud-Ahes through all her transformations and all her haunts. From the city of Ys to the Isle of Avalon, by way of the dragon's cave, is only the distance from one image to another. In all these transpositions of the same fundamental idea it is apparent that "the field of symbols can no longer be thought to be formulated by man, but rather as forming him" (Jacques Lacan). A study of *how man dreamed of woman, how he submerged her* and *why he did so* discloses a fundamental truth of human existence.

But, as Claude Lévi-Strauss comments, the symbol developed in myths is never absolute. When all has been said, there still remains just as much to be understood. The magnificent Irish epic of the *Courtship of Etaine* concludes in a significant way.[15] The god Mider abducted Etaine, wife of King Eochaid — though with her consent, which somewhat alters the picture — and took her to the marvellous universe of the *sidh*. In his attempts to find her, Eochaid ordered all the hills in Ireland to be hollowed out, but through Mider's trickery the woman he won back was not his wife but another, who had assumed her face. This ending is important. Once man has lost woman. he begins to understand what she was and what she represented. Unfortunately too late, for now other images come between him and objective reality. "The truth lies in a swing of the pendulum between those who speak it" (Jacques Lacan), and it is very difficult to grasp.

Perhaps the answer lies in a rediscovery of the language of our origins, the first structuring of the unconscious. But where should we start looking for it? Under the sea? The town of Ys is still there with its Submerged Princess, and, on the day when Ys comes to the surface, the first to hear the sound of the bell will possess the whole kingdom and Dahud-Ahes. And yet, where is the *real* town of Ys, above or below? When we look at the reflection of a town or forest in the waters of a lake, a river, or a sea, how can we be sure which is the real image? If the myth of the Submerged Princess raises doubts about the long-established opposition between *mors et vita*, because it highlights the anguish experienced on the borderline between dream and reality (the state of waking), we might well wonder whether it does not also highlight man's powerlessness to choose. In his imagination corrupted by centuries of distorted thinking (because exclusively male-oriented), the princess whom he has consciously repressed returns with more beauty and strength than ever in the image of a goddess he should never have ceased to adore.

Chapter 4

Our Lady of the Night

Every religion in the world has offered goddesses for the faithful to worship, and in the dim and distant past these goddesses were probably given pride of place as Water Mother, Earth Mother, and then as mothers of gods and men. But as ancient societies abandoned their gynaecocratic structure, the role of women was diminished and the worship of female divinities was transferred to male gods. Not entirely, however, for "the great patriarchal epochs preserved in their mythology . . . the memory of the times when women occupied a very important position" (Simone de Beauvoir); and "In the historical era one observes, notably in India and Iran, the remains of an ancient religion which seems to have been related to gynaecocratic institutions in the beginning."[1] So, according to the *Rigveda* of India, Aditya (Ardvi in the Iranian *Avesta*) is both the Great Goddess and the name of a mythical river which is the source of all the waters of the world; and the Indian cult of the goddess Kali, the devourer and the provider, dates back to pre-Indo-European times, at least to 3,000 B.C. In like manner, the Hebrew Bible echoes with the continual wars undertaken by the followers of the moon god Yahweh (Jehovah) against the "heretical" believers in the Semitic Great Goddess, probably the Babylonian Ishtar.

The Druidic religion was no exception to this rule. Its mythology, like all other mythologies, contains traces of a mother goddess. Its religious practices, like all others, reveal many instances of the worship of women. Images of goddesses are to be found on the decorated monuments of the Roman period in Gaul and Britain, and there are references in Irish and Welsh texts, which are the early mediaeval written records of an oral tradition, some of it fairly old. But though they continue to play quite an important role, these goddesses have fallen from greatness. Within the patriarchal framework they were often obscured, tarnished and deformed, and submerged in the depths of the unconscious. But they do still exist, if only in a dormant state, and sometimes rise triumphantly to rock the supposedly immovable foundations of masculine society. The triumph of Yahweh and Christ was believed sanctified for ever, but from behind them reappears the disturbing and desirable figure of the Virgin Mary, with her variety of unexpected names: Our Lady of the Water, Our Lady of the Nettles, Our Lady of the Briars, Our Lady of the Mounds, Our Lady of the Pines. But in spite of the veneration accorded her over the centuries and the public declaration of successive dogmas related to Mary, the authorities of the Christian Church have always made her a secondary character, overshadowed and retiring, a model of what women ought to be. Now the pure and virginal servant of man, the wonderful mother who suffers all heroically, she is no longer the Great Goddess before whom the common herd of men would tremble, but *Our Lady of the Night*.

THE QUEEN OF HORSES

To understand her fully, we must bring her out of the night, the cave, the oceanic darkness where the obsessed imaginings of men have buried her. For this we need the help of myths, which in their variety enable us to sketch a kind of composite picture of Our Lady of the Night. Our first landmark in the Celtic tradition is the story of Rhiannon, as told in three of the texts that make up the Welsh *Mabinogion*. *Pwyll, Prince of Dyvet* contains the essence of the myth; *Manawyddan, Son of Llyr* is a sequel to it; and *Branwen, Daughter of Llyr* offers some additional detail.[2]

Wales, *The Saga of Rhiannon*
Pwyll Penn Annfwn, King of Dyvet, was on the mound of Arbeth when he saw a young girl wearing "brilliant golden clothing" and riding a pale white horse. He sent one of his knights after her, but she disappeared. The incident recurred the following day. On the third day Pwyll himself ran in pursuit of her, but could not catch her, so he called out, "Young girl, for love of the man you love most, wait for me." The horsewoman stopped and told him her name was Rhiannon, daughter of Hyveidd Hen, and that she had come out of love for Pwyll, saying, "If you do not reject me I shall never want anyone but

you." The king agreed to marry Rhiannon and the wedding was fixed for a year later at the court of Hyveidd. But during the banquet Rhiannon's former suitor Gwawl arrived. He wanted Rhiannon himself and took advantage of the custom of having to give a present, but pretended he did not know of the occasion and so claimed Rhiannon for himself. But she managed to obtain a year's grace before marrying Gwawl and used this time to draw up a cunning scheme whereby Gwawl, defeated and dissatisfied, was finally put out of the running.

Rhiannon married Pwyll and a while later gave birth to a son. But that night, she and the women watching over her all fell asleep and the child was mysteriously abducted. To escape blame themselves the women claimed that Rhiannon had killed her child. She was tried by Pwyll and the wise men of Dyvet and sentenced to a strange punishment. "For the next seven years she was to stay at the court of Arberth, sitting beside a stone mounting block outside the entrance telling her story to all comers who seemed ignorant of it, and suggesting to guests and strangers alike that they should let her *carry them on her back* to the court." Meanwhile the child was just as mysteriously deposited in the stables of Teyrnon, a man of Gwent. Each year, on the night of 1st May, his mare used to foal a colt which always disappeared without anyone knowing what had happened to it.

That particular night Teyrnon mounted guard and found not only a new-born colt, but also a baby boy swaddled and wrapped in a richly ornate coat. Teyrnon brought up the child and gave him the name Gwri Gwallt Euryn (Gwri of the Golden Hair). By the age of three the child had made friends with the colt, tamed it and mounted it. Having heard of Rhiannon's adventure, Teyrnon decided to take the child to the court of Dyvet, where Rhiannon offered to carry them on her back. The child refused and Teyrnon told the whole story to Pwyll and Rhiannon, who then recognised their child. Rhiannon cried out that she was free of her "trouble" (*Pryderi*), so giving her son his final name, Pryderi.

He grew to be a handsome young man and after the death of Pwyll became King of Dyvet and married Kicva. After Bran's disastrous expedition to Ireland, he was one of the seven survivors, who continued to lead a magic life whilst hearing the song of the "birds of Rhiannon whose singing awoke the dead and put the living to sleep". He returned to Arberth with Manawyddan, son of Llyr, who married Rhiannon.

But a spell fell on Dyvet and the land became barren. Rhiannon, Kicva, Pryderi and Manawyddan were the only living souls left in the land, and when they had exhausted their provisions they set out to chance their luck elsewhere. They returned to Arberth with fresh supplies. One day, they saw a white boar disappearing into a fortress they had never noticed before. Pryderi chased it right into the fortress, which was deserted. In the centre of the courtyard stood a fountain with a gold cup fastened by chains which led into the air so that the ends could not be seen. Pryderi seized the cup and immediately lost his voice. His hands stuck to the cup. Rhiannon grew uneasy when her son did not return and, after reproaching Manawyddan for not going to his aid, herself entered the fortress. She tried to free Pryderi but the same thing happened to her. "As soon as night fell, there was a crash of thunder; a thick cloud enveloped the fortress and they disappeared with it."

Fortunately Manawyddan succeeded in breaking the spell on Dyvet; this had been cast by Llywyt, son of Kilcoet, to avenge Gwawl. It turned out that during their absence mother and son had been servants at the court of Llywyt, and that Rhiannon had worn round her neck "the kind of halters asses wore to carry in the hay".

The link between the horse, or rather the mare, and the character of the goddess is undoubtedly the most remarkable thing in this saga. Rhiannon first appears as the *horsewoman* who has come mounted on a *white* horse to seek the love of King Pwyll. This is the image of the goddess of the Other World, the fairy in love with a mortal, whom she comes to carry off into the land of eternal youth. The horse is a symbol of the sun, for it draws the chariot of the sun and travels through the space of night. But from this it follows that the horsewoman is an image not only of death but also of resurrection, since she comes from the night on a horse the colour of daylight. Pwyll first saw her on the magical mound of Arberth, where nobody could go without witnessing some marvel, a place like the *sidh* of Ireland where the Tuatha Dé Danann or the fairies live. And, since Rhiannon rose from this mound, she must be Our Lady of the Night.

Pryderi, her son, is clearly likened to a colt. He was found in Teyrnon's stable beside a newly born colt, which he broke in and rode by the age of three. His first name, Gwri of the Golden Hair, suggests that he had a head of yellow hair like the mane of a charger, an image not merely poetic but also symbolic of the sun.

Finally, Rhiannon herself is likened to a mare, both in her unjust punishment for the disappearance of her new-born child, and in the role of beast of burden she is forced to play during her captivity at the court of Llywyt. Ultimately, however, she is the Goddess of Marvellous Birds, as we shall see later.

For the moment we shall confine ourselves to examining the theme of the horse in the legend of Rhiannon. All mythologists are unanimous in establishing a connection between Rhiannon and the Romanised Gallic goddess Epona, whose cult assumed considerable proportions within the Roman Empire, and to whom many monuments and inscriptions were dedicated, chiefly in Gaul and the German Rhineland. Gallo-Roman sculpture portrays her in three different poses: sitting on a horse or colt, standing in front of a horse or between two or more horses, and, more rarely, lying half-naked on a horse. Sometimes she is carrying a horn of plenty, a goblet, or even an ordinary bowl. She is occasionally accompanied by a dog, an interesting association since all traditions make the dog the guardian of hell.[3]

Epona is not of Latin origin, which explains why her name is mentioned only by relatively late authors such as Juvenal (*Satires*, VIII) and Apuleius (*Metamorphoses*, III). From them we know that her image decorated the walls of stables and was embellished with roses. In the Roman world, she must therefore have been a patron goddess of horses, a fact corroborated by the recurrence of inscriptions in her honour found in the frontier regions with Germania, where there were the most horsemen.

But her position as patron goddess of horses was probably just a pale reflection of her former role among the independent Celts. She obviously shared the same fate as many of the Christian saints who originally stood for a specific concept given form by a symbol. Then, gradually, as the meaning of this symbol was forgotten, it was taken literally. St Barbara, for example, was represented by a tower, the symbol of virginity, but later became the patron saint of gunners (who demolish the tower), and consequently of firemen (who put out the fires started by the former). The absurd way in which so many mythologists present gods and goddesses solely as patron divinities results from the mistaken assumption that all the followers of ancient religions were simpletons. Thus Epona was relegated to a secondary role, though she was in fact the true image of the first mother goddess of the Celts.

At all events, she is associated in one way or another with horses. Even her name, Epona, comes from the Gallic *epo*, a derivative of the Indo-European *ekwo*, which also gave the Latin *equus*. She is therefore etymologically the "horsewoman" or, more literally, the "mare". Agesilaos, a Greek writer of the decline, relates a strange story about the birth of Epona.[4] "Phoulouios Stellos, who hated women, had relations with a mare. In time it gave birth to a beautiful little girl who was given the name Epona." Her equine origins could hardly be more specific. Surprisingly, however, the Greek text clearly states that the little girl did not receive her name from Phoulouios Stellos but from *the mare itself*, which was probably magical or divine, or simply the zoomorphic representation of a divinity.

This Greek anecdote has much in common with a very ancient custom of the Gauls relating to royal accession, and mentioned by

Giraldus Cambrensis, a thirteenth-century Welshman who wrote in Latin. Here is a translation from his *Topographia* (III, 25) of a passage concerning Kenelcunnil, a town in northern Ulster:

> "Once all the people had been assembled together, a white mare was led into the middle of the crowd. Then, in full view of everybody, this person of highest rank [the king] approached the mare bestially, not like a prince but like a wild beast, not like a king but like an outlaw, and behaved just like an animal, without shame or prudence. Immediately afterwards the mare was killed, carved up into pieces and thrown in boiling water. A bath was prepared for the king with the broth, and he sat in it while scraps of the meat were brought for him to eat and to share with the people around him. He was also washed with the broth and drank it, not with a cup or his hands, but directly with his mouth. Once this ritual had been performed, his rule and authority were assured."

This rite of sovereignty is not unique, for similar practices have occurred almost everywhere, notably in India, where *asvamedha*, or the sacrifice of the horse, was performed.[5] The ceremony took the following form: a horse was stuffed with fabrics; the king's wives walked several times around the corpse, and then the first wife stretched out beside it and they were both covered over. The woman then put the horse's phallus into her own sexual parts. Despite the difference between the Indian ritual of woman—horse copulation and the Irish ritual of man—mare copulation, both represent a sacred marriage in which the horse or mare are divinities bringing actual power to the sovereign.

In the light of this ritual, the marriage of Rhiannon and Pwyll also takes on the aspect of a sacrament in which the earthly powers accorded to king Pwyll by the will of his people were confirmed by Rhiannon, so that he became the divine chosen one, able to assert his dominion as far as his eyes could see, in the Celtic definition of kingship. So Rhiannon—Epona is the divine mare, who has brought her powers from the world of the mounds, where the new patriarchal institutions of society had confined her; but that society was like a son, brutally snatched from his mother. It was afraid of its responsibilities, and needed to share them with Our Lady of the Night, from whom it had usurped these powers.

There is a trace of Rhiannon—Epona in a folk-tale from the Vosges, a mountainous district in Germanic territory, which still bears the name of an ancient Gallic divinity.

Vosges, *The Princess of Anfondrasse*
    The Princess of Anfondrasse refused to marry an old king unless she recovered her sash lost in the wind and her diamond

necklace lost in the sea. Prudent, a young man who had boasted he could retrieve them, was given the task. With the help of his friend the mare and the King of the Fishes, he managed to bring them back. But the princess fell in love with Prudent and still refused to marry the king, who was furious and ordered that an oven be heated for twenty-four hours and Prudent thrown into it. The mare told Prudent to open a vein in her right leg and wash his whole body with the blood. So he spent three days and nights in the oven without coming to any harm. The king became increasingly furious and the princess increasingly in love. Prudent ran towards the mare and realised that she had turned into a beautiful young girl. Called upon to choose between the princess and the ex-mare he decided on the latter. (L. F. Sauvé, *Le Folklore des Hautes-Vosges*. p. 322 ff.)

There is no doubt that this story is of Celtic origin, because of the heated oven in which Prudent was placed. This is a reference to an ancient ritual, of which little is known, but which is usually linked with the feast of Samain. It is mentioned in many Irish texts, including the *Leabhar Gabala* (in which Partholon killed his father by setting fire to the house he was in); *The Story of Labraid* (in which Labraid shut up his uncle the usurper in a house stoked up to a white heat); *The Drunkenness of the Ulstermen* (in which Queen Medb heated an iron house to white heat and threw Cù Chulainn and the Ulstermen into it) and *The Death of Muirchertach* (in which the king escaped from an iron house but drowned in a great vat).

But, leaving aside this detail, the theme of Rhiannon is easily recognised, and the return to the mother is in the background. For, to preserve Prudent's life, the mare actually covered him with her own blood — that is, hid her son in her own womb to feed and protect him against the aridity of the oven (the catastrophe of birth). It is a perfect illustration of the analogy drawn by Ferenczi (in *Thalassa*) between the catastrophe of birth and the catastrophe that befell all species millions of years ago, when the great seas dried up and creatures had to adapt to a new life on dry land. In tradition, the whole process is symbolised by the flood (which is actually beneficial) and the conflagration of the world in the myth of Phaeton.

On the social level, the legend also represents the rebellion of the young man against the old king (his father) with the active involvement of the mare (his mother) and, most significantly, *the help of the King of the Fishes*, or followers of the ancient gynaecocratic order, the fish being the symbol of return to the mother. Prudent's final choice, of the former mare, also undoubtedly marks a return to the mother.

Although we have been examining Our Lady of the Night as she appears in the guise of a mare, or, at least, as associated with the horse symbolically, it would be wrong to assume that there was any totemism among the Celts. Certain tribes may have been classified under a specific name, taken sometimes from an animal, sometimes from a tree (for example, the Baiocasses or Bodiocasses were the warriors of the crow; the Eburovices, the people of the yew, the Arverni, the people of the alder; etc.), but for the Celts, as for other Indo-Europeans, animals had little more than symbolic significance. The few rare traces of totemism that have been discovered originated in pre-Indo-European aboriginal traditions preserved after the conquest. The Celts, however, did frequently use the horse as a religious symbol for iconographic and decorative purposes in a way perfectly consistent with their practice of breeding horses. Even at the time of Caesar, both the British and Gallic cavalry formed a select and highly efficient fighting force. The coins of the Redones, the Veneti, Curiosolites, Osimi and Baiocasses all portray the horse as a fantastic animal, sometimes ridden by a ghostly charioteer, sometimes itself given the head of a bird or a man: a clear indication of the importance accorded to this kind of representation, the examples of which are remarkably beautiful.

The fact that we have so far confined our studies of the goddess to her guise as a mare does not mean that she did not appear in the form of other animals, with their own specific meanings. There is a Gallo-Roman statue of a bear goddess, now housed in the museum at Bern, a town whose German name and coat of arms suggest the bear. This goddess, Artio, whose name is derived from the Gallic word for "bear", is represented sitting by a tree with short branches in front of a huge bear, with a basket of fruit on a small column beside her. Whether she was the patron of bear-hunters or actually a protector of bears hardly matters, for the basket of fruit and the fact that the bear appears to be her equal suggest that she was a goddess of plenty, a mother goddess of all life and food, and another instance of Our Lady of the Night.

In fact, the bear goddess is as rare in literary mythology as in the iconography of the Celts, though the Silvanecti did cast a bronze coin representing a bear devouring the goddess. She was probably replaced by a bear god at some comparatively early stage. Indeed, one of Mercury's nicknames was "Artaios".

Even so, it is worth pausing to examine one celebrated, though fairly late, mythological figure who became the subject of so much mediaeval European courtly literature. For the name of King Arthur, the character in question, might derive from the Indo-European root *ar*, "to plough", or equally from the Gallic word meaning "bear". It has also been suggested that the name Arthur is of Roman origin and developed from *arctus*, denoting the Little and the Great Bear, or *Arcturus*, the name of Bouvier's star; all of which leads us back to the root meaning "bear". The Arthur of our tradition is a mocked and cuckolded king whose wife Guinevere (Gwenhwyfar in Welsh, meaning "white shadow") symbolises true sovereignty according to Celtic belief; but she is often taken away from him by her lovers and it is not unreasonable to wonder whether Arthur is a later, *patriarchal* transformation of an ancient bear goddess. So changed and complex has his character become through additions to and confusions of his story, that we shall probably never know.

Meanwhile, we may simply conclude that there must have been a bear goddess and that she became blurred in the memory of the Celts, making way for other, more confused ideas.

IN THE PIGSTY

The theme of the wild boar enables us to discover one aspect of Our Lady of the Night that to this day mythologists have never understood. The wild boar is often portrayed in Gallo-Roman and even Gallic sculpture and coins. Soldiers often took the wild boar as an emblem, and there are inscriptions in honour of Mercury *Moccus*, which contains the Gallic name for wild boar or pig (Breton, *moc'h*). But perhaps the most interesting representation is the statue of the goddess Arduinna, whose name evokes that of the Ardennes, where she was discovered, and suggests a possible relationship to Artos, the bear. However, she is clearly portrayed riding on a wild boar, and her features are those of Diana the Huntress, who is, as we shall see, the ancient mother goddess of the Indo-Europeans. As Epona is represented astride a horse and virtually equated with a mare, this goddess *with* the wild boar must also have been a boar goddess, or rather a sow goddess; this assertion is confirmed by ancient, even prehistoric, traditions found in Welsh writings.

> Wales, *The Birth of Culhwch*
> "Kilydd, son of Prince Kelyddon, wanted a woman to share his life and his choice fell upon Goleuddydd ('Bright Day'), daughter of Prince Anllawd. Once they were living under the same roof, the whole country prayed that they might have an heir and, thanks to these prayers, a son was born to them. But the moment Goleuddydd became pregnant she went mad and shunned all inhabited places. When her time came she returned to her senses. She happened to be in the place where the swineherd kept his pigs and her fear made her give birth. The swineherd took the child and carried it to the court, where it was baptised with the name Culhwch because it had been found in a sow's lair." (*Culhwch and Olwen*, J. Loth, *Mabinogion*, vol. 1, pp. 244—5.)

According to the author of the narrative the name Culhwch would therefore derive from *cul* (pronounced "kil"), "narrow", or from *cil* (also pronounced "kil"), "hiding-place", "retreat", "corner", which is close to the Gaelic *cill*, "church" (as in Kildare, "the church of oaks", originally "the hiding-place of oak trees"); and from *hwch*, "pig" (but "sow" only in modern Welsh), related to *houc'h*, "pig" in Breton.

Joseph Loth states that this is a fantasy etymology analogous to ones found in most mediaeval writings. But this may be too hasty a judgement, for it seems likely that the anonymous author of this text, the first Arthurian romance, which dates in part from the ninth, if not the seventh, century, was following a perfectly authentic tradition.

It is undoubtedly a very strange story. A woman called "Bright Day" goes mad and lives far from human habitation, but comes to her senses when giving birth near pigs. On this point the text is clear: it is because she regains her sanity and realises that she is among pigs that she gives birth hastily *in a sow's lair*. Obviously she is the sow-mother, the sow goddess, and Culhwch is the young hog that she carried in her sow's hiding-place, her womb. The whole story resembles that of Rhiannon, whose son was found in a stable when a mare had just foaled a colt. There are also some connections between this and *The Story of Diarmaid*, a Gaelic legend from the Leinster cycle (Finn's cycle) and well known throughout Ireland and Scotland.

> Ireland and Scotland, *The Story of Diarmaid*
>
> Diarmaid was brought up in the home of the fairy king Oengus, and the son of Oengus's steward was his foster-brother. One day, when Diarmaid's father had come to visit his son, he accidentally killed the steward's son and was forced to make reparation. On the decision of Finn, the steward transformed his dead son into a boar without bristles, ears or tail and pronounced these words, "I put you under a magic bond to lead Diarmaid to his death; and your own life will not last a day longer than his." The boar got up and disappeared. Later it was known as the Boar of Ben Culbainn. (R. Chauvire, *Contes Ossianiques*, pp. 164–6.)

There is no mention of a woman in this curious story, though the wife of the steward might conceivably have had some connection with the sow.

So Diarmaid's fate was linked to that of the Boar of Ben Culbainn, who was his double, his magical projection. In some senses Diarmaid was the young boar, and though the version of the legend that has reached us may have been abridged and rearranged, it does contain the basic elements of the myth about a woman giving birth to a son who was likened to a boar.

The pig, or wild boar, played an important part in the life of the Celts. First, it figured in their daily life, for the Celts were great hunters and were very partial to the wild boar found in such abundance in the forests of Gaul, Britain and Ireland. They also bred large herds of pigs, and the position of swineherd was one of the most important in the social hierarchy. According to the Welsh Triads, two of the greatest swineherds were Pryderi and Tristan. A Gaelic narrative entitled *The Two Swineherds*[6] describes the magical feats of the swineherd of Munster and the swineherd of Connaught.

Secondly, the hog was a supernatural animal in Celtic mythology. When the Tuatha Dé Danann were beaten by the Gaels and banished into the hills and islands, they were fed, in a kind of feast of immortality, by the pigs of Mananann. In *The Destiny of Tuirenn's Children*, these had to take back to Lug, among other things, seven enchanted pigs, which could be killed every evening but would be restored to life the following morning. According to the Welsh Triads there were seven marvellous pigs in Dyvet which had been brought back from the Other World by Pwyll Penn Anwfn and entrusted to Pendaran, Pryderi's foster-father. The *Mabinogi of Math* says that they had been sent to Pryderi by Arawn, King of the Other World. "They are small beasts, but their meat is better than that of cattle. They are not tall and are in the process of changing their name. Now they are called *moch*."[7] This is obviously a reference to the introduction of domestic pigs into Britain, though these particular animals are also the subject of a magic battle between Gywddyon, the magician of the North, and Pryderi, chief of the South, who is custodian of the pigs and of the secrets of the Other World, which they symbolise. Gwyddyon used cunning to acquire them and the ensuing war ended in a duel between him and Pryderi, in which the latter was killed.

The image of the sow goddess seems to have survived for a very long time. A thirteenth-century French tale from the Round Table cycle, introduces a strange variation on the myth of the white pig.

Courtly romance, *The White Pig*

Guingamor, a Breton knight and the king's nephew, rebuffed the advances of the queen who had fallen in love with him. In revenge she had Guingamor appointed to go and hunt the wild white boar that roamed the forest and which nobody could ever catch. Indeed, none who had pursued it had ever returned. During the chase, Guingamor got lost and discovered a marvellous maiden bathing. She invited him to go home with her and granted him her love. But Guingamor wanted to return to his uncle's court, bearing the head of the white boar. The girl let him go with the warning that three hundred years had passed since his disappearance and that nobody would recognise him, but he was undeterred. The fairy of the white boar then advised him not to drink or eat as long as he was outside the fairy domain. He told his story to an old charcoal burner, but ate some fruit and fell down lifeless. Then the girl's servant came to fetch him back to their marvellous kingdom. (André Mary, *La Chambre des dames*, Bolvin, Paris 1922, pp. 243–252.)

The queen of the mysterious country in a way managed to attract the hero as a white pig, though once he reached the frontier regions between the two worlds she had only to appear in her friendly and attractive feminine guise to seduce him entirely. In this respect she was very similar to Goleuddydd, the sow goddess. But she could, on some occasions, assume a much more terrifying form. For, though much has been made of the destructive wild boar of Welsh legend, that formidable creature of the night, pursuit of which might cost one's life, no one noticed that the boar was really a sow, and stands as yet another image of Our Lady of the Night. Here are two versions of this legend.

Wales, *The Story of Twrch Trwyth*
    To obtain Olwen in marriage, Culhwch had to acquire a comb that was on the head of the wild boar, Twrch Trwyth. He had been promised help in the chase by King Arthur and his warriors, one of whom, Gwrhyr, an expert in magic, assumed the form of a bird and flew down over the lair where Twrch Trwyth lay with his seven piglets. Gwrhyr asked that one of them should come and hold talks with Arthur, to which one piglet replied, "We shall not speak to Arthur. God has done us enough harm in giving us this form without your coming to fight us." Arthur started the hunt. Twrch Trwyth devastated Dyvet and all of Wales. One after another, his piglets were killed, but he in turn killed a good many warriors and kings, and continued on his destructive path as far as Kernow (Cornwall). In the end Arthur stole the comb. "Then it [the boar] was hunted out of Kernow and pushed straight into the sea. No one ever knew where it went to." (J. Loth, *Mabinogion*, vol. 1, pp. 336–44.)

Wales, *The Story of Henwen*
    "One of Koll's sows named Henwen ('the Old White') was with young, and it had been predicted that Britain would suffer from her litter. So Arthur assembled the British army and set out to destroy her. The sow went to earth in Kernow and there threw herself into the sea with the great swineherd behind her. At Maes Gwenith ['Field of Wheat'] in Gwent, she gave birth to

a grain of wheat and a bee. From that day to this there has been no better land for wheat and bees than Maes Gwenith. At Llonyon, in Penvro [Pembroke], she brought forth a grain of barley and a grain of wheat. The barley of Llonyon has become proverbial. At Riw-Gyverthwch, in Arvon, she gave birth to a baby wolf and a baby eagle. At Llanveir, in Arvon, under Maen Du ['The Black Rock'] she bore a cat, which the swineherd threw from the rocks into the sea. The children of Palu, in Mon [Anglesey] fed it, which led to their misfortune." (Triad 63, J. Loth, *Mabinogion*, vol. 2, pp. 271—2.)

The sinister aspect of the sow goddess is evident in the destructive Twrch Trwyth and in the progeny of Henwen, the wolf, eagle and cat that were to be the scourge of Britain. Irish epic contains reference to the destructive sow Beo, which Finn killed, taking its head as a wedding present for Cruithne, daughter of the smith Locham (*The Childhoods of Finn*). Yet the animal is also clearly linked with fertility and abundance, as is shown by the grains of wheat and barley and the bee that Henwen bore. These are all mentioned as being particularly good. The sow goddess was therefore both good and evil, like the mother goddess of the ancient Mediterranean and Indian peoples, "the black Kali, adorned with the hands and heads of her victims dripping blood, and trampling underfoot the prostrate, corpse-like body of her master" as Zimmer calls her, "the mother of India, a beautiful and terrifying, gracious and murderous image by which eternal India symbolises the destructive and creative in the world, the eating and the eaten."[8]

The number of men killed by Twrch Trwyth inevitably suggests some kind of horrifying ritual like that associated with the worshippers of Kali, the insatiable devourer of human and animal victims, comparable to the sow, which sometimes devours its own young. This would explain the apparent barbarity of certain cults devoted to the mother goddess in the ancient world, both in India and round the Mediterranean. Until 1835, the Khonds of Southern India used to prepare a human victim, a *meriah*, over a period of ten or twelve days. After the *meriah* had been dedicated, unrestrained debauchery began; on the day of the sacrifice the *meriah* was inserted into the cleft of a sapling and the crowds hurled themselves upon him, tearing out shreds of his flesh. In Rome, during the festival of the Phrygian mother goddess, the priests formed processions which were accompanied by frenzied music and ended in orgies. At Argos, during the feasts to Aphrodite, the priestesses drugged and drank themselves to the height of mystical ecstasy. Flagellation played an important part in such rituals, notably in Sparta, where children were whipped before the statue of Artemis, a practice that replaced the child sacrifice evident in the legend of

Iphigenia; and in Rome, during the feast of Cybele and Attis and at Lupercal, when the priests used to flagellate the faithful, particularly the young women. Similar rituals survived into the Christian era with the mediaeval practice of mortification and corporal punishment, and the processions of flagellants.

So the sow goddess is thirsty for blood and cries of pain. The animal itself roots in the soil, tearing with its fangs and tusks. Naturally, the theme of the wild boar, or sow, is not peculiar to the Celts, for it underlies the myth of Aphrodite, one of the oldest goddesses of the Hellenic world. Although myth made her rise from the water, child of the foam and Uranus' testicles, her name is in itself significant, for it contains the word *Dite* (*Ditis-Daitis*), the name of a water goddess in Asia Minor and later the Tethys of Greek legend; and, more importantly, the term *Aphro*, which is related to the Latin word *aper*, meaning "wild boar".

All the obsessive male fantasies seem to have been condensed into the figure of the sow goddess or wild-boar goddess. The divine image associated with prosperity and love was repressed but the vilest, sexual images connected with blood and corruption were retained. In fact, the sow goddess became the "swine", with all the literal and metaphorical meanings the word conveys in contemporary speech. A "swine" is not merely a dirty man who does not wash, but a man who practises obscenities, some abnormal form of fornication. We might also note, in passing, that the low and vaguely slang word used in France to denote something dirty and ugly is *moche*, which derives directly from the Breton *moc'h* or possibly the Gallic *moccus*. Pornographic books are swinish books. A *mochete* is a dirty and ugly woman, the degenerate image of the sow goddess.

We have reached the crux of the problem. The goddess, i.e. the woman, is dangerous, unhealthy and frightening. Man keeps her submerged at the bottom of the sea or in the depths of a cave, and his conscious mind finds as much fault with her as possible, even as he secretly wishes she would rise again. She is a reminder of all cults of the mother goddess, which were conspicuous for their lack of modesty.

In his *Essay on Japanese Mythology*, N. Matsumoto recounts the tale of the goddess Ama-no-uzume, who was trying to make the sun goddess Amaterasu leave her hiding place in a cave. Holding a bunch of bamboo leaves in her hands, she climbed onto an upturned dugout canoe and started to dance. Possessed by divine spirits, she exposed her breasts and lowered her clothes down to her sex. The gods started to laugh and Amaterasu emerged from her cave.

This scene bears comparison with contemporary striptease shows and with the positively divine frenzy that drives girls at pop concerts to strip naked and dance in a kind of unconscious delirium. Then, of course, there are the witches' Sabbaths, whether factual or fictitious, when women dance with Lucifer, under the auspices of Diana-Artemis, often portrayed in sculpture lifting up her robe to show her sex to her worshippers. And behind all this lie the traces of sacred prostitution, an almost compulsory adjunct to the worship of the goddess in Babylon, where the daughters of the nobility offered themselves in the temple of the goddess Anahita. Herodotus wrote, "The worst of Babylonian customs is that which compels every woman in the country to go, once in her life, to the temple, in order to have sexual relations with an unknown man there. . . . The men pass by and make their choice. It matters little how much money they pay; the woman will never refuse, for that would be a sin, the money becoming sacred through the act. After this the woman is sanctified in the eyes of the goddess." And the goddess is Ishtar, the primordial "goddess of love and of life, courtesan and sacred whore of the temple", who proclaimed through the voice of her oracles, "I am a compassionate prostitute."

Clearly, "civilised" man cannot tolerate such memories within a male-ordered society based on monogamous marriage and on total faithfulness of the wife. To protect his patrilineal descent, his son must be the son of the father and not the son of the mother. His affairs will not endanger the male line of succession, but, given the same freedom, his wife might become pregnant by somebody else and restore the supremacy of matrilineal descent. Interestingly, female succession was clearly customary among the Celts, to judge by their mythological traditions. Still half-way between gynaecocratic and androcratic society, they were much more tolerant of female adultery than purely patriarchal societies. But, even in ancient Celtic traditions, the divine female being dressed all in white (Rhiannon on her white charger, Goleuddydd-bright-day, Gwen-hwyfar-white-shadow and her Irish counterpart Finnabair, the grey mare, the white hog or white sow) has become Twrch Trwyth, the destructive, or Henwen (white but old). It had been forgotten that the sacred whore was beneficent, that Acca Larentia, who brought up Romulus and Remus, gave her immoral earnings to the State, that the mother of Romulus and Remus was herself a Vestal virgin who prostituted herself in the temple and only chanced to become pregnant by the god Mars. Queen Medb of Connaught proved very generous with her body every time the interest of her *tuath* was at stake. Her husband, King Aillil, was never shocked at her lavishness with "the friendship of her thighs", but happy to announce that "it was necessary for the success of the enterprise".

It is the very freedom of the woman to use her sex as she likes that threatens masculine authority, since it implies that woman is capable of everything. In Indian theology, Siva, who personifies Brahma, the great immaterial Whole, is a passive, contemplative male figure who is powerless without his wife Shakti, who is energy in action. So, although man needs woman, he tries to keep her power under control, legislating against woman's free use of her sex in case she compromises the fragile but tenacious social structure of our patriarchal society. It goes further than we might think, as Herbert Marcuse remarked with reference to a thesis of Freud (both Freud's thesis and Marcuse's comments are given in full on pp. 148—9): "Free libidinous relations are essentially antagonistic to work relations; only the absence of full gratification sustains the social organisation of work. . . . Civilisation depends on steady and methodical work and thus on unpleasurable delay in satisfaction. *Since the primary instincts rebel 'by nature' against such delay, their repressive modification remains a necessity for all civilisations.*"[9]

The danger of free sexual relations, as symbolised in the goddess, Our Lady of the Night, lies in the possibility of their leading to total satisfaction of the instinctive desires of men and women, followed, if not by sleep, then by a state of inertia, close to *nirvana*, in which all will to live disappears. To put it another way, there would be a general *regressus ad uterum*, a return to true paradise in the real or imaginary protection of an ever-damp and nourishing maternal womb. This ultimate happiness towards which man aspires has been his incentive for thousands of years, but always it remains outside his grasp. In order that human society may continue to progress, he must remain in a state of permanent anxiety, which is equated with activity. So society feeds this anxiety by whatever means it has at its disposal, whether it is the promise of future welfare in capitalist countries, of egalitarian paradise in Marxist states, or the choice between heaven and hell after death offered by the Christian Church. Behind all these there is a deliberate attempt to associate feelings of guilt with man's natural, sexual impulses, to reject sex as shameful, disgusting, evil-smelling, dangerous and hellish. But, even in this, it is woman who is identified with sexuality, and banished into the darkness. And if she should rise again she will be covered in filth. Our Lady of the Night has become the great sow wallowing in the mud.

That is why the Celts invented Twrch Trwyth to complement Goleuddydd; why Arthur hunted the *Porcus Troit* in the ninth-century *Historia Brittonum*; why, in the *Mabinogi of Math*, the two sons of the goddess Don, having offended against their uncle Math, were condemned to assume the forms of a wild boar and a sow; why, in the imagery of the hagiographers, St Anthony the Hermit, who lived with a pig, was bound to be subjected to carnal temptation.[10] There followed a whole body of literature the aim of which was to bury this pig who slept so deeply in the night, for some things can be done in daylight and other, unmentionable things only at night. Racine's Phaedra, one of the incarnations of Our Lady of the Night, never oversteps the boundaries between darkness and sunlight, the brilliance of which she fears. When she dies, she returns the day she defiled to its former purity. The contemporary writer Francois Mauriac continues the same theme in *Thérèse Desqueyroux*, the eponymous heroine of which is herself a distant descendant of the sow goddess: "One evening in Paris, where they stopped on their way home, Bernard pointedly left a music hall because he was shocked by the show. 'To think that foreigners see such things! How shameful! And it is by that we are judged . . . .' Thérèse marvelled that this modesty should come from the man whose endless inventiveness of the darkened bedroom would be imposed on her in less than an hour."

This astonishing admission is reminiscent of the double morality of those defenders of our purity who flock to shows as insipid as *Hair* and *O, Calcutta!* in order to have the pleasure of protesting vigorously against the shocking things they have seen. In puritan periods it developed into a mania. Woman was depersonalised, desexualised, and trussed up in clothes that not only concealed the "obscenity" of her body, but were harmfully restrictive, because the object of sin must be punished. Molière's Tartuffe is, alas, no mere figment of the imagination, but savagely true to life. Women were told, "You have the divine in you, but you also have that intimate weakness inherited from your first mother's failings, which you must overcome despite all the unsettling temptations around you." At the turn of the last century, sinister characters like Dr Pouillet advocated a "binding belt" for the use of women, and cauterising with silver nitrate the sensitive parts of girls inclined to masturbation; and certain doctors practised clitorectomy, with the approval of the Church, presumably with the aim of removing the Devil from the woman's body. Such people were supported by treatises on marriage advising women to submit to the marital act, taking care not to "give way to sudden movements which might disrupt the sexual relations or seriously injure the male organ by twisting or bruising it".[11] All this would be laughable were it not for the disastrous effects it had on women's mentality.

Admittedly, some illustrious thinkers had set precedents for such attitudes. The Talmud (*Shabbat Tractate*, 146) said, "At the time when the Serpent entangled itself with Eve, it spurted defilement into her which continues to infect her children." Aristotle wrote, "One should touch one's wife cautiously and harshly for fear of arousing her so sensuously that her pleasure send her beyond the bounds of reason." Even Montaigne wrote that to caress a woman too well "is to shit in a basket and tip it over one's head".

Since man is conquered in the act of love, his partner becomes his unforgivable enemy; she can achieve an apparently limitless succession of orgasms, while he must recover before embarking on a second attempt. This extraordinary and amazing power disturbs him, for there must be magic in it, and from magic it is but a short step to the Devil. Clearly, therefore, the Devil is behind these obscenities, and has given woman the repulsive form of the sow, ever threatening, ever desirable, continually denounced by the brave fellow who comes to fear her in the end. In *The Second Sex*, Simone de Beauvoir quotes several revealing passages from an interview between a Dr Gremillon and Stekel, author of *Frigidity in Woman* (New York 1936). Gremillon says, "The normal, fertile woman has no orgasm. . . . The frequently concealed erogenous zones are not natural, but artificial . . . they are the stigmata of the fall. . . . Tell the man of pleasure all this and he will ignore it. He wants his partner in depravity to have an orgasm . . . he is working against himself by creating insatiability. A loose woman can exhaust any number of husbands without tiring. . . . A woman with 'zones' becomes different . . . sometimes terrifying, capable even of resorting to crime."

Given these frightening images of the devouring woman, it is easy to see why Drach, a nineteenth-century convert to Catholicism from the orthodox Jewish faith, might be perturbed by a modern Rabbinical commentary (Medrash Yalkut, on Jeremiah, article 315) on this ancient text of the *Zohar*: "Behold, Yahweh will create a new situation on earth: woman will embrace man." According to the commentary, the idea behind this was that, at the advent of the Messiah, woman would pursue man instead of man pursuing woman, as happens now. Horrified, Drach exclaimed that this was "a state of affairs as far from the sublime as the earth is from the sky and offends the morality of all nations and degrades woman. There is perhaps no more hideous sight than that of the timid sex rejecting the modesty that is her most beautiful ornament and chief guardian of her virtue."[12] After a remark like that it only remains for men to retire to the "local" and exchange the latest in dirty jokes, which always involve women.

For just as man invents the sow-goddess figure as a form of self-defence, so, for self-gratification, he finds substitutes that will not endanger his superiority or engulf him in the cave where Our Lady of the Night reigns. Starting from the coarse joke and the smutty story, he progresses to eroticism (very literary and well done) and pornography (sordid or witty). The remarkable thing about all these substitutes for sex is that none of them leads to anything. Take pornography, for example. The inconclusive, unsatisfied sexuality it provokes is an indispensable element of patriarchal and capitalist society, since it not only fosters the anxiety and guilt necessary to ensure production, but also represents the forbidden, and therefore the desirable, in an apparently austere society which can continue to be uncompromising about morality only if it tolerates and pursues deviations. For, in the words of Tertullien, "the palace is built over the sewer", and prostitution and pornography are as essential to good patriarchal society as the drains under its cities.

These reflections on capitalist pornography bring us closer to Our Lady of the Night than might be supposed, for patriarchal society knows very well that it cannot suppress her altogether. Every now and again she opens a safety valve, some minor means of momentary release, while reaping the benefit herself. But sometimes the trickle becomes a tidal wave that threatens to submerge man's world, as we shall see in connection with the revolt of the Flower Daughter. Meanwhile, we have yet to study some other aspects of Our Lady of the Night in Celtic tradition.

THE HIND OF THE WOODS

The Irish cycle of Leinster, or Finn, also called the Ossianic cycle, contains the clearest account of the legend of the deer goddess. This cycle is the most recent of the fairy-mythical collections that make up Gaelic literature, and some of its legends (for example, the story of Diarmaid and Grainne) have reached us in their entirety through oral accounts preserved in the folklore of Ireland and Scotland and collected in the eighteenth and nineteenth centuries. The fact that many Irish and Scottish tales tally on points of subject matter and characterisation indicates a very ancient oral tradition.

Ireland, *The Birth of Oisin*

Finn, king of the Fiana, and his men were out hunting when they caught sight of a hind and pursued it. But no huntsman or hound could catch it. Only Finn and his two bloodhounds, Bran and Scolan, "who had the 'minds of men', carried on the chase. Eventually the hind lay down in the grass, and the dogs, instead of attacking it, played with it and licked its face and body. Astonished, Finn led the hind back home with him, and that night a beautiful girl appeared to him, announcing that her name was Sadv and that she was the hind he had been chasing all day. She had been transformed into an animal by the magic of the Druid Fir Doirch, because she repelled his advances; but a servant of the Druid had explained to her that if she could manage to get inside the Fiana's fortress the Druid would have no more power over her. Finn fell in love with Sadv and found perfect bliss with her, and she soon became pregnant.

One day, when Finn was away, the Druid Fir Doirch disguised himself as Finn and came calling for Sadv outside the fortress. When she ran out to greet the man she thought to be Finn, the Druid changed her into a hind once more. Sadv tried to return to the fortress, but the Druid's two hounds prevented her and dragged her off into the woods. When he learned of this, Finn gave way to great grief and for seven years scoured Ireland for the hind with his bloodhounds. One day his dogs stopped by a small boy and lavished signs of affection on him. Finn was amazed at the resemblance between the child and Sadv. He took him away with him and brought him up. When the boy was able to speak he revealed that he had been reared by a hind, which had been taken away by a dark man who had touched it with his wand. Finn concluded that the young boy was Sadv's son and gave him the name Oisin (Ossian) which means "the fawn". (R. Chauvire, *Contes Ossianiques*, pp. 102—6).

The basic plot of this tale is strangely like the story of Rhiannon and Pryderi, and that of Goleuddydd and Culhwch. In fact Oisin is the fawn, just as Culhwch is the young hog and Pryderi the colt. Similarly, Sadv becomes the hind goddess. The whole story of Oisin is affected by the fact that his mother was changed into a hind and therefore belonged to the Other World, for he eventually became a poet of divine inspiration who did not die a real death. Indeed, the *Accalam na Senorach* ("Conference of the Ancients"), a curious twelfth-century collection of different Ossianic legends, tells how Oisin went to join his mother in the marvellous universe of the Tuatha Dé Danann.

This hind goddess also figures in Gallic or Gallo-Roman iconography. There exist several statues representing a woman with deer's antlers, notably the one housed in the British Museum; this portrays a seated goddess, holding on her knee a horn of plenty and on her left shoulder the head of a ram. Her face is entirely human except for the deer's antlers sprouting from her hair.[13] It seems very likely that this figure is Sadv. There is also a representation of a Gallic god in the guise of a young man who has one deer's ear,[14] and if we accept that the religion of the Celts spread throughout the area they occupied, it would not be too outlandish to see in this a portrait of Ossian. In fact, it has been possible to establish some connections between Irish divinities who became heroes of literary epics, and Gallic or Gallo-Roman divinities whose image has been preserved in stone carvings; for instance, the god Lug, hero of the Tuatha Dé Danann, was also the patron god of Lyons (Lugdunum) and of Laon, Loudon and Leyden.

There is another literary reference to the hind goddess in a mediaeval French text, one of the Lays of Marie de France, who is known to have worked from British and, more particularly, Breton originals.

Courtly romance, *The Lay of Guigemar*
Young Guigemar, son of the Count of Léon, was out hunting. "In the thick foliage of a thicket he saw a hind, which, with its fawn, had been driven out by the barking of the dogs. *It was an all-white beast with the antlers of a stag on its head.*" Guigemar fired an arrow which wounded the hind but then flew back at him and pierced his thigh. The hind then groaned, "You, vassal who has wounded me, will find no cure for your wound, neither

from herb, root, nor doctors, nor even from poison, until the woman who for love of you endures greater suffering than ever woman endured comes along." (P. Tuffrau, *Les Lais de Marie de France*, Épopées et Légendes, Paris 1925, pp. 9—10.)

The wounded hind, who has powers of speech and curses Guigemar, is a fairy creature who replaces, in the Christian and courtly world of Marie de France, the divinity present in an originally pagan legend. Note that the hind is white, accompanied by a fawn, and, above all, that she bears deer's antlers: a description that is no mere matter of chance, since in all her Lays Marie de France refers closely to an existing model and accurately describes every detail, even though it might shock a Christian audience. Another detail that points to Celtic sources is that of the arrow returning to wound Guigemar in the thigh. For, in all twelfth- and thirteenth-century courtly literature, a wound in the thigh is a euphemism for a wound in the genitals, as is evident from the mysterious Math ab Mathonwy (in one of the Welsh *Mabinogi*), who can only live with his leg in a virgin's lap, and from the Fisher-King, who, also wounded in the thigh, was rendered impotent, as a punishment for having uncovered the Grail without being entitled to do so. The hind's curse derives from the Irish *geis*, the goddess reserving Guigemar exclusively for herself by rendering him impotent until she, the one woman in the world, can cure him. This same idea occurs in the legends of Diarmaid and Grainne and of Tristan and Iseult.[15]

The theme of the goddess inflicting a wound on her lover extends well beyond the Indo-European sphere and is common in the Near East, particularly among Semitic peoples. It occurs in the story of Ishtar and Tammuz, Astarte (later Aphrodite) and Adonis, and, above all, in the story of Cybele and Attis, in which the goddess drove her lover-son insane in order to keep him. Then, in his madness, Attis castrated himself, an act preserved in ritual by the priests of Cybele, the *Galloi*, who, identifying with Attis, castrated themselves and wore female clothes.

Apart from these Semitic versions of the goddess, we should also examine the more Indo-European Artemis, whom the Romans likened to Diana, and who tallies on a number of counts with the ancient mother goddess of the gods. Artemis and her Indo-Iranian counterpart Arvi are very obscure in origin, but both derive from some older, probably pre-Indo-European, word. They are generally taken to be forms of the cruel and ancient Scythian Diana, the sun goddess of the people of the Steppes, who was worshipped throughout the periphery of the Mediterranean at the time of the Hellenic migrations. In earliest times, human sacrifices were made to Artemis at Sparta, a fact consistent with what is known of the cult of the Scythian Great Goddess. The reformer Lycurgus forbade such sacrifices and modified the ritual to flagellation of young people before the goddess's statue; and in this we find the myths of Cybele and Attis, Ishtar and Tammuz.

The fact that Artemis is represented with a hind in iconography says a great deal about the transformations of the original theme. For, although she was established in both literary and classical Greek mythology as Artemis the Divine Huntress and possibly given a hind as a sign of her patronage of hunters, the goddess probably initially stood as the patron of wild animals, particularly hinds, because she was herself in some earlier analogy a hind. This process, by which the notion of protection came after, and accorded with a symbolic representation, has already been observed with Rhiannon—Epona. Another argument in favour of this line of thought is furnished by the legend of Iphigenia. Though sacrificed to Artemis, the compassionate goddess carried her away and put a hind in her place. Later, Iphigenia became the priestess of Artemis in Tauris, and, in this capacity, had to sacrifice young people who came to her. Artemis is really the wild-beast goddess who sacrifices the young man, her lover and son.

The discrepancy between the position of Artemis as huntress and that of the Gaelic Sadv and Guigemar's hind as quarries is linked with social development. In the literary legends of classical antiquity, Artemis remained the firmly rooted image of the ancient goddess, as she had been at the height of her power within a gynaecocratic society. In the oral, and consequently more developed, Celtic tradition, however, there was time for the personality of the goddess to change and become obscure. With the reversal of ideas about femininity within new patriarchal social structures, the goddess was placed outside the lawful limits. Like the Submerged Princess in the punishment of the town of Ys, the huntress became the quarry, forced to hide in the undergrowth from the persecution of male huntsmen. A few heroes, such as Finn, who was a far cry from the hero of prowess of Indo-European tradition, continued to protect her, but the patriarchal order represented by the priesthood of all religions endeavoured to dismiss her for ever. So the Druid Fir Doirche ("Black Man") furiously pursued Sadv and transformed her into prey once more. Yet the image of the goddess is fixed so deep in man's subconscious that she still reappears, in more or less distorted forms. Sadv may have disappeared, but she leaves a new kind of character in her son Oisin, the fawn, who embodies the patriarchal ideal but represents through his lineage the ancient concept of the feminine divinity.

So, just as the mother goddess became the father god and the sun goddess became the sun god, the hind goddess naturally became the stag god celebrated in Celtic statues of a man with stag's antlers. We even know from a bas-relief on the altar of Nautes, now in the Cluny

Museum in Paris, that his name was Cerunnos. On another monument, housed at Autun, the god holds in his hand a goblet, towards which two snakes are stretching. The best-known representation of Cerunnos is on a bas-relief kept at Rheims: this shows him sitting in the position in which Buddha is generally portrayed, encircled by Apollo and Mercury and holding a kind of bag which spills out a stream, probably of coins, onto a bullock and a deer. He is also represented in one of the plates of the Gundestrup cauldron (kept in Copenhagen), which is of disputed age and origin but undoubtedly immensely valuable as an illustration of Celtic mythology. In this case he is surrounded by four animals, one of which is a stag and another a dog. In literary works that are comparatively late, though imbued with Celtic tradition, this stag god (and we stress that this is merely a convenient title, the animal symbolising the god just as the mare symbolises Rhiannon—Epona) reappears as a creature who is hunted to reap some reward, or even as a domestic animal who helps the man or woman who has tamed it.

Chrétien de Troyes, *The Hunt for the White Deer*

At Easter, King Arthur, who was holding court at Cardigan, announced that he wished to hunt the white deer "in order to revive the custom". Gawain, who was not in complete agreement, declared, "We all know about the custom of the white deer. He who kills it must give a kiss to the most beautiful woman of your court." (*Erec et Enide.*)

Wales, *Geraint and Enid*

At Pentecost, King Arthur held court at Caerleon-on-Usk. A knight arrived and told the king he had seen in the forest "a deer such as I have never seen before. . . . It is all white, and out of dignity and pride in its kingship, it does not run with any other animal." Arthur decided to go and hunt the white deer, and Gwalchmai (Gawain) suggested that he "allow whoever saw the deer during the hunt, whether horseman or foot-follower, to cut off its head and give it to whomever he wished, whether his own mistress or his companion's". (J. Loth, *Mabinogion*, vol. 2, p. 124.)

Wales, *Merlin's Deer*

When Merlin had gone mad, he went to live in the Kelyddon Forest, and even said that his wife Gwendolyn could remarry on certain conditions. He learned of her impending marriage and arrived riding on a deer and driving a whole herd of the animals before him. When he called to her, Gwendolyn appeared at her window and was greatly amused at the sight of him. When her future husband also came to look, Merlin tore out the antlers of the deer he was riding and hurled them at him, smashing his skull. Then he went back to the forest, still on his strange mount. (*Vita Merlini*, analysed in J. M., *L'Epopée celtique en Bretagne*, p. 118.)

Brittany, *Edern and Genovefa*

Edern, a character in Arthurian romance who had become St Edern in Brittany, arrived at the Mountains of Arrée "riding on a deer, with his sister Genovefa up behind him". There they settled, one at Loqueffret, the other at Lannédern. The deer helped with transporting loads and they each built a hermitage. To define the boundaries of their respective domains, Edern had until the first cock-crow to cover the greatest possible area whilst mounted on the deer. When Genovefa saw that the deer was running faster than expected, she arranged to make the cock crow. It is claimed that the woods in that vicinity are still inhabited by the descendants of St Edern's deer. (A. Le Braz, *Annales de Bretagne*, vol. 8, pp. 404—7).

Though the hunt for the white deer in the first two of these stories seems to be some kind of magico-religious ritual to honour a woman, the deer of Merlin and Edern have lost this quality. Nevertheless, there is universal agreement that the deer brings plenty and fertility, as the Gallic or Gallo-Roman representations of a god furnished with a cup or bag streaming coins appear to prove. But, since plenty and fertility are associated with women, the image of the deer god or god of deer must have concealed an older image of the hind goddess or goddess of hinds. Indeed, the motif of deer antlers is of very ancient, pre-Indo-European origin.

The cave drawings of the Camonica valley, which date from the fifth century B.C., represent a divinity with torcs and deer antlers; a picture in the Three-Brothers Grotto, dating from Palaeolithic times, portrays a partly human, partly animal person with antlers. In Mesolithic sepulchres on the islands of Teviec and Hoedic (Morbihan), antlers were discovered on the skulls of dead men. The peoples of Northern Europe had a special cult of the deer, obviously as the animal that represented the hunt. Some of the shamans of Siberia dress up as deer and wear antlers on their heads. In fact, it is possible that the deer or hind was the sacred animal of Arctic civilisations, and that during the ice age it spread south with them to the Mediterranean area.[16] In addition, there is the very important point that all these practices and beliefs have much in common with those of the ancient Scythians. In fact there have been finds in many tombs of the Asian Scythians, particularly in Eastern Asia, of statues representing men or animals adorned with antlers, and even of antler-like ornaments designed for horses' heads, notably at the site of Pazirik, east of Altai.[17]

So we are back with the Scythian Diana, the Greek Artemis, the sun goddess of early times who relinquished her solar position to a male god. One can, moreover, trace the course of this process in the Hellenic world and transfer it to the Celtic tradition. Originally Artemis was identified with her mother, Leto (or Latone) in the same way that Kore—Persephone was the double of her mother Demeter. In the myth of renewal she was the young and powerful rising sun, in contrast to the old, setting sun of Leto (just as Kore was the young daughter, or young earth, as opposed to Demeter, the old). Because it was impossible to wipe the former, feminine aspect of these divinities from men's minds, even after the goddesses had become gods, the character of Artemis was preserved, but alongside a male equivalent, her brother Apollo, who monopolised the solar office while she was banished into the night and made moon goddess. Similarly, in Egypt, Osiris replaced Isis as the setting sun, while Horus became the rising sun. Note also, in passing, that Isis was the goddess of the cow, and that the cow and the bull are the Mediterranean equivalents of the hind and the deer. So, although the moon was originally masculine and the sun feminine, as is still true of Semitic, Germanic and Celtic languages, and in the popular superstition that the moon impregnates women, a major upheaval took place in mythical and religious symbolism, and the sun mother-goddess, Leto, was replaced by her male and female children. Juno—Hera did all she could to prevent those children (the products of Zeus' adultery and therefore of patriarchal privileges) from being born, evidence that she tried to prevent society changing from a gynaecocracy to a patriarchy.[18]

We can claim, not unreasonably, to recognise the children of an ancient sun or deer goddess in Merlin and his sister Gwendydd on the one hand, and in Edern and Genovefa on the other. For Merlin, though married to Gwendolyn, was chiefly involved with Gwendydd and seems to have shared the world with her. At the end of the *Vita Merlini*, Geoffrey of Monmouth's curious twelfth-century work, Merlin passes all his magical and prophetic powers to his sister Gwendydd, which would tend to indicate a certain re-evaluation of gynaecocratic ideas. St Edern, on the other hand, who is really the son of the Celtic god Nudd, or Nodens, and brother of Gwynn, the gatekeeper of hell in Welsh Christian tradition, contended fiercely for his territory with his sister Genovefa, who, though attributed with "saintliness", as her brother is, is also represented as a character of great cunning and malice. But, following the Christian doctrine of male superiority, she failed to oust her brother, because he possessed the deer and with it the symbolic power of its antlers, and was in addition the new sun of a male-oriented society dedicated to the defeat of the sun goddess.

Various practices associated with the deer survived into the Christian Middle Ages, particularly the custom of walking in

procession wearing deer-masks. Césaire of Arles, in his Lives of
St Hilaire and St Pirminius, described this custom as "the vilest
wickedness", and it took very little to move from that kind of
censure to dressing up the Devil in deer's antlers. So Cerunnos
became the Devil, and this convenient diabolic mask covered
everything forbidden by the new religious and social dogmas, that is
to say, all traces of the mother goddess.

Perhaps the most convincing arguments about the hind goddess
can be drawn from a thirteenth-century text:

> Courtly romance, *The White Deer with the Golden Necklace*
> Launcelot and Guinevere were in a forest when "suddenly
> there emerged a white deer with an escort of four lions behind
> it. A golden chain glittered around the neck of the sacred
> animal, whose coat was whiter than freshly blooming clover."
> (Xavier de Langlais, *Les Romans du roi Arthur*, vol. 3, p. 61.)
> Later, when Galahad, Percival and Bohort, the three heroes
> of the Grail, had met together, the white deer appeared once
> more, led by the four lions, and the three heroes followed it
> into a chapel where a priest was about to officiate. The deer
> then appeared to change into a man, and three of the lions into
> an eagle, a bullock and a man. "They took the pew where the
> deer was sitting . . . and left through a stained glass window
> without breaking it or damaging it in any way." (*Quête du Saint
> Graal.*)

The Christian interpretation of this story is quite clear, and all
commentators are unanimous in stating that it concerns Christ and
the four evangelists, who are enacting an ascension worthy of them.
But this explanation is over-simple, for there still remains the
disturbing fact that the four evangelists were represented by four
lions. For, while it might be argued that the author was attempting
to improve on an original and add to the unusualness of the tale,
bearing in mind the contemporary fashion for lions (such as Yvain's
lion in Chrétien's romance), the lion was actually used, like the dog,
as a symbolic guardian of the Next World. And, in any case, behind
its almost exaggeratedly Christian exterior, the Quest for the Grail is
really just a vast pagan epic, its ancient text showing through the
Cistercian ornamentations. Every detail, every anecdote in this
inspired work is a mere travesty of the Celtic quest for the
submerged woman represented by the Grail. Once we realise that, it
is hard to take the white deer with the golden necklace at face value.
In its whiteness it is like the deer hunted by Arthur in *Erec et Enide*,
and the white hind of Guigemar. Its golden necklace is obviously a
symbol of the sun. It may be argued, correctly, that Christ was also
invested with solar symbols, but the Christian image-makers were

inspired by pagan sources. For the golden necklace is surely the golden torc worn by ancient Gallic chieftains, and which the god Cerunnos had around his neck as the insignia both of his divinity and of his solar origins. No commentator has ever linked the white deer with the golden necklace to the Cerunnos of the Gundestrup cauldron, who sits, with his deer's antlers on his head and his torc round his neck, encircled by four animals; nor pointed out the analogy between these two representations of the god and the image of the hind with the antlers of a stag seen in Sadv, whose fate was influenced by four dogs — Finn's two bloodhounds, Bran and Scolann, who drew her from cover, and the two hellish bloodhounds of the Druid Fir Doirche who drove her back again.

For ultimately everything leads back to the story of Sadv, the hind in the woods, who was pursued so fiercely by the Black Man, the Druid who represented the social and religious order, but protected by Finn and the Fiana, the last champions of Our Lady of the Night. For Finn's real name (Finn, "handsome", "white" or "fair", being a nickname) was Demne, which suggests an ancient *dam-nijo* ("small deer"); his son was Oisin, "the Fawn"; and Oisin's son was called Oscar, which means "he who loves the deer". A part of Leinster bears the name Osraige, meaning "people of the deer". Indeed, the whole epic cycle of Finn, or of Leinster, is placed under the symbolic patronage of the deer, whereas the cycle of Ulster is under the sign of the bull or cow.[19] All this is enough to make Sadv and the story of Oisin particularly significant; for the hind goddess, or goddess of hinds, is related to the most ancient image of Artemis—Diana, the sun goddess of those peoples who came to Western Europe before the Indo-Europeans.

THE GODDESS OF BIRDS

We have mentioned that Rhiannon was as closely connected with birds as with horses. In fact the "birds of Rhiannon" are celebrated throughout Welsh tradition. In the tale of *Culhwch and Olwen*, Yspaddaden Penkawr demands fantastic gifts from Culhwch in return for the hand of his daughter Olwen, and includes among these "the birds of Rhiannon, which bring the dead back to life and put the living to sleep. I want them to re-create that night for me" (J. Loth, *Mabinogion*, vol. 1, p. 307). The same marvellous birds also appear in the *Roman de Jaufré*, an Arthurian romance that contains many points of interest but is little known.

Provence, *Brunissen's Orchard*
    After strange adventures in the Forest of Brocéliande, Jaufré came across an orchard "surrounded by a marble wall" and full

of birds. This orchard was attached to the Monbrun Palace, where the young orphan Brunissen lived in seclusion. "She was dressed in a high and elegant silken bodice. Her fine, fair hair was charmingly tied with a golden thread. She had a beautiful and delightful face.... It was naturally very pure and her perfection never faded, neither at dawn nor at dusk; rather, it seemed to heighten, to shine and gleam, illuminating all who walked beside her. She had put on her head a hat of peacock feathers, and held in her hand a splendid flower which gave off a fragrant smell." Brunissen had been grieving for seven years, and she and her companions revealed their sorrow in tears four times a day and four times a night. Only the singing of the birds could relieve her anguish. (*Roman de Jaufré*, lines 3040 ff.)

From all the evidence, the enigmatic Brunissen is a sun goddess. The radiance of her face proves it, though it does not suggest the sun of the living world, but rather the "black sun" of the Other World, which shines more brightly at sunrise and sunset. Her name is also expressive, for Brunissen is the Brown Queen, despite the blonde hair that mediaeval fashion gave her, though this may have been intended to underline the sun idea. The name of the Monbrun Palace in which she lives probably means "dark mountain", unless it is a Provençal distortion of an original Celtic word, *Maen-Brun*, meaning "stone of the crow". But we know that the crow, despite its blackness, is the bird of Apollo, just as it is associated with the Celtic god Lug, whose name means "white". It is also connected with the actual name of the British hero Bran Vendigeit, "the Blessed Crow", whose head, together with the birds of Rhiannon, makes the feast of immortality possible. Apart from these considerations, Brunissen, with her hat of peacock feathers, closely resembles Juno, whose symbolic bird is in fact the peacock, though the Juno in question is not Juno- Hera, who belongs to the day, but the rather disturbing Juno- Lucina, who is banished into the shadows and called *Mala Lucina* ("Evil Lusine"), the "Melusine" of Poitou. We have found another face of Our Lady of the Night, secluded in the Monbrun Palace, carrying in her hand a marvellous flower which is the flower of immortality.

In this case there are some very curious points to be examined. Brunissen is grieving over some tragic events, and she and her household show their sorrow in tears somewhat reminiscent of the weeping and wailing that Peredur witnessed in the Castle of Marvels (Castle of the Grail) during what must have been the original Procession of the Grail. That Brunissen was consoled for seven years by the singing of birds is no coincidence, for both the *Roman de Jaufré* and the tale of Branwen are related to the same tradition, thereby affording us a fairly precise description of the goddess with the birds, another aspect of Our Lady of the Night.

Irish epic literature contains an equally well-known character, the goddess Morrigane or Morrigu, whose name suggests Morgan, and who also appears in the form of a bird. We should perhaps point out, however, that any identity between Morrigan and Morgan has more to do with their palpably similar roles than with any common linguistic origin, Morrigane (*Morrigu* in the nominative) apparently meaning "queen of nightmares" or "nocturnal demon", and Morgan suggesting the Welsh *Morgwen*, old Celtic *morigenos* ("born of the sea"), which would be rendered in Gaelic as *Muirgen.*

In fact, Morrigane almost always appears in the company of her two sisters, Bodb and Macha, and is often confused with them, especially with Bodb. Macha is the mare goddess, whom we have already considered, but the name of Bodb (or Badb), which tends to be used in Gaelic tradition as a generic term for the bad fairy, recurs in the name of Cathuboduae, a Gallic goddess of war, known from a Gallo-Roman inscription discovered in Savoy.[20] This name can be broken down into *cathu* or *cath*, "fight" (Welsh and Breton *kad*), and *bodu*, "rage, fury, violence", which is further suggestive of the historic queen Boudicca, who was the leading light of British resistance against the Roman invaders.

Indeed, Morrigane, Bodb and Macha are always shown in a wild light, as the warlike furies who harried combatants and urged them to fight. Morrigane is even called "daughter of Ernmas" ("Murder") which is highly expressive in itself. In the great epic of the *Tain Bo Cualnge*, she joined in the fighting after she had stolen the bull, the cause of the war, and openly offered herself to Cú Chulainn with a promise to help him. But, as he refused, she tried to avenge herself on him by appearing successively in the form of a cow, an eel and a she-wolf.[21]

D'Arbois de Jubainville suggests that the Gallic monument at the Cluny Museum in Paris, which represents a bull with three cranes (*tarvos trigarranos*) flying overhead, is an illustration of this theme, because Morrigane and her two sisters usually appear in the form of crows. In *The Death of Cú Chulainn*, Bodb, daughter of Calatin, who seems to be another version of Morrigane, came in the form of a crow to the top of the house where Cú Chulainn was and uttered the magic words that were to lead the hero to his downfall. Then, when he had fallen and she wanted to make sure he really was dead, she approached the hero's corpse "in the form of a crow, sweeping down from the highest reaches of the heavens to utter three cries over him, then settled in the foliage of a hawthorn opposite, so that thicket in the plain of Muirthemne is known as the 'hawthorn of the crow' ".[22]

The History of Ireland, which John Keating drafted from old documents in the seventeenth century, quotes Bodb, Morrigane and Macha as being the three goddesses of the Tuatha Dé Danann. *The*

Battle of Cnucha, an epic in the Ossianic series, describes the "Bodb on the breasts of men"; *The Battle of Mag Rath* speaks of the Morrigane "with grey hair"; *The Destruction of the House of Da Choca* has "Bodb with red mouths". In the *Book of Conquests*, a vast scholarly compilation on the mythological origins of Ireland, the mention of "Bodb, Macha and Ana (or Anand), the three daughters of Ernmas", is contradicted immediately afterwards by a poem in which Morrigane replaces Ana.

The Gaelic Morrigane, like the Morgan of the *Romans de la Table Ronde*, has the ability to change herself into a bird, and is accompanied by her sisters, who can also take the same form. But Our Lady of the Night may appear with other birds, or herself be a bird other than a crow. A great number of Celtic epics relate stories of bird-women.

Ireland, *The Birth of Cú Chulainn*

Dechtire, sister of King Conchobar, ran away with fifty young girls, without asking leave of the king. They reappeared one day in the form of birds and all the Ulstermen rushed in pursuit. Their chase led them into rather mysterious houses where strange music could be heard. Finally, Bricriu, one of the Ulstermen, learned that Dechtire and the fifty girls were there, and the next day a tiny child was discovered asleep on Conchobar's chest. It later transpired that he was Dechtire's son, Setanta, who was to be given the nickname Cú Chulainn. (Second version, D'Arbois de Jubainville, *L'Épopée celtique en Irlande*, p. 22.)

Ireland, *The Story of Derbforgaille*

"Derbforgaille, daughter of King Lochlann, fell in love with Cú Chulainn through all the fine stories told about him. She and her servant set out from the east in the form of two swans and reached Lough Cuan, joined together by a golden chain." Cú Chulainn, who was there with his foster-brother Lugaid, threw a stone from a sling at the birds and it lodged in the body of one of them. The birds resumed their human form and Cú Chulainn sucked the wound of Derbforgaille to extract the stone. But, as he was then joined to her blood, he could not unite with her and gave her to Lugaid. (J. M., *L'Épopée celtique d'Irlande*, pp. 106—7.)

Ireland, *The Illness of Cú Chulainn*

One day of Samain, when the Ulstermen were assembled, the women asked Cú Chulainn to catch for them the birds gliding over the lake. Cú Chulainn performed this extraordinary feat, but, very soon after, two birds linked by a red-gold chain arrived at the lake and sang a sweet song that put to sleep all the Ulstermen except Cú Chulainn, his concubine Ethne and his driver Loeg. Cú Chulainn took his sling and attacked the birds, but for the first time in his life he missed his mark. He then threw his spear and pierced the wing of one of the birds, both of which disappeared under the water. Then Cú Chulainn felt ill, leaned against a stone pillar and went to sleep. He had a horrible dream during which two young girls came and struck him. He was ill and bed-ridden for a whole year. Then he had another dream, in which one of the two women came to tell him that her companion, Fand, wife of King Manannan, was in love with him and hoped he would come to her fairy land. (G. Dottin, *L'Épopée irlandaise*, pp. 123—43.)

Brittany, *The Magician's Daughter*

The young shepherd, Pipi Menou, who kept his flock near a pond, had noticed that sometimes large birds flew down to rest there. But the instant they touched the ground, they turned into beautiful young girls, who bathed and frolicked in the sun, completely naked. Then, at sunset, they resumed the form of birds and disappeared into the air. He inquired about this of his grandmother, who replied, "They are the swan-women, daughters of a powerful magician, who live in a beautiful palace gleaming with gold and precious stones and held above the sea by four golden chains." By a cunning trick, Pipi Menou forced the three daughters of the magician to lead him to the enchanted palace, and there he hid in a basket with access every evening to the room of the one who pleased him most. But the other two sisters threatened to reveal everything if Pipi did not visit them as well, so he and the young enchantress fled, Pipi astride the back of the bird-girl, though not before he had carefully loaded himself with precious stones. (Told in the isle of Ouessant to J. M. Luzel, *Bulletin de la Société archéologique du Finistère*, vol. 9, 1882, pp. 88—92.)

Wales, *The Birds of Gwenddoleu*

The two birds of Gwenddoleu, who wore a golden yoke, were scarcely ordinary creatures, for, not content with just guarding their master's treasure, they devoured two men for their dinner every day and the same number for their supper. (J. Loth, *Mabinogion*, vol. 2, p. 256).

Wales, *The Birds of Drutwas*

Drutwas, son of Tryffin, one of the knights at King Arthur's court, had married a fairy woman, who gave him three marvellous birds that could understand human speech and do everything that was asked of them. Drutwas took them off to war and they worked marvels. But, having challenged King

Arthur, he sent the three birds in his place with orders to kill the first person to appear. Arthur was prevented from coming, so Drutwas was the first to arrive and was torn to pieces by his own birds. (Iolo manuscripts, p. 188. J. M., *L'Épopée celtique en Bretagne*, pp. 262—3).

The birds of Drutwas were obviously fairies, as were the birds of Gwenddoleu, who "devoured men", and clearly feminine, representing the Kali-like, devouring aspect of the goddess who dominates. Note also that all these birds were linked to each other by a golden chain while flying through the air, but resumed their woman's form as soon as they touched the ground, unlike the children of Lir, who were condemned by their stepmother's curse to remain birds for ever. It was also in the form of a swan that Mider abducted Etaine from her husband King Eochaid, and they both fled from hill to hill after the king had ordered the hollowing-out of all the hills in Ireland to catch them (*The Courtship of Etaine*).[23]

The swan motif is also reminiscent of the Brittano-Germanic legend of Lohengrin, son of Parzifal, King of the Grail, who was forced to betray his secret to the woman he loved and flee, mounted on a swan, to his father's mysterious kingdom. European folklore is full of stories about princes and princesses changed into birds, especially swans, either as the result of a curse, or simply in order to enter regions where they could not go in human form.

There are also references among classical writers to unusual Celtic customs associated with birds. Strabo (IV, 6), for example, quoting a tradition described by Artemidorus, tells how, in an oceanic port, when two people were arguing about something, they would put two cakes on a plank in a raised place. Crows with white right wings would then hurl themselves at the cakes, and whoever's cake was knocked over was declared the winner. There are many other stories about birds, including one, in particular, related by Livy (VII) about Marcus Valerius, who won his nickname of Corvinus from the crow that protected him, and another told by Justinius (XXIV) about the great Gallic migrations across Illyria following the flight of birds.

But all this merely reinforces the idea of the bird as a celestial guide, a light, aerial creature whose mystery lies in its capacity to scale the highest reaches of the atmosphere and lose itself in the blue of the sky. It is elemental that the bird should be associated with woman, the mysterious and disturbing creature who belongs to forbidden regions like the sky. She has the power to engender, the power to cure, the power to re-create within each man the primordial paradise that he lost as a result of the great catastrophe.

The bird-woman, or goddess of birds, therefore forms one of the essential faces of Our Lady of the Night, though obviously a more serene, more reassuring aspect than that of the horse, the bear, or the deer. But, despite all appearances to the contrary, men have not really forgotten the derisory and devilish disguise they have imposed on woman, and have yielded to the occasional but irresistible pressure of the subconscious. For, deep down, the bird goddess must surely represent hope, or, more plainly, temptation. We should not forget that it was Pipi Menou's grandmother who explained to him who the swan-women were and how he could reach the castle held above the sea by golden chains. For it is always the mother or one of her substitutes who points out to man the road he must travel. As she brings up her child, the mother is bound, willy-nilly, to develop in him all his erotic instincts and consequently to shape his eventual power as a man. It is this that lies behind all myths about the mysterious and transforming power of woman, particularly the myth of Keridwen.

For this goddess (who might just as well be called Rhiannon, Laudine, Sadv, Dechtire, Macha, Bodb, Morrigane, or Morgan) is at the heart of the problem of the myth of woman. Not only does she change her own appearance, but she also transforms others: her male and female children, of course, and also the men who are her lovers. She is Circe, the divine enchantress, who changed seamen into animals, and *Kirke* is simply the feminine form of *Kirkos*, the wheeling falcon. So Our Lady of the Night is the sparrow hawk, the devouring bird-woman perhaps, but also the one who gives another life, on another level, in another world. As man is never sure of meeting her, he dreams up the different aspects of her that mythology has preserved for us. She is not just submerged in the sea, in a lake, or in a deep cave, as Our Lady under the Water or Our Lady Underground; she also makes the odd appearance in broad daylight. But, by her nature and because man wishes it so, she is elusive, constantly changing her appearance. Who really is Our Lady of the Night?

Chapter 5

The Great Queen

Since the time of the early nineteenth-century Romantic poets, very little attention has been paid to describing the divine woman. In fact, most descriptions have become worn-out clichés, fit only for display in a museum of banalities. There has also been a deplorable lack of interest in the "Litanies of the Virgin", which form part of the remnants of Catholic ritual. They have been recited apathetically in Latin over the centuries, with scarcely a response in the subconscious of the faithful. They are actually the symbolic and poetic transposition of a basic truth which is an indelible part of the souls of the people, despite all prohibitions and threats. Patriarchal society suppressed the mother-goddess, replacing her, sometimes by force, with a warlike father god; he was jealous of her superiority, and popular thought re-created her in the role of Mother of God and men; she was constantly invoked, ever-present and ever-triumphant. The official Church had to go along with the movement, like it or not, though it tried to empty the idea of any meaning and make the *Theotokos* an asexual and "virginal" being whose female nature was evident only in her role as the admirable mother who was a slave to her son. Mediaeval Christian society, the heir to the Roman Empire, deliberately contained this revival of a very ancient myth within the confines of a psychological *tour de force* intended to deflect spiritual and intellectual strength away from its original objective and make it a pliable instrument for the domination of one caste (the faithful) by the wealthy, the priesthood and the nobility. Most of these were complete atheists, but were careful to manipulate the paradise that they promised others (provided they were obedient) for their own personal profit in this world.

Meanwhile the worship of the Virgin Mary carried the seeds of revolution, both from a spiritual and a social point of view. At first this meant a return to the natural and instinctive cult of the mother. Then it was recognised that if a woman (Eve) had caused the downfall of humanity, another woman (Mary) had helped to save it; this realisation not only restored woman to a position that, though theoretical, was nonetheless accepted, but also showed that what had been rejected as unlucky, shameful and dangerous could, within a very short space of time, become an object of hope and reverence. This raised doubts about traditional ethics of absolute good and evil, and even about the unproductive system of logic that scholasticism had inherited from strict Aristotelianism and the most elementary Manichaeism.

The religious traditions that developed alongside the Established Church reflect the unconscious thought of the masses terrorised by hell and the stake, and are also the only link with earlier periods. Why, after the thirteenth century, and particularly during the fourteenth, should there have been so many theatrical works devoted to "miracles" attributed to the Virgin Mary? In these she snatches from Satan his binding pact with the clergyman Theophilus; and, when a nun leaves her convent to lead the life of a prostitute, she takes her place, so that her absence will not be noticed until she decides to return to the fold. The good Virgin was apparently protecting people who, as a rule, did not deserve it; though it is difficult to say whether her actions were intended to be an illustration of charity or resulted from a transference of unconscious longings in a population harassed by the Inquisition and by the idea of an omnipotent and vengeful male god whose political image was the king. All these questions can be summed up in one: is there still a kind and welcoming mother goddess who begs her son to show tolerance and rebels against the tyranny of her divine husband reincarnated in the son?

As we have seen, she goes back very far in time. In the purely Celtic sphere, the countless number of statues or statuettes produced in the Gallo-Roman era and protraying mothers, or, more accurately, *matres* and *matronae*, proves that the mother goddess was still worshipped among the Gauls. One of these statues, supposedly worshipped by the Druids, stood in an underground sanctuary on the site of Chartres cathedral and later became Our Lady Under the Ground and an object of reverence for Christian pilgrims. Even if too much has been read into that particular statue, the Gauls did worship the divine mother and under a variety of names, as Christians still do Our Lady (for example, Our Lady of the Road, Our Lady of Sailors,

Our Lady of Lourdes, of Chartres, of Pontmain, of la Salette, of Fatima, and so on). One of the very few extant texts written in Gallic consists of two invocations to the mother goddess. They are worth quoting in their entirety, first as an archaeological curiosity, and secondly because of their resemblance to a Catholic prayer, like the expressive "Litanies of the Blessed Virgin".

> For love of the spirit ever persisting, O Caticatona, be thou for thy servants a powerful wave, for thy servants worship thee. Be favourable, O Dibonna, charming goddess. With this one, with this one, O pure and joyful, Sucio worships thee with this one, eternal daughter, his servant Pontidunna, daughter of Vousos.

> Prosperity! We pray today, outstretched towards thee, today before thee by this precious offering. We drink to this, to thine own source: thou hast loved us. Stretched towards thee, worshipping each day at noon. To prosperity! We pray to thee through this offering, Imona, be kind to thy servants soon.

If the people worshipped the goddess with prayers like these, they must also have related the adventures of the mother of gods, for every known cult has been supported by mythological narrative, even in the earliest recorded eras of civilisation. This goddess, mother and virgin, as we shall see, had her own story rooted in the Gallic soil, particularly in Poitou, the region from where the two invocations just quoted originally sprang. This story was the legend of Melusine.

Many people have tried to make Melusine a purely historical character, supposing her to have been a "Scythian" woman, from Central or Eastern Europe, who married Raymond de Lusignan, Count of Poitou. At the end of the fourteenth century, they say, Jehan d'Arras, in a literary work of subsequent fame, transformed the real, non-Christian woman into a fairy woman who built monasteries and churches, was the benefactress of Poitou, and gave the Lusignan family their letters of nobility, according them divine or supernatural ancestry. It goes without saying that this historical explanation is not very convincing. Jehan d'Arras, who wrote his *Roman de Melusine* in about 1380 A.D., did indeed write it to glorify the family of his patrons, the Counts of Auvergne and the Duke of Berry, but he certainly did not invent either the character or the name Melusine, who came, according to some, from Lusignan. She is too complex to be the invention of a man of letters, but stems from a fund of myth that must have been preserved in Poitou for centuries.

Melusine was unlike the other fairies of the French countryside, in that she was half snake and half woman. Rabelais, who was always very closely in touch with popular traditions, particularly those of Poitou, described her in the *Quart Livre* (XXXVIII), obviously with his own brand of humour, but insisting on her original character nevertheless. "Visit Lusignan, Pathenay, Vouant, Mervant and Pouzauges in Poitou," he writes. "There you will find witnesses of great age who will swear on the arm of St Rigome that Melusine, their first founder, had a female body as far as the breasts, and below that a snaky sausage, or even a sausagey snake. Yet she had a bold and elegant gait, of the kind still imitated by Breton clowns dancing their *trioriz* [dances in treble time]." Note the comparison of Melusine's movements with those of a popular Breton dance; this might well point to the great age of some of these dances. It is no mere chance that Rabelais makes this comparison, for the legend of Melusine abounds with assimilations of this kind. But Rabelais continues his extraordinary dissertation on sausage shapes with a comment of considerable interest: "The Scythian nymph Ora also had a body half woman and half sausage-shape. Yet she seemed so beautiful to Jupiter that he slept with her and they had a fine son."

So Rabelais, the remarkable transcriber of oral legends of the people, introduces a reference to the land of the Scythians. The legend of Melusine made her sometimes a princess from Scythia, sometimes a fairy from Scotland, though in the Irish tradition *Scotie*, meaning Scotland, is often confused with Scythia because of a similarity in pronunciation.[1] This would suggest that the legend was Irish in origin, especially as various episodes of the *Roman de Melusine* take place in Ireland, or Scotland, a country inhabited by the Gaels of Ireland. On the other hand, Rabelais' citing the Scythian nymph Ora, who has a child by Jupiter and is therefore classed as his wife, or as a mother goddess, ranking equally with Juno, points to two conclusions: either Melusine—Ora is what folklore made of the Scythian Diana, the sun goddess Artemis, whose worship spread with the arrival of the Indo-Europeans in the Mediterranean basin at the same time as the cult of Apollo at Delphi and Delos; or else she is one of the faces of Juno, who is sometimes called the Evil Lucina, *Mala Lucina*, which we must accept as the original form of the name Melusine, unless we resort to whimsical Celtic etymology. If Mala Lucina is the Evil Midwife, the Evil Mother, so too in a certain sense are Melusine and the Welsh Arionrod, her divine counterpart among the island Celts. That, however, is a digression, and we should return to the main lines of the legend.

Jehan d'Arras, *The Story of Melusine*

Elinas, the King of Scotland, a widower, met a mysterious girl called Pressine by a fountain. She would not say who she was or whence she came, and married Elinas on condition that he would never try to find out. She gave birth to three daughters, Melusine, Meliot and Palatine. But Elinas, prompted by curiosity and jealousy, did not keep his promise. Pressine cursed him and declared that her descendants, with the help of her sister, the Queen of the Lost Island, would avenge her. Then she disappeared, taking her daughters with her to the Lost Island.

Fifteen years later, Melusine decided to avenge her mother and with the help of her sisters used her magic powers to shut her father away in an inaccessible part of the Brandebois mountains. Furious that her daughters should take vengeance without her, Pressine laid curses upon them, the worst one on Melusine, as instigator of the conspiracy. Meliot was to be imprisoned in an Armenian castle, Palatine in a mountain together with her father, while Melusine was to become a "snake up to the waist" every Saturday. If anyone wished to marry her, he should remain ignorant of her secret.

Melusine left the Lost Island and arrived in Poitou. She met Raimond de Lusignan beside a fountain, rescued him from some desperate plight, and married him on condition that he never try to find out what she did every Saturday. Ten healthy boys were born of their union, but all were afflicted with strange physical defects. For example, one of Urian's eyes was in the middle of his cheek, and Geoffrey had a very long eye-tooth, which was why he came to be nicknamed Geoffrey Big-Tooth. One day Raimond could no longer contain his curiosity: he had noticed that each of Melusine's absences coincided with the apparently magical building of a castle, a monastery or a church. So he followed his wife into the cave to which she withdrew every Saturday. There he saw Melusine, her lower body like a snake, bathing in a green marble tub. When she realised she had been found out, she wept and stretched out her arms, which turned into wings; finally, she disappeared into the air, uttering a terrible cry of affliction. Her son Geoffrey Big-Tooth later became the hero of extraordinary adventures in Britain and Ireland and master of the lands of his grandfather, Elinas.

It looks as though the story of Pressine and the story of Melusine were originally one and the same, but were repeated so that the legend, which undoubtedly originated in Ireland, could be transferred to Poitou, an ideal region for further development. Pressine's sister, the sovereign of the Lost Island, closely resembles Morgan, Queen of Avalon, and the whole legend revolves round the theme of the mother goddess who alone can assure the prosperity and happiness of men, but on the strict condition that they do not know exactly who she is. This prohibition, naturally broken, like all warnings, is not unlike Yahweh's command to the Hebrews never to look him in the face, for they would not be able to stand the absolute vision of the divinity. It proves that Melusine (or Pressine) is a primordial divinity who has retained the nature of the originally female and later decidedly male god who presided at the birth of the world, its construction and organisation. Her name, *Mala Lucina*, is further evidence. Finally, there is the fact that she gave birth to ten boys who all bore the mark of the supernatural. For all these reasons, we are bound to look upon this traditional character as one of the most compelling images of the mother goddess of gynaecocratic cults. Melusine's imprisonment of her father, Elinas, can be explained only as the last rebellion of femininity against a society that had recently become male-dominated.

The theme of the forbidden exists in a number of legends, all of which refer to the union of the goddess with a mortal. Originally such a union was dangerous for the mortal, as in the legend of Cybele and Attis; Attis must surely have been metamorphosed because he had seen the goddess unveiled. The theme is identical in the stories of Venus and Adonis, Ishtar and Tammuz, Venus and Anchises; and also, as we shall see with regard to another aspect of the female divinity, in the strange adventure of the Fisher-King, Keeper of the Grail, who was wounded in the thigh — that is, made impotent. But, in those versions of the legend where pure folklore outweighs the religious element, the breaking of the prohibition results not in a wound for the mortal, but in the disappearance of the fairy.

Wales, *The Legend of Llyn y Fan*

A young man who kept his herd close to Lake Fan noticed on its waters a beautiful young girl and fell in love with her. Having overcome his shyness, he managed to engage her in conversation. The young girl's father, who also lived under the waters of the lake, set him a test which he managed to pass. He was able to marry the Lady of the Lake on condition that he did not lay a hand on her three times without reason. He became very rich because of the herd of marvellous cattle brought by his wife. But, after several years, he quite unintentionally touched his wife for the third time without reason. Lamenting, she disappeared under the waters of the lake, taking her herd with her. She came back only once, to see her sons and teach them the principles of medicine. (*Meddygon Myddfai*. J. M., *L'Épopée celtique en Bretagne*, pp. 273—6.)

This legend also derives from the relocalisation of a much older myth. The Lady of the Lake, whose name remains unknown, must not be touched *without reason* more than three times, for to do so would be the equivalent of perfect vision, knowledge being acquired not only by the eyes and ears, but also by touch. This prohibition attached to Melusine and the Lady of the Lake is reminiscent of the legend of Orpheus leading Eurydice out of Hades. Her stay in the

Other World had given Eurydice a supernatural, even divine quality, which meant that she could no longer be looked at by human eyes, at least not while she continued to shine with the strange brilliance of the domain of Hades. This explains why Orpheus was told not to turn back to look at her until after they had crossed the frontier between the living and the dead worlds: a warning that would otherwise remain inexplicable.

There was a different kind of prohibition attached to the lady of courtly love, who was regarded as inaccessible by many troubadours; she was so divine, so frighteningly beautiful that it was almost impossible to look at her, except after a gradual initiation process, namely a learning of habit and custom. All religious and philosophical initiations are obviously based on the idea that it is dangerous to survey the divinity without due preparation. Thus humanity has sought since the dawn of time to contemplate what cannot be contemplated and express the inexpressible after all.

Early man believed that he had nothing to do with the phenomenon of parturition, which was the specific function of woman. This statement is not mere conjecture, for the same belief still persists in certain practices of contemporary societies, such as those studied in Oceania by Bronislaw Malinowski: "The husband is not regarded as the father of the children in the sense in which we use the word; physiologically he has nothing to do with their birth according to the ideas of the natives, who are *ignorant of physical fatherhood*. According to native belief, children are inserted into the mother's womb as tiny spirits, generally by the spirit of a *deceased kinswoman of the mother*. Her husband has to protect and cherish the children, to 'receive them in his arms' when they are born, but they are not 'his' in the sense that he has had a share in their procreation."[2]

This archaic belief is characteristic of a society that we are all too ready to consider primitive in the derogatory sense of the word. In fact it is primitive only in a chronological sense, and represents a stage of civilisation that is not necessarily worse than the purely patriarchal stage of Roman civilisation, or the hybrid stage of our day. Again with reference to Oceanic peoples, in this case the Trobriand Islanders, Malinowski commented that in matrilinear civilisation there are fewer emotional conflicts than in patrilinear societies, because, on the one hand, the father is forced to win his children's affection rather than expecting it as a right, and, on the other, he is that much more prepared to let his fatherly instincts develop, since he is freed of the burdens of ambition and economic responsibility.

By stressing the biological role of the father, patriarchal society reinforces all the sources of conflict of an Oedipean nature and destroys the balance of basic instincts that survives in matrilinear societies, for in these the relationship with the father is bound to be disinterested and free from all authority or abuse of it. There lies the nub of the problem concerning family relationships, for the family is the basic unit of society. The introduction of a patriarchal structure does not therefore seem to have been an improvement on the previous, gynaecocratically inclined structure, even if the latter was not exactly perfect.

There is evidence of matrilinear descent in various mythological traditions, particularly those concerning the founders of religions or originators of great religious theories: the most famous came from humble origins and traced their descent through the mother. Though we are told that Moses was a Hebrew, he was rescued from a wicker basket floating on the waters of the Nile by the Pharaoh's daughter, who then brought him up. Clearly this was a symbolic way of saying that Pharaoh's daughter was his mother, as she discovered him and presented him to the world. His father was obviously Hebrew, but the princess could not acknowledge him. The text of Exodus actually mentions "a man of the house of Levi", who was supposed to have married a woman of the same House, but Exodus was inspired, if not written, by Moses himself, and he could hardly have admitted that his own mother was Egyptian. Yet the teachings of Moses bear the undeniable imprint of both Jewish and Egyptian inspiration, and his rejection of his mother might explain the patriarchal tendencies of his Law.

Then we have Jesus, the purest example of a gynaecocratic society, whose only link with mankind, since he had no fleshly father, was through his mother's line, which went back to King David. Joseph was exactly like the fathers of Oceanic societies, a foster-father and an emotional father, but no more. Christianity, at least in its early days before St Paul rearranged it, was a *revolution* in a patriarchal background, an attempt to restore the mother to her true role. Jesus' intentions to destroy the religion of the father (Judaism) and replace it with the religion of the son (Christianity) are characteristic of the Oedipean rebellion. It was to the Virgin Mary, standing at the foot of the cross, that Jesus gave John as a son, a substitute for himself and the symbol of humanity.

These considerations lead us to the problem of the Virgin who bears a child. An extraordinary amount of childish and foolish nonsense has been applied to the *Virgo paritura*; and yet it is through this theme that we shall arrive at a true understanding of the concept of the mother goddess.

Note, in passing, that it is the most patriarchal societies, and consequently those most ready to regard women as a "machine for pleasure and reproduction", that have laid most stress on the sacrosanct virginity of girls. The young virgin is the most glaring symbol of the prey reserved for the exclusive use of the owner, namely the future husband, the pivot of this society. In this connection, there is a Welsh narrative containing a curious story which, though slightly confused, testifies to the mixture of two types of society.

Wales, *The Story of Arianrod*

King Math ab Mathonwy had an infirmity almost incompatible with kingship. In peace-time he could not live unless he had his feet in the lap of a virgin; in time of war he could live only by riding his horse. Now his nephew, Gilvaethwy, son of his sister Don, was in love with the young virgin "in service" and with the help of his brother Gwyddyon, who got Math out of the way by launching a war, he managed to "do violence" to the girl. When the war ended Math returned, but the girl could no longer perform her duties and told Math what had happened. Furious, Math avenged himself on his two nephews, but nevertheless asked their advice about replacing the virgin so necessary to his existence. Gwyddyon suggested his sister, Arianrod, daughter of Don. Math summoned the girl and asked her if she were a virgin, to which she replied that she was. But Math wanted to make sure, so he took his magic wand, bent it, and told her to step over it. "She took a stride over the enchanted wand, and, at that very moment, dropped behind her a strong, fair child. At the infant's cries she made for the door and simultaneously dropped something else behind her, also like a young child. But, before anyone could get a second glimpse, Gwyddyon snatched it up, rolled it in a 'straw' coat and hid it at the bottom of a chest."

Meanwhile Math had the first child baptised as Dylan and "hardly was the ceremony over than he made for the sea. Immediately he entered it he was at home there and became as good a swimmer as the fastest fish. So he was known as Dylan Eil Ton ['Son of the Wave']." Gwyddyon brought the other child up in secret, then one day took him to Arianrod's citadel. She welcomed her brother and asked who the child was. When Gwyddyon told her "he is your son", she became angry and accused her brother of bringing her further shame. When she finally asked Gwyddyon the name of *his* son, and he replied that he had none, Arianrod pronounced this curse: "By my oath, he is destined to have no name until I have given him one", which meant that she refused to give him a name.

Gwyddyon went away with the child and used his magic powers to return to the citadel disguised as a shoe-maker, accompanied by the child, who had also become unrecognisable. Arianrod received them, admired the shoes and tried them on. At that moment a wren flew by and the child killed it with one thrust of a javelin. Arianrod laughed at this and cried out, "The *child* has a really *sure hand* to have hit it." Immediately

Gwyddyon broke the spell that had changed their appearance and told his sister that she had just given her son a name; henceforth he would be called Lleu Llaw Gyffes, which means "child with the sure hand".[3] Furious, Arianrod uttered a second curse, to the effect that the child would have no weapon other than she gave him. When Gwyddyon contrived to break this taboo as well, Arianrod was even more furious and made a third curse: "I vow that this young man will be fated never to have a wife of the race which peoples the earth at this moment." Then Gwyddyon, with the help of Math, and by magic, made a woman out of flowers, who was to be Blodeuwedd. (J. Loth, *Mabinogion*, vol. 1, pp. 190—9.)

This story, and indeed the whole collection of narratives of *Math ab Mathonwy* from which it is taken, seems considerably adulterated, but the details that hold good are unusual enough to merit some comment. The magic wand is the attribute of Math, whom many other Welsh texts describe as master of the magic of the Britons. He is also said to have taught his magic to his nephew Gwyddyon, which would fit with a matrilinear tradition, in which the inheritance passes from maternal uncle to nephew. But by making Arianrod stride over his wand Math gave it a distinctly phallic significance. This, together with the fact that Math was suffering from an infirmity resembling the impotence of the Fisher-King, made his act a ritual of sexual magic connected with several very obscure beliefs about virginity. Note that Arianrod claimed to be a virgin and appears to have been the first to marvel that she had given birth to two children, whom, moreover, she refuses to acknowledge, especially Lleu Llaw Gyffes. Here we stumble on a complete mystery, for the context suggests that the father might well have been Gwyddyon, making the children the products of fraternal incest, a kind of sacred union between the children of the goddess Don. Yet Gwyddyon seemed quite certain of his sister's virginity, for he had no hesitation in recommending her to his uncle as a replacement for the girl Gilvaethwy had wronged. These confused and contradictory details obviously require some clarification.

The explanation might well arise from a discussion of "virginity", since the term appears to have meant different things at different times, even to different people within one social body. The story of Arianrod, a virgin without being so, a mother without the help of man (except, possibly, her brother) touches on the fundamental problem of the mother goddess. When society was gynaecocratic the goddess was alone, the primordial goddess of beginnings. Then, as society gradually became patriarchal, she was represented alongside a father god, with whom she shared the responsibility for the world and all life. Finally, in the majority of cases, once memories of the former, gynaecocratic order had been suppressed, the goddess disappeared altogether, leaving her throne to an omnipotent god, such as Jupiter or Yahweh, who is the paradigm of the male warrior figure whose cult eventually eliminated the worship of woman. But, because the unconscious retains such memories for longer and stores them in the form of symbolic images re-enacted and carried over into a new framework, the goddess reappears in patriarchal cults, as is testified by the Christian worship of the Virgin Mary. The story of Arianrod actually seems to cover this entire development, which would explain its inner contradictions.

For, ultimately, what is a virgin? The word comes from the Latin *virgo* and was first introduced into common parlance as a religious term denoting certain saints of the Christian calendar. In fact the Latin word means "young girl", "unmarried woman", with no other qualification and certainly no inference of chastity. To describe a physically pure young girl, the expression *virgo intacta* was used. The word *virgo* led to the Breton *gwerc'h*, "young girl," and *Gwerc'hez*, "Virgin" in the Christian sense, and to the Welsh *meirch*, "young girl". The Celtic root corresponding to the Latin root of *virgo* is *wraki*, recognisable in the Breton derivative *gwreg*, "wife", and the Welsh *gwraig*, "woman". Another derivative of *wraki* was the Celtic *wrakka*, which led to the Breton *grac'h* (or *groac'h*) "old woman", later "witch", and which can been seen in the Gallic *virago* adopted by the Romans before being borrowed in the same form by the French. All these words appear to be connected with an ancient Indo-European root *werg* meaning "to enclose". This would make the virgin a "woman enclosed upon herself", a concept that might easily have been associated with virginity, but only in its narrowest and ultimately most uncertain sense.

The root *werg* also gave rise to the Greek ἐργον ("action"), as well as its derivatives ἐνεργειε ("energy"), ὀργιον ("religious ceremony", "orgy"), and ὀργανον ("instrument", "organ"); and is connected with the Gallic *ver* ("great", "powerful"), which probably led to the Welsh augmentative prefix *guor*, Irish *for* and the Breton preposition *war* ("above", in the sense of the Latin *super*). The Latin *vis* ("force", plural *vires*) and *vir* ("man"), Irish *fer* and Breton *gour* must surely stem from the same root. So, according to etymology (and all etymology can be challenged), the virgin may well be related to concepts of *force*, *action*, and *confinement*, all associated with femininity and perfectly compatible with the ancient notion of the feminine as divine and creative, solely responsible for prosperity and parturition. This linguistic research, based upon analogies, which are often indicative of mental attitudes, strengthens the belief that the virgin mother was the first divinity to be worshipped by man.

We can learn a great deal about the definition of the virgin from a close look at the Bible and the Rabbinical tradition. The Bible uses three different terms, *naara*, *betula* and *alma*, to describe what we call by just one word. *Naara* stems from a root expressing movement, disturbance, hurrying, and denotes "a young girl, married or unmarried", *virgo intacta* or not. It seems very vague. Deuteronomy (XXII, 15—16) uses the word *naara* to speak of a married woman accused of having lost her innocence before marriage. In Ruth (II, 16) it applies to a widow who has not remarried. It is the name given in Genesis to Rebecca, who is *virgo intacta*, though in the same book (Genesis XXXIV, 3) the term *naara* obviously denotes a girl who has lost her innocence against her own will, since it occurs in an account of Shechem's rape of Dinah. Note also that the masculine form of the word is *naar*, used to mean "boy", "adolescent", then "slave" (in the sense of the Latin *puer*), and having no connotations of chastity whatsoever. So it seems safe to conclude that *naara* is a name that can be given to all young women, as opposed to old.

Betula, on the other hand, seems to denote any woman, young or old, who is *virgo intacta*. In Leviticus (XXI, 1—3), the High Priest is told that he must not approach an inanimate human body, but that he may perform the last rites for his sister if she is *betula*, never having married. Note that the root of the word *betula* means "distance", "separation", and that one of its derivatives, the plural form *betulim*, denotes the hymen. So a *betula* is possibly a woman who still has her *betulim*. But there any speculation must end. Indeed the Jewish commentators on the Bible had a great deal of harmless fun with this theme, for it is a medical fact, of which the ancient Hebrews were well aware, that a woman who has "known" a man may retain that part of the mucous membrane known as the hymen, which never has exactly the same shape, size or suppleness in any two women. Taking this membrane as the usual sign of physical virginity would, in a sense, sanction those dreadful pimps who have traded in false *virgines intactae*. The Talmud (*Kettubot Tractate*, folio 11) makes allowances for a situation in which a woman could lose this precious part of her body by accident, through a fall onto some projecting object or by wounding herself with a piece of wood. This last possibility implies the existence of defloration and other practices, also hinted at in Genesis (XXX, 14—15), where, from the intrigues of Leah and Rachel, it appears that mandrake roots had a specific use.

The third term, *alma*, stems from a root that means "to hide, screen from sight" and denotes a young girl of the utmost innocence who is sheltered from the eyes of men.[4] The word recurs in Phoenician with the meaning of *virgo intacta* (St Jerome, *Comment.*, VII), though it in fact appears to have suggested a virginity more moral than physical, for the masculine form *elem* denotes a young man who is unmarried and therefore only theoretically a virgin. The Rabbinical commentaries on this topic are rather confusing and rely for the most part on very specious sophistry. One reads in the Talmud (*Hagigah Tractate*, folio 14), "Can a *betula* who is pregnant be the wife of the high priest? . . . For Shemuel [Samuel] says: 'I can know a woman several times without her losing her virginity' ", an interpretation consistent with Leviticus (XXI, 13—14). Moreover, in Proverbs (XXX, 19—20), this curious passage appears: "there be three things which are too wonderful for me, yea, four which I know not: the way of an eagle in the air, the way of a serpent upon a rock, the way of a ship in the midst of the sea, and the way of a man with a maid [*alma*]. Such is the way of an adulterous woman; she eateth and wipeth her mouth and saith, I have done no wickedness." The Talmud (*Kettubot Tractate*, folio 6) categorically states "the majority of men are trained to approach a woman without damaging the signs of her virginity". There is even a commentary on this point containing a solemn list of instructions for such activities. A commentary by Ibn Ezra on Genesis (XXIV) points out that "Rebecca was *betula*, and no man had approached her". It is not likely that this was a deliberate tautology intended to exclude unnatural practices, but the meaning is that she had not been defiled in any way. For a girl could remain *betula* while completely surrendering to a man and even becoming pregnant.

From all this it is apparent that the virginity of Mary may be keenly disputed even within an entirely biblical context, as no one agrees on the actual meaning of virginity and there is a variety of words meaning different things according to circumstances. This should give us a better understanding of the enigma contained in the story of Arianrod, that rather isolated figure of the Great Mother Goddess among the island Celts.

For the story of Arianrod is based on a confusion of meaning. When Math asked her if she were a virgin, and when, later, Gwyddyon mocked his sister's anger at having lost her reputation for chastity, the term used was *morwyn*, which simply means "little girl" (like the Latin *pucella*, diminutive of *puella*), though it presumably has some connection with the Breton *morgan*, which denotes a mysterious fairy being who lives in the sea bed, as in the name of King Arthur's sister. This word *morwyn* obviously meant one thing for Arianrod and another for Math and Gwyddyon. For her it signified "free young girl, outside all male constraints", namely woman defined according to the criteria of a gynaecocratic society; for Arianrod is still the image of the ancient goddesses of female-oriented structures. But for Math and Gwyddyon, the representatives of the new patriarchal system, the term denotes only physical virginity.

However speculative this explanation may seem, it does enable us to understand why Arianrod was able to stride over Math's wand *in all innocence*, though it is difficult to see why she then fled, abandoning her two new-born sons and refusing to acknowledge them. One answer seems obvious: as a virgin, which in her own definition is a woman free of man's control, Arianrod had nothing to do with her children, for they belonged by right to the *tuath* or tribe, and its chiefs, her maternal uncle and her brother, were responsible for them in the name of the community. Another answer could be that Arianrod, representing the old law, no longer had a role in the new, male-dominated society, which allowed her only the subordinate position of a *mother* subject to patriarchal authority.

It would also be as well to reflect on her required role as "foot-stool", for it is in this connection that some glimmers of light begin to emerge from her rather confused story. *The Laws of Hywel Dda*, a mediaeval development from early Celtic law, mention among the officials of the king's court a person called a *troediawc*, which means "foot-stool". It was his job to hold the king's foot on his lap from the moment he sat down at table until he went to bed. During this period he was also supposed to scratch the king and protect him from any mishap. He was rewarded with free land, a horse provided by the king, and the opportunity to eat from the same dish as the monarch. If anyone did him any kind of wrong, they had to pay him one hundred and twenty cows in compensation, while his own personal value was put at one hundred and twenty-six cows. Finally, and significantly, he could protect a guilty person by letting him go free during the period when the king's foot was in his lap (*Ancient Laws*, vol. 1, pp. 622, 660, 678).

Note first of all that during the time the king had his feet in the lap of the *troediawc* his royal duties were suspended and *he was no longer truly the king*, since his law of justice was withdrawn from him in favour of the "law of clemency" exercised by the *troediawc*. This explains why Math could not live in time of peace unless his feet were in the lap of a maiden. He was suffering from an illness that prevented him from ruling (sexual impotence) and, in order to save face, had always to be in some way between the start of a meal and going to bed. This very unusual and highly specious way of interpreting the prohibition allowed him to remain king while putting his royal duties in abeyance.

A second observation is even more revealing. The position of *troediawc* is an odd one, to say the least, and like all strange institutions it seems to have very ancient origins, probably misconstrued by the tenth-century editors of the laws, for whom, as members of a patriarchal society, the office would naturally be entrusted to a man. But the *Math ab Mathonwy* narrative represents an older tradition, in which a woman, rather than a man, fulfils the duties of *troediawc*. This sheds an entirely new light on the matter, since it shows that the story was set, not in an earlier epoch, but within memory of that epoch. That, and the clear evidence of a matrilinear régime in the *Mabinogi* narrative, places Math at the cross-roads of two types of civilisation.

The image of the impotent king with his feet in the lap of a "maiden", a *morwyn*, meaning a fairy being originating from the sea, a *morgan* if you like, is simply the image of the king emerging from the womb of woman. So the royal authority, which Math embodies so imperfectly, stems in a direct line from his female ancestors, from woman, who is the true sovereign, being maternally the custodian of life. Sovereignty, which is usually personified in Celtic legends by a woman, resides in the "maiden" on whom Math must keep his feet or lose his power to reign. When he learns that his nephew Gilwaethy, helped by Gwyddyon, has violated the girl who held that noble office, he is forced to replace her, for sovereignty cannot be wronged with impunity. Moreover, the man who committed this outrage was the son of his sister; another example of matrilinear descent and the superiority accorded kinship through the womb. This idea recurs in other, better known legends, such as that of Tristan and Iseult, in which the nephew abducts the sovereign Iseult from his maternal uncle King Mark, and the story of Guinevere and Arthur, in which Gawain (who is replaced by Launcelot in the Christian version) and later Mordred become the lover-abductors of the queen, the true custodian of sovereignty.

The impotent Math could not have a wife and had to be content with the "maiden", who was a substitute for the mother, the last incarnation of female power. This was the only way to bring legality and universal recognition to a king who was really of the patriarchal type, but caught in the contradictions arising from memories of the earlier régime. The "maiden" is the very source of his power, or lack of it, which paradoxically amounts to the same thing. She is the exact image of the Virgin Mary of mediaeval mysteries and legends, who acts as mediator between men (her sons) and Jesus (her son—husband) on behalf of the unfortunate, but also for robbers, perjurers and murderers. If one really thinks about it, she was empowered to free the guilty from the first moment she held the feet of Jesus in her lap, exactly like the *troediawc* of Welsh legislation, or, rather more, like the maiden who enabled Math to live. There are any number of memorable representations of the Entombment of Christ in which the Virgin is pressing her son's feet against her breast, and in which Christ, who is not really dead but in a state of dormancy, must surely correspond to Math in the *Mabinogi* narrative.

These curious observations highlighting the Celts' use of the "maiden" as a symbol of divinity bring to mind all those highly mysterious characters who populated the worlds of Irish and Welsh legends and the *Romans de la Table Ronde*. The maidens encountered somewhere along the journey, guardians of fountains, beautiful but forlorn ladies of the manor, prisoners of wicked lords, the

Maiden of the Grail herself, and the disturbing Empress in *Peredur* were all indisputably "virgins" in the broadest sense of the word, meaning they were not under the thumb of a husband, *not subject to the authority of a man*. For, ultimately, both in the Celtic tradition and in all pre-Christian Mediterranean traditions, virginity is not physical but purely moral, and concerns only the independence of the woman from man. The non-Christian virgin is the free woman, ever available, ever fresh, ever possible, a dazzling symbol of renewal, youth and, by inference, of sexual freedom. Her very name is derived from the word for force and strength, for the power that in the nature of things is constantly changing hands. So she becomes the prostitute, the royal whore, always generous with her body. Men compete for her favours because they are the token of the strength and the supreme authority that she holds, biologically, through her power to give life.

She is a kind of Amazon who refuses marriage, though not lovers, and rejects enslavement by man but holds men in slavery. From there it is but a short step to the kind of courtly love that makes Chrétien's lover-knight Launcelot a submissive subject of female supremacy. The authors of courtly romances were dimly aware of the dangers inherent in this attitude, as is borne out by the French version of the story of Merlin and Vivienne, probably taken from a Breton source, though the original mythical figure of Merlin came from the north of Great Britain.

Courtly romance, *Vivienne and Merlin*

    Merlin the wizard, adviser to King Arthur, came to the Forest of Brocéliande in Brittany. There, beside Barenton fountain, he met a young girl called Vivienne, whose father was Dyonas, "god-son of Diana, goddess of the woods". Diana had granted him a gift that his first daughter would be desired by the wisest of men, who would teach her all his magical powers and then be subject to her. Merlin fell in love with Vivienne, who would not accept his love unless he revealed his secrets to her. So gradually he fell into her trap, though perfectly aware of his fate and determined to follow it through. After several journeys in Brittany, Merlin returned to the Forest of Brocéliande. One day, while he was sleeping, Vivienne pronounced a spell upon him and he found himself in an invisible castle, her prisoner but perfectly happy to be with the woman he loved. (*Estoire de Merlin*.)

Note that Merlin resolutely accepts his fate, which means being eternally subject to Vivienne. She is a virgin in the sense that she is mistress not only of her own fate, but of Merlin's as well, because he is her serving knight, her "servant of love", in fact her *worshipper*.

For Vivienne is placed on a level with the exclusive and jealous divinity to whose service man is dedicated. She is also one of the faces assumed by the ever-virginal mother goddess.

In fact she is a very mysterious character. We have said that this legend is probably Breton in origin, but it is only on the continent that Vivienne appears in this courtly form, so well aligned with twelfth- and thirteenth-century codes of love. She has an island model in the original legend of Merlin, which clearly comes from the north of Britain, near the Scottish border. The French Vivienne is a courtly adaptation, retaining several aspects of the original, a character whose ambiguous relations with Merlin were too morally shocking for the continental romance writers, because she was Merlin's sister, called Gwendydd in the Welsh texts and Gandieda in Geoffrey of Monmouth's Latin text *Vita Merlini*.

Wales, *Merlin and Gwendydd*

Merlin (Myrddyn) became mad after a battle and lived wild in the woods, making prophecies and shunning men. Only his sister Gwendydd, wife of King Rydderch, could come near him, and several times she made him return to court. Finally, when he had given his own wife her freedom, he withdrew to the woods for ever, accompanied by some "wise men" and his sister Gwendydd, to whom he passed his gift for prophecy. (*Vita Merlini*.)[5]

The character of Vivienne certainly appears to have been modelled on Gwendydd, though it seems that she also acquired some additional features. She changed from sister to mistress, though we know from other instances that her story bears the traces of a time when fraternal incest was not forbidden, at least not in the case of exceptional people who thereby re-created the perfect couple. But Vivienne is also linked with the myth of Diana, through her father Dyonas, the goddess's god-son, and Diana gave her the power of making a man forever captive. It is hard to say whether this particular goddess is the chaste Artemis of watered-down legends, in which she was content to hunt animals in the woods, or the original Scythian Diana, the cruel and voluptuous goddess of the sun, whose worship spread in a roundabout fashion throughout the Indo-European world. In the event, however, the Scythian Diana would seem more appropriate, if only because of Vivienne's cruelty in stealing the man she loves from the real world and keeping his love jealously for herself. But there is another reference to the goddess in the *Estoire de Merlin*. In the Forest of Brocéliande there is a Lake of Diana, and the author of the courtly romance explains the origin of this name in a very curious story.

Courtly romance, *The Lake of Diana*

Merlin led Vivienne to the shore of Lake Diana, where there was a tomb on which the epitaph of Faunus was inscribed.

Merlin then told the story of Diana, who "reigned at the time of Virgil". She settled in Brocéliande and had a manor built at the edge of this lake. She had a lover, Faunus, and had made him vow to give up all the world for her. Later she loved another knight called Felix and considered getting rid of Faunus. One day, when he was injured, she made him go down into a grave on the pretext of curing him, but replaced the stone over him. So Faunus perished, but when Diana told Felix what she had done he cut off her head, and ever since that time the place had been called the "Lake of Diana". (*Estoire de Merlin.*)

Apart from the moralising end to this story, which indicates a distinctly masculine and patriarchal attitude on the lines that men are the unfortunate victims of wicked women who must be punished, it is easy enough to recognise in the legend of Faunus and Diana both the story of Merlin and Vivienne and traces of the ancient cult of the Scythian Diana, as seen in Ishtar, who killed her lover; Cybele, who made Attis insane and reduced him to self-castration; and Aphrodite, who arranged to have Adonis killed by a wild boar. However far removed she may be from the stereotyped image of the chaste Diana, this savage and sensuous divinity is the true face of the goddess, her cruelty a statement of the obvious fact that it is the mother goddess who both gives life and takes it away. In the same way, she grants her favours and withdraws them as she wishes. In her the dual nature of the goddess who is mother and virgin, ever available and totally free, becomes duly authenticated.

It is clear that Vivienne has much in common with the mythical Diana; that is, the original Scythian goddess, rather than the pleasant and soothing figure that Roman and Renaissance statues have bequeathed us. Even Racine understood the fundamental weight of the ancient myth. For the only reason why Hippolytus is sacrificed in *Phèdre*, despite his obvious virtues, is because he is a priest of Diana, who cannot forgive him his treacherous interest in Aricia, as she herself has exclusive rights over the young man. The whole tragedy of *Phèdre* is basically a sacrifice of atonement, which is perfectly consistent with the purposes for which ancient tragedy was written.

So Vivienne is the jealous virgin who demands exclusive worship. This should suggest new pointers for the study of courtly love, the many commentators on which have tried to link it with doctrines brought from the Far East. In fact, courtly love contains, among other things, a very clear trace of the cult of the Indo-European mother goddess. The archaic aspects of this cult would otherwise be incomprehensible in the Christian twelfth century, especially the inexplicable submission of the man to the woman, which is related to the concept of original female supremacy, the woman being the priestess of the goddess who once held absolute power.

There are bound to be objections that, though Vivienne may be considered a virgin according to our definition of the term, she was not a mother, as Arianrod, Rhiannon and Keridwen were. However, another episode in the *Romans de la Table Ronde*, this time quite clearly of Breton origin, and concerning the childhood and education of Launcelot, shows that she was.

Courtly romance, *The Lady of the Lake*
King Ban of Benoic, at war with his neighbour Claudas of the Moor, fled secretly from his fortress of Treb to ask for help from King Arthur, taking with him his wife and their baby son. When he reached the Forest of Brocéliande, Ban climbed a hill and saw his fortress aflame in the distance. He died of grief, and the queen, completely overwhelmed, left her son at the foot of a tree. She returned to see a beautiful woman snatch up the child and disappear with him into the depths of a lake. The mysterious woman was Vivienne and "the lake was merely the result of a spell that Merlin had cast for her not long before: at the place where the water appeared to be deepest, there were lovely, rich houses". It was in this country that the child, who became Launcelot, was brought up. "Whether the Lady of the Lake was affectionate to Launcelot, we need not ask: had she carried him in her own womb, she could not have brought him up more tenderly." (*Lancelot en prose*: "The Childhood of Lancelot".)

Apart from the fact that Vivienne appears here as yet another "Lady of the Lake", among so many others who haunt Celtic legends, she is also given the role of Launcelot's mother. Obviously it is possible to see in her action the much-used folklore theme of the fairy who takes a child, but Vivienne's cruelty in snatching the child from his real mother, knowing that she will die of grief, is persuasively close to the image of the Scythian Diana. Indeed, Vivienne is acting as a goddess, for she knows that the child is destined for great things, that he will eventually have to go to the Castle of the Grail, and that he will be the father of Galahad. Her mission in abducting the child from his natural mother is divine, for as the second mother she will give Launcelot a new birth of intelligence and valour, just as Keridwen, by bearing Gwyon Bach a second time, made him Taliesin, the universal bard.

Note that the adventures of Vivienne and Merlin, Diana and Faunus, and Launcelot and Vivienne all take place in Brocéliande. But this forest is also the home of a well-known character who, according to the island tradition, usually lives in a lost island in the middle of the sea. This figure is Morgan, the "haughty fairy" of continental folklore, King Arthur's sister and all-powerful sovereign of the Isle of Avalon.

In Brocéliande. however, Morgan takes on a rather different aspect, quite unlike the usual idea of her, and she may well have been confused with Vivienne. Yet, in the midst of a tradition heavily imbued with patriarchalism, she does stand as the expression of female rebellion against male authority, a rebellion necessarily crushed by the protective measures of mediaeval patriarchal and Christian society. In the light of this observation, we might also point out the extent to which the feudal system exploited fundamental Celtic ideas for its own ends, distorting them in the process. In this the influence of the Anglo-Angevin dynasty of the Plantagenets was at work. Henry II may have contributed to a wider knowledge of Celtic myths by encouraging the writers of his time to work on Arthurian themes, but he also dug the grave of early Celtic tradition, by reducing what had been the last remnants of an ancient philosophy to a series of stories for the amusement of a feudal society that had to be distracted from the machinations of his wealthy family's excessive ambition. In short, he wiped Ireland from the map of the world.

To return to Morgan, as she appears in the courtly romances inspired by the Plantagenets and their allies, there is a fairly detailed description of her in the *Estoire de Merlin*, which points out her real character and the close links she retained with the original mother goddess:

> "She was the sister of King Arthur, very gay and playful; she sang most agreeably; though dark in the face, very well made, neither too fat nor too thin. with beautiful hands, perfect shoulders, skin softer than silk, engaging of manner, long and straight in the body: altogether wonderfully seductive and, besides all that, the warmest and most sensual woman in all Great Britain. Merlin had taught her astronomy and many other things, and she studied them so well that she became an excellent scholar and was later called Morgan La Fée because of the marvels she wrought. She expressed herself with gentleness and delightful sweetness, and was more good-natured and attractive than anyone else in the world, when she was calm. But when her anger was roused against someone, she was very difficult to appease. . . ." (*Estoire de Merlin.*)

This is undoubtedly a portrait of the ambiguous, original mother goddess, both good-natured and spiteful, the very image of the divinity who gives and takes away, "warm and sensual" like the great Eastern goddess, but a "virgin" nevertheless, because unwilling to submit to masculine authority. Note also, that Merlin is supposed to have taught her magic, as he did Vivienne. In fact, from other versions of the story, now lost, but of which traces can be found in the fifteenth-century English *Morte d'Arthur*, Thomas Malory's vast collection of Round Table romances, we get the impression that Merlin was Morgan's lover before becoming Vivienne's. This makes it feasible to suppose that Morgan and Vivienne were one and the same person. So it is to Malory's text, which represents a somewhat different tradition from that known through the French *Lancelot en prose*, that we look for the more interesting facts about Morgan. She is portrayed as mother of Yvain and wife of Uryen, but she is an unruly wife who finds it difficult to bear the narrow confines of marriage and takes a number of lovers. This last fact is consistent with *Lancelot en prose*, though this portrays her as unmarried.

> Courtly romance, *Morgan and Uryen*
> One day when Morgan came across her husband, King Uryen, asleep on his bed, it occurred to her to get rid of him. "Then she called a servant in whom she had complete trust and told her to 'go and fetch my lord's sword, for I have never had a better opportunity to kill him'." But the servant, frightened by Morgan's plan, went to find Yvain, the son of Morgan and Uryen, told him everything and asked him to intervene. Yvain advised her to comply with Morgan's request. Then when Morgan raised the sword above Uryen's head, Yvain, who was lying in wait, rushed forward and wrenched the sword from the hands of his mother, mistress of the house. Morgan begged his forgiveness, claiming to have had a momentary fit of madness. (*Morte d'Arthur*, IV, 13.)

Morgan's attempt to murder Uryen is typical of the goddess who does not want to be encumbered with a husband, or too exclusive a lover. It is the story of Diana and Faunus. But equally interesting is the battle of wits between Morgan and her brother Arthur, for it seems to contain the same theme as that of Gwyddyon and Arianrod. One day, when Arthur was unarmed, Merlin took him to the shore of a lake on which there was a damsel, the Lady of the Lake, i.e. Vivienne, who gave Arthur his famous sword Excalibur (*Kaledvoulch*, "hard and sharp"). Morgan seems continually to have been stealing Arthur's sword, or its scabbard, for the benefit of her lovers. So, if Morgan appears in this case as Arthur's enemy, then the Lady of the Lake, called Nimue by Thomas Malory, is, in contrast, the king's protector. This dividing of the one character into two may well be symbolic of the goddess's basic ambiguity, her goodwill and her spite, her giving and her taking away.

> Courtly romance, *Morgan and Arthur*
> Arthur had to yield the scabbard of his sword to Morgan, his sister, and she loved another knight much more than either her

husband, King Uryen, or King Arthur. She would have liked her brother Arthur to be killed. So by magic she made another scabbard, which looked exactly the same, and gave the Excalibur scabbard to her lover, Accolon. (*Morte d'Arthur*, II, 11).

Morgan arranged that Accolon fight Arthur, who mortally wounded him, though before he died he revealed Morgan's treachery. Then she, distressed by Accolon's death, sought vengeance upon Arthur, and sent him a rich coat that had the magical property of burning all those who had the misfortune to try it on. But, when Arthur was about to put this coat on, the Lady of the Lake appeared and told him of the impending danger. (*Morte d'Arthur*, IV, 14—16.)

If we accept that Morgan, the king's sister, represents gynaeco-cratic authority and the distaff side of the family, it is easier to grasp the meaning of this struggle between brother and sister, which is comparable to the even fiercer battle of wits between Arianrod and Gwyddyon. In any case, the king received his power (represented by the sword Excalibur) from a woman, the Lady of the Lake. This detail from Malory's work explains one of the last scenes of the French *Lancelot en prose*, in which Arthur, mortally wounded after the Battle of Camlann, asks Girfleet (Gilvaethwy, son of Don) to go and throw the sword in the lake, where it is caught by a mysterious hand. Having obtained his authority from the Lady of the Lake, Arthur had to return it to her to dispose of as she wished, to the advantage of a man of her choice.

If the mother goddess gives her lovers sovereign power, she also gives them the opportunity to be reborn as her sons. Patriarchal society, being based on violence, exploitation of aggression and consequently on war and death, tries by every means to deny the marriage with a divinity (the *hierogamos*), at least between mortal and lover-goddess. The hippies' slogan "make love not war" is regarded as anti-social, because it is a denunciation and a categorical rejection of the aggressive attitudes of this society. But, once men want to become the sons of their mistresses, they will forget that the official aim of legal mating, or marriage, is procreation, and society will be well on the way to disappearing.

This very idea is contained in the Apocryphal Gospel of the Egyptians, in a little known passage that is bound to cause comment. There is an ambiguous conversation between Christ and Salome in which she asks him how long death will prevail. Christ replies, "As long as you, women, bear children, for I have come to destroy the work of women." Naturally Salome does not understand and asks for an explanation. Christ replies that these things will come to pass "when you trample upon the clothing of shame, when that which is two becomes one, when the male with the female will be neither

male nor female."[6] Advocators of sexual repression will quite
naturally conclude that Christ is condemning the work of the flesh,
which is true enough; but beyond that he is really speaking out
against that work of the flesh *whose purpose is procreation*, which is
totally emptied of its original, instinctive content.

For, in the mythical traditions of every land, procreation appears
to be linked with death, in the sense that death practises a necessary
natural selection by eliminating the old in favour of the new-born.
But, again within myth, if man cannot perpetuate himself through
his children, death loses this compulsory quality and human beings
can become immortal. Consequently, in ancient traditions, particularly in Genesis, it is possible to acknowledge the existence of a
concept of human immortality *before the sin*, which is to say *before
the first birth*, a sinful event because it broke with the established
order, destroyed the work of God (the sole creator) and, according
to certain Rabbinical commentaries, put a full stop to divine
creation. This would explain the curse transmitted to man (and to
woman) from the far distant time when, because of circumstances we
shall never know, the human being created by God (as Genesis has it)
set himself to create a necessarily imperfect creature on his own
account. The Jewish tradition argues that the origin of our troubles
was a contamination passed on to Eve by the serpent; this
engendered Cain, *synonym of death*, who passed it to his descendants.

This is an important point in traditional Jewish thought and comes
close to the Cathari's belief that the world of the flesh was a creation
of the Devil. It suggests that the serpent (i.e. the spirit of evil, or the
spirit of rebellion) slid the contamination (the ability to reproduce)
into Eve, whereas previously she could have enjoyed sexual relations
free from the possibility of subsequent pregnancy. This would
explain Christ's ambiguous words in the Gospel of the Egyptians,
where he said that he came to destroy the work of woman. If this
was indeed his teaching, it was never put into effect, although Jesus
came to defend the new woman (Mary) against the old, contaminated woman (Eve) in a struggle that should be examined more closely,
while remembering that Eve was not the first mythical woman, but
took the place of the unacknowledged Lilith, whom we shall be
studying in a later chapter.

Curiously however, Eve, according to various Hebrew texts, was
not particularly conscious of her contamination. On the contrary,
she seems to have regarded what happened to her as a blessing: "And
she conceived and bore Cain, and said I have gotten a man from the
Lord." Eve's exclamation clearly suggests that there had been a
hierogamos, and is, moreover, consistent with the primitive belief
that man has nothing to do with parturition, which occurs through
the intervention of a god. The birth of Cain, therefore, strangely
prefigures the birth of Christ; though, whereas Cain was the evil

child, Jesus was to be the child of charity. From that point, as psychoanalysis shows, the young man, the son, becomes the mythical equivalent of the bridegroom, who is the old father. In addition, the aim of woman is always, if only by transference, to replace the old man by the young, which explains why Morgan wants to kill Uryen, and why Rhiannon, widow of Pwyll, marries her son Pryderi's friend, Manawyddan.

Thus we can infer that the conscious or unconscious aim of the young man. the young son, is to return to the mother, whether by removing the father and appropriating her (as Oedipus did), or by identifying with her spiritually or physically. It is this last, lesser-known point that requires examination.

In fact, the Celtic myth of woman takes on an entirely new light once we take into account both the psychoanalytic evaluation of identification with the mother, and the traces of matrilinear descent evident in all Irish or British literary writings of the period. In legal terms, the Celtic family was agnatic, or related through the father's side, but not invariably; for the privileges reserved for women testify to a wavering between the agnatic family and the cognatic, i.e. the family based entirely on the wife as the undisputed centre of all relationships and inheritance.

Nostalgia for the cognatic era is as evident in Irish and British law as in myth in general. This is evidence of a stifling of the secret longing to return to the old system, if not in fact then in a kind of metaphysics combined with a very subtle eroticism that only psychoanalysis can satisfactorily explain.

Since the Celts are, after all, Indo-Europeans, let us first consider the concept of feminity among the ancient Indians. All Brahmin mythology appears to be based on the fact that the male divinity can do nothing alone but must be complemented by a female divinity. There is no unique male god, jealous of his authority, among the Indians, nor among the other early Indo-Europeans. A summary of the theogony of the Vedas will make things clear. In the beginning was Brahma, the immaterial Whole, the Absolute, which, being absolute, was incapable of action. This Hegelian statement leads to the supposition of a relative form of the absolute and immaterial divinity, one in which a phase of Brahma is enacted, and this is Siva. But since there can be no being without its opposite or its complement, and Siva is male and the typical legislator of a patriarchal society, he can exist and be effective only when opposed by a feminine principle. She is Shakti, who assumes the face of the ancient pre-Aryan goddess Kali, and, for that matter, the face of every other goddess. She is Siva's wife and etymologically "energy in action", "dynamism of time". While Siva sits in inner contemplation, outside time and space, the *passive* aspect of eternity, it is Shakti who sets him in motion as the *active* aspect of eternity.

What are regarded as the normal roles of men and women have

been reversed. The concept of active femininity never for one instant
occurs to the men who believe that they dominate the world and
regulate the established order. Yet it may well explain why, in those
languages that have retained traces of earlier epochs, the Germanic,
Celtic and Semitic to name but a few, the sun is feminine and the
moon masculine. For the sun represents the active heat that falls on
the earth and gives life to the sterile moon. There are superstitions all
over the world about the moon impregnating women. And the
relation, popularly established, between the moon and the menstrual
cycle, and therefore between the moon and periods of fertility in
women, suggests that the female, solar fertility needs an opposing
lunar passivity. All this is, after all, only a dialectic argument, but the
opposition of feminine activity and masculine passivity is the basis of
the story of Tristan and Iseult, which gave rise to all Western
interpretations of love.

It goes without saying that the concept of Shakti is behind the
many realistic representations of sexual union on Brahmin temples,
all of which evoke, to varying degrees, the union of Siva and Shakti.
Theirs is the *hierogamos*, towards which all people unconsciously
aspire, because they are aware that it leads to the *maya*, the world of
illusion, which for Europeans becomes the world of apparent reality
or relativity.

The heroes of Celtic epics are no exception to this universal
tendency. While sailing over the sea, Maelduin discovered the
enchanted island where the *queen* lived. Launcelot sought sacred
union with *Queen* Guinevere, as did Tristan with *Queen* Iseult.
Peredur pursued his roving course towards the Castle of the Grail
guided by the different manifestations of the *Empress*. To take the
fortress of Curoi (the Dog-King of the Other World) Cú Chulainn has
first to seduce Blathnait, Curoi's wife, and therefore *Queen* of the
Other World. When the same Cú Chulainn went into the Other
World, it was at the summons of *Queen* Fand and for love of her.
There are any number of further examples of this divine woman, if
only in the mysterious maidens who wait for travellers in some castle
along the dark, winding road that all heroes of adventure must travel
in search of the sacred union that will make them *king*. For even the
hero of prowess of the male-oriented system is in the image of Siva,
the passive being who can do nothing alone.

It is also for this reason that all Celtic legends contain instances of
identification of son with mother, which, like that between two
lovers, is a kind of spiritual substitute for *hierogamos*, and results in
the odd couples of ancient mythology — Owein—Yvain and his
mother Modron, Rhiannon and her son Pryderi. Very often these
couples survive only in terminology, as in the case of Gwyddyon son
of the goddess Don, Conchobar son of the warrior woman Ness. For
the mother—son couple, too shocking and provocative in a patri-

archal society, was replaced by the lover—mistress couple, in which
the same identification nevertheless occurs. The love that unites two
people like Tristan and Iseult or Diarmaid and Grainne is the
symbolic incident by which they attain divine nature. Theirs is the
age-old theme of a mortal who obtains the favours of a goddess and
consequently ascends to divinity.

The same notion of identification lies behind the wearing, by
priests of many cults, of distinctly feminine garments and ornaments;
these, used especially for ceremonies, make their wearers glaringly
different from common mortals. In certain cases this goes beyond
external imitation and becomes total identification, which is perfectly consistent with the idea of priests, of whatever religion, being
bound to identify with their divinity. Herodotus, who spoke from a
wide knowledge of mysterious Eastern cults, said that the Scythian
priests, the Ennarees, were hermaphrodites; and we have established
the similar origins of the Scythians and the Celts. Like the Ennarees,
the Druids foretold the future with the help of a wand (the former
using willow, and the latter preferring yew or mountain-ash).
According to *Herodotus* (Histories, I, 105), the Ennarees owed their
gift of divination to the goddess Aphrodite, who had punished them
for pillaging her temple at Ascolon by inflicting upon them a
"woman's disease". This disease, which became hereditary, is clearly
reminiscent of the "illness of the Ulstermen", inflicted by the
goddess Macha to punish the Ulstermen for an outrage they had done
her.

The Ennarees also have something else in common with the Celts,
for their name appears to stem from Inara, an Indian and Hittite (and
therefore Indo-European) goddess, who is a kind of Calypso seducing
mortals and shutting them away in her house. This theme of the
captive lover, beloved of courtly and Renaissance poets, and
brilliantly expressed through Calypso and Circe in the *Odyssey*, was
one of the most common elements in Welsh and Irish literature. It is
the story of Fand and Cú Chulainn, of Bran, and of Maelduin with
the queen of the mysterious island, of Condle, son of Conn, of St
Guengalc'h of Tregurier, of Morgan and Launcelot. We even find it in
Celtic folklore, for many Irish songs are laments of a fairy who could
no longer keep prisoner the mortal she loved.

In a discussion of vaguely related and rather Celticised peoples,
Tacitus mentions the Maharvali, who had a wood dedicated to an
ancient religion where they worshipped a divine couple, whose priest
was dressed in female clothing (*Germania*, XLIII). Though Tacitus,
admittedly with reservations, identifies this couple as Castor and
Pollux, suggesting an extremely male-oriented society, the gods in
question were probably a male—female couple. The fact that the
priest wore feminine garments is significant enough. He was
obviously identifying with the goddess, in the same way as the priests

of Cybele (the *Galloi* who wore women's clothes and were also castrated); the eunuch priests found in Uruk, among the Hittites, and in Ephesus, Cyprus and Lydia; and the shamans of ancient Europe and present-day Asia, whose connections with the Druids are beyond doubt.

However, it would be a great mistake to confuse this trans-vestitism with homosexuality, for, although homosexual practices were widespread even in earliest antiquity and formed part of certain rituals, homosexuals being regarded as intermediaries, like drunkards or lunatics, and therefore gifted with supernatural powers, the religions in question were centred upon the Great Goddess. It is here that the process of identification of created man, son and lover, with creating divinity, mother and mistress, comes into full play.

Although early man may have envied woman her mystery, her basic ambiguity, her ability to give life, modern man, through his completely male-oriented education, has forgotten this metaphysical longing for the divine woman, though it still exists in the subconscious of every person. Poets and artists express it in their works, other people in apparently inexplicable or quite clearly aberrant behaviour, such as physiological imitation and clothing fetishism. "Man comes closest to the state of femininity during the Carnival. There we have the transvestites who have undergone what they call the 'big operation' (castration followed by the creation of an artificial vagina). Here is a link with the second origin of castration fears discovered by Freud, namely that desire for femininity can lead a male to want castration. . . . In fact, the ideas that prompt men to such behaviour *throw some light on the mystery that femininity presents to men*. This dressing up corresponds to the erroneous interpretation made by a brother when he realises the little girl has no penis."[7]

The real problem has nothing to do with the Freudian idea of penis envy in women, but rather with approaches to femininity, which despite appearances, is just as mysterious for the girl as for the boy. The priest who officiates in his ceremonial robes of feminine origin, and the transvestite, whether castrated or not, are both obeying the same wish to *understand the mystery*. The lover's unveiling of a woman's body is a sacred gesture as old as man himself. In our rationalised world, which no longer believes in ritual but which constantly and unwittingly re-creates it, this act has become the strip-tease, an aberrant form of religious worship debased to the level of commercial spectacle.

If we go back to the mythical origins of mankind (the myth symbolically summarising the psychological evolution of man), the same act is contained in the story of Adam and Eve. "Eve was the first to be aware of sexuality and she forced Adam to make it appear that he was revealing it to her . . . this fact, which is not unlike the stimulation of the penis of a baby boy by his mother, gives Eve the status of Adam's mother ... the account specifically states that Eve came from the man ... an assertion that does not fit in with the story but is the end result of a misrepresentation; this leads to the conclusion that Eve is an entirely man-made representation of woman. To a certain extent she is Adam in disguise."[8]

So, although Adam sees the naked Eve, he sees her as an emasculated version of himself. She was created *ex Adamo*, as Genesis puts it, but was the product of his imagination rather than the rib, which is only symbolic of the part of him that created her, as the divine woman is born of the testicles of the father in other mythological accounts. Eve, the mother of mankind, is merely the castrated version of Adam. This line of argument still persists in everyday life: "The little boy who secretly puts on his mother's clothes and masturbates in front of a mirror (a commonplace practice) would be greatly surprised to hear that in so doing he was recreating Eve and denying her castration."[9]

By rejecting the solutions to man's anxiety that femininity brought, mankind has become totally neurotic. "This small boy was forced into such practices because he was not given a dress to wear when he was little, as used to be the custom. A stupid and rigid notion of virility has put an end to it; the custom stems from unconscious motives and is infinitely preferable to that destruction of love which so-called educators try to achieve through their so-called sex education."[10]

Once again, the future of our whole society is at stake. By making society male-oriented, we have lost sight of the emotional bonds that unite the members of one family, of one clan -- the bonds based on the parent—child relationship, especially the mother—child relationship, which are fundamental to psycho-social relations. By suppressing the idea of the divine mother, or subordinating it to the authority of the father god, man has upset the mechanism of instinct, which originally kept the balance. But instinct is what is natural to us, and in denying it man opens the way to all those mental disorders that affect partiarchal societies. In fact he can no more determine woman's position in society, or his position in relation to her, than any law of reason can influence the law of nature.

Whatever else we may have achieved in this study of the feminine principle among the Celts, we have at least succeeded in showing that instinct is of prime importance and is responsible for progress and evolution. And yet it is fearful, because strong and inescapable. It is the sole driving force of our feelings and actions, and yet hard to look in the face. For the truth is shocking, especially to minds hide-bound by morality. If we dare assert that all relations between man and woman, conjugal, filial or otherwise, *are necessarily incestuous relations between mother and son*, we are bound to incur fierce criticism and accusations of obsession. And yet . . .

Man is in fact incomplete, and he realises it. In his fear of attraction to the bottomless pit (the nothingness from which he comes) and his fear and vertigo in the face of death (the nothingness to which he will go), he searches for security *at all costs*, and this security is represented by the mother, for woman as for man. Yet, both in a physical and an emotional sense, man has the means to return, if only temporarily, into the mother, to re-enact, through the act of love, an imaginary return to paradise.

Every woman is actually or potentially a mother. Man is therefore biologically subordinate to woman, whether he likes it or not. He is the *contained*, while she is the *container*. So he is bound to feel inferior and can only try to assert his superiority by behaving in an apparently forceful way, by violence and fighting, by setting himself up as sole protector of the species. He has even succeeded in persuading women of this superiority, which is symbolised by the recognition of the infant penis at birth, either by his mother or by any other woman helping at the confinement. The birth of a girl is accepted, the birth of a boy is cause for rejoicing.

Yet, the container, the mother or woman, is paradise re-created. She re-creates this paradise in two ways within a single idea, by containing both her child and her lover. Although her vagina may not be recognised at birth, it will be acknowledged at some point by man. So woman needs man to assert herself, to become conscious of what she is and, above all, of what she can do. The two sexes are inextricably linked. Man needs woman, woman needs man. Translated into mythological terms this becomes: man needs a goddess, and the goddess needs a man. That is why the ancient cults of the feminine divinity still continue, in a variety of ways.

We have seen her among the Celts behind the various faces, or rather the various masks, men have given her. Whatever name she is given, she remains unique, the primordial mother, the original goddess, the Great Queen of Beginnings.

Yet she is exposed, not only to men's sarcasm, but also to their will to power, their egoism, their sense of property. It is men who have invented the woman-as-object, tricked out in endless fineries, but a prisoner just the same. Some day this woman, the goddess, the Great Queen imprisoned in the shrine, is going to shake off her chains, and her rebellion will be terrible, for she is a direct threat to the society that men have built without her.

Chapter 6

The Rebellion of the Flower-Daughter

ur industrial society, whatever we think of it and however much we try to ignore or reject it, is the logical consequence of the patriarchal society established with the beginnings of agriculture; this society sanctified the division of labour and the sharing of power and wealth among the different members of the community. It is based on labour and therefore on a degree of effort and suffering, which are directed towards the production of goods and food. But to achieve the maximum production, those immediate interests that tend towards instant consumption must be sacrificed in favour of some provision for a wider and more varied yield and therefore superior consumption in the future. There is an imbalance between immediate, *instinctive* and future, *rational* interests; this reinvokes the eternal argument between instinct and reason. Yet, despite classical philosophers' claims of a basic difference between the two concepts, reason appears to be an intellectual evolution of instinct; the spurious opposition of the two continues to poison our society because we have forgotten the series of links between them. Thus, disregarding the fact that instinct has given birth to reason in order to gratify itself, we serve the cause of reason alone; hence the position in industrial society (the direct heir of patriarchal, agricultural society), which is entirely based on the *repression of instinct* and the *glorification of reason* as an autonomous factor. But all that reason can do is to revolve vacuously, victim of the extraordinary momentum of a civilisation that has lost its genuine objective. the gratification of instinct, and must continue along its course if it is not to perish and drag the human race with it, or so it is believed.

The instinct that we label sexual, sensual, erotic, and therefore base, is merely the search for that state of internal bliss known as happiness. That is the goal; it is not necessarily reached, but our action in searching for it must have some kind of result; though this has nothing to do with either ends or means, but is the outcome of an incomplete act, doomed to failure. We call it pleasure, and in some ways it is the imperfect form of what we believe to be happiness and is all that is left to man in his attempt to gratify his instincts. One might well ask whether man still has an instinctive life, though that is bound up with questions of man, nature, environment, the mental stability of mankind, and even the function of our sensory organs — to discuss all of which would take too long.

This instinct, which civilisation deliberately erases from our minds, and about which the various systems of education maintain a wilful silence despite man's fundamental nature, is clearly symbolised by women in patriarchal societies. If it is opposed to production, women, being instinctive, feeling and intuitive, is fatally opposed to man, who is reason, logic, a builder, producer and organiser. There are also the ancient fears about woman; these are still very much with us, and spring from the idea that woman is love, which is sinful, though it stems from an irrepressible sexuality and must therefore be tolerated, if only as a means to procreation. This makes love a practical instrument, a means of production for providing society with the labour force it needs to pursue the infernal cycle of its development; it enables the land-owners and managerial classes to maintain their control.

Another, and totally disinterested, kind of love is the emotion that can unite two people and is not necessarily followed by procreation. Whilst not actually forbidden, it is disparaged, because it threatens society. As Freud very rightly said in *Civilisation and its Discontents*, "Sexual love is a relationship for two in which a third person can only be superfluous or play the part of kill-joy, while civilisation necessarily implies relationship between a large number of people. When love is strongest there remains no interest in the surrounding world; the lovers are enough for each other, not even needing a common child to be happy." The same argument extends to "communal" love, for, however large the group, it is still separate from the much larger established order.

Obviously the organised community, unable to tolerate the lovers' deliberate retreat into another world, will fight against sexuality and imagination. "Free libidinous relations are essentially antagonistic to work relations; only the absence of full gratification sustains the social organisation of work. Even under optimum conditions of a rational organisation of society, the gratification of human needs would require labour, and this fact alone would enforce quantitative and qualitative instinctual restraint and thereby numerous social taboos. No matter how rich, civilisation depends on steady and methodical work and also on unpleasurable delay in satisfaction. Since the primary instincts rebel 'by nature' against such delay; their repressive modification remains a necessity for all civilisation."[1] All one can add to Herbert Marcuse's argument is that mythology, through the play of symbols and structures, reachers virtually the same conclusions.

"The sexual power of woman", says Otto Rank, "makes her a danger to the community, the social structure of which is based on the distress which, once inspired by the mother, now arises from the father."[2] Once dangerous, woman is set apart, buried in the deepest caves, masked, and even occasionally made male. The mother goddess has become the father god. As man still needs woman all the same, he takes the easy way out and creates her in his own image, as God created man. At this point, the myth of Pygmalion becomes significant, for man's creation escapes him, the woman rebels, bursting rudely from the oblivion of the unconscious into the conscious mind, to fulfil her necessary role as the transformer of energy into activity. There is no knowing what may result from this, but throughout the history of our present patriarchal society man has been put on guard against female rebellion. The struggle between the two is discernible in one of the strangest myths of the Celtic tradition, an apparently trite, but emotive, story told in the fourth section of the Welsh *Mabinogion* and fragmentarily in a poem attributed to Taliesin, the *Cad Goddeu*.

Wales, *The Story of Blodeuwedd*

Arianrod, daughter of Don, gave birth to two sons, Dylan and Lleu, whom she refused to recognise. Dylan threw himself into the sea and drowned, while Lleu was brought up by his uncle, Gwyddyon, Arianrod's brother and probably also her lover. She had pronounced a curse on her son to the effect that he would have no woman of the race of men. So, with the help of his uncle, the magician Math, Gwyddyon tried to find a way of overcoming the taboo imposed by Arianrod. "They gathered the flowers of the oak tree, of broom and of meadowsweet, which they used, with their spells, to fashion the most beautiful and most perfect maiden in the world", whom they married to Lleu Llaw Gyffes.[3]

He and Blodeuwedd led an uneventful life until, one day, when Lleu was away, she offered hospitality to a group of huntsmen led by Gronw Pebyr, lord of Penlynn in Merioneth.[4] When Blodeuwedd and Gronw met, "from the moment she looked at him her entire being was pervaded with love for him; glancing at her, he too was overcome by the same feelings". They spent the night together and the following day Blodeuwedd refused to let him go. So deeply did they love each other that they considered getting rid of her husband, who had now become a hindrance. Gronw told the young women to try and find out from Lleu himself how he could be killed, and when Lleu returned, Blodeuwedd managed to make him tell her. The conditions were none to easy to fulfil: he had to be on the bank of a river with one foot on the back of a he-goat and the other on the rim of a tub, in which a bath had been prepared for him. The only weapon that could kill him would need a year to make and, even so, it could be worked on only during Mass on Sundays. Blodeuwedd passed this information to Gronw, who began to make preparations. After a year, Blodeuwedd asked Lleu, as if from idle curiosity, to show her how he could stand on the back of a he-goat and the rim of a bath-tub at the same time. When he did so, Gronw hurled a javelin at him. "Lleu flew away in the shape of a bird, uttering a strident and terrible cry and was seen no more."

So Blodeuwedd was able to spend many happy days with Gronw Pebyr. But Gwyddyon searched throughout the land for Lleu, until one day, while following a sow that was behaving strangely, he came to a tree where an eagle perched. As the eagle moved it dropped worms and food, which the sow ate. Gwyddyon realised that he had found Lleu, and charmed him back to human form. When he had nursed him back to health, he took him to wreak vengeance on Gronw and Blodeuwedd. Gwyddyon set out first and, when she heard of it, Blodeuwedd took fright. "She travelled over the river Kynvael, towards a court on the mountain. With her were her servants, who were so afraid that they could only walk with their hands turned to look backwards and so fell into the water. All were drowned except Blodeuwedd. Gwyddyon then caught up with her and said, 'I shall not kill you, I shall do worse by letting you go in the shape of a bird. To punish you for the shame you have brought to Lleu Llaw Gyffes, you will never dare show your face in the daylight for fear of all the other birds, whose instinct will drive them to strike and despise you wherever they find you. You will not lose your name, but still be called Blodeuwedd.' Indeed, the owl is still called Blodeuwedd to this day, which is why it has come to be hated by all birds." (J. Loth, *Mabinogion*, vol. 1, pp. 199—210.)[5]

The first point of interest in this myth is the curse his mother pronounced on Lleu, that he should have no woman of the race of men. This taboo, comparable to the Irish *geis* practised by the ancient Druids, seems less strange when we remember that Arianrod is one of the faces of the mother goddess. So her son, the first man, as Adam was, born of the divinity, cannot have a wife from the race of men because he is their integral representative. Moreover, the divinity, which can be so only when opposed to non-divinity, namely man, needs no other man to interfere in the harmony-cum-opposition between itself and its creation. The mother goddess Arianrod jealously guards for herself her son Lleu, who will also be her lover. Here the myth is analogous to the myths of Ishtar and Tammuz, Cybele and Attis, Aphrodite and Adonis. An ideal projection of the same relationship was brought to life in the Mary—Jesus couple, most usually symbolised as the Madonna and Child, a representational form that existed long before Christianity.

The second point of interest is the creation of Blodeuwedd, who is *manufactured* from flowers, namely from nature at its most fully evolved, by the spells of Gwyddyon and Math, who is the master of magic, therefore the mounter of the forces of nature. But, since he is wounded in the thigh (i.e. impotent), it is Gwyddyon who assumes the role of demiurge, and later of father, usurping the powers of his uncle and eventually finding himself in the same position as Prometheus, who stole the fire of heaven from Zeus and created Pandora, the first woman. Note that in the creation of Pandora, as in the creation of Blodeuwedd and that of the mysterious Lilith, to whom we shall return, the mother goddess no longer has any part to play, for man has assumed the creative function. This is the mark of a myth constructed within a masculine society, where man tries to rob woman of her independence and her exclusive ability to procreate because through them she becomes an untamed enemy who must be brought under patriarchal law. The creation of Blodeuwedd, Pandora and Lilith must surely be symbolic of the great upheaval that took place in some distant and hazy period of antiquity or prehistory, when the cult of the father god replaced the cult of the mother goddess, and male-oriented, partriarchal society replaced a female-oriented gynaecocracy. On a higher, philosophical level, this is to say that the *civilisation of reason*, which builds, organises, divides, legislates and geometrises, replaced the *civilisation of the instinct*, which is essentially feminine and based on feeling, emotion and sexuality. By manufacturing Blodeuwedd outside the maternal womb, Math and Gwyddyon deny sexuality and create an entirely new woman fashioned in their own masculine image. The father has triumphed over the mother and made a manufactured object of a woman, which he will be able to possess and use for his own ends. Implicit in this creation is the education of woman according to the desires of man, who requires that she submit, remain in his shadow, obey him, renounce all male social functions, and use her sexuality solely for purposes of procreation.

The third factor is the marriage of Lleu and Blodeuwedd. Created solely as a companion for Lleu, as Lilith and then Eve were created solely as companions for Adam, Blodeuwedd is the hallucinatory projection of Lleu and his narcissistic double, in the same way as Eve is the castrated image of Adam. Thus she has no choice in the matter and is given by Gwyddyon, the father and representative of the patriarchal order, to Lleu, his son. Lleu and Blodeuwedd are therefore in the same position as Adam and Eve, and are indeed given, by Gwyddyon and Math, a kind of earthly paradise far from all care and want, where they can be perfectly happy within the restrictive, patriarchal conception of happiness, as the family couple. For the family has replaced the "clan" (for want of a better word) as the nucleus of the new society, and, being based on monogamy, is restricted to two people, the husband and the wife. The woman in isolation, so perfectly exemplified in Arianrod, the mother—daughter whose children were brought up by their maternal uncles, has gone. Now we have the couple.

The fourth factor is Blodeuwedd's refusal to accept her situation, the rebellion of the Flower-Daughter. Rejecting her alienation, she claims her right to freedom and chooses her man because she loves him. Though the conflict between instinct and reason becomes critical, Blodeuwedd, being in love with Gronw Pebyr, chooses instinct. Gronw Pebyr ("the Strong Young Man") admirably symbolises the son whose active support the woman seeks in her struggle against patriarchal authority (Gwyddyon) and its successor, marital authority (Lleu).

The fifth factor is the murder of Lleu by the two lovers. This should not be brushed aside as just another commonplace incident, for the rebellion of the Flower-Daughter can be complete only if she goes as far as killing her husband. If Blodeuwedd and Gronw had been content to love each other in secret (like Tristan and Iseult, Launcelot and Guinevere) they would to a certain extent have endorsed the patriarchal society that alienated them. The cuckold may be a figure of fun, but is never a real obstacle. So the lovers rid themselves of Lleu, not through any personal malice, but because the unfortunate man represents all the social taboos of Gwyddyon's patriarchal authority. Lleu may be killed (or, rather, spirited away, since he does not really die), but it is Gwyddyon who suffers the affront, which explains why he tries so hard to find Lleu, and why he takes his revenge in the way that he does.

The sixth element is the defeat of Blodeuwedd's bid for freedom. As the apotheosis of the powers of patriarchal society, Gwyddyon employs both magic and law to re-establish the threatened order. He is the father—shaman, the victor over death, priest, demiurge and legislator. But, though he punishes the reckless young man for his involvement with the woman, *he cannot rid himself of Blodeuwedd,*

*who is his own creation, but has to be content with changing her into
an owl.*

That Gwyddyon's powers are limited to metamorphosis may seem
astonishing, but can be explained by the fact that, as his own
creation, who has risen from his thoughts and still lives in his and
others' memories, Blodeuwedd retains a much stronger reality than if
born of his flesh. One can deny matter but not thought, for through
denial it is reaffirmed. So there is only one solution open to Gwyddyon, to change Blodeuwedd into an owl, a bird of the night, thereby
banishing her into the shadows. To put it more simply, the father
expels the rebellious daughter into the shadows of the subconscious.

Once a thought is formulated it becomes independent of its
author. Honoré de Balzac's strange theories about the existence of
our thoughts outside ourselves (which he borrowed from
Swedenborg and elaborated in *Louis Lambert*) have been sadly
ridiculed by generations of expert but imperceptive rationalists. For,
behind the symbols, Balzac was in fact arguing that every valid
thought formulated by the conscious mind exists for ever and can
challenge other thoughts arising from the same consciousness.
Psychoanalysis has since proved this by showing that even those
distant thoughts formulated in our childhood and hidden in the
depths of the subconscious can, at any moment, rise to the level of
consciousness and create disturbances by contradicting other
thoughts.

Just as Blodeuwedd could rise at any time from concealment in
Gwyddyon's subconscious to his conscious mind, so the rebellion of
the Flower-Daughter poses a constant threat to the foundations of
patriarchal society, even if it remains unmentioned or condemned by
reality. This is one of the reasons why man is so frightened of woman
and why he deliberately leaves her in a state of inferiority and
unconsciousness of her powers. It is better that she never knows she
can rebel, nor realises that the myth of Blodeuwedd is the myth of
every woman, and that there is indeed a *Blodeuwedd complex* about
which the anti-feminist Freud never spoke.

The legend of Blodeuwedd has many points in common with the
story of the mysterious first woman, Lilith, the subject of an obscure
and suppressed tradition that has survived in para-biblical texts
carefully edited out of the official version.

Jewish tradition, *The Story of Lilith*
    At the same time as Yahweh created Adam, he created a
woman, Lilith, who like Adam was drawn from the dust of the
earth. She was given to Adam as a wife, but was dissatisfied
because her expectations were not fulfilled; she quarrelled with
him, uttered the ineffable name of Yahweh, and flew up into
the air. Asked by Adam to return his wife, Yahweh sent the

three angels Senoi, Sansenoi and Samangloph to find her. They
caught her on the shores of the Red Sea at the place where the
Egyptian force was later drowned on the orders of Moses. But
Lilith refused to return to Adam's side, so the three angels told
her, at Yahweh's orders, that she would lose a hundred of her
own children every day if she did not return. When she accepted
these conditions, the angels tried to drown her in the Red Sea,
but Lilith pleaded her cause and was allowed to live on
condition that she never harm a new-born child on whom she
could see her name written. Finally Yahweh gave her to Samael
(Satan), and she was the first of the Devil's four wives and the
persecutor of the new-born. (Drach, *De l'Harmonie de l'église et
de la synagogue*, vol. 2, p. 319.)

Like Blodeuwedd, Lilith is the creation of the demiurge, is given
to Adam as wife-object, but rebels and refuses to obey Yahweh, the
Father. And just as Gwyddyon cannot rid himself of his own
creation, Yahweh cannot rid himself of the woman he created at the
same time as Adam; he can only remove her.

Unlike Blodeuwedd's, Lilith's role does not appear to have ended
when she was banished — in Lilith's case to Hell, where she became
Satan's wife. On the contrary, according to the *Zohar* (*Ḥadash*, Yitro
section), she then takes part in the fall of Adam, to whom Yahweh
has given a second wife, Eve, born of Adam's rib as his castrated
image. "After the Tempter had disobeyed the Most Holy One,
blessed may He be, the Lord condemned him to die. Then he said
'What shall I do? If I die Adam will take another servant.' For the
Tempter and his companion are slaves. So he and his wife went to
seduce Adam and the Tempter seduced Eve." The Kabbalah echoes
this tradition in the book of Emek-Ammeleh (XI) and specifically
states, with regard to a passage of Isaiah (XXVII, 1) that Samael will
be punished: "On that day Yahweh with his terrible sword will visit
Leviathan, the creeping serpent who is Samael, and Leviathan, the
winding serpent who is Lilith."

This last quotation makes it clear both that Lilith is included in
the supreme punishment inflicted on Samael (unlike his other three
wives), and that she too assumed the appearance of a serpent, not
unlike the "serpent" Melusine, whose ambiguous nature we have
already discussed. The vengeance that Yahweh now proposes to
wreak on Samael and Lilith is equivalent to the vengeance of
Gwyddyon on Blodeuwedd and Gronw Pebyr. We shall have to
return to psychoanalysis to grasp the deeper significance of the myth
and its repercussions on the memory of patriarchal types of society.

In fact Lilith does not disappear completely, but is only driven
back into the subconscious to rise again into the conscious mind at the
slightest opportunity. And "when Lilith appears again and leaves the

shadows of rejection, patriarchal law is confounded. So, when Eve prepares to turn Adam from the true path, it is really Lilith reappearing, and, being the mother of Adam, she feeds him and, occasionally, in tender and erotic mood, plays with his child's penis."[6] The suggestion that Lilith is Adam's mother may seem extravagant, but he must have had a mother to be a human being. Even if he never knew a physical mother he had to create his own image of her; and her flight from him can surely be interpreted as weaning him. The disturbing idea that Lilith was both wife and mother to Adam may explain why she has disappeared from the authorised versions of the Bible. In any case, there is a definite equation between wife and mother. "The idea of prohibition had been transferred from that game with the genitals to sucking the breast (eating the apple). . . . The real meaning is 'one may eat the apple but it is forbidden for a son to play sexual games with his mother. . . .' Who then is Lilith? For Adam she is a first object of love, whom he must not remember, who revealed his sex to him. . . ."[7]

As we have seen, the *Zohar* and the Kabbalistic tradition liken Lilith to the serpent, which makes her the image of the fairy with the serpent's tail (or fish's tail, like the mermaids). Psychoanalytically speaking, the serpent's tail would symbolise the original scene when the head of the serpent entered her. "With whom did Lilith make love? It can only have been with God and in this sense Lilith must presumably have preceded Adam. We might go even further . . . God made man in his own image, which included giving him a penis like his own. Surely the human image of God arises out of its separation from its feminine part, thereby, according to the Platonic myth, discovering its sex."[8] We can compare this notion with the Indian tradition of the *Brhadarauyka-Upanishad* (I, 4): "In the beginning only the *Purusa* existed. He was as wide as a man and a woman embracing, and divided in two, from which came the husband and the wife."

The image of Lilith with the tail of a serpent or a fish (both may have the same phallic significance) would then be the "androgynous image of the original god of the previous existence, undoubtedly an omnipotent god, but thereby non-existent, because unaware of desire."[8] For, as Heraclitus and the pre-Socratic philosophers, who formulated the theory of synthesis long before Hegel, recognised, the absolute and undivided is equivalent to the void. This image, then, is a relic of the original Lilith, who has since become a bird of the night and flown away to disappear into the shadows. Her second form, corresponding to an image unhampered by earthly considerations, is the one she takes on in the memory. Besides, this myth is not particularly theological, but essentially social. In a patriarchal society, Lilith has been driven out to make way for Eve, *who*

therefore represents woman as seen, educated and moulded by man.
But she is incomplete and lacks that dimension of Lilith in rebellion
that Eve assumed when eating the apple, and the Virgin Mary later
assumed by giving birth to a son who rebelled against the law of the
father and established the Gospel ("the good word") of the son (and
of the mother). Here we have a complete picture of the transition
from Judaism (patriarchalism) to primitive Christianity (matern-
alism), which was then immediately brought back under patriarchal
control and diverted from its true goal.

In fact, Eve the woman is *alienated*. Her personality is incomplete
because she "will only be the image of the castrated form [of
Yahweh and Adam] and not the image of the feminine side of God.
Thus one half of the former divine omnipotence no longer expresses
its essential desire and becomes as silent as the vagina of a little
girl."[8] In addition, psychoanalysis stresses the fact that the penis of
a little boy is solemnly and openly acknowledged by his parents,
especially by his mother, while the daughter's vagina is consistently
overlooked. So Eve is the voiceless woman, the ghost of woman,
almost a delusion, like the Blodeuwedd of Celtic myth. But when, in
rebellion, Blodeuwedd adopts the aspect of Lilith, the real woman,
she is no longer alienated, and, once her links with the earth are cut
and she becomes a bird of the night, she will be able to appear to
all men in their dreams, when sleep allows the subconscious to
unfold.

For every man, basically but secretly unsatisfied, dreams of a
Lilith—Blodeuwedd, who alone could fulfil his longing for the
infinite, because the Eve alongside him is the mere caricature of
femininity he has made her. This point can be illustrated by two
examples of comparatively recent literature which appear to derive
from the same preoccupation, and which, in any case, concur totally
with the myth.

The first is the *Histoire de l'oeil*, by Georges Bataille, a
pornographic work if ever there was one, but a work of such beauty,
such poetic merit and such depth as to warrant reinstating this
literary genre, which has fallen into money-grabbing and sordid
hands.

Georges Bataille, *Histoire de l'oeil*

Two adolescents, the narrator and Simone, indulged in sexual
games reflecting the author's own obsessions about family and
society. One day, during a wild storm at the seaside, Simone
and the narrator were involved in one of their games when they
were surprised by another adolescent girl, Marcelle ("the purest
and most moving of our friends"), whom they made join in
their activities in a frenzied and insane atmosphere. On another
day they invited some young boys and girls to an impromptu

party, which ended in an orgy. Marcelle was there ("We had found the sight of Marcelle blushing disturbing when once Simone and I had been certain that nothing would ever make us draw back"). During the orgy Marcelle shut herself *in a cupboard* to reach orgasm on her own. But she became mad and was sent to an asylum.

The narrator lives secretly in Simone's room, where they continued to indulge in their *childish* sexual games, which never finished in the act of love because Marcelle was missing. So they imagined her there in their obsessions: "Besides, the swampy regions of the arse, which can only be likened to days of rutting and storm or the suffocating fumes of volcanoes, and which, like storms and volcanoes, burst into activity only to cause disaster, those discouraging regions that Simone, in an abandonment that could only foretell violence, allowed me to look at as if hypnotised, were for me, from then on, simply the subterranean empire of a Marcelle tormented in her prison and prey to nightmares".

One night they made an initial expedition to the asylum where Marcelle was confined, returning later to take the girl away and bring her back to their room. But Marcelle shut herself in the same cupboard and hanged herself. Simone and the narrator performed the carnal act on Marcelle's corpse and were then bound together by a mysterious force. Deprived of Marcelle, they wandered the earth in search of increasingly complicated and cruel sexual games, without ever being able fully to gratify their desires.

Leaving aside the specific context of Bataille's illusory world, this tale highlights the alienation of the couple who cannot fulfil their desires because the woman is lacking some facets of her real personality. Marcelle and Simone are merely the two opposite and irreconcilable sides of one woman, which even the imagination and perversity of the man (his rebellion against the state of affairs) cannot make into one whole figure. Simone is confusedly aware that she is merely an Eve, the castrated form of Adam. She is haunted by the image of Lilith and calls to her longingly. But, in the guilt-ridden context of our society, Lilith is forbidden, or, in Bataille's unconscious symbolism, hidden in a cupboard, interned in an asylum, and hanging herself in the cupboard. Despite her attempt to rebel, Blodeuwedd is still a bird of the night; and Marcelle, likewise, is merely a ghost that will haunt the lovers' memory insistently, reminding them that their search for satisfaction is hopeless because Simone lacks her forbidden dimension. This tale is much more than a simple anecdote or transcription of Bataille's obsessions; it is the enactment of all the delusions of man in search of equilibrium, which the patriarchal intolerances of our present society keep continually out of his reach. So long as Blodeuwedd remains an owl through the wishes of Gwyddyon, that is how it will be.

The second literary illustration of this theme is from Rémy de Gourmont, a writer who cannot really be classified with the naturalists or the decadents of the late nineteenth century, though his work, imbued with the symbolist mentality, is rather curious and very clearly *fin de siècle*. He actually wrote an unperformable play entitled *Lilith*, based on the Rabbinical tradition of Satan's wife. This play is the last word in bad taste, yet paradoxically, because of that, it borders on the brilliant. The eroticism with which Rémy de Gourmont peppers his text reveals an authentic vision of the myth of Lilith, though this has been masked and completely distorted by the attitudes of the masculine society in which he lived. While unquestionably attracted by the character of Lilith, whom he attempts to bring out of the shadows, his terror leads him immediately to hide her behind words like "perverted", "depraved" and "vicious", so pandering to his guilt complex.

Rémy de Gourmont, *Lilith*
Yahweh (Jehovah) created Lilith, the first woman. She immediately asked him for a male and he gave her to Satan.

"SATAN. Greetings, companion given me by the inexperience of Jehovah! Greetings, beauty happily escaped from his aging fingers! Greetings, whore! Greetings lewdness! I lacked that vice. Ha! This is a more pleasurable pasture than pride! Pride is hollow. . .
(*Freely caressing the breasts of Lilith, who offers no resistance and closes her eyes.*)
This is full, this is warm, this is soft!

(*Lilith is charmed by these manual greetings and falls back, writhing and arching her body. But, confronted by a woman he does not know, Satan becomes suddenly stupid and begins to knead her like heavy dough. He dribbles and his eyes grow bloodshot. Like a madman he growls, barks and bites. Then Lilith tames him with a skilful caress. Kneeling solemnly, she kisses and adores the male, then lies down, dragging with her the enlightened demon, who has finally seen which acts and profanations Lilith desires.*)

SATAN. Yes, this is how our first embraces should be, we two! We have corrupted love for ever! We have turned it upside down! Female, I love you!
LILITH. Male I love you!
SATAN. Female, to you my ejaculation of the evening.
LILITH. Male, to you my morning prayer.

SATAN. I shall inhale your sex like a bunch of lilac.

LILITH. I shall feed your sex as if it were a little bird.

SATAN. My universe is there, under that shadow.

LILITH. My joys fill my hand.

SATAN. We have tasted both the bread and the wine . . . You do not understand? In four or five thousand years that joke will hit its mark. You will see, it is rather blasphemous.

LILITH. O my daily bread!

SATAN. O my cup of new wine!

LILITH. I am hungry for your flesh, O my he-goat.

SATAN. I am thirsty for your blood, O my she-wolf.

> (*They fall on each other, as though onto their prey, and writhe in frenzied curves. Then they sink down, shattered, their mouths open, their fingers like hooks curved into their palms.*)

LILITH. (*Speaks first in a sensuously weary voice, which dies away in a caress after each invocation.*) *Iod*, O male, God and Phallus, axis of the world and axis of the spirit, I worship you Iod O male!

SATAN. *He*, O female, matrix and beauty, spiritual indolence, lasciviousness, I worship you, *He* O female!

LILITH. O Copulation, female and male, spout and calyx, obscurity of tomorrow, I worship you, *Va* O copulation!

SATAN. *He*, O female!

LILITH. Do not call me *He*, call me Sterility. Am I not the infertile woman?

SATAN. No, your son will be Sodom and your daughter Gomorrah.

LILITH. May they be blessed, but may they be the only ones — and I shall be the happiest mother among mothers. Amen. O Father of future vices, give me the joy of my lips."

(Rémy de Gourmont, *Oeuvres*, vol. 6, 1891—92, p. 31.)

Behind these litanies of Satan and Lilith may be discerned the profound and everlasting ambiguity of man's desire, in his attraction to and terror of the woman and the portrait sketched by his subconscious dreams of the *unalienated* woman, unadulterated by the imprint of masculine society. Rémy de Gourmont is denouncing the taboo imposed on the type of love that consists of the total possession of two people without any biological purpose. But since, within this kind of love, woman would regain all her alarming powers, the taboo has to be reinforced more severely. Like Blodeuwedd and Pandora, who poured out over the world the evils and vices locked in her box, Lilith can bring only an *accursed* love.

There are other examples of the spirit of Lilith at work in the Judaeo-Christian tradition. It inspires the daughters of Lot to intoxicate their father so that they may continue their threatened line unbroken (Genesis, XIX, 31—2). The instinct for preservation is at work here and may seem to contradict the theme of the "infertile" Lilith, but the fact that Lot's daughters rebel against patriarchal law symbolises an equivalent feminine strength in the exclusive affirmation of a future. The Rabbinical tradition is also aware of this aspect of the problem, and some texts highlight the importance of woman's capacity for actively exciting man's desire, as first Lilith and then Eve gave Adam his sexual education. We have already quoted the passage from the *Zohar* (Bereshit section) that describes how "Yahweh will create a new situation on earth: woman will embrace man", and which modern Rabbis take to mean that, with the coming of the Messiah, woman will seek out man instead of man seeking out woman, as happens now. Thus the basic problem is only too clear: while woman still lacks some part of her personality and is alienated, the eternal struggle between the daughters of Eve and the daughters of Lilith will continue in the mind of man. But the stakes are high, being no less than the stability of a society incapable of resolving its own contradictions.

There is also the disturbing story of Salome, the inspiration of so many poets, painters and musicians, who alone realised that the story contained the seeds of the Blodeuwedd—Lilith rebellion. Here again, however, censorship has intervened and made Salome the epitome of the perverted woman. Oscar Wilde was almost the only man to reveal the fundamentally revolutionary quality of Salome's eroticism, possibly because as a homosexual he understood the feminine problem better, while expressing it through masculine means. His Salome defies every prohibition to gratify her desire to possess Jokanaan, the divine prophet and therefore the representative of the divine word. Since he eludes her, she plays on the unbridled lust of the aging father-figure, Herod, and forces him to renounce his power to her by giving her Jokanaan's head. Woman has triumphed over man. But, by carrying her desire to its conclusion and kissing the lips of the dead Jokanaan, Salome achieves an even more important victory in regaining her own personality, formerly diminished and castrated by the patriarchal law of the living Jokanaan and the feeble Herod. When he realises that he has been outwitted, Herod, in a final burst of energy, has Salome crushed under the shields of his soldiers. Her ephemeral triumph turns to a cry of agony, but a cry that will be heard by Herod and all fathers for a long time to come.

The collection of early myths from Latium, which forms the Roman pseudo-history of our origins, contains another example of feminine rebellion, also stifled under the shields of soldiers (a highly significant act, since the patriarchal order relies on the army). This is the story of Tarpeia, who, according to some sources, betrayed Rome to the Sabines for love of the Sabine king, Tatius, who then had the girl put to death. Florus (I,1) makes the strange comment that she acted "less from motives of treason than for the sake of a vanity natural at her age", suggesting that Tarpeia's deed was motivated by more than love. Indeed, the fact that the victor and actual beneficiary of her "treason" condemned her to death points to a definite rebellion on her part against the established, patriarchal order. The very name Tatius contains the Indo-European word for "father" (*tat* or *tad*). It is also worth noting that, according to Plutarch, Tarpeia betrayed Rome to the Gauls and not to the Sabines.

The Celtic heritage offers us a number of legends on this theme of the supposedly treacherous. but actually rebellious, woman who opens the door of a fortress or mocks the authority of the royal upholder of the established order.

Ireland, *Blathnait and Curoi*

After an expedition into a mysterious fortress, the Gaels Conchobar and Cú Chulainn, and one of the Tuatha Dé Danann, Curoi mac Daere, returned with rich booty, comprising a magic cauldron, some cattle, enchanted birds, and a girl named Blathnait. Because Conchobar and Cú Chulainn forgot to share the trophies with Curoi, he seized the lot and insulted Cú Chulainn. One day the latter arrived at Curoi's fortress and met Blathnait, who had become Curoi's wife. "He loved her long before she had come from the lands of the sea and arranged to meet her round about the night of Samain." At the appointed time, Cú Chulainn returned with an army of Ulstermen. Blathnait advised Curoi to send his warriors to build another fortress, so that he would be left alone. Then she washed him in a tub, tied his hair to the rails of the bed, drew his sword from its scabbard, and went to open the fortress to the Ulstermen. Curoi managed to free himself, but too late, and seeing his fortress in flames he drowned himself in the sea. The Ulstermen recovered Curoi's treasure and Cú Chulainn was taking Blathnait away when Curoi's poet "threw himself on Blathnait, grabbed her so tightly in his arms that her ribs cracked in her back, then carried her towards the cliff just ahead, leapt into space, and both were smashed on a rock." (J. M., *L'Épopée celtique d'Irlande*, pp. 130—1.)

Brittany, *The Body without a Soul*

A young man was invited to the house of a washerwoman, the wife of the Body without a Soul, a kind of ogre who slept twenty-four hours at a time. Asked by the young man why she called her husband the Body without a Soul, she replied, "Because he has a terrifying lion, inside which is a wolf; the wolf has a hare in its stomach and the hare a partridge; the partridge has thirteen eggs and the thirteenth contains his soul. I should like to meet a man brave enough to remove the eggs from the body of the partridge. For this wicked giant stole me away and I do not love him at all." The young man agreed to the test and, with the help of the washerwoman, managed to kill the lion, the wolf, the hare and the partridge. Then the woman broke the egg containing the soul of the Body without a Soul; he died; and she was able to marry the young man. (P. Sébillot, *Contes populaires de la Haute Bretagne*, vol. 2, pp. 126—31. Told in 1879 by a joiner from Collinée in the Côtes-du-Nord.)

The tale of the Body without a Soul contains a clear picture of the woman abducted by man, and in this case by a brute with no soul, presumably himself a victim of the alienation of society. In fact, there is not much difference between this folk-tale and the very ancient and complicated mythology inherent in the story of Curoi. For the role of Curoi is not well defined. He is one of the Tuatha Dé Danann, a character from the Other World, whose name contains the word "dog" and connects him to the myth of Cerberus. In basic opposition to him stands the human Cú Chulainn, the "Dog of Culain", Culain being the name of the blacksmith (also from the Other World) for whom the hero has promised to act as a guard dog. The name Blathnait contains the Gaelic word *blat* ("flower"), suggesting that, like Blodeuwedd, Blathnait meant born of flowers. Brought back by the expeditionary leaders from the Fortress of Ghosts with a mysterious cauldron reminiscent of the Grail, she, like Blodeuwedd and the wife of the Body without a Soul, rebels against masculine authority, here represented by Curoi, to assert her freedom of choice for Cú Chulainn, whom she loves. But, again like Blodeuwedd, she falls a victim to masculine law, for Curoi's poet, setting himself up as judge, condemns and kills her. Strength must remain on the side of the law, as is shown in another legend, included in the *Romans de la Table Ronde*.

Round Table romance, *Grisandole and the Wild Man*

The Emperor, Julius Caesar, had a wife of "noble lineage and marvellous beauty, but more lewd than any woman in the land of Rome". And the worst of her vices was that she "kept with her twelve squires whom she dressed as maidens so that no one should have the slightest suspicion about what she was doing with them". Now Julius Caesar's steward was a girl disguised as a man and called Grisandole. One day a "wild man" laughed a great deal at the false Grisandole and the so-called maidens, and, when called upon to explain himself, revealed the truth to the

Emperor, who had the Empress burned and the false squires hanged, and married his former steward. (J. Boulenger, *Romans de la Table Ronde*, Plon, Paris, 1948, pp. 27—31).

This tale, which could almost have been written by Boccaccio, is a perfect illustration of the sexual rebellion of woman and her subsequent repression. There is obviously some recollection of the excesses of Messalina and a curious invocation of Julius Caesar, but, then, the epic *Huon de Bordeaux* makes him and Morgan the parents of the dwarf Oberon. But the "wild man", who is Merlin, takes us back to the legend of Lailoken, which belongs to a fairly ancient tradition and originated in Scotland; this describes how the heroine shakes off the conjugal yoke by committing adultery until betrayed by the "madman of the woods". Adultery, however, is not indispensable to rebellion, though it is generally used by women seeking freedom from marital law.

There are other tales in which a daughter or a sister commits some "treason", which may be beneficent or maleficent according to the circumstances. For example, in Chrétien's *Chevalier à la Charrette*, the daughter of Baudemagu, sister of Meleagant, betrays her brother by freeing Launcelot. This girl, who is the Hideous Maiden of the Mule, Kundry the Witch, the Empress, of recognised supernatural origins, is a sort of wild, even bloodthirsty virgin who pursues her victims like the Lilith of Hebrew tradition. During the night she takes on a number of different appearances, both forbidding and attractive. But most important is her open rebellion against fraternal authority, for Meleagant represents cruel necessity and death, but a death practically sanctioned by law. When she asks Launcelot to give her the head of the Knight of the Gué (the Gué being the frontier between the two worlds), she may quite possibly be asking him to break down the barriers between life and death, in order to free passage between the two domains, which have a common border but no fixed access from one side to the other. Certainly Chrétien offers no other justification for her request, and was probably, in any case, using some source that he did not understand or that interested him only as an episode to explain Launcelot's eventual rescue. Nevertheless, in this case Launcelot becomes the champion of femininity, not his usual role in the stories of the Round Table, for, despite his education by Vivienne, he is the archetypal hero of prowess, the defender of the patriarchal society represented by King Arthur. Though he has removed that part of Arthur's supremacy that Guinevere symbolises, it is she who initiates the rebellion and not Launcelot.

In face we have only a truncated image of Queen Guinevere, whom the French authors, with the exception of Chrétien when he is correctly interpreted, made totally insipid, and who has become the paradigm of a woman passionately, almost romantically, in love. Nothing could be further from the true face of the queen as she appears in the oldest Welsh texts and in Chrétien's *Lancelot*.

There is also a strange passage in Chrétien's *Perceval* that is usually overlooked by mythologists, yet gives us a rather arresting miniature portrait of Guinevere's real nature. It explains the manner, of absolute mistress, that she adopts towards Launcelot in the *Chevalier à la Charrette*, and her demands, which might otherwise by regarded as the whims of a courtly tradition enjoyed by idle women. The passage in question is part of 'an adventure of Gawain, who, having reached the Castle of the Miracle, comes before King Arthur's mother, who asks him to speak to her of Queen Guinevere. He replies, "Ever since the first woman was formed from Adam's rib, there has never been a lady of such renown, which she deserves, *for, just as the wise master teaches young children, my lady the queen teaches and instructs every living being. From her flows all the good in the world, she is its source and origin.* Nobody can take leave of her and go away disheartened, for she knows what each person wants and the way to please each according to his desires. Nobody observes the way of rectitude or wins honour unless they have learnt to do so from my lady, or can suffer such distress that he leaves her still possessed of his grief." (*Perceval le Gallois*, trans. Foulet, Stock, 1947, p. 191.)

This passage scarcely requires comment. First, Guinevere appears as an *initiator*, which for the ancient Celts was bound to include sexual relations, a role to which we shall return in a later chapter. But we should also stress that Gawain, who was the queen's lover at some time or other, gives her the attributes of the mother goddess, the source of all good in the world. Since Chrétien's source material clearly contained many archaic elements, this description of Guinevere furnishes further evidence that the cult of the Grail and, particularly, the ritual of the Quest hold traces of the cult of the ancient goddess represented in this case by the queen. As a woman she has control over life, over the food that makes life possible, over procreation, in fact total supremacy, which is administered by the king, her husband, or her lover-knights. In the light of this reflection, courtly love, its code and laws can hardly be just a form of amusement for the mediaeval nobility, but, rather, the poetic form adopted in the twelfth and thirteenth centuries by the cult of the *Magna Mater Omnipotens*.

At this point, we are inevitably drawn to a comparison between Guinevere (Gwenhwyfar, Winlogee or Guenloie) and a well-known Irish heroine, Medb, Queen of Connaught. In their more pagan context, the characters of Gaelic epic are less refined than those of French adaptations of British legends. Queen Medb is distinctly nasty, but the authors of the epic deliberately stressed that side of her character, which was shrewish and *virago*-like in the etymological sense of that Celtic word. Medb is the warlike woman, the warrior woman, daughter of the King of all Ireland; she will not bow down to any man, least of all her husband, King Ailill, who plays a slightly fawning role in this legend. She discusses with Ailill which of them has the greater fortune and boasts of having more than he, since she would then, in accordance with Celtic custom, be able to order the business of the household. On realising that he does not have a bull, she is anxious to swing the balance in her favour by obtaining an extraordinary one for herself. She asks Dare, son of Fiachna, to give her his famous Brown Bull of Cualnge, in exchange for which she will give him land and a chariot and, above all, receive him into her bed.

The last proposition is no mere detail. As daughter of the King of all Ireland and Queen of Connaught, Medb has supreme control, or rather *is* supreme control and power, and any man who sleeps with her, like the mortals of Greek mythology who acquire divine powers by becoming the lover of a goddess, is bound to come into contact with that power. Besides, Ailill always turns a blind eye when his wife is lavish with "the friendship of her thighs", as the authors of the epic so delicately put it. In fact, whenever Medb yields some of her supremacy to a man, it is in order that he will serve the interests of the queen and, through her, of the kingdom. This is clear in the passage of the *Tain Bo Cualnge* where Medb, having failed in her negotiations with Dare, decides to take the bull by force through war with Ulster; needing warriors, particularly the formidable Fergus, an exile from Ulster, she lavishes very special attention on him. One day they are caught together by one of Ailill's servants, who tells the king what he has seen. But, although in this instance the king is content to say, "For her it is necessary, she has to act in this way to insure the success of the expedition", Ailill does become jealous on a number of occasions and, finally, when confronted by the sight of Medb bathing in rather indecent fashion before Fergus, orders one of his men to throw a javelin, which kills the hero.[11]

In *The Feast of Bricriu*, Queen Medb is clearly represented as the holder of supreme power. As there is nothing to choose between the three Ulster heroes, Cú Chulainn, Conall and Loegaire, as candidates for the "part of the hero", they are sent to submit to her judgement. She declares Cú Chulainn the best of all warriors, though later, when he beats her during the battles for the Brown Bull of Cualnge, she makes painstaking preparations to kill him, by initiating the children of Calatin who murder the hero. Medb cannot bear to remain at a disadvantage. In *The Drunkenness of the Ulstermen*, she offers strange hospitality to the drunk and bewildered Ulster warriors. Sitting beside Ailill, but also beside Curoi mac Daere, who appears to be one of her lovers, she is persuaded by Curoi to kill the Ulstermen, whom Ailill tries in vain to protect in the name of the sacred laws of hospitality and honour. With Cú Chulainn's help, they manage to escape their desperate situation, taking Ailill with them in their flight, as he prefers to live in exile than remain in the shadow of his formidable wife. Obviously the Irish story tellers paint an exaggerated portrait, almost a caricature of her, but they were writing in a distinctly patriarchial context. Ailill's lack of authority must be considered deplorable and Medb's behaviour scandalous. Of her former role as queen, representative of supremacy and strength, virtually nothing remains but the outward appearance of a prostitute and a harpy.

Yet a comparison between this queen (whose daughter is called Finnabair, the exact Gaelic equivalent of the Welsh Gwenhwyfar) and Guinevere gives us a better grasp of the authentic role of Guinevere in the primitive tradition that formed the basis for the *Romans de la Table Ronde.* She too represents sovereignty and power, but these have been usurped and alienated by man (King Arthur) when, theoretically, they should be inalienable. For the queen, as mother of the people, perfectly symbolises the collective sovereignty of which Rousseau spoke in his *Contrat Social.* According to him, sovereignty is in the hands of the collective social body, the actual nation, which is a feminine kind of moral being (*patrie* in French is a paradoxical word, feminine but derived from the word for "father", which proves that nobody properly understood the word, which should be replaced by *matrie*).

So, when Guinevere takes lovers, it is not to share her power nor to alienate her supremacy, but to transmit her strength and enable the man to work for the exclusive good of her sovereignty. This explains the way in which Launcelot performs his death-defying feats at the thought of Guinevere, whose haunting image finally becomes the very driving force of all his actions. But, in so doing, the queen transgresses the taboos imposed by patriarchal society and deliberately places herself outside the law: hence all the trappings of mystery surrounding her affairs, the shadow of complicity, the secret meetings, which are so many golden opportunities for story-tellers to show their audience the tantalising charm of the forbidden and the unparalleled attractions of royal adultery.

Like Medb and Blodeuwedd, Guinevere rebels against the established social order, so set in its routines and with its many contradictions. Her rebellion is dangerous: she narrowly escapes execution, though Blathnait did not escape Curoi's avenger, nor Blodeuwedd Gwyddyon's curse, nor Lilith Yahweh's curse.

However, Irish literature possesses one very strange tale that suggests that rebellion could go a long way and, in part, succeed. The main theme of the story is that of a tragic but fascinating confrontation between triumphant Christianity and a Druidism no longer officially acknowledged in Christianised Gaelic society. It had become, as in the ancient Celtic countries of the continent, the concern of certain women, who continue to practise it secretly in the popularised form of witchcraft.

Ireland, *The Death of Muirchertach*

Muirchertach, the King of all Ireland, was out hunting when he met a girl with whom he fell madly in love. At his entreaties, she agreed to follow him to the royal house of Cletech, but only on condition that the king submit to her entirely and that no priest should ever set foot in the house while she was there. When the king asked her name, she replied that she was called Sin, that is "sigh", "rustling", "storm", "rough wind", "winter night", "cry", "tear", "groan". Once installed in Cletech, the first thing she did was to turn out the queen and her children. The queen went to complain to the holy Bishop Cairnech, who came and threatened Muirchertach, ordering him to send Sin away. The king refused and Cairnech cursed him in a ritual that was more Druidic than Christian. However, the men of Ireland sided with the king, and therefore with Sin, against the bishop. One day, when asked by the king where her strength lay, Sin replied that she was a witch and gave him some examples of her magic powers. As time passed Muirchertach began to feel suspiciously weak and went to confess to Cairnech, promising to leave Sin. But when he returned, he again fell under the girl's influence; she bewitched him with fantastic visions. Muirchertach had a presentiment of his approaching death, but too late to escape the clutches of Sin. During the night he woke suddenly and saw the house on fire. He tried to catch hold of a vat full of wine to protect himself from the fire, but fell into it and drowned. It then transpired that Sin was the daughter of a man whom the king had murdered, and that she had been avenging her father. But, as she had really fallen in love with Muirchertach, she died soon after, unable to bear her grief. (Edited and translated into English by W. Stokes; see *Revue celtique*, vol. 23, p. 396 ff.)

Although this story unfolds almost like a play by Corneille, with Sin, torn between love and vengeance, nevertheless fulfilling her duty and bringing death to the guilty, the myth expresses a great deal more. Setting aside the theme of vengeance, which appears to be an *a posteriori* rationalisation of the real aim of the "witch", the story is about a definite rebellion against the king, which takes on a more subtle twist because of the method used. The Bible contains similar examples: Delilah deprived Samson of his strength, Judith murdered Holofernes, though their actions were justified by the background of struggles between rival nations. This myth also differs from the classic rebellion of son against father, which, however important it may be individually and socially, is, in fact, the simple wish to replace aging authority with a fresh young version, and an affair between men. People have dwelt at length on the rebellion of the son, sometimes supported by the mother, and have even looked for its causes in the primitive tribe, where the chief was always the strongest man; but the rebellion of daughter against father remains unexplored.

This is because the son's rebellion does not threaten the structure of patriarchal society. On the contrary, it is essential that some internal danger revitalise inert energies and lead to a resolution in which the establishment is reaffirmed rather than changed. By the laws of nature, individuals pass away while the institution goes on. Though the rebellion of son against father (disputation, youthful protests and political movements) may elucidate the malaise affecting our present society, it merely hands over industrial society's fundamental anxiety to the next generation. This anxiety is based on the assertion that woman is both forbidden and desirable. The rebellious son transgresses taboos for his own ends, only to reimpose equally exorbitant demands when he has succeeded in usurping the father's position. Nothing has really changed, and the laws instituted to protect the new father's rights are still put forward as being the best for humanity's welfare.

The whole process is but a vast fraud at the expense of the sons and, more especially, of the daughters. Education has, over the centuries, successfully reduced daughters to total dependence and spiritual alienation by terrorising them with injunctions not to meddle in men's affairs, not to be sensual, and so on. When daughters open their eyes to what the law of the father, aided and abetted, albeit unconsciously, by the mother, has made of them, moral rebellion will become possible.

Its practical application, however, is hard to envisage, since everything has been organised to prevent it. Sin can achieve her rebellion against royal authority only through cunning. The traditional mistrust of hypocritical women, who use indirect means to achieve their ends, is surprising, because it is the rules of patriarchal society that force them to do so. Meanwhile, the rebellious daughter is inevitably looked upon as a monster of ingratitude, or just a monster, possibly even a person with harmful magic powers who may conveniently be condemned to the stake as a witch.

Sin, with her combination of cunning (witchcraft), charm (a watered-down version) and intelligence certainly succeeded in her rebellion. She not only secured her own triumph, but also led the father-king to his downfall. She made a laughing-stock of authority and showed the true face of the hero of prowess as society had shaped him: above the common run yet weak as a baby, a creature stuffed with pretentions and bloated with wind. It was a harsh lesson.

Occasionally, however, these heroes themselves accidentally lent a hand in women's rebellion. The *Rigveda* contains a legend that appears to be the oldest version of the theme; in this, Indra frees the cows shut in a cave by the Panis. It is easy to decipher this myth: Indra had to overcome an aversion for women, which had driven the cows (i.e. women) into the darkness of the cave (i.e. vagina), which he then had to explore to bring the women out into daylight (free them vaginally), so that they could express their sexuality openly and shake off their alienation. The Iranian *Avesta* gives the same adventure to Thraetana, who frees two young girls of miraculous beauty from a grotto; while, in a Graeco-Latin context, Livy (I,7) echoes this same myth in a story about Hercules. Cacus the shepherd had stolen Hercules' herd and shut them in a cave while the hero was asleep, taking care that the cows entered the cave backwards so that Hercules did not know what had become of them. This deceit was more than mere cunning; it was a complete inversion of the female polarity, an alienation of the female personality. But Hercules heard lowing from the cave, killed Cacus and freed the cattle.

The Celtic story most reminiscent of the Indra—Hercules legend occurs at the end of *The Education of Cú Chulainn*, a text that is fairly recent in form but very old in content. On his return from a visit to Scotland, where he had been improving his skill as a warrior, Cú Chulainn saw a solitary young girl on the shore. She explained that her father, the king, had offered her as tribute to the Fomors, who were a mythical marine race, enemies of the Gaels and the Tuatha Dé Danann. Cú Chulainn killed the giant Fomor and saved the girl. In this story, as in the legend of Theseus and the Minotaur and the legend of Tristan as victor over the Morholt, who came to raise tribute from the people of Cornwall for the King of Ireland, the hero is releasing the girl, or girls, from the patriarchal law that forced them to become sacrificial victims.

There is a similar strain in the Welsh tale of *Owein or the Lady of the Fountain* and in Chrétien's *Chevalier au Lion*; in these, Owein—Yvain rescued the maidens whom Luiton (a kind of demon representing the father) had imprisoned in the Castle of Pesme-Aventure. The deed takes on a new form in the Christian *Quête du Saint Graal*, where Galahad freed the girls shut up in a kind of hell called the Castle of Maidens. All in all, the knights of the Arthurian romances who rescued girls imprisoned by giants or demons were performing an identical act of liberation for a female character alienated by the father, or some other representative of the patriarchal society. There is a direct link between them and Don Quixote, who wanted to save a Dulcinea existing only in his imagination, as well as all the fairy stories in which the hero, usually a Prince Charming, comes to save the Sleeping Princess with a kiss.

But these heroes of prowess are the natural product of patriarchal society. This particular attitude is rare or incidental: after their brief aberration, they revert to their true nature. The girl who has been freed either marries her deliverer, which reconfines her, sometimes more restrictively, or is forced to continue alone her fight for total freedom from the male yoke. Traces of this struggle, through its various stages, are discernible in most myths and popular traditions.

A typical example is the myth of Apollo, sun god of the Greeks, who was Nordic in origin and introduced to the Greek peninsula by the Indo-Europeans. An analysis of the legends connected with Delphi reveals a series of changes in the cult corresponding to changes in society and its attitudes. When ,Apollo arrived at Delphi, he attacked and killed the great snake Python, which clearly represented the earth and therefore a female divinity. The feminine earth cult was replaced by a masculine heaven cult, as a male-oriented structure replaced the more female-oriented order within Greek society. But the victory of Apollo was ambiguous, for, as soon as he had vanquished the snake, he was nicknamed Pythian; and the *Pythes*, who were women, were given the duty of interpreting his words through the famous oracle at Delphi.

Through these myths, the importance of *Pythes*, sybils, fairies and witches can be seen in a proper perspective. Their world officially denied their role or punished them when they exceeded the permitted limits of vague, ineffectual prophecy. Patriarchal society has hounded witches with such determined cruelty because they are creatures of the Devil, who had a feminine nature to begin with, as the many legends about the Devil and his dam show. She was the personification of the ancient mother goddess; and the witches' Sabbaths, which re-enacted the bacchanalias of antiquity, the orgies associated with the worship of Demeter and Isis, retained the last traces of the rebellion of the Flower-Daughter.

All strange and secret sects have, over the years, been concerned, consciously or otherwise, with restoring woman's rights and privileges in a new human society. The taboos and prohibitions of patriarchal society drive all such rebellions underground. That is why Christianity began as a secret society based on the mother—son couple — a reintroduction of love and harmony between man and woman; the first precept of Christ, "to love one's neighbour", was essentially contrary to the hierarchical and patriarchal Roman State and its axiomatic notions of war and aggressive tension. The Romans were well aware of this; the Christians' rejection of patriotism and refusal to sacrifice to the gods of the Roman State provoked a bloodthirsty persecution. It was not until the government had taken over the Christian religion and incorporated it into the Roman judicial system that it was given official recognition and freedom to expand, with the loss of its revolutionary ideals. By preaching obedience to the established order and riddling women with guilt, it has since then become the most zealous supporter of patriarchal society.

Apart from a tendency to restore the ancient mother goddess in the guise of the Virgin Mary, there have been a great number of heresies within Christianity itself that have sought to implement the female rebellion. The third-century Gnostic sect of the Phibionites saw in the ritual of the Last Supper the ingestion not only of male sperm but also of female secretions, especially menstrual blood. By rejecting procreation as the purpose of sexuality, they allowed women to enjoy their bodies fully once more. All these practices were based on the Nicolaitan and Archontic syllogism, itself Manichaean in origin, on which the later twelfth-century Catharist doctrine was based. This syllogism stated that "everything created by God was good, but that a lesser god [the Devil] added evil to it; consequently, in order to fight evil it is necessary to destroy creation, hence the need for contraception and abortion".[12]

The Black Mass is quite unlike the ceremony described by sensation-seeking writers, for, however strange the motives of the participants and however depraved the ritual, a penetrating analysis reveals its deliberate resistance to the repressive course of male, patriarchal society and its desperate attempt to rediscover an ancient, more female-oriented order. That a woman serves as the altar and that she (particularly her sexual parts) is the object of adoration is proof enough. The same argument applies to the "backward" Mass, which involves saying the holy texts from finish to start, thereby betraying, in a deliberately blasphemous context, an attempt to return to the early days preceding the dominance, in the Euro-Mediterranean world, of the great male god of the Jews. These are undoubtedly forms of Devil worship, but only in so far as he, being etymologically the one who "throws himself across", prevents things from happening according to the current norm. So Black Masses and so-called Devil worship are not adorations of evil, their only blasphemy lying in the denial of established values.

The myth of the Fisher-King as he appears in Celtic tradition, which mediaeval Christians regarded as very important without really understanding it, can also be examined in connection with blasphemy. Chrétien's *Perceval*, Wolfram von Eschenbach's *Parzival*, though not the Welsh *Peredur*, present the Fisher-King, guardian of the Grail, as lame because wounded in the thigh. We have already mentioned that this was a euphemism for a wound to the genitals, producing impotence in the king and making him unfit to rule. But the texts vary as to how he received this wound. According to the *Quête*, the king tried to approach the Grail too closely and, being unworthy to look upon it, was struck by a mysterious weapon. This explanation will not do, for it contains an implicit desire to justify the presence of a bleeding spear in the Procession of the Grail. Its purpose can be understood only after a detailed study of the Gaelic mythology of Ireland. In any case, the Christian morality inherent in the idea that the king was in a state of mortal sin and therefore unworthy to touch the blood of Christ is too glaringly obvious. One might, of course, be tempted to believe in a play on words between sinner and fisher (Latin, *peccator* and *pescator*; French, *pêcheur* and *pêcheur*). But Wolfram's text contains the key, along with many other ancient details within his thirteenth-century German muddle of esoteric ideas: "One day, the king [Amfortas] . . . seeking adventure and feeling greedy for love, hoped to obtain a loving reward for his delight. In a strange fight, he was wounded in his manly parts by a poisoned spear." From this passage it emerges that Amfortas was wounded for breaking his vow of chastity. His accomplice was Kundry the Witch, a strange character integral to the legend of the Grail, and forming an almost divine couple with the king, rather like the pairs of gods found among antique statues.

The change from worship of the goddess to worship of the god through worship of the divine couple (the god becoming equal to the goddess and then eliminating her) gives the outline of development of the royalty invested in the Grail: in the beginning the goddess was guardian of the Grail (and originally the Grail herself); then there was a king—queen couple (Pelles—Kundry or Amfortas—Kundry, who correspond to the Welsh Rhiannon and Pwyll); and, in the end, just a king, Pelles or Amfortas. But the king retains a wound, namely a guilt, from his past, because he tried to wipe out all traces of the previous situation, which if not gynaecocratic, was at least based on the harmony of the couple. However, this line of argument is a digression and belongs to a specialised study of the deeper meaning of the Grail and the Quest, to which we shall return. At this point it is enough to realise that the sexual union of the Fisher-King and Kundry is a blasphemy, inasmuch as it recalls a situation too dangerous to be restored. It is interesting that the word "blasphemy" derives from the same Latin root as the word "blame".

The rebellion of the Flower-Daughter has led us to examine various legends in which the woman rises against the established order and blasphemes. She tries in various ways to escape the man who created her through education and conditioning. While adultery may not be the most common form of rebellion, it at least seems the one most brutally aimed at the man. But the full significance of adultery as a reaction against the idea of woman-as-object contains the rebellion against the father, whether husband or sovereign.

This rebellion is not merely an egoistical whim on the part of a girl who wants to marry against her father's wishes, nor the banal adultery of a woman dissatisfied with her marital lot. It is the vital assertion of woman seeking control of her personality and freedom to use her intelligence (reason) and her emotions (instinct) as she wishes. However, she must first strip off the fancy costume man has given her: despite its attractive appearance, it is a badge of slavery. For, in patriarchal society, woman is merely the imaginary creation of an allegedly rational person, who sets himself up as the original creator. Gwyddyon, son of Don, figures largely in all men, and Blodeuwedd in every woman.

Chapter 7

The Grail, or the Quest for Woman

f all Celtic myths, or myths incorporated into that context, the myth of the Grail has been the most persistent, and has given rise to the greatest number of variations and interpretations. The Grail itself has meant whatever one wished it to mean, both in the Middle Ages and in modern times; and, though undoubtedly a pagan object, it was transformed by early thirteenth-century Cistercian mysticism into an esoteric sacred vessel alleged to contain the blood of Christ and symbolising the divine spirit and heavenly riches promised to men of goodwill. The lengthy study required to condense all existing theories about the Grail would be outside the scope of this work, which is concerned with the role of woman in Celtic civilisation; our aim is to examine this on a sociological and a mythological level, the latter representing the ideal female character seen through the whirlpool of changing beliefs and historical vacillations.

It has already been stated that the Grail and its legend appear originally to have stemmed from a Celtic theme of *vengeance by blood*.[1] This is not a supposition, but an observation based on a study of the Welsh tale of *Peredur*, which, though not the oldest version of the legend, contains most archaic features. Joseph Loth refers to it in a note to his French translation of the *Mabinogion*, as does Mary Williams in her *Essay on the Composition of the Welsh Romance Peredur*, which influenced many Celtic and Arthurian scholars into accepting that the original Quest for the Grail was pagan and masks some mysterious ritual clearly connected with bloody vengeance. As we shall see, certain apparently incomprehensible details that have survived in other, much more recent texts without the authors' knowing to what they referred are explicable only by this basic fact about the pagan origins of the Quest, though it would be foolhardy to suggest that it is only a tale of vengeance. Our basic task is to discover what lies behind this confused story, which was adjusted to suit twelfth- and thirteenth-century Christian society.

Many scholars have stressed that the Quest constitutes a test, which has parallels in all the Welsh and Irish tales about mysterious voyages or expeditions into the Other World. It may be compared with the practices of shamanism, many traces of which can be found in what remains of Druidic mythology. Others have emphasised the object of the Quest, seeing it as a kind of initiation into kingship and sovereignty, or have interpreted the chosen knight's reclamation of the Land of the Grail as a kind of fertility ritual analogous with prehistoric customs still clearly remembered in Mediterranean and Nordic religions. In a series of debatable but exciting works,[2] Jessie Weston suggested that the different items in the Procession of the Grail all have some symbolic and ritual value and that, more specifically, if the bleeding spear represents the masculine element, the Grail, or chalice, is its feminine counterpart, these two basic elements uniting to restore the waste and infertile Land of the Grail to its ancient richness and fertility.

The sexual symbolism of the Grail itself is obvious. As a cup or chalice it is the breast bestowing food; but, more than that, it is a container into which the Christianised versions put the blood of Christ, and so presumably represents his mother, the Virgin Mary. So the Grail—chalice is the uterus of the mother goddess, which will give life to all the creatures of the world once it has been fertilised. But, since the Fisher-King has been wounded in his genitals, the Land of the Grail is waste and arid, waiting for the chosen knight, who is to restore its lost fertility. This simple equation of the Grail—chalice with the maternal womb furnishes a conclusive argument in favour of the femininity of the Grail.

There is another argument. As the Quest is a descent into hell, an expedition into the Other World, it is really a *regressus ad uterum*, an attempt to re-create the state of paradise that preceded birth. The challenge inherent in this pursuit of sovereignty, which in Celtic myths is always represented by a woman, must therefore be an attempt to approach femininity in its most essential form.

We can therefore conclude that the Grail, whatever shape the various texts may give it, is a feminine symbol, and that the quest that the knight undertakes is a search for femininity. Study of the various versions of the legend will support this idea and enable us to discern the exact role of the myth in early mediaeval European society.

The basic text, Chrétien de Troyes' *Perceval*, is the earliest to contain the famous Procession of the Grail, and, if not the oldest version, it did at least initiate all later development of the legend. It is important to note, first, that Chrétien's text presents the raw material of the myth and makes the Grail a common noun denoting an everyday object; and, secondly, that he did not finish his book, so we have no idea how his story of Perceval was to have ended. All elaborations on the theme were made by his continuators, though they did refer to fragments of Celtic tales, which had reached them by extremely diverse routes.

> Chrétien de Troyes, *Perceval*
> "Torches made the hall so bright that a more brilliantly lit house could not be found in all the world. While they talked leisurely, a servant appeared from an adjoining room, holding by the middle of the staff a dazzling white spear. . . . A drop of blood welled up at its steel point and ran down to the hand of the man who bore it. . . . Then came two other, very handsome men servants, each carrying a candlestick of enamelled gold in which there burned at least ten candles. Then, following the servants, a *grail* appeared, borne with both hands by a beautiful, graceful, finely dressed maiden. At her entrance such brightness spread over the room that the candles grew pale as do the stars and the moon when the sun rises. After her came another maiden bearing a silver platter. The grail which went before her was of the purest gold, and set with precious stones, the richest and most varied to be found in the earth or the sea. No gem could be compared to that of the grail."

This Procession of the Grail makes precise reference to three items of the greatest importance: the *grail*, the *spear* and the *platter*. Moreover, both the grail and the platter are held by a woman, but, while the platter is silver, the grail is made of gold, or at least looks like gold, and *shines like the sun*.

It is easy to see the spear that trickles blood as one of the miraculous objects of the Celtic Quest, despite the later Christian interpretation of it as the spear of the centurion Longinus. The Tuatha Dé Danann brought back from the "Islands of the North of the World" "the spear that Lug owned. The woman or man who held it could not be conquered in battle."[3] "It had such destructive force that its head had always to be immersed in a cauldron so that the town where it was being kept did not go up in flames."[4] It is also the "spear of Assal"; "the man whose blood it spills is dead. So rare is it, that it will not miss its mark if one says to it *ibar*, and it comes back to the thrower's hand if he says *athibar*."[5] This is also the spear of the Irish hero Celtchar, son of Uthechar, a rather strange character who appears in some of the secondary epics of the Ulster cycle. In *The Pig of Mac Datho*, the assembled warriors are quarrelling over the "part of the hero" when Celtchar lays claim to this honour; he is challenged by Cet, son of Maga, who says, "I came to the door of your house, where I was shouted at. Everybody arrived, including you, who went and found me in a narrow pass and threw a javelin at me. I threw another, which pierced your thigh and the top of your testicles. Since then you have had a bladder disease and have fathered neither sons nor daughters."[6]

Clearly Celtchar is suffering from the same infirmity as the Fisher-King, which is why he cannot claim the "part of the hero", meaning the role of king, kingship being incompatible with sexual impotence. More interesting still is the fact that Celtchar owns a formidable spear like that of Assal, and that it is through his spear that he later dies.

> Ireland, *The Violent Death of Celtchar, Son of Uthechar*
>
> Celtchar's wife, Brig Brethach, deceives him with Blai Briuga; so, while her lover is in the royal palace watching Conchobar and Cú Chulainn playing chess, Celtchar kills him, by thrusting his spear into the other's body "so deeply that a drop of blood from the tip of the spear fell onto the chessboard." This drop of blood is important, because the place where it falls indicates whether Conchobar or Cú Chulainn was closest to the victim and, consequently, which of them should take revenge on Celtchar for violating the right of asylum and hospitality in the royal house. In the end, Celtchar is condemned to ridding Ireland of three scourges. The first is Conganches mac Dedad, Curoi's brother, who is ravaging the country and against whom neither spears nor swords have any effect. Celtchar arranges to marry Conganches to his daughter, who has the strange name of Niam, which means "heaven" in the religious sense (from Breton *Nenv*). When Niam contrives to find out how her husband might be killed, he replies, "Red points must be thrust into the soles of my feet and my calves".[7] So Niam tells her father Conganches' words and Celtchar kills him. (Note the similarity between this episode and that in which Blodeuwedd makes her husband Lleu Llaw Gyffes reveal the way in which he might die.)
>
> Celtchar tackles the second scourge, an infernal dog, which he manages to kill by cunning. But the third scourge, also a fearsome dog, brings about Celtchar's death. Though he does in fact kill it, as he withdraws his spear from the animal's body and brandishes it in the air "a drop of blood trickled onto the shaft of the spear and rolled across him to the ground, causing his death".[8]

The theme of the drop of blood at the top of the spear is so emphatically expressed in this instance that it cannot possibly be mere coincidence. It seems likely that the Procession of the Grail contains traces of the mysterious story of Celtchar or some other tale of the same nature. Not only is there a distinct similarity between the destruction wrought on the land of the living by the infernal dog, a kind of malevolent Cerberus, and the desolation of the waste and infertile Land of the Grail; but there is obviously also a connection between Celtchar and the Fisher-King: Celtchar, wounded in the genitals and the victim of his own spear, through a drop of blood that runs from its tip, bears comparison with the Fisher-King, wounded in the same place, who introduces a spear with a drop of blood at its tip into the Procession of the Grail. Finally, there is a story of bloody revenge behind Celtchar's misfortune, as in the original legend of the Grail.

The name of Celtchar's daughter, Niam, points to his having connections with the Other World, as did the Fisher-King. Indeed, Niam may even be the same mythological character as the king's daughter who bears the Grail and, later, in the Cistercian Quest, becomes the mother of Galahad the saviour.

It would also be valid to compare the story of Celtchar with that of Yspaddaden Penkawr in the Welsh tale of *Culhwch and Olwen*. Asked by young Culhwch for his daughter in marriage, Yspaddaden throws a kind of spear, a prehistoric stone weapon, at him, three times in succession; but, thanks to his and his companions' alertness, the spear is turned back on Yspaddaden and seriously wounds him. Yspaddaden "Large-Head" has several connections with the Fisher-King, as the father of a daughter destined for higher things and as the inhabitant of a mysterious castle in the Other World. His head, which is eventually cut off, is reminiscent of certain aspects of the Grail—head, as we shall see in the tale of *Peredur* and in more recent texts.

The sexual symbolism of the spear, as of all incisive and other weapons of combat, is indisputable and needs no further emphasis. Chrétien de Troyes, who obviously saw it as the weapon that had wounded the Fisher-King, naturally gave it a place in the Procession alongside all the other instruments of the suffering borne by the king and, through him, by the dying kingdom he embodies.

The silver platter is certainly much more interesting, and, though hard to account for in Chrétien, resumes its true role in other versions of the legend. For the moment, however, we shall keep to the Grail itself, since it was regarded as the essential element by the readers of the tale of *Perceval*, by Chrétien's continuators, and by all those scholars who have contributed to the never-ending succession of questions about its mysteries.

The word "grail" presents no difficulties, being a common noun of Provençal origin (*gradalis* or *gradale*), which goes back to the Latin *cratalis*. It occurs in the documented will, dated 1010 (a hundred and seventy-odd years before Chrétien's work, of Count Ermengaud d'Urgel, who left to the abbey of Sainte-Foy de Conques *"gradales duas de argento"* (two plates of silver). The word *gradal* is also used — in the *Roman d'Alexandre*, which dates from around 1150 — to mean "plate"; and, at the beginning of the thirteenth century, the monk Helinand de Froidemont compares *gradalis* (i.e. "grail") to the Latin *scutella* ("basin"). The Cistercian version of the legend, which was probably written by Robert de Boron and developed in the *Estoire dou Saint-Graal*, makes the Grail the basin from which Christ ate the lamb of Passover and which Pontiùs Pilate gave to Joseph of Arimathea, who used it to catch the blood of Christ when he came to enshroud him.

So Chrétien's grail is a basin, a receptacle. According to Giraldus Cambrensis, a writer usually well informed about thirteenth-century Wales, the Welsh commonly used remarkably wide and deep basins. If Chrétien worked from a Welsh model, or, as seems likely, translated from Welsh, he must have found a perfectly ordinary, common noun. His conciseness in describing the Procession of the Grail suggests that his grail is just a simple receptacle containing something which the author did not yet wish to put a name to, but was intending to do so at the end of his work. For in Chrétien's section of the text of *Perceval* he says nothing specific about the Grail or its contents, and never claims that the Procession of the Grail was a religious ceremony, as it later became in the Cistercian version of the Quest. However disappointing this may be from a mythological standpoint, it is a tribute to his literary ability and his gifts as a story-teller that, while drawing from a fruitful source, he contrived real suspense to hold his readers' interest.

But before the theme of the Grail was adapted, or rather rehabilitated, for purely mystical and Christian ends, it passed through a number of other stages, of which the two most important are contained in the German Wolfram von Eschenbach's *Parzival* and an anonymous Welshman's *Peredur*. Both these works were written in the early thirteenth century and appear to be based on an archetypal source which we continually recognise without being able to give it a definitive form. It is in *Peredur* that we find out what the receptacle known as the Grail contained.

Wales, *Peredur*
"He saw two men coming across the hall and into the room bearing an enormous spear from the neck of which three trickles of blood ran down to the ground. At this sight the whole company began to weep and sigh.... After a few moments silence, two maidens entered bearing between them a great plate on which lay a man's head swimming in blood. Everyone then let out such shrieks that it was difficult to stay

in the hall with them." (J. Loth, *Mabinogion*, vol. 2, pp. 64—5.)

"You went to the court of the lame king, where you saw the young man with the red spear tipped with a drop of blood that turned into a running torrent as it fell on his fist; you saw other marvels there but you did not ask their meaning or reason! If you had done so, the king would have won good health for himself and peace for his estates; instead of which all he will see from now on is fighting, wars, knights being killed, women made widows, ladies without means to live. And all this because of you." (Ibid., vol. 2, pp. 104—5.)

This strange, ceremonial parading of a decapitated head on a plate (the Grail) and the famous and formidable magic spear is a far cry from the pious, contemplative atmosphere of Chrétien's procession. It seems to have more to do with a story of vengeance for a murder as yet unpunished, the memory of which arouses lamentations that those present find dreadful to hear. If we accept the argument that the *Peredur* represented popular beliefs of the time concerning the Grail, it is probably more authentic, or at least traditional, than the continental versions distorted by literary additions and by theological or philosophical preoccupations.

The sophisticated text of Wolfram von Eschenbach, though the product of a rather bewildering muddle of different streams of thought, contains as many strange, equally revealing and probably very old details, which are scarcely compatible with Cistercian theology.

Wolfram von Eschenbach, *Parzival*
"A squire suddenly stepped over the threshold carrying a spear from the point of which blood spurted and ran the length of the wood to his hand and away into his sleeve. Then tears and sobs filled the air. . . . The squire, bearing his mournful burden, walked all round the room and back to the door, through which he suddenly disappeared. . . . At the end of the hall a steel door opened to admit two young girls of noble bearing . . . they were white virgins. . . . . Each held a golden candlestick in which burned a candle . . . after them came a duchess with her peeress, carrying two ivory pedestals. Immediately there followed eight other ladies, four of whom bore great torches, while the others effortlessly held up a precious stone pierced by the rays of the sun, its name derived from its brightness. Two deliciously adorned princesses arrived in their turn, their palms supporting two sharp knives of extraordinarily white silver. . . . The queen followed them, her face so brilliant that everyone thought dawn had broken. On a

cushion of green emerald she bore the Grail, that root and crown of every hope about Paradise, and above all earthly ideal. Repanse de Schoye was the name of the maiden permitted to carry the Grail."

This long-drawn-out description of the Procession of the Grail has too superficial a veneer of Christianity and far too many maidens to be clearly orthodox. *Except in Ireland and Brittany*, women were never allowed to participate in Christian religious worship during the Middle Ages. Yet, for Wolfram's precursor Chrétien, for the anonymous Welsh author, and, above all, for Wolfram himself, women played a considerable part in the Procession: an observation all the more perplexing in that the rest of Wolfram's work displays very distinct Christian and mystical leanings. Be that as it may, a woman carries the Grail in *Perceval* and *Parzival*, and the *head* in the *Peredur*, proving beyond doubt that in this mysterious and almost incomprehensible ceremony the role of officiator devolved on a woman.

The spear appears in all three texts. In Wolfram's it is merely said to pour blood, in Chrétien's work it produces a single drop, while in *Peredur* there is a contradiction: to begin with, the narrative mentions three streams of blood, then goes on to talk of a drop of blood that turns into a torrent. But apart from these differences of detail, the anecdote is identical in all three cases. The silver platter appears only in Chrétien's version, with tables performing the same role in Wolfram's, and nothing to match it in *Peredur*. Finally, both Chrétien and Wolfram stress the astonishing light that emanates from the object and from the woman who carries it, while Wolfram and the Welsh author emphasise the cries of grief and mourning from those present, which are scarcely compatible with a Christian religious ceremony, and may be more suggestive of the theme of vengeance. At the end of *Peredur* there is an attempt to explain: "The head was that of your first cousin, whom the witches of Kaerloyw killed. They also crippled your uncle. . . . It is foretold that you will avenge them."[9] Strangely enough, the idea of vengeance reappears in Wolfram's sophisticated version, though it is completely absent from Chrétien; this suggests that Wolfram may have had some direct contact with Breton or Welsh writers, possibly through "Kyot the Provençal" the translator whom he continually names as his source.

When Parzival meets the hermit Trevrizent, he discovers, and we with him, what is on the emerald cushion (that is, plate).

Wolfram von Eschenbach, *Parzival*
"All their food comes from a precious stone, which in its essence is all purity. If you do not know, I will tell you its name

is *Lapsit exillis*, and by virtue of this stone the phoenix perishes and becomes ashes from which life is reborn. Through this stone, the phoenix changes its feathers to reappear in all its former brilliance. There is no man so ill that, once before this stone, will not be certain of avoiding death for a whole week after the day he saw it. Whoever sees it stops growing old. After the day on which it has appeared to them, all men and women resume the appearance they had at the height of their strength; and were they to stay in its presence for two hundred years they would not change except that their hair would turn white, for it gives such vigour to man that his skin and bones immediately return to their youthfulness. The stone has the name Grail. . . . Every Good Friday [a dove] brings it the capacity of providing the best of food and drink. . . . Paradise contains nothing more delicious. . . . The stone also procures game of all kinds for its guardians."

Note that Wolfram does not tell us very much more than Chrétien. For both of them the Grail is a container, a golden bowl or an emerald plate. Only the author of *Peredur* makes specific reference to the contents as a man's head. Yet, while Wolfram seems to suggest that the active power of the Grail is inherent in the stone container, the Welsh author obviously considers the head, the contents, more important. Leaving aside the Cistercian version, which avoids the issue by making the contents the blood of Christ, we must find a way of reconciling these two apparently contradictory ideas.

The myth of the severed head goes back a long way in mythology and in Celtic history. There is incontrovertible evidence of it in Latin and Greek authors, Livy in particular, and in the museums of southern France, which house strange hooks for skulls. The Gauls, and presumably the other Celtic peoples, used to cut off the heads of their conquered enemies and keep them not only as trophies of war, but also as sacred objects.[10] This practice would appear to have something in common with the presence of a head on a plate held by two girls in the tale of *Peredur*. The best known historical example of this custom concerns the Roman consul Postumius, who was conquered and killed by the Gallic Boii, who then covered his skull in gold and used it as a ritual vessel (Livy, XXIII, 24). This golden vessel is not unlike the Grail itself.

THE ARCHETYPAL EPIC OF THE GRAIL

The second section of the *Mabinogion* is about a severed head, and, since it is one of the oldest Welsh narratives, representing the British tradition before the separation of the Bretons, deserves further examination. It is the story of Bran the Blessed, a mythological character of some importance, whom certain scholars have identified with King Ban of Benoic, Launcelot's father. He is, in any case, one of the many faces of the Fisher-King.

Wales, *The Head of Bran*

The expedition to Ireland mounted by Bran and the British, to avenge the injury to his sister Branwen and to recover a magic cauldron that brings the dead back to life, struck disaster. Bran, *wounded in the foot by a poisoned spear*, asked the seven surviving Britons to cut off his head and carry it with them, which they did. Together with Branwen, they reached Harddlech, where they settled. "They began to lay in a wealth of food and drink and consume it. Three birds came to sing them a song, which made other birds they had heard seem dull. This meal lasted for seven years, at the end of which they left for Gwales in Penvro." There they stayed in a great hall with the head of Bran fully displayed. "They remembered nothing of all the suffering they had seen and all they had experienced, nor of any pain in the world; they stayed for twenty-four years and it seemed to them the best and most agreeable time in all their lives. They felt no more tiredness and none of them could see that the others had aged at all since the time they had arrived. The presence of the head was no more painful than when Bendigeit Vran was alive." After the twenty-four years, they opened a door and immediately their memories returned along with their tiredness and sufferings, and they went to carry out Bran's last wishes that his head should be buried in the White Hill in London. (J. Loth, *Mabinogion*, vol. 1, pp. 142–9.)

This strange story, "The Hospitality of the Sacred Head" has many analogies with the Procession and the Banquet of the Grail. First of all, there is a cauldron that brings the dead back to life, and, having failed in his attempt to recover it, Bran gives his head to his companions as a kind of substitute. Bran is wounded in the foot with a poisoned spear and, like the Fisher-King, becomes impotent and, therefore, unfit to rule. Then the vengeance aspect is clearly evident in the fact that the expedition to Ireland was mounted to avenge the injury to Branwen. There is also much in common between Wolfram's Grail and the head, which brings food and drink to Branwen and the seven survivors, making them lose all idea of time and preventing them from growing old. Thanks to it they reach a kind of paradise (comparable to the Land of the Fairies so often described in Irish literature), where there is neither death, suffering nor disease. It is the paradise they lost at birth. This is clear proof of the head's maternal, feminine function, supported by the presence of the birds of the mother goddess Rhiannon, and also of Branwen, whose name means, among other things, "white breast". She may well have been the bearer of the head, therefore the bearer of the Grail.

This passage from the tale of Bran would appear to be one aspect of the original archetype of the Grail. Certainly mediaeval authors were familiar with the legend of Bran's severed head, since it occurs in works about the knights of the Round Table and the Quest for the Grail.

Manessier, *Third Continuation of Perceval*

During the tribulations of the Quest, Perceval had to fight a certain Partinal of the Red Tower, whom he beat, cutting off his head and hanging it from his saddle (like the Gauls described by Diodorus of Sicily, V, 29). Perceval returned to the Castle of the Grail, where the Fisher-King, wounded and lame, *rose to his feet, perfectly cured, as soon as he caught sight of the head*, which Perceval gave to him. The king thanked him *for having taken revenge* on his enemy, and had the trophy placed at the top of the highest tower. (Potvin edition, lines 48, 340 ff.)

The theme of vengeance appears essential to this anecdote, since the Fisher-King is cured simply by looking at the head, which symbolises it. However much we discuss the excessive imagination of Chrétien's continuators and criticise their distortions of the original aspect of the Grail, they must still have had access to written or oral legends of Celtic origin. There is no other possible explanation for the persistence of the theme of vengeance associated with the king's wound, the severed head, and the feast in the castle. All these elements occur in a fourteenth-century work written in Latin by Pierre Bercheur. This concerns an adventure of Gawain, who appears, from a number of references, to be one of the oldest of Arthur's companions and, in addition, the hero of the original Quest.

Pierre Bercheur, *Reductorium Morale*

Galvagnus (Gawain) had escaped his enemies by diving into a lake, where he discovered a submerged palace, which he entered. In a hall "there stood a table covered in food; there was an empty seat waiting. But he could see no way out. Being hungry, he had begun to eat when he suddenly saw the head of a dead man on a dish, and, lying on a stretcher near the hearth, a giant, who leapt to his feet, hit the ceiling with his head and shouted to Gawain that he must not touch the food. So he could not eat and, after many marvellous things, he managed to escape, though he never knew how. (1521 edition, book XIV, folio 319.)

It is tempting to equate the giant with Bran the Blessed, who was so huge that he could even, when needed, act as a bridge over a river for his warriors. In any case, there is no doubt about the head placed on a dish and a banquet being prepared, though Gawain is unworthy to touch it, as he is in the Cistercian Quest. The seat standing ready for the hero is amazingly like the Perilous Seat of the Round Table; this is reserved for Galahad, who eventually brings the adventures to a successful conclusion. Meanwhile, Gawain's adventure is not unique, for it appears again in slightly distorted form in one of the sequels to Chrétien's *Perceval*.

Pseudo-Wauchier I, *First Continuation of Perceval*

Gawain made his way into the castle of Bran de Lis, which stood on the bank of a river, and reaching a great hall, noticed a meal lying prepared. But when he went to eat he discovered more than a hundred boars' heads on a dish. Terrified, he crossed himself, and then saw lying on a bed near the fire a knight, Bran de Lis, who woke and attacked him. (Roach edition.)

Bran de Lis ("Bran of the Court") is obviously Bran the Blessed and also the Fisher-King. A text entitled *The Elucidation*, which can be taken as a preface to Chrétien's *Perceval*, though it was written later, specifies that the Fisher-King was a man "qui moult savait de nigromance qu'il muast cent fois sa semblance" ("who knew so much magic that he could change his appearance a hundred times"). This, and the fact that his daughter (the Maiden of the Grail) or his sister (Branwen) or his mistress (Kundry) can appear to the heroes of the Quest in so many different assumed shapes, proves that he belongs to the Other World.

In the French romance *Perlesvaux*, based on the tradition of Robert de Boron and dating from around 1200 A.D., Launcelot encountered, in a deserted castle, a richly equipped knight, who told Launcelot to cut off his head with an axe or submit to beheading himself. In any case, Launcelot was to return to the castle in a year to be beheaded by the same knight. Launcelot agreed, cut off the knight's head and left the castle. Then he realised that both the head and body had disappeared.[11]

The "game of the beheaded man" obviously meant very little to the author of *Perlesvaux*, though he obligingly related it. The Irish tale of *The Feast of Bricriu* contains a complete archetype, if not an explanation.

Ireland, *The Game of the Beheaded Man*

The three Ulster champions, Cú Chulainn, Loegaire and Conall, were quarrelling over the "part of the hero", which was

to be given to the most valiant of them. After submitting to
various judgements, all of which gave first place to Cú Chulainn
but were contested by the other two, the three champions went
to obtain the judgement of Uath Mac Immonainn ("the Terrible
Son of Great Fear"), a wild and formidable giant, who said to
them, "I have an axe. Let one of you take it in your hand and
cut off my head today, and I shall cut off his head tomorrow."
Conall and Loegaire refused to accept this deal, but Cú
Chulainn agreed. "After pronouncing an incantation over the
blade of his axe, Uath laid his head on the stone before Cú
Chulainn, who took the weapon and cut off his head. Then
Uath left and dived into the lake, holding his axe in one hand
and his head against his chest with the other." When, the
following day, Cú Chulainn came as arranged and laid his head
on the stone, Uath, who appeared to be as well as ever, was
content to brandish his axe three times over the neck and back
of the hero, declaring him worthy of the honour he claimed.
(D'Arbois de Jubainville, *L'Épopée celtique en Irlande*,
pp. 133—5.)

Any precise interpretation of this anecdote would be risky, but
two things do emerge clearly. First, there is a kind of mutual
sacrifice, which ends in a sham (sacrifice of a substitute victim or
through some ritual symbolic gesture), and suggests real bloody
vengeance according to the *law of retaliation*. Second, the giant
whose head is severed is not really dead, but resembles those
cephaloferous saints who abound in Christian epic, taking their
decapitated heads under their arms and continuing their Masses or
finishing whatever else they had started doing. In fact, the giant
(Bran, the Fisher-King, Master of the Other World) knows nothing of
death because he is, in some ways, the god of death and of life. So
completely did the author of *Perlesvaux* misunderstand this, that his
Launcelot, returning after a year to meet the giant he decapitated, is
met by the dead man's brother, and escapes his beheading only
because two maidens intercede on his behalf.[12] There is an almost
identical adventure in *Sir Gawaine and the Green Knight*, an English
romance of the fourteenth century, in which Gawain is the hero.

The severed head must be of exceptional importance. A strange
passage in Chrétien's *Lancelot* introduces the Maiden of the Mule,
who, in this case, is the sister of Meleagant and belongs to the Other
World. She demands from Launcelot the head of the knight he has
just beaten, and carries it away with a promise to recompense the
hero for his gift by helping him whenever he wishes. Chrétien gives
no explanation as to the meaning of this gesture.

Pseudo-Wauchier's *First Continuation of Perceval* contains the
same story, but in this case the protagonist is Caradoc, one of

Arthur's most long-standing companions and certainly a Breton.[13] An unknown man, arriving at the king's court, challenges all those present by asking that one of them should cut off his head, provided he allows his own head to be cut off after the passage of a year. Caradoc, son of the King of Vannes, accepts the ordeal and after a year submits to mock decapitation by the unknown man, who then reveals himself to be the wizard Eliavres, Caradoc's real father. Later, when his mother wishes to wreak some strange vengeance on her son, a snake winds itself round Caradoc's arm and sucks the life from him. He can be saved only by the sacrifice of a virgin. This last theme is repeated in the Quest for the Grail, when Perceval's sister gives her life-blood to cure a leper woman.

There may well be a link between decapitation, or mock decapitation, and feminine vengeance, though this particular case of maternal vengeance on the son is difficult to explain without recourse to the curse uttered by Arianrod against her son Lleu Llaw Gyffes, and is obviously a kind of counterbalance to the main theme of paternal recognition of the son. When Eliavres officially acknowledges Caradoc, his mother is abandoned and takes her revenge by withdrawing from her son the life she had given him. It marks the passing from a maternal, gynaecocratic order to a patriarchal, androcratic state.

This change-over is brought about through the game of the decapitated man, an ancient and bloody ritual, of which the severed head on a dish is the last relic. It is reminiscent of circumcision and all ceremonies of initiation into adulthood, practices characteristic of so-called primitive civilisations.

There are also references to such practices in the works of classical writers about the Celts. In Pomponius Mela (III, 2) we find these useful lines: "Gaul is inhabited by proud and superstitious peoples who once carried savagery so far as to sacrifice human victims, regarding such offerings as the most effective and the most pleasing to the gods. [The Romans and the Greeks tended to forget the similar sacrifices practised by their early ancestors, as witness the legend of Iphigenia.] This atrocious practice has been abolished in their land, but traces of it still remain: *for, although they refrain from taking the life of those men whom they consecrate to their divinities, they still lead them onto their altars and wound them slightly*."

So the severed head borne on a dish appears to have connections both with the game of the decapitated man and with the last traces of an act of vengeance that, though entirely ritualistic, allows us to glimpse behind it the face of the mother, the original goddess. But, since the head represents the earliest aspect of the Grail and Wolfram's stone the most recent, we should try to establish some connection between the two.

In the tale of Branwen, the last task of the seven survivors is to bury Bran's head in the White Hill in London, thus returning the essential part of his body, and therefore of the whole creature, to the maternal breast of the earth. But the head must be buried in a specific place where it can achieve something, where the head of the country, its capital will stand, a true omphalos from which life and intelligence will radiate. The Romans had a similar legend. "While digging on that mountain to hollow out the foundations of the building, the head of a man was found", wrote Pliny the Elder in *Naturales Historia* (XXVIII, 2). In *Contra Gentes* (VI), Arnobius asked, "Which man does not know that the tomb of Tolus Vulcentanus is in the Capitol at Rome, and that while digging the foundations they found the head of a man which had been buried there a short time before, although it was alone and had been separated from the other parts of the body?" Denys d'Halicarnasse wrote, "Tarquinius Superbus had a temple to Jupiter built on the Capitoline Hill in 509. . . . Under ground they found the head of a man who appeared to have been killed recently, and warm, red blood still flowed from it." This explains why the hill that was to become the head of Roman authority acquired the name *Caput Tolis*.

And yet the key to the problem must be sought in Ireland, in the tales of the Ulster cycle about King Conchobar and the "clan" of the Red Branch. (The word "clan" is not strictly accurate here, but it is used for want of a better term to describe what was in fact a kind of warriors' society, a mystico-religious, political organisation whose members were blood-brothers.) The "Red Branch" or "Red Bough" actually denotes one of the buildings in which the king of Ulster used to assemble his warriors. "Conchobar had three houses, the Red Branch, the Variegated House and the Bloody Branch. Heads and spoils lay in the latter, while the Red Branch was red with kings, and spears, shields and swords were kept in the Variegated House."[14] There is something rather strange about three halls of this kind; indeed, the one kept for spoils and, more specifically, for heads, recalls the "skull hooks" discovered in the sanctuaries of the Celto-Ligurians (particularly the Salyans) of the south of France. But, more than that, the ritual of "brotherhood" that ordains meeting in one hall, storing heads in a second and weapons in a third relates to the happenings in the Castle of the Grail, where, in the presence of its inhabitants (the initiates into the "clan") and the traveller (who is undergoing some kind of initiation test), there is a procession parading a platter for the banquet, a dish carrying a head, and a spear. It might be argued that this is just a matter of coincidence, or over-enthusiastic interpretation out of tune with scientific methods in current use; but scientific progress itself relies on people who are prepared to leave the beaten track and have the courage of their convictions. Besides, the ceremony of the Grail, which is generally agreed to be Celtic in origin, can hardly have arisen from nothing at all. Indeed, two of the tales of the Red Branch, *The Seat of Dun Eadair* (or Howth) and *The Death of Conchobar*, considerably illuminate this point.

Ireland, *The Head of Mesgegra*

Because of the poet-Druid Athirne the Importunate, the Ulstermen had to make war on Mesgegra, King of Leinster. Conall Cerach lost two of his brothers in the fighting and to avenge them he pursued the King of Leinster, whom he overtook when he was alone with one of his servants who had just cut off his fist as the result of a quarrel. Conall fought Mesgegra and cut off his head, which he then placed on a stone at the edge of the ford. "A drop of blood fell from the neck onto the stone and ran across it to the ground. Then he put Mesgegra's head on another stone; the head passed through the stone."[15] Conall took the head and placed it on his own, but it fell onto his shoulder and "his eyes began to squint".[16] Mesgegra's wife, whose name was Buan ("Eternal") arrived, and Conall tried to force her to come with him on the pretext that the order came from Mesgegra's head. But she refused, gave a great shout and died. Conall then tried to take hold of the head again and told his servant to carry it, but it was impossible to lift. Then he said to his servant, "Take out the brains with your sword, take them away and mix them with earth to make a ball for a sling." (*The Seat of Dun Eadair*.)

This ball was then exhibited in the hall of the Bloody Branch. One day when the Ulstermen were drunk and Conchobar could not restore peace among them, Conall had the "brains of Mesgegra" brought to him. This inspired such terror that when he challenged the other warriors to single combat with stone and sling no one would oppose him, and the "brains" were put away again with harmony and brotherhood restored. But Cet, son of Maga, a warrior from Leinster, who was always in search of an evil deed (an Ulsterman's head to cut off), knowing that "Mesgegra had predicted that his death would be avenged by his own head", seized the "brains" and managed to throw them at Conchobar's head. Conchobar's doctor refused to remove the ball and would only tie it to him with a golden thread. Conchobar was disabled in some way and could only remain seated and watch the others. After seven years he lost his temper, the "brain of Megegra" burst from his head, and he died. He was later avenged by Conall Cernach, who killed Cet, son of Maga, and cut off his head. (*The Death of Conchobar*. D'Arbois de Jubainville, *L'Épopée celtique en Irlande*, pp. 368 ff.)

This epic tale is rather unusual. In keeping with the trophies of the Bloody Branch, it introduces protagonists of some stature and, moreover, revolves round a series of acts of vengeance. The Ulstermen originally went to war with Mesgegra to avenge the poet-Druid Athirne, whose magic orders Mesgegra had disobeyed. Conall avenged the death of his two brothers at the hands of the Leinstermen by killing Mesgegra, whose death was then avenged by Cet on Conchobar. Finally, Conall avenged Conchobar's death by killing Cet. The first link in the chain was Mesgegra's refusal to give his wife, Queen Buan, to Athirne.

Then there is the drop of blood that falls from Mesgegra's neck and is very like the drop that falls from the spear in the Procession of the Grail. It is dangerous and has corrosive powers, even causing infirmity, since Conall becomes cross-eyed. Indeed, the whole head is dangerous and passes through the stone. It has to be mixed with earth to be neutralised. Nevertheless, it remained the instrument of vengeance.

This extraordinary legend, which might well be the original, archetypal epic of the Quest for the Grail, endorses, if not an identity, then an analogy between the head and the stone. This we have already noticed in the fact that the head of Bran had to be carefully buried in the White Hill in London.

So it comes as less of a surprise that Wolfram von Eschenbach's German version should have a stone Grail as counterpart to the head in the Welsh *Peredur*. In fact, *Peredur* does contain a reference to a magic stone, which has both benevolent and destructive powers. "In this cairn there is a snake and in the tail of the snake a stone, which has the property that whoever holds it in one hand may have in the other all the gold he can wish for."[18] Peredur killed this snake in the end, but not before fighting an *addanc* and also a kind of dragon, which he succeeded in killing only with the help of another stone, which was given him by a mysterious woman and made him invisible.[19]

Another magic stone famous in Irish tradition is the Stone of Fal, which is the Stone of Sovereignty. *The Battle of Mag Tuireadh* says that, "The Stone of Fal, which was at Tara, was brought from Falias, and it cried out under each king who governed Ireland." *The Race of Conaire the Great* mentions "The Stone of Fal, the Penis-Stone . . . when a man was to accede to the throne of Tara, it cried out . . . so that everybody could hear it." "Conn saw a stone at his feet. He climbed onto it and the stone cried out so loudly that it could be heard across Tara. When he asked the *fili* why the stone had cried out and what kind of stone it was, they asked for a delay of fifty-three days before replying. Finally they said that the name of the stone was Fal and that it came from the island of Fal in Tara, in the land of Fal. It should have been at Tailtiu, where the famous games had taken place, and a chief who had found it on the last day of the feasting there would be dead within the year. The number of cries the stone had emitted when Conn had put his foot on it signified how many kings of his race would rule over Ireland."[20] A commentary on this passage reads, "*Fo-ail*, meaning 'under-rock', or 'rock under a king' ". There have been attempts to establish an analogy between the name Fal and the word "phallus", as the stone is called *Fal ferb cluiche* ("Fal, phallus of stone") in some texts. But it has no phallic characteristics whatsoever, and its association with sovereignty suggests, on the contrary, that it is feminine.

Our search for the archetypal epic of the Quest for the Grail ends here with the Stone of Sovereignty and the story of Mesgegra. The Quest for the Grail is essentially a bloody struggle for sovereign power between the members of a community. This sovereignty is woman, as queen or goddess, the symbolic image of the omnipotent mother whose children we all are. Mesgegra loses his life and his head because he has refused to give away his wife, Buan, the *eternal*. The ensuing acts of vengeance, marked by a row of heads, is the struggle between the successors. Since both Mesgegra and Buan are now dead, the head represents all that remains of former sovereignty, and it is both dangerous and beneficent, bleeds and kills. As power passes from woman to man, the sovereign-head is transformed into an aggressive weapon and forges the structures of the new masculine society. Just as Queen Guinevere's successive lovers each took their share in her sovereignty, so the strongest man claims ownership of the head, until justice, the voice of the earth, the voice of the goddess, can make itself heard through the Stone of Fal, and restore a temporary balance. Meanwhile, the possessors of sovereign power apparently continue to kill each other, leaving the enjoyment of their power to the immediate victor. This emerges clearly from Chrétien's *Chevalier au Lion*, in which Yvain, having killed the Black Knight, immediately marries his widow, who has a characteristic double in the Magic Fountain, which brings rain and fertility.

We now have to discover the deeper meaning of this quest that makes men fight for the possession of woman, and to find what meaning should be given to the concept of "sovereignty". Only then can we explain the epic quest, in which symbolic objects like the spear that bleeds, the dish, the head or the stone are merely ideographs. It is this that makes it so convenient to interpret the Quest as a religious or mystical ritual, as twelfth- and thirteenth-century Christian authors did. The fact that they had no difficulty in doing so proves that the basic outline already existed, but as a mystical, pagan theme dating from the dawn of time.

THE MYSTICAL ARCHETYPE OF THE GRAIL

In all the texts relating to the Grail, the characters who live in the

Castle of the Grail, or those who are linked to them in some way, appear in continually changing and varied forms. The Fisher-King was not the only person who could change his appearance at will. Kundry the Witch is both the Hideous Damsel of the Mule and the queen who bears the Grail. Similarly, in all Celtic epics, Gaelic and Welsh, the hero often assumes many different forms and names. The Grail itself varies, from Chrétien's bowl, to Wolfram's stone, to the dish or head of *Peredur*. It may be many other things besides: a vessel in the *Quête du Saint Graal*, a chalice in the *Morte d'Arthur* of Thomas Malory. We should also remember that one archetype of the Grail is the famous ritual and magic cauldron that appears throughout the legends of the Celtic islands. Its significance merits careful study.

From proto-historic and Celtic archaeology we learn that the cauldron was in everyday use in Gaul and in the British Isles. Although prehistoric man began roasting game (having hitherto eaten it raw), it was not until the Neolithic era that receptacles that could stand in the fire began to appear. Thus the introduction of the cauldron was a definite improvement in cooking methods and marked a refinement in civilisation. Celtic cauldrons varied greatly in size and material, often being made of bronze, copper or silver, and sometimes richly decorated with engraving, like the Gundestrup cauldron. When there was no metal available they were probably made out of clay. According to Posidonius, "Those who serve the drinks carry cups shaped like cooking-pots and made of clay or silver, as are the plates and bowls containing meats, though some are bronze and sometimes baskets woven from cane replace the bowls." In all, the cauldron was a domestic implement, though we know from Strabo (VII, 2) that there were also sacred cauldrons used as objects of worship. Obviously, its religious and symbolic significance led to the cauldron itself becoming part of mythology.

Without going into detail, it is useful here to quote the two chief properties of the magic cauldron in Irish and Welsh writings. A Welsh poem by Taliesin describes a "cauldron that does not boil the food of a coward" and refers to a tradition also evident in an Irish poem that describes how Cú Chulainn went with Curoi into a mysterious fortress to fetch a "cauldron streaming with gold and silver". The Welsh cauldron of Tyrnog also would not boil the food of a coward, while the *basin* (cauldron) of Diwrnach the Gael seems to have provided food in abundance. Again, amongst the Thirteen Jewels of Britain, there is the magic basket of Gwyddno: "If food for one man was put in it, when opened up it offered food for a hundred." When Keridwen, the mother goddess, wanted to give her son (Avanc-Du) intelligence, and prepared a cauldron of inspiration for him, three drops of her brew fell by chance of the finger of Gwyon Bach, who immediately possessed knowledge of the past, present and future, and as a result became the bard Taliesin.

But the cauldrons of Dagda in Ireland and of Bran and Peredur in Wales are the most interesting, because of both their function and the context in which they are found. They are true archetypes of the object called the Grail, and are probably the direct source of the significance given to the Grail in its Christian setting.

Ireland, *The Cauldron of Dagda*

"The cauldron of Dagda was brought from Murias; no company departed without being grateful to it." When Dagda went to the camp of his enemies, the Fomors, they made him eat the contents of a huge cauldron, which they had emptied into a hole dug in the ground. Dagda managed to finish this phenomenal meal. (*The Battle of Mag Tiureadh.* D'Arbois de Jubainville, *L'Épopée celtique en Irlande*, pp. 426—7.)

Wales, *The Cauldron of Bran*

"I will make full amends by giving you a cauldron whose properties are as follows: if one of your men is killed today, you have only to throw him into it and tomorrow he will be as well as ever, except that he will no longer be able to speak. . . .

"The Gaels began to light a fire under the cauldron of resurrection and threw the corpses in it until it was full. The following day they rose again, warriors once more and formidable as ever, except that they could not speak." (*Branwen*, J. Loth, *Mabinogion*, vol. 1, p. 129.)

Wales, *The Cauldron of Peredur*

"He went to the court of the sons of the King of Sufferings and, entering, saw only women, who rose to greet him and made him very welcome. He had begun to talk to them when a horse approached with a corpse in the saddle. One of the women rose, took down the corpse, washed it in a tub full of warm water which was deeper than the door, and applied some precious ointment. The man was restored to life and came to greet him with a joyful face. Two more corpses arrived, borne on saddles; the woman restored both of them to life in the same way." (*Peredur.* J. Loth, *Mabinogion*, vol. 2, p. 94.)

The Celtic cauldron has at least two characteristics: it provides abundantly and it restores to life. The Christianised Grail also provides abundantly, as those who participate in the Banquet of the Grail receive on their plates the food they most prefer. Similarly it provides immortality, bringing the dead back to life by giving them eternal life, but on an entirely new plane which has nothing to do with their past existence. That is why the corpses resurrected after treatment in the Cauldron of Bran cannot speak — they belong to the Other World.

This sheds new light on the head swimming in blood on the dish presented to Peredur, and, in a general way, on all the severed heads of Irish or Welsh epics. The rebirth of life comes through vengeance by blood, just as the *sacrifice* of the Christian Mass is basically the ritual repetition of the sacrifice of Christ, who gave his blood that men might live. Thus it is easy to see why the Grail was so speedily absorbed into Christian thought: there was no inherent contradiction in the process.

But we should not lose sight of the original, feminine aspect of the Grail. A short Irish narrative provides a link between the barbaric ritual of death by hanging over the basin, and the goddess who is always in shadow, in that Other World that is the Castle of the Grail.

Ireland, *The Adventure of Nera*

While at their house in Cruachan, Ailill and Medb asked those present at the feast to go to the torture house and apply the willow to the feet of one of the prisoners whom they found hung by the feet. (Julius Caesar refers to certain tribes that "have dummies of colossal proportions, made of *woven cane*, which they fill with living men and set fire to, so that the men fall victim to the flames" (*De Bello Gallico*, VI, 16).) Those who went in order to win the promised reward returned very quickly because they were afraid, but Nera went bravely and the prisoner said to him, "Take me on your back so that I may go and drink with you. I was very thirsty when I was hung." Nera agreed and carried him into a house where "there were tubs to bathe and wash in and in each of them a brew . . . from which the prisoner drank a mouthful, blowing the last drop through his lips over the people in the house so that they all died."

Nera took the prisoner back to the torture house, but on his way back to Cruachan he saw the hill burned before him and a pile of severed heads, the heads of his men. On the hill there was also a band of warriors, whom he followed into the depths of Cruachan. His presence was noticed in the *sidh*, and the king said to him, "Go into that house, where a solitary woman will receive you." That was how Nera was "married".

He stayed in the *sidh* until the day when his wife told him that the destruction of the fortress of Cruachan had been an illusion. "It was an army of ghosts that came towards you, but it will all come true unless you warn your men." When Nera asked how he should do this, she replied, "Get up and go towards them; they are still around the same cauldron and its contents have not yet subsided." Nera was dumbfounded, for "it seemed to him that he had been in the *sidh* for three days and three nights (a symbolic, rather than a literal number, often used in Irish epics to express a lapse of several months.) The woman advised him to tell his men to be ready to destroy the *sidh* on the day of Samain, or its inhabitants would destroy the fortress of Cruachan. She told Nera that she was expecting his child and persuaded him to return, before his men destroyed the *sidh*, to take away herself, their son and her cattle.

When asked by his men where he came from, Nera replied, "I was in lovely lands, with great treasures, precious things, rich ornaments, good food. . . ." On the day appointed by Ailill, he returned to the *sidh*, left it with his wife, his son and the cattle. Then "the man of Connaught and the black army of the Exile (Fergus mac Roig) entered and destroyed the *sidh*, seizing all they found there." Among their trophies was a marvellous crown. Then Nera returned to the *sidh* and stayed there. (Egerton, *Cahiers d'histoire et de folklore*, vol. 6, 1782, pp. 66—72; quoted in Lengyel, *Le Secret des Celtes*, pp. 268—70).

This is a revised version of the story of Nera and appears somewhat confused, though interesting. Note first of all the challenge, which is comparable to that of the Grail in that it involves performing an act of vengeance upon a mysterious prisoner, probably from the Other World, who is hung by the feet in the position of those consecrated to Teutates and, like them, probably condemned to be burned. But, helped by Nera to quench his thirst before the sentence is carried out, he takes a drink out of every vat, the last harmful drop killing all those upon whom it falls. This has obvious links with the three drops from the cauldron of Keridwen that give Gwyon Bach perfect knowledge, while the rest of the contents poisons the river; and is reminiscent of the drop that flows from Celtchar's spear and poisons him, and of the wound of the Fisher-King and the curse that befalls the inhabitants of the Castle of the Grail.

Yet Nera performed the challenge, and found himself in an *elsewhere* that was not *spatial* but *temporal*; or, more accurately, *outside time*, in the Other World.

What makes the Celtic Other World so distinctive, and quite unlike Mediterranean or Nordic concepts, is its location alongside the normal universe of humans. To reach it, one has only to cross a wood, a hill, a river or a stretch of the sea, always provided one knows the password and has passed some test, as it remains unrecognisable, invisible to the unaware. The only exception occurs when, during the feast of Samain, the mounds (or megalithic monuments) known as the *sidh*, the Other-World dwelling places of the Tuatha Dé Danann and the refuge of ancient gods and dead heroes, are opened to permit communication between the two worlds. Then the people of the *sidh* can invade the world of humans and humans the Other World. There are no special privileges for those who have passed the test on the night of Samain, for it is the great Celtic feast of the unity of the two worlds, which are really only separated by appearance and *co-exist*. The Christianised version of Samain, the Feast of All Saints on 1st November, provides food for thought about the permanence of traditions; for one can find no better evidence of the essential unity of the two worlds of the living and the dead than in this festival dedicated to the memory of the departed through their presence in the minds of the living.

So Nera, suddenly thrown into the Other World and outside time, imagined he saw the ruin of the fortress of Cruachan. Like Taliesin after he had drunk the three drops from the cauldron of Keridwen, he had knowledge of the future but was not aware of it. He saw everything round Cruachan burned, like the waste land surrounding the Castle of the Grail ("Gradually the fields around Perceval became more desolate; he could find neither villages nor ploughed fields, but all around him fallow land and dried grass; in the deserted orchards no tree bore fruit. . . .") So, like Perceval, a prey to despondency, Nera followed the band of ghosts and entered the *sidh*. There the king greeted him amicably, because he had passed the test and probably also because he had helped the prisoner. He was admitted to the universe of the *sidh* and given a wife. This part of the story is reminiscent of Launcelot of the Lake being welcomed into the castle of Corbenic by King Pelles, *who gave him his daughter*, Helen, bearer of the Grail, by whom he later had a son. It would be unreasonable to suppose that these similarities are a coincidence.

Nera's wife provided him with everything — affection, riches, even glory. She also had total authority in the world of the *sidh*, higher even than that of the king, because it was her decision to tell Nera to alert his men, thereby entailing the destruction of her own race, or, more precisely, the destruction of everyone who was not regenerated by contact with Nera. Basically she was acting for herself and her future son and represented sovereignty and power, riches and fertility. Nera was only her agent. So, although he would be able to regain his domain unchallenged after the destruction of the *sidh* and become King of the Grail, like Perceval, *the Queen would still be there*.

Nera's story probably contains the basic factors of the original, mystical Quest. A state of permanence has to be achieved, involving the resolution of the life—death dilemma and the abolition of time, with its inherent concepts of beginning and end. Having succeeded in his epic quest (which in this story is still represented by heroism and a warring expedition), Nera was no longer in one world or the other, but in both at once. When he returned to settle in the *sidh* after its destruction by Ailill and Medb, basically nothing had changed for him: the future was only the infinite prolongation of the past, or, rather, as time had been abolished, there was neither past nor future but a different state, which defies the verbal explanations of traditional logic. In the image of the divinity that is both life and death and neither one nor the other, Nera found himself in a state of being and non-being, which is the subconscious longing of all mankind, though it may have tormented the Celts more than anyone else. It is significant that even in fairly recent times Breton story-tellers used to begin their tales with the following reflection, which is profound rather than strange: "Once upon a time, there was no time, and it was then that . . .".[21]

This contradictory style expresses a whole mentality, a whole system of thought, represented by the taste of baroque intellectuals for the "world inside-out", the "game of opposites" beloved of the surrealists, the works of Lewis Carroll, or the mania of Breton story-tellers for systematically jumbling the tenses of verbs in a tale or a poem and transposing certain nouns in the sentence. For example, "Tomorrow I went to the pig to sell my village. I shall not see the man I met but he bought me a table at the inn-keeper's glass. Besides I had wet my river while crossing the shirt and I shall be soaked when I mistook the wind while observing the direction of the road. . . ."

Nera had attained the stage of non-temporal kingship reached by Wolfram's Parzival, but with the help of woman, just as Parzival was guided by Kundry, the double of Condwiramur, and Peredur was haunted by the Empress of many faces. Peredur—Parzival had been through long initiatory travels (an internal journey towards understanding), which took him from the castle where his mother secluded him (the maternal womb) to the mystico-sexual union by which he became King of the Grail (a return to the maternal womb). As René Nelli has shown,[22] there is an "eroticism of the Grail" which is not unlike the eroticism of the troubadours, though it gained from a wide variety of Celtic contributions regarding the specific interpretation of the role of woman as initiator. In a remarkable work on the troubadours,[23] Robert Lafont points out that "for them, death may well be something quite different from a halt in living time, a milestone to pass, a mystery to elucidate. It seems to be a reality that is experienced daily." That this poetic transcription of the experience of death is inseparable from love becomes clear when one reads the works of the troubadours. The same notion applies in the Celtic tradition, particularly in the legend of Tristan, and in Chrétien's and Wolfram's versions of the Grail legend, where the themes of the Provençal troubadours and the Celtic bards appear to mingle harmoniously.

In psychoanalytic terms, the Quest for the Grail can be explained as the return of son to mother. When Peredur—Perceval escaped from his home and fled from his mother, he went through his birth, which cost his mother her life, because she died as soon as he crossed the bridge. But Perceval could not grasp this, because he was still too affected by his egocentric, if temporary, intoxication with freedom and existence. His action, however, had serious repercussions, for ultimately it was the weight of the sin of his mother's death that prevented him from curing the Fisher-King and restoring fertility to the Land of the Grail at his first attempt. Meanwhile, he embarked on his long quest, with almost every stage marked by women. To expiate the death of his mother, meaning his own birth, he had to find on his own the road that would lead him to the Castle of the Grail, which was *surrounded by water and invisible most of the time*. The castle is an obvious symbol of the new mother, who can be approached only by a *son* or a *lover*. These, however, are one and the same, since every lover is unconsciously a son, just as every mistress is a mother.

Having failed the initiation test of his first journey to the Castle of the Grail, Perceval set out on his quest. The women he met, who bear an astonishing resemblance to the "fairies" and divinities encountered by the heroes of Celtic expeditions, all seemed to behave like the pieces in a game of chess, the object being to beat the king in order to take his place. But, both in the Quest for the Grail, seen as the *quest for woman*, and in a game of chess, the king can be beaten only with the co-operation of the queen, which, of all the pieces on the board, is *the only one that can move in any direction and assure victory*. This versatility of movement on the part of the queen, who is woman as sovereign, takes on a wide variety of guises in the Celtic epics and the Quest for the Grail.

Many versions of the Quest for the Grail pinpoint the role played by women in the long search for the sacred object. The various authors may have been following the mediaeval fashion of returning to women their long-lost importance; but there are too many incomprehensible details apparently rising from the distant mythological past to warrant accepting this conclusion. In all such texts woman is both *one* and *many*, both stable and changing, and the heroes are very preoccupied with sexuality, even though their adventures have been censored to a point; the clear and explicit eroticism is surprising in a mystical quest for a vessel filled with the blood of Christ. For many of the attempts to transpose and translate the original nature of the Quest are so clumsy that eroticism reappears, showing through the disparate muddle of adventures.

Mythologically, the Quest for the Grail is an attempt to re-establish a displaced sovereignty, usurped by the masculine violence of the despoiling knight, while the kingdom rots and the king, the head of the family, is no longer the executor nor balancer of forces, but impotent. Only a strong young man who has proved his powers as a warrior and therefore as a man will be able to restore the original situation; and he is the appointed successor, the nephew of the wounded king. This theme, which is probably very old, appears well disguised in the loves of Launcelot and Guinevere, originally Gawain and Guinevere, and in the relationship of Tristan and Iseult, the wife of Tristan's maternal uncle.

Unfortunately, we have no way of knowing exactly what took place in the Castle of the Grail. We have, however, seen that the Grail is light, just as woman is light, and that both are the light of the sun. The image of the sun woman is also emphasised in some texts (such as the *Quête du Saint Graal* and later works) in which the Grail is actually a chalice; but, strangely, while it is intended to convey an increasingly Christian message, the reference is nevertheless extremely pagan and Celtic. For the motif of the chalice or cup appears in several Irish legends about sovereignty.

In *The Adventures of Art, Son of Conn*, which appears to be one of the versions of the Quest for the Grail, the theme of the perilous cup is interwoven with that of tasks to be overcome before reaching the goal of the journey, the chosen woman who represents sovereignty. Art also needs her to fight the influence of a *geis* that is affecting the kingdom of Ireland and is clearly analogous to the spell affecting the desolate Land of the Grail. Since this version of the story is outside any Christian sphere, we are better able to analyse the different episodes in terms of their intrinsic value.

> Ireland, *The Adventures of Art, Son of Conn*
> Because King Conn of the Hundred Battles had taken as concubine Becuna Cneisgel, a woman of the Tuatha Dé Danann exiled from the Land of Promise for some mysterious crime, Ireland was struck by infertility. The people tried sacrificing a child, for which a cow was substituted. But because the king could not send away his concubine, for he was bound to her by a *geis*, he still lacked a third of Ireland's harvest. One day, Becuna Cneisgel won a game of chess against Conn's son Art and forced him with another *geis* to bring back and marry a mysterious Delbchaen, the daughter of Morgan, who was on a distant island. Art left and had to overcome fantastic trials in his search for the fortress in which Delbchaen had taken refuge. He was received by her mother, who made him drink the contents of a cup; he had to choose between two, one full of poison, the other of wine, each held by a woman. Forewarned by a fairy queen, Art chose the right cup and then all he had to do was cut the head off his lady-love's mother, seize all the treasure in the castle, and take Delbchaen back to Ireland. Then Becuna Cneisgel gave up and left Ireland, which immediately returned to its former prosperity.

Note that the pivot in every stage of this story is a woman. A woman imposes the tasks upon Art; another is the object of his search; yet another, a mysterious queen, comparable to Peredur's Empress, who might well be just another face of Delbchaen, helps Art in his ordeal. An *evil* woman is responsible for Ireland's infertility through her relationship with the king; this had shaken the natural balance he controlled, just as the forbidden amorous adventure of the Fisher-King had rendered him impotent and his land barren. Finally, a woman holds the cup through which Art finds victory, for it contains the wine he drinks to give him the courage and strength to fulfil his quest.

There are traces of the same theme in the French romance *Huon de Bordeaux*, in which Oberon the dwarf, wishing to give power to Huon, entrusts him with his goblet, which fills up with wine at will. But nobody can drink from it unless he is pure; as soon as an evil man tries to take it in his hand, he destroys its properties. This may possibly explain why the Grail loses its power when in unworthy hands, just as the Cauldron of the Abyss described by the bard Taliesin cannot boil the food of a coward. For the drink is reserved for those who have deserved it, having first accomplished some deed of valour and performed all the tasks imposed on them.

The Elucidation[24] is very exact on this subject: once, when the Castle of the Grail was visible to everyone and could be visited, maidens used to receive travellers and offer them a reviving drink from golden cups. But one day king Amangon threatened one of the maidens and stole her cup; since then the kingdom lay barren, the leaves disappeared from the trees, the fields withered, the waters receded, and the Castle of the Grail and its maidens disappeared, so that nobody knew the way there any longer. The only man who could restore things to their original state was the one who could find the way and recognise the Fisher-King behind his many guises. The maidens are obviously reminiscent of all the fairies in Celtic legends who bring drinks for lost travellers and are often perched on hillocks, or occasionally found inside a dark, almost impenetrable fortress. The same theme clearly persists in the image of the Bearer of the Grail, daughter of the Fisher-King, who controls the omnipotence of sovereignty in the sacred drink and can offer it only to the privileged.

So, from whatever angle one analyses the legend of the Grail and all its many versions, some permanent and fundamental themes emerge: *vengeance by blood*, after some action that has shaken the balance of the world and led to the infertility of the kingdom; *the impotence of the king* who can no longer rule; *ritual sacrifice*, whether human or animal or through simple substitution of the victim or offering; *tasks* inflicted on those who set out on the Quest; *female characters* who belong to a fairy world and guide those who take part in the Quest; and the *queen, princess or empress* who controls the drink of power and sovereignty, which is given only to the man who has overcome all the tasks (the name Galahad probably comes from the Celtic *gal*, meaning "power"). The Quest for the Grail is inextricable from the quest for woman. Whoever finds her finds the Grail; and she who, while her land was cursed, grieved alone and infertile in the depths of her hidden castle, can form part of the ideal and perfect couple with the man for whom she was waiting. The languishing and impotent Fisher-King will be succeeded by the new, young King of the Grail, who can restore fertility to the surrounding countryside and symbolically to the woman who holds the cup, the dish or the stone, the priestess of a cult whose true meaning we may never know.

Of one thing we can be certain, however: we have again come face to face with the memory of the worship of some ancient goddess dethroned by male gods. This is clear from King Amangon's violent treatment of one of the divine maidens of the Castle of the Grail: he shaped his own fate by bending feminine power under his blind and brutish male force and stealing her sovereignty symbolised by a cup. In fact he was the father who had imposed his exclusive authority. Society has been in search of harmony ever since, and will not be able to find it until the young son of the mother comes and kills or castrates the father to restore her long-lost sovereignty. As an ideal, a myth, and long before the myth was absorbed into Christianity, the Quest for the Grail was the glorification of the chosen woman, the eternal divinity of many faces who still reigns in the underground caverns of the world. There she waits for her youngest son, in order to rise again into the open air and resume her title of Great Queen (Rhiannon-Matrona), restoring harmony to the society of her disunited sons, who will be reconciled in their love for the mother.

Chapter 8

Iseult, or the Lady of the Orchard

The hero of Julien Gracq's novel *Le Rivage des Syrtes* entered one of the half-abandoned gardens scattered about the town of Orsenna expecting to meditate in solitude, when he suddenly came across a girl leaning on her elbows at the very place where he usually did this. He was totally confused: "I was less affected by the beauty of that half-hidden face than by the feeling of heightened *dispossession* which seemed to grow within me from one second to the next. With the peculiar harmony between that dominating profile and a privileged place, and the dawning impression of a singular presence, I became increasingly convinced that the *queen of the garden* had just taken possession of her solitary domain. . . . It was not until much later that I understood her superior ability to become immediately inseparable from a landscape or an object. . . . Things opened up for Vanessa. She would take possession with a single gesture, or with a marvellously easy, yet unexpected inflection of the voice, like the word captured unerringly by a poet, and with the same loving and privately consented violence as a leader whose hand hypnotises a crowd."[1]

This is the theme, translated into poetic, but extremely expressive, terms, of the initiating and transforming woman, a theme that the Celts seem to have cultivated with brilliance and originality. Immediately she appears in a landscape, the woman transforms it and consequently its observer as well; he will never fully belong to himself again, for she has imperceptibly asserted her domination over the universe to which he belongs. This is one of the reasons why woman always appears a formidable creature to some men, who seem unable to distinguish between her real ability to possess and their idea of this. But they also want to be possessed, because woman brings them something they lack before meeting her. Leaving aside the romantic aspects of the love story, this argument forms the basic plot of the legend of Tristan and Iseult.

Tristan and Iseult, the best known of the Celtic legends, has come down to us from the twelfth century through writings that, though fragmentary, all interconnect along the main lines, thereby proving the existence of an original source, which is now lost. A pan-Celtic legend, it contains Breton, Welsh, Cornish, Pictish (in particular the name Tristan) and Irish elements, all of which blend together into a great epic tableau of unquestionable poetic beauty. The legend of Tristan has become one of the literary masterpieces of mankind.

The oldest texts are French, actually Anglo-Norman, pointing to either a Breton or British origin, since the Norman rulers of England were constant intermediaries between the twelfth-century British and Bretons, and the French. There are equally fragmentary German versions and an abbreviated Scandinavian version.[2] Strangely, the only written Celtic-language material that deals specifically with the legend of Tristan relates to various late episodes in the story, a notable example being the *Ystoria Trystan*, a very short Welsh narrative about the forced reconciliation of Tristan and Mark (J. Loth, *Revue celtique*, vol. 34, p. 358). By combining all these texts, however, one can approximate a reconstruction of the original legend.

Tristan and Isolde

Son of Rivalen de Loonois (in Wales) and of the sister of King Mark of Cornwall (Kernow), young Tristan was an orphan, brought up by Rohald le Foitenant and entrusted to the care of the squire Gorvenal. He learned the skills of war and the chase; also music and poetry, excelling at the harp, singing and composing "lays".

At the age of fifteen he was sent to Tintagel, where King Mark welcomed him to the court without knowing who he was. Three years later the day of reckoning came for the tribute Mark owed the King of Ireland. Three hundred boys and three hundred maidens were claimed every five years by the Morholt, the formidable warrior-brother of the Queen of Ireland,[3] unless a knight from Cornwall should venture to oppose him. But Tristan was the only man prepared to risk his life, and, resolved to go and fight the Morholt, he revealed his identity to his uncle. During the fight on the Isle of St Samson, Tristan was wounded by the Morholt's poisoned sword, but he wounded his opponent fatally, leaving a fragment of his sword in the other's head.

On his return to Cornwall, Tristan received a hero's welcome, but his wound in the hip (symbolic, like the Fisher King's wound in the thigh) became worse, despite the efforts of the doctors. He then asked leave to depart in a small boat equipped with a sail, provisions and his harp, intending to leave his voyage to chance and the mercy of God as to whether he found death or cure.[4] On the fifth day he landed in Ireland, where he was cured by the queen and her daughter Iseult. He had concealed his identity and pretended his name was Tantris. By way of thanks to the queen, he gave singing and harp lessons to the young Iseult, and then returned to Cornwall. There King Mark, who was not married, planned to make him heir to the throne, as was customary in matrilinear relationships, Mark being Tristan's uncle and therefore not only his adoptive father, but also a trustee for his mother's property. But the barons, jealous of Tristan, called upon the king to marry. To placate them, Mark swore that he would marry only the girl to whom belonged the golden hair a swallow had just dropped. Tristan, recognising the hair as belonging to Iseult, suggested to his uncle that he should go on his behalf to ask for her hand in marriage.[5]

He left Cornwall disguised as a merchant and arrived in Ireland. There a dragon, an enormous "crested snake" was creating havoc in the country. The king had promised his daughter to whoever rid Ireland of this scourge, so naturally Tristan went off to find the monster, and after a hard struggle managed to kill it. But he was wounded by the poisonous breath of the snake and an impostor claimed his victory. Then the queen and Iseult, suspecting some betrayal, sought to discover the truth and found Tristan unconscious. While nursing him back to health they discovered that the sword of "Tantris" had a piece missing and that the gap matched the piece of metal found in the Morholt's head. Iseult grabbed Tristan's sword and tried to avenge her uncle by killing him, but she yielded to Tristan's persuasions and forgave him, which suggested that she already loved him. Finally, Tristan asked for her hand for his uncle King Mark, to which the King of Ireland agreed, as such a marriage would restore peace between the two countries. A date was arranged for their departure and the queen gave Brangwain, Iseult's maid, a philtre containing a love potion that she was to pour out for the newly-wed couple on their wedding night, so that they would love each other for ever.

On the ship scudding along towards Cornwall, Iseult lamented the fact she had been promised to a king whom she did not know, and gave every sign of violent hatred towards Tristan, further evidence that she loved him and was terribly disappointed that he should have asked for her hand on behalf of another man. One very hot evening Tristan asked for a drink, and Brangwain mistakenly gave him and Iseult the love potion in a goblet. No sooner had they drunk it than they felt an irresistible love for each other and spent the night together, to the great despair of Brangwain. However, on their arrival in Cornwall Iseult was married to King Mark, and that night, under cover of darkness, Brangwain took Iseult's place in the king's bed so that he would suspect nothing.[6]

An ambiguous situation, worthy of the most vulgar music hall jokes, ensued. Tristan and Iseult used to meet whenever they could, even under the king's nose, but their favourite spot was an orchard, which, being enclosed, was an ideal place for the lovers. The orchard is obviously a symbol for the paradise (the Persian word for "orchard") that lovers re-create by their meeting. When Tristan wanted Iseult to meet him he would throw shavings of wood or bark into a stream which flowed from a source in the orchard, and passed close to the royal palace, where Iseult could see the signal. But the barons and the king's dwarf (the *gelos* and *losengiers* of the Provençal troubadours), aware of the lovers' tricks, warned the king, who decided to surprise them by lying in wait in the pine-tree that stood in the middle of the orchard. But Tristan and Iseult caught sight of his reflection in the fountain and cunningly avoided the danger. Later, however, they were actually caught in the act and condemned to death by King Mark, who was furious at his betrayal by the nephew he had regarded as a son. But Tristan escaped, freed Iseult, who was about to be handed over to a group of lepers, and the two lovers fled to the Forest of Morois, where they hid for several months.[7]

One day King Mark discovered the lovers asleep with Tristan's sword between them, but he decided not to kill them and, having exchanged his own sword for Tristan's, went away without waking them.[8] Then the two lovers, overwhelmed by Mark's show of mercy and realising that the situation could not continue, determined to make their peace with him. Tristan solemnly returned the queen to his uncle and went into exile,[9] finally reaching Brittany, where, after winning great fame, he married the daughter of Duke Hoel, *because she was called Iseult*.

But the marriage between Tristan and Iseult of the White Hands[10] was never consummated,[11] because he could not forget the woman to whom he was indissolubly bound.[12] He returned to Cornwall several times in various disguises in order to meet Iseult the Fair, and on each occasion their love reached new heights. (His brother Kaherdin, who accompanied him on one occasion, fell in love with Brangwain.) One day he entered the court of King Mark disguised as a fool and held an apparently irrelevant, though actually suggestive, conversation with the king, ending with the proposal, "King, I have a very beautiful sister whom I will give you in exchange for Iseult, whom I really love." Mark thought this very entertaining and asked the fool how he intended to treat the queen, to which Tristan replied with this parable: "Up in the air I live in a great and splendid glass hall, in whose very middle the sun's rays burn hot. It is suspended in the air and hangs in the clouds; whatever wind is blowing it neither sways nor swings. Next to the hall is a room made of crystal and richly panelled. When the sun rises tomorrow, a great brightness will spread over it."[13] After these preliminaries, Tristan made himself known to Iseult and was able to see her in secret. When he returned to Brittany he had as perfect a statue as possible made of her, and kept it in a castle to which he knew the hidden paths.[14]

After returning from his travels,[15] Tristan had to go to the help of a certain Tristan the Dwarf, whose sweetheart had been abducted by Estout the Proud of Castel-Fier.[16] But the expedition met with disaster, Tristan the Dwarf being killed and Tristan "wounded by a blow from a poisoned spear which passed through his kidneys, though he managed to relieve his anger by killing the man who wounded him."[17]

So Tristan asked Kaherdin to leave for Cornwall and bring back Queen Iseult. If his mission succeeded he was to put a white sail on his boat, if he failed a black sail, so that Tristan would be able to see from afar whether the Queen had come to his aid. Kaherdin went, and was returning with Iseult when first a storm and then a calm unfortunately delayed their voyage, much to Iseult's distress. Finally, when they were speeding towards port, Iseult of the White Hands, who had overheard Tristan's instructions to Kaherdin, and was consumed with jealousy, told her husband that the sail was black.[18] Tristan died, lacking the will and the strength to carry on living, and when Iseult reached the palace there was nothing left for her but to die as well. So the two lovers, united in death, were buried side by side in separate graves, and a vine and a rose-tree grew up, one from each, closely intertwining.[19]

Any interpretation of a legend so complex, and with such a poetic and philosophical range, is bound to be hazardous. First, the reconstruction from different texts is sure to be influenced by our twentieth-century attitudes, which means that we may even be misrepresenting the authentic structure. Secondly, while there is every reason to believe that the legend existed long before, the texts we have used date only from the twelfth century, when the story had already been adapted to suit a mediaeval audience whose pre-occupations differed greatly from those of Welsh, Breton or Irish Celts in the fifth and sixth centuries, when the action is supposed to have taken place. The motivations of Béroul and Thomas are very different, while Gottfried von Strassburg, like his contemporary and compatriot Wolfram von Eschenbach, betrays a certain sophistication. In any reconstruction of the legend of Tristan one is continually brushing against the original text without ever really coming to grips with it.

Of the subsequent adaptations of the legend, it is best to ignore the insipid fables written by the Comte de Tressan in 1782, in an era scarcely suited to an understanding of the myth; we should rather concentrate on Richard Wagner, whose grasp of its meaning enabled him to transpose the myth successfully. But, though he gave magnificent expression to the Germanic myths of the Ring cycle in both his libretti and his music, and showed a real understanding of the Celtic myth of the Grail, as revised and amended by Wolfram, he misconstrued the myth of Tristan. For it is hard to recognise the structure of the legend in the Schopenhauerian and Buddhist rigmarole of his opera, *Tristan und Isolde*, with its unspecified "sublimation", "transfiguration" and "annihilation". His two lovers become the symbols of suffering and discordant humanity, and find the ultimate solution in the motionless and peaceful unity of a nirvana, all will to live destroyed. This mixture of philosophies, together with the unquestionable beauty of Wagner's music and the rather esoteric aura of German romanticism, has misled us all into thinking of the story of Tristan and Isolde (or Iseult) as the loveliest and most moving, but also the most significant love story of the Western world.

The value of the Tristan legend is beyond doubt, but as a reflection of our Western, Mediterranean and Christian world it falls short. There seems to have been a deliberate attempt to make the story either a *justification of adultery* as a necessary contingent of monogamous society, or a *justification of masochism* (the *Liebestod*), closely linked with Germanic "melancholy". In this respect the heights of lunacy are reached by the diplomat-poet Paul Claudel, a purveyor of works dressed up in religious trappings for the enjoyment of snobs, who actually wrote, in a letter to Jacques Rivière, "How ridiculous the romantic fumes of purely carnal love and the braying of that great ass Tristan appear to me! Human love has no beauty unless unaccompanied by satisfaction."

This is the trap into which most of the adaptors of and commentators on the Tristan legend have fallen, notably Denis de Rougemont, who, nevertheless, displays great sensitivity and lucidity in his very beautiful book *Passion and Society*. In this work he makes an admittedly clear, accurate and valuable statement concerning

Western psychology: "The astounding success of the *Roman de Tristan* reveals in us, whether we like it or not, a hidden preference for unhappiness." Perhaps we have not really understood the *Roman de Tristan*, but superimposed upon it the preoccupations of Romano-Judaeo-Christian Western society, which are diametrically opposed to those shown up by an analysis of the actual work.

"It is unbelievable," Denis de Rougemont writes, "that Tristan should ever be in a position to marry Iseult. She typifies the woman a man does not marry; for once she became his wife she would no longer be what she is and he would no longer love her. Just think of a Mme Tristan! It would be the negation of passion" (*Passion and Society*, p. 45). This comment is inaccurate in that Iseult is married to King Mark and he does not cease to love her. The problem is that, for various reasons, she does not love him, chiefly because she was married against her own wishes. She is therefore rebelling against the patriarchal society that forces her to obey laws for which she is not responsible. She is the equivalent of Blodeuwedd, the Lilith-woman, who will probably take a lover to defy society.

But as Iseult takes her lover before she is married, this is not the basic reason. Here we encounter the argument, explored by all the troubadours and extensively propounded by the *Précieuses* of the seventeenth century, that love, being an uncontrollable feeling that belongs to the sphere of emotions, is incompatible with marriage, a social and legal institution governed by laws. It is possible to make a person marry or remain married, but not to make someone love, at least not within our present system of logic which derives from the classical Mediterranean. The Celts' system of logic, however, throws a different light on the problem, as we shall see.

The mistaken attempts of Western society to graft love and marriage together have led to openly expressed love becoming an object of censure in European literature, though adultery remains the hub of all "dramas of passion". "In the eyes of the Ancients," says Denis de Rougemont, "marriage was a utilitarian institution of limited purpose. Concubinage was allowed by custom. . . . But Christian marriage, inasmuch as it is a sacrament, imposed on the natural man a constancy that he found unbearable." This type of marriage, which, since it constitutes the legally recognised family, forms the basis of the present patriarchal society, has a social purpose only. This is to "make" children for the survival of that society and to look after them so that they can join the rat-race with the best possible start. It is hard to see where love comes into all this.

It is interesting to compare the modern, Western family with the ancient Greek family, in which the father married in order to have children and perpetuate his race, but found love with courtesans, sex with prostitutes of the lower classes, and total emotional and sexual satisfaction in paederasty, which tended to become a social institution. A comparison between both these kinds of family and the Celtic family, based on unconventional relationships between husband and wife and permitting concubinage and temporary marriages, reveals a great disparity between the pagan era and the Christian. It should not be forgotten that the Church began by preaching chastity though tolerating marriage, as it could prevent neither sexuality nor the propagation of the species. It simply denied sexuality by confining it to reproduction, and that was strictly supervised by the codifications of marriage. The priest even shrugged off all responsibility for the marriage by leaving the couple to administer the sacrament to each other.

Naturally, by restricting sexuality, the Church succeeded in restricting the whole psycho-emotional system of the human being. But the energy suppressed by the stunting of any human love not directed towards reproduction had to be put to some use. Hence the frenzy of mystical, discarnate love that has enflamed centuries of Christianity, and its absorption into the complicated and disturbing metaphysics evident in the writings of the great mystics.

The "courtly" love or *fine amor* of the troubadours and courtly writers of the twelfth and thirteenth centuries fits perfectly into this framework. Mysticism and sensuality co-exist happily in all their works, just as large drops of paganism seep through their Christianity. The legend of Tristan and Iseult, in the form it has reached us, is an expression of this; to be understood fully, it must be stripped of its "courtly" mask. To do otherwise would be to deny love itself, as the courtly authors apparently tried to do. Denis de Rougemont said, without even realising what a corrupt comment he had made, "Tristan and Iseult do not love one another.... *What they love is love and being in love.* They behave as if aware that whatever obstructs love must ensure and consolidate it in the heart of each and intensify it infinitely the moment they reach the absolute obstacle, which is death."

In other words, if love is pure abstraction, Tristan and Iseult would be victims of a delusion, which they pursue endlessly without ever being able to reach it. So death, which no longer stands for "meeting in death", loses its significance as the "triumph of love over life" and becomes, on the contrary, a brutal checkmate. The fact may have been overlooked that love is nevertheless real when both partners *act*, their respective actions being manifest in *effects*. Given that the concept of love is inseparable from the concept of harmony and agreement, these effects can only be complementary and *not identical*. This line of reasoning can be illustrated by a simple comparison with electrical phenomena: lightning can flash only when there are two antagonistic and complementary forces present. So in love there must first of all be an *exchange*, which is inherent in the concept of altruism. Tristan has something to give to Iseult, who has something to give to him. This is obvious on the purely sexual level, and equally so on the intellectual, psychological and spiritual planes.

Denis de Rougemont was aware of this solution: "If the lady (of courtly love) is not simply the Church of Love of the Cathari, nor the Sophia-Maria of the Gnostic heresies (the feminine principle of divinity), why should she not be the *anima*, or, more precisely, man's *spiritual* element, that which the soul imprisoned in his body desires with a nostalgic love that death alone can satisfy?" (*Passion and Society*, p. 90). Obviously the Gnostics have little to do with the interpretation of a Celtic work, and any possible connection between Celtic legends and Catharism (as envisaged by de Rougemont) must be immediately ruled out. Known Celtic thought is the absolute opposite of Manichaean dualism, the formal distinction between good and evil, the division of the universe into two opposing forces, the existence of two separate worlds. For the Celts dualism is resolved: their Other World is neither above nor below, but *beside*, and can be entered when one wishes, provided it is seen through the eyes of instinctive intelligence.

The value of de Rougemont's comment and its relevance to the truth of the Tristan legend lies in his pinpointing the decisive role of woman in courtly love, and consequently in the writings that concern us. As members of a patriarchal civilisation where the principal offices are held by men, we are too obsessed by the character of Tristan, the heroic knight "sans peur et sans reproche", his betrayal of Mark excused as the fault of the love potion. Yet, in the final analysis, Tristan is a sorry figure of a man, and it is Iseult who takes the lead in everything right from the beginning. This is clearly evident in an Irish legend,[20] older than that of Tristan and generally considered to be one of the archetypes of the *Roman de Tristan*.

Ireland, *The Pursuit of Diarmaid and Grainne*

The old king of the Fiana, Finn mac Cumail, requested in marriage the hand of Grainne, daughter of the King of all Ireland, Cormac mac Airt; but, to deter him, the young woman asked him to give her as a present a pair from every species of wild animal to be found in Ireland. Cailte, Finn's nephew, collected the animals,[21] so Grainne could not refuse to marry Finn; but she showed terrible hatred towards her husband.[22]

Then Cormac organised a great feast to which he invited the Fiana. Grainne asked all of them their names, then called her maid and asked her to go and fetch a cup made of gold and precious stones and which she filled with a magic brew.[21] She had the cup taken to Finn and the chiefs of the Fiana, and asked them to drink. Except for Oisin and Diarmaid, all of them went to sleep after they had drunk. Obviously the magic potion was selective in its effects; and, since Oisin and Diarmaid alone succeeded in the test, they were the only men whom Grainne could love without shame. Grainne then suggested to Oisin that he run away with her, but he refused, alleging that a *geis* (prohibition) prevented him from taking a woman who belonged or was promised to his father. She did not insist but turned instead to Diarmaid O'Duibne,[24] making him the same proposition, which he also refused. Then Grainne pronounced these highly significant words, "I place upon you a *geis* of danger and destruction, O Diarmaid, unless you take me with you out of this house tonight before Finn and the chiefs of Ireland wake from their slumber." As Diarmaid could not withdraw, he asked the advice of Oisin and the other Fiana, who all replied that he had no choice. So he fled with Grainne, who explained that she had been in love with him for a long time.[25]

On waking, Finn was furiously angry and set off in pursuit of the fugitives, followed by the reluctant Oisin, Cailte, and the Fiana, who were prepared to forgive Diarmaid as a victim of the *geis* rather than a traitor to the king. Diarmaid and Grainne took shelter in a grotto, where they were betrayed by an old woman, herself deceived by Finn, but managed to escape. Oengus, Diarmaid's foster-father, then protected the two fugitives, taking Grainne into the folds of his magic cloak and giving Diarmaid the gift of invisibility, which enabled him to pass through the Fiana unseen.[26] Finally Diarmaid and Grainne were reunited. Oengus wasted on them the advice never to stay in the same place if they wished to escape the vengeance of Finn. Diarmaid gave vent to his despair at finding himself in a predicament he had never looked for, and revealed that Grainne and he had not yet had sexual relations.[27]

One day, when Diarmaid and Grainne were walking over marshy ground together, some mud splashed up between her thighs and she exclaimed that it was bolder than Diarmaid. Asked by him to explain, she replied with another *geis*, tantamout to an accusation of impotence, which he had to obey. So they became lovers, and Diarmaid felt none the worse for it because he discovered her true love for him.

Meanwhile, Finn, still hoping for vengeance, pursued the lovers for seven years, even seeking reconciliation with his mortal enemies as long as they were prepared to help him. Only the Fiana, and more especially Cailte, Oisin and his son Oscar, appeared indifferent to this search for a vengeance that did not concern them. But all things come to an end. Diarmaid and Grainne had taken shelter in an underground cave where they thought they were quite safe; but the stream that flowed through the cave and provided them with water also took away their refuse,[28] and this showed Finn the way to the cave. He craftily planned to destroy Diarmaid by surrounding him with an inescapable network of *geisa*, thereby relieving himself of any personal responsibility for Diarmaid's death. In fact there was no reason why Finn should not kill Diarmaid, who, after all, had broken his oath of loyalty to the king. It is possible that Diarmaid, like Tristan, could not be killed or wounded without the man who killed or wounded him also being killed. One of the constraints placed on Diarmaid was that he could not hear the baying of a hound chasing game without joining in the hunt. So Finn had only to make his dog bark near the cave and Diarmaid came out.[29]

Finn pretended to make up his quarrel with Diarmaid and asked him to accompany him on a hunt for the boar of Ben Culbainn. Now Diarmaid had another obligation never to refuse a request of one of his companions (which Finn had now become by patching up their quarrel), but the boar of Ben Culbainn happened to be Diarmaid's own foster-brother transformed into an animal, whose fate was linked to his own. They set out to hunt the boar, which Diarmaid had no choice but to kill, thereby transgressing another of his taboos which was never to kill a boar. Finn, furious that he was still safe and sound, persuaded Diarmaid to go and examine the animal, but its venomous bristles inflicted a fatal wound in his foot. However Finn was able to cure any man he personally brought water to drink, so his son, nephew and grandson urged him to fetch water as quickly as possible. Though unable to get out of it, he took his time and scooped water into his hands in such a way that if flowed through his fingers. Finally, when his grandson Oscar threatened him with single combat if he evaded his duty any longer Finn returned with the water, but too late, for Diarmaid had just died.[30]

The end of Diarmaid's story varies according to different versions. One has Oengus coming to mourn the death of his adopted son and Grainne alerting Diarmaid's sons, who launch a merciless fight against Finn. He, deserted by all the Fiana, has to make honourable amends for Diarmaid's death, but manages to persuade Grainne to live with him. In another version Grainne dies of grief when she hears of Diarmaid's death, and is buried in the same grave as her lover.[31]

This vast epic tableau, which has so many details in common with the legend of Tristan and Iseult, is structurally based on three essential elements, all instrumental in revealing the deeper meaning of the Tristan legend. First there is the Irish *geis*, a virtually untranslatable word, which can be passably rendered as "prohibition", "taboo", "magic and religious constraint". Next there is the exceptional part played by the woman in the story. As the real driving force, able to influence the man effectively and bring about his complete psychological and spiritual metamorphosis, Grainne is an *initiator* and a *transformer*. Finally, there is her indispensable solar nature, which makes her both sought-after and feared as a kind of *tyrannical* goddess, queen and mistress of the orchard into which the man has come. These three mutually complementary and interdependent elements give the key to the story and offer a definitive explanation of the whole myth of woman among the Celts. It is therefore important that we study them in some detail.

THE GEIS

We know from Irish epic writings and various codes of law on the powers of the Druids that the *geis* is primarily a *modus operandi* put at their disposal to ensure their personal authority and the efficacy of their edicts. In a religious society like the Celtic, the powers of certain privileged men came from the gods, who dictated the laws and punished every infringement of the rules. The use of the interdict and excommunication during the Christian Middle Ages springs to mind, though the comparison with Druidic practice is not strictly valid. There is another example in the formal, State religion of the Romans, a religion of material ends rather than metaphysical considerations, and aimed at confining the citizen rigidly within the political framework, though resorting to supernatural sponsorship in order to win respect. It was believed that King Numa Pompilius, the first Roman law-giver, had decreed his laws on the advice of the goddess Egeria, with whom he had frequent conversations. The concept of the divine right of kings is obviously a product of the same determination to make many men accept one man's authority, by putting this under the reassuring and fearful protection of a heavenly power in which they may or may not believe.

The problem of accepting authority was more likely to arise in Celtic society, which, unlike the Roman, had no firmly established judicial foundations and, from its early days, lacked any coherent identity. Only the Druidic religion could unify peoples scattered all over the continent of Europe and the British Isles. So, as all contracts and agreements were liable to be disputed by somebody or other, these were placed under the direct protection of the divinities, with the Druidic priests officially safeguarding their application. This is why there were so many oaths sworn to sanctify treaties, and, consequently, why there were so many divine "curses" dealt out to those who broke their oaths and contravened those treaties. It is in the light of these facts that we should examine the theoretically excessive power of the Druids and the means of action vested in them.

Their power of divination is hardly worth discussing; though obviously an excellent way of making others behave as was foreseen and therefore determined, it was not unique to the Druids, but used by priests of all lands and all religions. It would be equally fruitless to examine the "magic powers" that enabled the Druids to act on nature, as any shaman or wizard can do this by his powers of suggestion or para-psychological talents. But two particular powers make the Druids different from their counterparts in other religions: the *glam dicin* and the *geis*, which are so similar that it is hard to distinguish between them.

The *glam dicin* is a kind of satirical incantation directed against a particular person and having the strength of an obligation; it is in fact a curse which can be pronounced for such valid reasons as infringements of divine or human laws, treason, breaking a contract, and murder, and also as a result of mere personal desire or animosity. The poet Athirne was tolerated by his fellow Ulstermen because they were powerless against him and feared his unjust and hateful *glam dicin.* For it could be used not only by the Druids, but also by the *fili*, or poets, who, even in pre-Christian times, tended to usurp the powers of the Druids and take their place in society. In all respects the *glam dicin* was to be feared, because it pitched the victim of the satire into a state of shame, sickness or death. Rejected by society, he was beyond further help, even if pitied.

The *geis* is more complex. Since it influenced the whole fate of its human (and sometimes animal) victim, it was not cast lightly, but only when justified by a very serious reason. It was a kind of prohibition, imposed on a particular person as a result of certain events, and it left a definite mark. Anyone transgressing a *geis* was exposed to serious trouble and finally to a painful death, which was also hateful and shameful, because the moral and social weight of the prohibition placed the offender outside the established social order. There are endless examples of *geisa*, to which a human being was already exposed at birth. King Conaire the Great, for example, was subject to a whole series of complicated, interdependent prohibitions, so that the transgression of a single *geis* entailed the transgression of a whole chain of other *geisa* and inevitably led to his downfall.[32] When given the name "Dog of Culain" Cú Chulainn's most important *geis* was that he should never eat a dog. Trapped by his enemies, he eventually had to eat dog flesh, because he was imprisoned in a whole network of *geisa*; he could not avoid every one of these, and, since the transgression of one geis involved the fatal infringement of all the others, the magic gifts of the Druids and satirists led him to his inevitable death.

Besides this negative, prohibitive quality, the *geis* could also compel someone to perform a deed on pain of punishment. When Grainne placed Diarmaid under a *"geis* of death and destruction", she meant, "If you do not come with me you are not only a dead man but also dishonoured." This became clear when even Oisin and some of the Fiana, all of whom were bound to have respect for the established order and be obedient to Finn, advised Diarmaid that there was nothing he could do but go with Grainne, though this went against all human and divine law. The power of the *geis* was above divine and human jurisdiction and appeared to brush aside all previous rulings, establishing a new order through the wishes of the man or woman controlling it.

Although the use of the *geis* was originally reserved for the sacerdotal class, the Druids and *fili* (magicians like the shamans of Asia and Eastern Europe possess similar powers), the most recent texts contain evidence of *geisa* cast by ordinary people. In the story of Diarmaid and Grainne, the woman uttered the magic incantation, and, given the traces of a gynaecocratic system apparent in Celtic society, it is not unreasonable to suppose that her action recalls some former age when women, as priestesses, law-givers, or even witches, were able to impose their will by ritual, religious and magic means.

In the historical narratives about the founding of Marseilles, there is a reference to a related Salyan custom (the Salyans were a race classed as Celto-Ligurian). During a feast, the king's daughter would herself chose which of her suitors was to marry her. Similarly, in the Indian ceremony of *svayamvara*, the girl chooses her husband from the assembled suitors. Even the *Odyssey* may have preserved some trace of these gynaecocratic institutions; otherwise Penelope's attitude in receiving her suitors in the palace every day would be inexplicable. She may have delayed making a choice as long as she could, using the famous tapestry as an excuse, but in fact, she was there to *choose*, and none of the suitors was mad enough to force himself upon her. That would have been illegal.

So the *geis* cast by Grainne on Diarmaid must be viewed within the social context inherited from a former civilisation with gynaecocratic leanings. There are many other examples of such *geisa*, the best known being cast in virtually the same circumstances by the heroine Deirdre on Noise, son of Usnech, as the starting point of one of the most melancholy stories in the great collection of Celtic legends.

Ireland, *The Murder of the Sons of Usnech*

When Deirdre was born, the Druid Cathbad prophesied that the girl would be the cause of many murders among the Ulstermen, who, after these warnings, wanted to kill the child. But King Conchobar opposed their plan and took the girl under his protection, declaring that he would see to her education and keep her as a wife. (Conchobar's attitude here is neither a free choice nor prompted by a desire for possession, but connected with a belief dating from earliest prehistory. The prophecies made about Deirdre are in the nature of a *geis*, which affects her whole future, and the unhappiness of curse that she brings on herself would fall on the Ulstermen were they to kill her. Only the strength of the king can stand the weight of it, which is why he not only orders that she be kept alive but also takes her away from any contact with men.)

So Deirdre became a beautiful young woman and Conchobar made sure that no man saw her. One day, she saw in the snow a crow drinking the blood of a wounded animal and exclaimed, "The only man I shall love will wear these three colours: hair like the crow, cheeks like the blood, and body like the snow." Soon after, Deirdre happened to meet Noise, son of Usnech, who was the exact image of her ideal lover, and initially she offered herself to him openly. But he, like Diarmaid, had principles and rejected her, for he could not look at a girl who was promised to King Conchobar. Then Deirdre fell on him, took him by the ears and said, "These will be two ears of shame and mockery if you do not take me with you!" (A ritual of the *geis* showing that it is essentially a threat to honour; Deirdre probably grasps Noise by his ears because they can turn red with shame.) "Noise tried one last time to ward off the *geis* and said, 'Go away from me, woman', to which she replied, 'I will be yours.' Immediately he let his voice be heard in a cry of lamentation, for he had just transgressed the *geis* affecting Deirdre, and at the sound of it the Ulstermen began to fight among themselves." Noise's brothers came at the news, and when he told them what had happened they said, "Evil will come of this; but whatever happens you will not be exposed to shame as long as we are alive, for we shall go with her into another country".

Noise and his brothers did indeed leave the country with Deirdre, and after many adventures in Scotland they were invited to return by Conchobar, under the guarantee and protection of the hero Fergus mac Roig. But it was a trap, and Conchobar massacred the sons of Usnech, provoking the anger and exile of Fergus. Deirdre became Conchobar's concubine and constantly bewailed her unhappy lot and mourned the fate of the sons of Usnech. To carry his vengeance still further, Conchobar then gave her as concubine to Noise's killer. That was more than Deirdre could stand. She leapt from the chariot in which she was riding and broke her head to pieces against a rock. (From the French translation in G. Dottin, *L'Épopée irlandaise*, pp. 76—85).

There is a surprising force in the woman's pronouncement of the (so to speak) "sacramental words" that bind her definitively to the man she loves. Her *geis* incontrovertibly involves him in an adventure, which is usually fatal for him but which, basically, he does not regret, since it enables him to discover the nature of love, of which he previously knew nothing. It is this implacable *geis* that became the "love potion" that Tristan and Iseult drink on the ship taking them to Tintagel and, beyond that, to their fate. In twelfth-century France, the *geis* as such would not have been understood without its first being made material in the convenient form of a witch's potion or an aphrodisiac, to be elevated into the cause of the whole drama, the reason for the lovers' irresponsibility, and even to be used as a deliberate diversion from Iseult's love for Tristan. Since Christian morality could not allow that King Mark's future wife be aware of her state and perform the fatal gesture herself, her role devolved on her maid, the mysterious Brangwain, the real goddess of love; though, in fact, goddesses and gods are only the formal and external representation of what is really happening inside man.

Modified in this way, the theme obviously becomes dull and devalued. In his film *L'Éternel retour*, Jean Cocteau, who succeeded in transposing the legend by keeping the essential point of the myth, showed the philtre as an ordinary object, in the effectiveness of which no one really believes, least of all the audience. And yet his object, a bottle marked "poison", is a catalyst for the hidden energies of Tristan and Iseult, and stands as the material expression of Iseult—Nathalie's knowledge that she does love Tristan—Patrice, but does not wish to admit it for fear of succumbing.

The philtre excuses many things, adultery in particular and even incest; for some way had to be found to make a pair of lovers consisting of aunt and nephew not merely acceptable but also sympathetic to a twelfth-century Christian public. On the mythological level, this kind of incest is normal and not at all shocking. Mark is a substitute for the father, Iseult for the mother whom Tristan never knew. In Tristan's relationship with Iseult there is the same ambiguity as in Jean-Jacques Rousseau's relationship with Madame de Warens, the woman whom, in accordance with local practice but very appropriately, he called "Mummy".

The flavour of incest persists throughout Celtic myths. In the oldest tradition Guinevere, having already had many lovers, took as a lover her nephew Gawain who was chastely overshadowed by Launcelot. The author of *La Mort le roi Artu* resolved the difficulties he experienced in describing the collapse of Arthurian institutions when Guinevere succumbs to the charm of the *wicked nephew* Mordred (who also turns out to be the incestuous son of Arthur!) by making the queen Mordred's prisoner, a condition totally at odds with the original, mythical and psychological character of Guinevere.

In this respect the Greeks went much further, without always solving their problems. Hippolytus is unshakable in the face of his stepmother Phaedra's advances, though she resorts to persuasion, curses and threats, because he does not understand her propositions, as we shall see later. All such stories of aunt and nephew, stepson and stepmother, brother and sister (displaced images of the mother—son couple) relate to a fundamental reality absolutely foreign to Christian and even Jewish thinking, namely the transgression of the incest taboo among the Indo-Europeans.

Indeed, while the Semites are endogamic (it is common among the Jews of the Old Testament to find a widow marrying her brother-in-law, an uncle marrying his niece, not to mention Lot's daughters), the Indo-Europeans are exogamic, meaning they cannot have sexual relationships with members of the same family or even the same clan. This prohibition is general among the Celts, as among the Greeks and Romans, and applies to the population as a whole. But the *heroes*, the exceptional characters who identify themselves with the gods in the sense that they are unlike other men, are allowed to transgress the prohibition, for the moral order is human rather than divine. The heroes enact the annual or seasonal festive ritual of the clan, during which every excess is not merely permitted but also positively recommended. The heroes have been removed from all ritual context and retain only their exceptional character, in which, nonetheless, there is transgression.

The *geis* had to be replaced by the love potion so that all traces of the past could be reassuringly obliterated and Tristan and Iseult cleared of all blame. The lucid determination of Grainne and Deirdre suggests overwhelmingly that the spirit of the myth has been falsified, and that the original Iseult, perfectly conscious of what she was doing, compelled Tristan to love her.

Besides, as a fairy or a witch, she must surely be divine. Blonde like the sun goddess, she uses magical powers to change herself into a bird, so that she can come and hover around Tristan, and she cures him of two incurable wounds. Supreme queen of the orchard, i.e. paradise, she possesses all the powers of the mother goddess and can force her serving knight to obey any command she may make. Clearly there are connections here with the generally accepted definition of the lady of courtly love, absolute mistress of her lover's behaviour. So when, during a tourney described in Chrétien's *Launcelot*, Queen Guinevere orders the hero to behave in a ridiculous fashion before giving him permission to win, he does not bat an eyelid, for the shame he feels when subjected to the mockery of the other knights is nothing to what he would feel if he even hesitated to obey the orders of Guinevere, whose absolute will is equivalent to the Irish *geis*.

Another example of this kind occurs in *The Death of Cú Chulainn*, where the Ulster hero grapples with the sons and daughters of Calatin

who have sworn to bring about his death and intend to enclose him
in a network of *geisa* while the Ulstermen are suffering from their
magic disease. King Conchobar entrusts to the women, who alone are
in good health, the duty of protecting Cú Chulainn and preventing
him from falling upon the fighting men created by the magic spells of
his enemies. Niam, daughter of Celtchar and "Cú Chulainn's
favourite", takes chief responsibility for this mission and drags the
hero into her fortress, where she makes him drink. But one of
Calatin's daughters, a witch who can change her shape and seems to
be very like Morrigane, takes the form of Niam and says to Cú
Chulainn, "O my soul, O warrior, O Beautiful Dog ... the armies
have reached as far as Emain, and the noblemen of the province
blame me for *keeping you and not allowing you to avenge the
province and drive back the armies.* And I know that Conall will kill
me *if I do not give you permission* to protect the province and attack
the men of Ireland" (*Celticum*, vol. 7, p. 517).

The idea that Cú Chulainn, who could stand against four
confederated armies on his own, should be entirely dependent on the
wishes of a woman seems out of this world. Like Launcelot he is in
the presence of an unquestionable and unquestioned authority
stronger than himself, since it derives from the loved woman, the
"mistress", the "favourite". This is one of the many forms of the
geis.

In the *Book of Conquests* (ed. and trans. R. A. S. Macalister,
vol. 3, pp. 41—2), there is a strange story about Algnat, wife of
Partholon, one of the original conquerors of Ireland, who invites one
of her servants to sleep with her. When he refuses out of fear of
Partholon, the woman "shames" him into obeying, by questioning
his virility in a *geis* directed at his sense of honour. On hearing of it
Partholon forebearingly remarks, "When the desire for copulation
comes it is not easy to resist!"

In *The Education of Cú Chulainn*,[33] the hero goes to learn the
martial arts from the witch Scatach. Her daughter, Uatach ("Very
Terrible") is in love with him; but when she slips into his bed Cú
Chulainn pushes her out and even breaks one of her fingers. Then the
girl puts him under a *geis* of destruction unless he agrees to keep her
with him, and Cú Chulainn has to submit, though he extracts from
Uatach the promise of a reward. In *The Illness of Cú Chulainn*,[34]
the hero is struck by a mysterious disease when he misfires while
hunting two birds, who are really two fairy women. He can be cured
only by going into the world of the fairies at the summons of one of
the two women, Fand, who is in love with him. This particular aspect
of the *geis* pronounced by a woman on the man she loves reappears
in the song of the Sirens, who drag their chosen sailor with them to
the bottom of the sea; and, more particularly, in the Irish story of
Condle the Red, who is given an apple by a fairy woman and cannot
resist the call of the Other World.

Finally the woman can, without pronouncing a true *geis*, perform an equivalent act. The young Derbforgaille, who, without ever seeing Cú Chulainn, has fallen in love with him because of his reputation for valour, comes to him in the shape of a bird. Cú Chulainn wounds her and, when she resumes her human form, he sucks blood from the wound to extract the ball shot from his sling. The blood tie that binds them means that Derbforgaille can belong only to Cú Chulainn, though he *gives* her to a friend of his choice.[35] The *geis* has created an indissoluble bond between them, so that later Cú Chulainn does all he can to avenge Derbforgaille's death.

Distinct and precise in the Irish tradition, the *geis* appears in an attenuated form in the British and, therefore, in the Arthurian traditions. When Peredur goes to fight the monstrous *addanc* at the bottom of a cave (note in passing the analogy between this episode and Tristan's killing of the crested snake to win the hand of Iseult), he meets the mysterious "Empress", who offers him a magic stone that will enable him to win provided he promises to love her more than any other woman in the world (J. Loth, *Mabinogion*, vol. 2, pp. 94–5). The obligatory nature of this exchange clearly allies it to the *geis*. The Empress is taking advantage of the situation, knowing very well that Peredur cannot refuse, and binds her to him symbolically through the stone, the materialisation of the magic powers of her words, like the love potion drunk by Tristan and Iseult. Moreover, the Empress reappears throughout the tale under different forms, and on every occasion she *compels* Peredur to do something. As the Hideous Damsel of the Mule (Wolfram's Kundry), she pronounces a kind of anathema on Peredur—Perceval, accusing him of failure in his mission and forcing him to begin his quest again.[36] As the Châtelaine of the Chess Game, then as the Black Girl, she makes him go towards the Castle of Miracles,[37] facilitating the end of the Quest.

In the Welsh tale of *Owein*, as in Chrétien's *Chevalier au Lion*, there is also a kind of *geis* binding the hero of the adventure to the maid Luned and thereby to her mistress, the Lady of the Fountain. Indeed, Owein is in great distress, for, though he has just mortally wounded his adversary, the latter has dragged him inside his fortress, where he is now a prisoner sought by men-at-arms. But he is saved by a "girl with curly blonde hair, her head adorned with a golden band, clothed in yellow *paile*, wearing ankle boots of speckled *cordwal* on her feet", who says to him, "It would be a woman's duty to help you. I have certainly never seen a better young man for a woman. You would be the best boy friend for any girl friend you had; a mistress could have no better lover than you; so I shall do what I can to rescue you. Take this ring, put it on your finger, turn the stone to your palm and close your hand over it. As long as you keep it hidden, it will keep you hidden."[38] Luned then takes Owein into a secret room from where he can see his victim's widow, with whom he falls hopelessly in love. Finally Luned arranges for him to marry the Lady of the Fountain.

This ring of invisibility is clearly reminiscent of that of Gyges, and yet it is included among the thirteen marvels of Britain. It is equally apparent that Luned is a fairy gifted with magic powers; like Brangwain, she plays the role of go-between, even that of a real goddess of love. Here the story becomes interesting, for the confused and inexplicable play between Luned and Laudine (the Lady of the Fountain) and between Brangwain and Iseult, as between the maiden Saraide and Vivienne, the Lady of the Lake in *Lancelot en prose*, suggests that the two women are two, interchangeable faces of the same woman, as Brangwain's taking Iseult's place in Mark's bed shows. It is possible that the fairy Luned loves Owein and for that reason binds him to her by pronouncing the incantation of the *geis* over him, but that she will give herself only under the sovereign form of Laudine. When narrating the same story, Chrétien de Troyes carefully rationalises Luned's attitude as gratitude owed to the knight Yvain for once helping her in King Arthur's court. But this justification does not explain all the necessary contact between Luned and Owein—Yvain. At the end of the romance, when Luned is virtually condemned to the stake, Owein—Yvain, abandoning all other considerations, rushes to help her. The bond of obligation between the hero and the fairy servant through whom he reaches Laudine, the personification of sovereign power, is connected with the theme, much used in Celtic tradition, of the fairy offering omnipotence to a man who is not worthy to live unless he accepts. This is nothing but a *geis*.

Similarly, when Merlin first meets the young Vivienne, he is already under a *geis*; for, even though he knows that she will eventually "dominate" him, he cannot stop himself returning to see her and teaching her his magic, so enabling her to bind him for ever by ritually walking nine times round the foot of the tree under which he sleeps. The castle of air (or glass) to which Vivienne transports him, and from which he will never be able to return, is undoubtedly a materialisation of the psychological and social state of the man on whom the *geis* has been pronounced.

There are traces of all this in folklore and fairy tales, which are simply the old myths in a new dress, and in the superstitions and practices of witchcraft. We have already spoken of "Saint" Guengalc'h, enraptured by a "mermaid"; despite his confession and exemplary life, he died a year later, the victim of the magic act she had performed to bind him to her for ever. There are also many strange customs concerning marriage.

The folklorist Paul Sébillot mentions the widespread custom of young girls, wishing to marry at any cost, speaking to the statue of a saint and behaving as if it were a real, flesh and blood substitute for the man they love. So, in the Minervois, around 1850, girls used to file past the statue of St Sicre and raise a fork over its head, chanting a rhyme to the effect that they would strike it if they had not found a sweetheart or a husband within a year.[39] This ritual gesture, which takes effect from the moment it is performed, signifies a threat to the young man represented by the effigy of the saint; he must therefore obey and respond to their call or be dead and *dishonoured.* In the Ain, girls used to threaten to throw St Blaise in the Rhône; at Sorbey in Meuse, they would stone St Vildbrock; and in Portugal, they would throw a stone at the statue of St Elisha on Mount Lucia.[39] In Perros-Guirec in the Côte-du-Nord, girls dig pins into the nose of the unfortunate St Guirec, asking him to find them a man. In sixteenth-century France, a girl would burn a laurel-tree, sacred to Apollo, with the wish that her sweetheart should burst into flames and be consumed with love. In the south of England, the girl would throw salt into the fire at night three Fridays running, pronouncing, "It is not this salt that I wish to burn, but the heart of the man I love. . . . May he have no peace nor happiness until he has come and spoken to me!"[39] In Cornwall and Sussex, at midnight on Midsummer Night, the girl washes one of her garments and silently puts it to dry on a chair in front of the kitchen fire, leaving the door open. The man who turns the clothing over will be her choice. County Donegal, in Ireland, has the same custom, but it happens on All Saints' Eve, the old Celtic festival of Samain, and the girl uses her nightdress, which she washes three times in running water.[40] All this is close to witchcraft, especially the clothing fetishism, which is as common among women as among men.

Also in County Donegal and at the feast of All Saints, the girl wishing to marry, or at least become involved with a man, walks all the way round a haystack befory thrusting into it a knife with a black handle and uttering the name of the Devil. The man who takes out the knife will be her choice.[41] Note that the Devil has been insinuated into a magic custom because he symbolises what is forbidden. Yet the act of driving the knife (the man) into the haystack (the woman) bears the stamp of an erotic ritual, and beyond that the mark of all beliefs about the night of All Saints, the festival of Samain, when the world of the dead (the *sidh* here represented by the haystack), opens its doors to the living — the hero who has passed the test, here represented by the knife.

Obviously the erotic aspect of the *geis* is only to be expected and is not peculiar to Celtic peoples. To overcome the resistance of Odysseus, Calypso had to make nasty comments about his virility. Ruth certainly used the same kind of provocation on Boaz. The oath *in testiculis* must surely be one form of the universally prevalent *geis*. One wonders which prudish author replaced testicles with ears, when describing how Deirdre grabbed hold of Noise to pronounce her *geis* on him; though obviously ears too had a symbolic meaning and the moral weight of the *geis* is in no way diminished by the change.

The erotic nature of the *geis* has persisted in popular superstitions, finding very crude expression in a number of cases. In Fougères in Ille-et-Vilaine, girls wanting a husband used to sit down on a hollow stone called the "Devil's Pulpit".[42] In Carnac in Morbihan, they used to lift their skirts before sitting on the surface of a dolmen called the "Hot Stone".[43] Similarly, in Dinan, girls used to climb onto the menhir of St Samson.[43] In Provence, behind the church at Bonduen in the Bouches-du-Rhône, there was a rock that formed a sloping surface and had become polished by "flaying" (by naked girls rubbing themselves against it to ask for a man).[43] The same kind of rubbing or sliding took place on the Great Menhir of Locmariaquer in Morbihan; in this case contact between the naked flesh and the stone was absolutely essential.[44] In the Grenoble district, girls and widows wanting to marry prayed before the oratory of Brandes, holding between their knees "the stone of St Nicholas".[44] There are many other examples of such customs, in which a woman had contact with a rock, a tree, a statue or a menhir.

Another extremely interesting ritual has been observed in a number of places, in Aunis in Saintonge, in Gironde, in the Deux-Sèvres, in Vendée, around Rennes and Dinan, and particularly in Plessala in the Côtes-du-Nord. The woman spits into the mouth of the man she loves and so can be assured that he will belong to her.[45] This appears to be an inverted and anticipated form of the act of love, the woman spitting her saliva into the man's mouth because she wants him to spit his semen into her womb. It is an authentically magic gesture able to spark off physiological reactions in the man, a form of provocation as the *geis* invariably is. A kiss on the mouth, pushing in the tongue and the mingling of salivas belong to the same category of both psychologically and purely physically expressive gestures. So, also, in everyday life, a woman may try dressing in such a way as to attract — even though the motive be subconscious — the eyes and the desire of a man, to intoxicate him quite literally with the use of perfume and seduce him. This also applies to the religious life: in antiquity, the image of the goddess was often represented with her robe quite shamelessly lifted to exhibit her genitals. This, in its ancient form, as in its present "perverted" form, is nothing other than *exhibitionism*. Yet it almost certainly contains a very attenuated and altered form of the *geis*. Even if her education has made her unaware of the role she is playing, the woman who gradually reveals herself is leading the man, even if, as in courtships displays, the male is apparently the stronger.

The man can do nothing but be caught up in the game. The magic power of saliva, evident in its aggressive and negative aspect in the expression "to spit in the face of someone", is as great as that of the love potion drunk by Tristan and Iseult. This is, quite simply and honestly, the mixture of their own salivas, and is drunk with delight. This idea may seem repugnant, but the act of love itself would, to put it bluntly, be a repulsive performance if one did not love and want to *mix with* one's partner, wiping out all negative concepts of retreat like modesty or disgust. As the logical outcome of the *geis*, it may be that the man finds himself spellbound by the emanations of the woman; this becomes real fetishism, a word with religious connotations of compulsory adoration. As Jean-Jacques Rousseau wrote of Mme de Warens, "How many times I kissed my bed, as I dreamed about her sleeping there; I dreamed that my curtains, all the furniture in my room belonged to her whose lovely hand had touched them; even the very floor on which I prostrated myself as I dreamed that she had walked there. . . . One day at table, just as she had put a piece of food in her mouth, I exclaimed that I could see a hair on it; and when she spat it back onto her plate I seized the morsel greedily and swallowed it" (*Confessions*, I,3).

If Rousseau appears to have an unhealthy mind, then read Michelet, the historian and moralist, who wrote, "Woman caters for man's needs, tiredness and known temperament; prepares his food, humanises it with fire, with salt and with *soul*. She blends herself into it, adds the scent of the beloved hand. . . . Any action requiring a touch by that same hand is desirable and charming, because it imparts her emanations. Such pastries, cakes and creams can be made only by the woman one loves and is greedy for" (*L'Amour*, II,6).

The magical charm exercised by the woman on the man is not a figment of the imagination, but, on the contrary, is based on one of man's fundamental, biological instincts. Taken to extremes, it would become a longing to taste again the milk and skin of the mother, an idea that conjures up all manner of strange pictures. A woman merely has to present the man she has chosen with a sensual whole built up with sight, sound, touch and smell to spark off the subconscious process of recreating his early happiness. Knowing that man is forever bound by his memories is woman's strength, enabling her to use the *geis*. The various objects involved, the philtre, the ring, and her utterances are all simply a material prop for a psycho-physical act committed in the face of all constraints, taboos, and moral laws, human or divine; the triumphant reassertion of instinct over reason.

Chateaubriand, that most Celtic of writers in French, has surely captured the essence of the myth in *Les Martyrs*. It hardly matters that Velleda, the name of his Druidess, is really the name of a Germanic priestess or that his supposed Gallo-Breton backdrop is so much junk, for the way Velleda makes Eudore love her against the weight of both his laws and hers can only be the result of a *geis*. When she sees him appear she says, "I knew that I would draw you here. Nothing can resist the strength of my words", and continues with a magic invocation: "I am wandering round your castle, sad that I cannot go in. But I have prepared some charms and shall go and find the Selago: first I shall make an offering of bread and wine; I shall be dressed in white, my feet bare; my right hand, hidden under my tunic, will tear out the plant and my left hand will take it from my right. Then nothing will stand in my way and I shall slide into your house on moonbeams, take the form of a wood-pigeon and fly to the top of your tower" (*Les Martyrs*, X). When Velleda throws herself into the waves, Eudore holds her back by her veil and cries out the "You will be loved" she had been waiting for. Naturally, within the context of his book, Chateaubriand adds, "Hell gave the signal for this fatal marriage", as any magic practice is bound to be under the aegis of the Devil. But the fact remains that Eudore and Velleda are a reconstruction of the original couple seen in Tristan and Iseult, Diarmaid and Grainne, Noise and Deirdre.

Behind Velleda one can also see the fantasies of Chateaubriand, and of Western man in search of his feminine ideal. For him, particularly if a Celt, love, as the strongest taboo of all, consists of transgressing another, lesser taboo. Velleda transgresses the taboo of her sacred virginity, unlike Atala, who, although the same character for Chateaubriand, kills herself rather than take such a step. Throughout his life, Chateaubriand struggled against the taboo on incest, which he could bring himself to transgress only in daydreams, either by gracing his mistresses with the charms of his sister Lucile, or by giving her features to some awesome fairy, Druidess or divinity who compels one to love her hopelessly, though her veil must not be raised. His heroines have the demonic charms of Grainne, the melancholy of Deirdre.

The woman enchantress, whatever her name, reigns triumphant in the dreamworld of her almost inaccessible orchard by virtue of her supremacy and magic words, those intonations that change the appearance of things and the essence of people. This explains the power of the *geis*.

NEW BIRTH

Literature always presents the consequences of man's acceptance of the *geis* as dreadful and invariably resulting in a tragic end; this might discourage any belief in "happy love", always supposing that the concept of happiness could ever fit in with an act that is inherently disruptive. The act of love may lead to happiness, but at that moment it becomes a memory. The great legends about love do not tell us about the search for happiness (whatever that is) but about what love can bring to a human being, particularly a man. For woman appears from the very beginning to have held the fearful secret that both attracts and repels man. "In the context of the creation, the primacy of the male is continually stressed; the subsequent theory that man reveals sexuality to woman is a logical outcome of the narrative. Yet the serpent, which was not initially forced to crawl upon the earth, appears to Eve first and suggests to her that divine authority can be questioned, that there exist things that are devilishly interesting. And the informed Eve makes Adam commit the original sin. Keeping to the sexual symbolism of the serpent, *Eve was the first to be aware of sexuality and compels Adam to make it seem that he is revealing it to her.* So the unconscious theme behind the story is the revelation of sexuality to man by woman."[46]

Whether the text of Genesis is taken literally or not, woman is seen as responsible for man's changed situations; and both the biblical and a number of other traditions that were originally mythical and then made into history describe this change of situation as retrogressive, as a *fall*. The Indo-European counterpart to the Semitic Eve is Pandora, the woman created by Prometheus, who lets out of her box all the evils from which humanity suffers. In Christian thinking, woman is a diabolic creature, made to tempt man and to humiliate him. But a whole stream of thought contradicts this apparently unassailable attitude. It has been sadly stifled by esotericism, but is evident in the troubadour Uc de Saint-Circ's declaration "One reaches God through woman"; in the fact that medieval sinners prayed to the Virgin Mary that God would relent; and in Goethe's exclamation in *Faust*, "The Eternal Feminine carries us on high". So which of these two attitudes to women is right?

The outward consequences of love in the stories we are discussing tip the scales against happiness. The love of Tristan and Iseult leads to adultery, treason, lies and death; the love of Diarmaid and Grainne to disloyalty, treason and crime; that of Noise and Deirdre to perjury and crime. In every case, disaster strikes not only the two lovers but also anyone directly or indirectly involved in the story. Decidedly, "there is no happiness in love". Any wishes for the future happiness of young couples who have just entered *lawful wedlock* refer not to their love, but to a stable life within the socially and legally established household, which is the basic unit of society. Any confusion between *emotional love* and *lawful marriage* is deliberately sustained by censorship, for the patriarchal social set-up demands that love be conditioned to submit to marriage and that everything that threatens to divert love from the path of moderation be unequivocally condemned; for, as Marcuse rightly remarks, "Beyond its legitimate manifestations, love is destructive and leads to very little productivity and constructive labour." The myths of Tristan and Iseult, Diarmaid and Grainne, Noise and Deirdre are therefore attempts to free love from its legal and socially obligatory shackles in order to make it whole and strong once more; for, once unchained, love enables men and women to discover *devilishly interesting things*.

From the logical structure of the legend of Tristan and Iseult, it soon becomes evident that Iseult falls in love with Tristan right from the beginning, but is unable to escape the law of the patriarchal régime. She has to wait until Tristan asks for her hand in marriage, or at least begs for her love, which he finally does in the name of another man (who can only be the omnipotent father, here represented by his king-uncle). Contrary to appearances, Tristan must also be in love with her, but is either unaware of it or afraid to infringe patriarchal law. In any case, he is not free, because freedom is knowledge and he has no knowledge of what is happening to him or passing through Iseult's mind. At this point in the story, the heavy burden of prohibition (fear of the father, respect for his oath, fear of incest) provides him with an ideal pretext for keeping a clear conscience, though in fact he has no conscience at all. Tristan is a man enamoured of logic, or at least educated in the logic of what is done and what is not.

Iseult, as a woman, knows through intuition, the dominant characteristic of her sex, what is happening in her own and in Tristan's mind; her knowledge makes her free actively to arouse Tristan from the apathy of his unconscious, using the philtre to replace the original *geis*. It is only then that Tristan notices *devilishly interesting things* at the bottom of the silver goblet and can transgress the prohibition, replacing the established with the underlying values and adopting an attitude that is "devilish" because contrary to the normal order.

Tristan, awaking after his first night with Iseult, the official fiancée of his king-uncle, is no longer his former self — awkward, ignorant and imprisoned — but the new Tristan — skilful, wise and free, given a new birth through the act of love with woman. For she is intended to bring life into the world, whether it be a child born of her body or a man nourished by it and swallowed up in her like the earliest creature in the primordial waters. Iseult provides Tristan with a second birth of a kind biologically and psychologically impossible for his real mother. The basic plot of Tristan and Iseult can be explained in this way: after considerable effort from the woman (comparable to the labour of childbirth), man can reach the decisive stage that will make him a real man, but only on condition that he breaks all links with the past and transgresses the original prohibition.

The legend of Diarmaid and Grainne is identical in structure, with variations in detail. The woman's share of the responsbility appears greater (and in the final analysis closer to the original myth of

Genesis), for Grainne matches her love for Diarmaid with a real rebellion against the patriarchal order and is basically involving him in this struggle. But he is slow to be born again, submitting only to the superficial aspect of the *geis*, their flight and therefore rebellion against Finn. Indeed, in an oral version of the legend collected in the Highlands by Campbell, Diarmaid refused to follow Grainne at first, saying, "I shall not go with you; neither by gentleness nor severity will you persuade me to take you. I shall not lead you into my house, nor take you away; I shall not take you on horseback, nor on foot." He returns home with dignity, only to see Grainne appear before his door one morning standing on a bench, therefore neither on foot nor on horseback. So he can no longer refuse. (Loys Bruyere, *Contes populaires de la Grande-Bretagne*, pp. 168—9.)

After this Diarmaid is content to live with Grainne, carefully avoiding sexual relations as if afraid of waking something devilish inside himself. One version of the legend even specifies that at the doorway of the cave or cabin he occupied with Grainne he used to plant a stake into the ground every evening and on it a haunch of game to show his respect for the wife of Finn, who did not intervene until the day when Diarmaid put out no stake, showing that his union had been consummated. (Compare this with Tristan's sword between the two lovers when Mark finds them asleep.) So Grainne had to take the decisions and pronounced another *geis* on Diarmaid, making him love her. Diarmaid's real metamorphosis dates from that point, as old King Finn was well aware. For even if it meant transgressing other taboos, Finn had to destroy the danger of a Diarmaid to whom Grainne had disclosed those *devilishly interesting things* that only Finn was entitled to know. For Diarmaid himself, transgression of the patriarchal taboo was a painful process and would never have occurred without the power of the woman.

This new birth of the man through the woman in the act of love is inseparable from her own new birth brought about by the man she has chosen. Man's actual unconscious longing is to make real his paradise, be it lost or imagined, by penetrating the maternal universe of the woman. But since his whole being becomes centred in his penis, he can do so only by allowing himself to be *contained* in a whole that is greater and necessarily more powerful than he; this induces in him a feeling, even a "complex", of inferiority, and a need to dream up self-deluding claims to dominance. But the woman, for her part, also re-creates the state of paradise by giving shelter both to a child, when she is a mother, and to a man when she performs the act of love. For as psychoanalysis has shown, any feelings of inferiority in woman spring solely from her parents' refusal to acknowledge her vagina, while parental recognition of the penis enables a boy to occupy a real position in society. The moment that the man's penis is in her vagina, and, thereafter, when the child is in her womb, woman feels the acknowledgement of that vagina as the triumph of her real entry into the social world. That is why a married woman enjoys an importance, and a widow or divorcee is allowed a freedom, denied to a young girl. The fact that she has been deflowered, then that she is a mother, constitutes woman's new birth; and whether she finds fulfilment in her love-life or in motherhood, woman has as much interest in new birth as man has.

In Celtic legend, however, and in old traditions of the other Indo-European races, woman appears to play the essential role, while man emerges from the experience more obviously transformed. This notion is manifest in the very old myth of Circe, which in the *Odyssey* had already been adapted to suit a patriarchal society. It used the formidable power of women, as represented by Circe, as an argument against them; for such power was bound to be considered negative if through it Circe could change her lovers into animals and keep them in a kind of museum. Even so, she fared better than Antinea, who had her lovers mummified; or Dahud-Ahes, who had them cast into a ravine; or Marguerite of Burgundy, who had them thrown into the Seine, which, even then was strongly polluted. It was to be expected that that paragon of patriarchal society, the cunning Odysseus, who was returning to Ithaca to find lasting power (symbolised by the father) would resist Circe's charms. Indeed he fought against her and managed to free all the men caught in her trap, so taking from woman, as symbolised by Circe, the goddess and magician, the gift of creation, the power to transform man. This reactionary idea has thrived, and is to be found wherever there are stories — such as the Breton tale paraphrased below — about "bad fairies", "witches" and other creatures of the Devil. Though suspect, for its collector Emile Souvestre had a lively and over-romantic imagination, the following story is none the less characteristic of a state of mind and useful in this discussion. However, it has not been dated.

Brittany, *The Groac'h or the Isle of the Lok*
Houarn Pogamm decided to seek his fortune before marrying Bellah Postik, his betrothed, who on his departure gave him two relics (magic objects): the bell of St Koledok, which, when the man who carried it was in danger, could be heard from any distance by all his friends; and the knife of St Korentin, which broke all spells. Bellah kept for herself a third relic, the staff of St Vouga, which could take its owner wherever he or she wished.

Houarn went to the Isle of the Lok, on which there was a lake where lived the Groac'h, who kept fabulous treasure and whose marvellous palace was accessible by a boat in the shape of a swan. There the witch welcomed Houarn warmly, gave him

a drink and suggested that he marry her. He was about to accept
when he heard the fish that she had just put into the pan to fry
mumbling something incomprehensible, and, by touching them
with his magic knife, he turned them into men who told him
that they had been enchanted by the witch after marrying her.
At that moment the Groac'h returned and threw her steel net
over Houarn, changing him into a frog.

But the bell of St Koledok rang right in the ears of Bellah,
who,-dressed as a boy, used the staff of St Vouga to effect a
speedy arrival. The Groac'h, not seeing through her disguise,
expressed a desire to marry Bellah, but she, instead of replying
directly, asked to catch one of the fish jumping in the pond
with the net the Groac'h wore at her waist. She threw it over
the Groac'h, turning her into a hideous queen of the mush-
rooms, and went to throw her into a well. Then, with the help
of the knife of St Korentin, she restored Houarn and all the
Groac'h's unfortunate husbands to their former shape and to
freedom. Finally, she and Houarn took the treasure stored in
the Groac'h's marvellous palace. (E. Souvestre, *Le Foyer
breton*, re-edited in Gwenc'hlan le Scouëzec, *Histoires et
légendes de la Bretagne mystérieuse*, pp. 131—43.)

The background details of this legend are all borrowed from
mythology. The Groac'h (etymologically "old woman", and thus
"witch") is a fairy of the waters, living in a palace under a lake in an
island. The geographical site is expressive, since the woman in the
middle of the waters represents both the mother and the mother
goddess, who takes back her children and changes them, so giving
them a new life. But the Groac'h also stands for the old matriarchal
authority, meaning gynaecocratic custom. When, conscious of his
danger, Houarn decides to go and find the witch in her enchanted
palace, he may either be returning to his childhood world of dreams,
or even his pre-natal condition; or else, knowing in his heart that he
is not in full possession of his power and feeling constrained to find
it, looking for it in the matriarchal universe of a still gynaecocratic
society. The Groac'h's hoard is obviously the treasure of the Other
World, which is not a future paradise but a place continually skirted
and into which one must dive to find the as-yet undeployed
resources despised by male-dominated societies. Houarn's search is a
return to the source.

But he is not free, being attached to Bellah, who is woman as
patriarchal society sees her: the legitimate wife who respects male
laws. If she lets him go, the thread will be broken. So talismans, the
bell and the knife are introduced, enabling Bellah to intervene and
save a situation endangered by Houarn's succumbing to the charms
of the Groac'h — in other words, his wish to try the gynaecocratic

experience. The present version of the tale has hidden Houarn's
acquiescence behind a flood of eloquence, to the effect that it was
not his fault, the wine he drank excited him, lowered his resistance,
and so on. This much-used excuse only underlines the element of
temptation involved with the monster-woman, the snake-woman, the
ogress. The Groac'h's throwing her net over Houarn is obviously a
metaphor for her returning her son to her womb in the shape of a
frog (or fish). In the existing story, this regression to an earlier state
is regarded as a curse; so the re-establishment of the present situation
is a matter of urgency, demanding the character of Bellah, who as
wife (legal, naturally) or daughter, and therefore subject to patriarchal law, wins the fight against the mother.

The transformation undergone by Houarn and the Groac'h's other
temporary husbands is a return to gynaecocratic society, in which
stability comes from a different set of emotional relations, based on
that celebrated mother–son complicity that Christianity, at least in
the beginning, tried to reinstate with the Mary—Jesus couple. The
legend we are now discussing may well contain some conflict
between the old kind of Christianity, represented by the Groac'h,
and the new, as represented by Bellah; for, however shocking such a
suggestion may seem, the true Christian religion, in its pure and
ideological form, was often concealed behind the ugly mask of the
Devil by the efficient patriarchal system of repression that has made
our "civilised" society entirely fraudulent.

Behind the symbolism of the Groac'h and hidden in the depths of
the subconscious, lies not only the genuine Christianity of the
Mary—Jesus couple, but also the archaic principle of relations
between man and woman, reimbodied in the love of Tristan and
Iseult, Diarmaid and Grainne, Noise and Deirdre — a love expressly
opposed to the legality of the king, be he Mark, Finn or Conchobar.
In this case, the Groac'h restores to Houarn that former kind of
relationship no longer tolerated by the present, patriarchal society,
which represses the instinct so as to sustain the lack of satisfaction
necessary for productivity. So Bellah, the woman-as-object created
by this society, comes to the rescue, having had the foresight not to
let Houarn go without giving him the *thread of Ariadne*.

We can now see that we have been basing our ideas on a total and
nonsensical misunderstanding of the myth of Ariadne, and, therefore, the myth of Phaedra. These continually underly the legends we
are studying. In fact, *the thread of Ariadne is not the umbilical cord
attaching Theseus (man) to Ariadne (his mother), but the un-
breakable thread binding man to the patriarchal society.*

When Ariadne gave Theseus the thread to unravel, she did so not to
help him slay the monster, nor to show him the way through to the
inside, but, on the contrary, to show him the way out, meaning to
help him return to her. This is a crucially important assertion, not

because it challenges the meaning of a myth, but rather because it explains how man is decieved by the ready-made images provided for him by a hierarchical and repressive society. The labyrinth is the obvious maternal symbol, and going to kill the Minotaur, the monstrous, hybrid product of the unnatural union of Pasiphae and the bull (feminine fertility and masculine strength), is an attempt to go back to the source, to return, under the cloak of the maternal womb, to a point at which relations between the two sexes can be rethought. But, though Theseus is the hero of the drama, Ariadne, woman-as-object, is the real power behind it; for, while appearing to give man freedom, she is really holding on to him, so that he will be forced to return and submit to the authority she personifies.

Yet Theseus, rebelling against this enslavement, abandoned her to the fate she deserved. For, though usually pitied, Ariadne, being an object, lasts only as long as a commodity that, when no longer needed, is thrown in the dustbin. And Theseus marries Phaedra.

The impressive, if complex, character of Phaedra also affords an opportunity to interpret the myth in an entirely new light, if we are prepared to examine it objectively and open-mindedly. The woman Theseus marries represents freedom and initiation. She undoubtedly showed him a vessel full of magic brew with some *devilishly interesting things* at the bottom; otherwise he would not have left Ariadne for her. But, as his father's successor, *King* Theseus cannot but play his allotted role of defender of the society that made him king. He deceives Phaedra and has a number of amorous adventures, which are really symbols of his infidelity to the authority, based on sensitivity and instinct, that she represents, and symptomatic of his fresh pursuit of the woman-as-object that previously revolted him. So Phaedra, terribly disappointed that her hero should stoop to mediocrity, has no choice but to look elsewhere, and naturally her glance falls on the young Hippolytus, a hero who, admittedly, has not proved himself, though he may prove capable of anything. He is the new face of Theseus, as Jean Racine so brilliantly expressed it:

"Yes, Prince, I pine, I am on fire for him.
I love King Theseus, not as once he was,
The fickle worshipper at countless shrines,
Dishonouring the couch of Hades' god;
But constant, proud, and even a little shy;
Enchanting, young, the darling of all hearts. . ."
        (Translation by John Cairncross, Penguin Classics)

In psychoanalytic terms, this is a "transfer" phenomenon. But the rest of Phaedra's declaration to Hippolytus expresses much more. Racine has intuitively touched the very core of the myth, delineating the real situation in an instant, and bringing out the underlying motives to justify Phaedra's attitude, both morally and meta-physically.

> "Why could you not, too young, alas, have fared
> Forth with the ship that brought him to our shores?
> *You* would have slain the monstrous Cretan bull
> Despite the windings of his endless lair.
> My sister would have armed you with the thread
> To lead you through the dark entangled maze —
> No. *I* would have forestalled her. For my love
> Would instantly have fired me with the thought.
> I, only I, would have revealed to you
> The subtle windings of the labyrinth.
> What care I would have lavished on your head!
> A thread would not have reassured my fears.
> Affronting danger side by side with you,
> I would myself have wished to lead the way,
> And Phaedra, with you in the labyrinth,
> Would have returned with you or met her doom."
>   (Translation by John Cairncross, Penguin Classics)

It is amazing that Racine, that most classical of the classical dramatists, should have written this when Cartesian logic and triumphant reason were in full flower; and paradoxical that we should be using his *Phèdre* to demonstrate a whole thesis about the Celtic woman. Admittedly, the Celtic woman is the universal woman, *before the eclipse*, and Racine, seeking universality above everything, must inevitably have come face to face with this fundamental myth. But that alone would not explain why he was able to feel and express it so exactly, and indeed superbly in the original French.

Phaedra's speech says it all. If Hippolytus — or a Theseus worthy to be led into the heart of the labyrinth — had arrived, he would have been helped not by Ariadne, woman-as-object and creation of patriarchal society, but by Phaedra, who specifically says that because of her love she would have walked *before* Hippolytus to guide him and share his fate, rather than attach a thread to the hero's wrist, as a collaborator with society would do. It is this that changes the whole face of the myth and gives the lie to the rather foolish, but generally accepted, notion of Phaedra as a Christian woman lacking in grace. For Phaedra is an initiator and transformer, in the same way as Iseult, Grainne and Deirdre, a descendant of the sun (as was Grainne, whose name comes from the Irish word for "sun", and Iseult the Fair, an eminently solar character). She leads the hero into the dark folds of the labyrinth (the maternal womb) in search of the truth in its depths. Instead of an accused, vicious woman, the seducer of a minor, there appears a fairy, offering to light man's path through the dark regions because she alone knows the way. And hers is *not the way of the return journey, but of the going in.*

Naturally Hippolytus does not understand the message any more than Theseus, and runs away from Phaedra in horror, as Tristan flees Iseult, Diarmaid refuses to follow Grainne, and Noise drives away Deirdre because she is promised to Conchobar. They are all offshoots of patriarchal society and frightened by the real woman, restored to her full authority. Because he is blind to the possibilities open to him, Hippolytus is eventually destroyed.

Nevertheless, Phaedra was very distant. Even in Racine's tragedy, which reconstructs the early myth, Phaedra pronounces what amounts to a *geis* on Hippolytus, by provoking him:

"Avenge yourself, punish me for an odious love. . .
Here is my heart, which your hand must strike."

But he does not understand its significance. So she insists,

"Strike. . .
Or, if too vile a blood would darken your hand,
Instead of your arm lend my your sword;
Give it me"

and takes his sword, keeping it to produce as evidence when later accusing Hippolytus of attempted rape, and thereby using it as an actual materialisation of the *geis*, just like the philtre in *Tristan*. But though Tristan, Diarmaid and Noise had the opportunity of reaching truth through love, Hippolytus' refusal to obey the obligations of the *geis* destroys him immediately, before he is entitled to any part of the knowledge.

The situation created in the Greek legend was intolerable, and had to be resolved in the death of the antagonists. The unnatural Phaedra had to suffer the fate of all traitors to society; while Hippolytus' death at the hands of Poseidon, patron god of Theseus and therefore of androcratic institutions, was the result both of Phaedra's revenge and of the necessity to eliminate anybody who might be contaminated by the dangerous disease she represented.

A Celtic version of the legend gives a completely different twist to the story and appears to underplay the theme of incest.

Ireland, *The Flood of Lough Neagh*

A king of Munster had two sons, Rib and Ecca. "Ecca, who was restless and unmanageable, his manners greatly displeasing the king, told his brother that he had decided to leave their father's house and conquer lands for himself in a distant part of the country. Rib vigorously tried to dissuade him, but, though he succeeded in delaying his departure, could not prevent his leaving altogether. Finally Ecca, manipulated by his stepmother Ebliu, seriously insulted his father and fled Munster with all his men, his brother Rib, and his stepmother Ebliu." When the Druids said that the brothers must separate, Rib went and settled on a plain "where the water of a spring gushed from the earth" and drowned him and his men. Meanwhile Ecca settled on another plain and built a fortress and a town. It was not until much later that the waters of a spring swept over the plain and drowned everyone except Ecca's son-in-law and Libane, the daughter he had had with Ebliu. (J.M., *L'Épopée celtique d'Irlande*, pp. 39—43.)

The remarkable thing in this story, which is also one version of the legend of the town of Ys, is the joint opposition of Ecca and his stepmother Ebliu to the authority of the father. In fact, they achieve what Phaedra and Hippolytus did not, by replacing the solely masculine authority of the King of Munster with a new and much more feminine system, based on a balance between man and woman, son and mother (Ebliu, like Phaedra, is equivalent to the real mother). But the success of Ecca and Ebliu cannot last because they have mocked the Celtic patriarchal structure.

With the characters of Phaedra, Ebliu, Iseult, Grainne and Deirdre, we are continually bordering on the theme of the rebellion of the Flower-Daughter, Blodeuwedd, the Lilith-woman who reappears behind the mask of Eve. The bond they set up with their lovers is fearsome, magical and definitive. The main lesson to be drawn from this is that all these legends appear to be arguing the *absolute and corrosive power of love*, which destroys any organised society by isolating two beings who are sufficient unto themselves and rise against the existing judicial structure.

Yet Phaedra, and many others like her, failed. She avenges herself by leading Hippolytus to his death, accusing him of what he has not done. The infernal machine is in motion and nothing can stop it; for a *geis* that is not observed leads to the swift and irrevocable downfall of the man who has failed in the difficult task of refuting, in one gesture or one word, all the attainments of patriarchal society. What Phaedra proposes to Hippolytus is a kind of blasphemy, the transgression of a secular prohibition on incest, and a return to some former situation. Iseult makes the same proposition to Tristan in the depths of the philtre, Grainne to Dairmaid when she threatens him with destruction if he will not obey her, and Deirdre to Noise when she pulls him by the ears; because *afterwards* there were devilishly interesting things to discover.

In Welsh mythology, these *things* are also to be found at the bottom of the cauldron of the witch-goddess Keridwen, who, as we

shall see, is very like the Groac'h, and also has much in common with
Iseult, Grainne and Deirdre.

Wales, *The Story of Taliesin*
   Keridwen lived in the middle of Lake Tegid, and, having a
revoltingly ugly son, decided to give him perfect knowledge, for
which she boiled up a "cauldron of inspiration and knowledge".
The procedure was to last a year, and she asked a certain
Gwyon Bach to watch over the cauldron. Then one day, "three
drops of the magic liquid flowed from the cauldron and fell on
his finger, which, because of their scalding heat, he put up to his
mouth; and as soon as he tasted the marvellous drops he saw
everything that was to come."
   Keridwen, furious that her labour had been in vain, pursued
Gwyon, but with his perfect knowledge he changed himself into
different animals in order to escape her wrath. She also changed
herself into different animals, finally into a hen, which
swallowed Gwyon Bach, who had transformed himself into a
grain of corn.
   "And according to the story, she was with child. When the
time came for her to be delivered, she did not have the heart to
kill the child, because of his beauty, and put him into a leather
bag and threw it into the sea . . . ." That child was to be the
bard Taliesin, the true incarnation of Druidism, and famous for
his knowledge of the world. (J.M., *L'Épopée celtique en
Bretagne*, pp. 94- 7. Cf. J.M., *Les Celtes*, pp. 341—82: the
chapter on Taliesin and Druidism.)

   The cauldron of Keridwen is clearly one of the original forms of
the Grail, dispenser of intellectual riches, and equally clearly
connected with the philtre from which Tristan and Iseult drink: both
contain a liquid forbidden to those for whom it is not intended. But
Gwyon Bach, like Tristan, drinks it *inadvertently*, and like him
transgresses a prohibition. By drinking from the philtre, Tristan binds
himself absolutely and unconditionally to Iseult, who transforms him
into a new man, who is both her son and her lover. By drinking the
three drops of the cauldron prepared by Keridwen, Gwyon Bach
binds himself absolutely and unconditionally to her, and though he
tries to escape he cannot succeed, because the three drops have the
properties of the *geis*. So Keridwen swallows him. Obviously this is
an image of the sexual act, in which the mistress swallows up the
lover as the vagina absorbs the penis. Gwyon Bach returns to his
mother's womb for a new period of gestation and is reborn in the
new form of Taliesin. This is the most vivid illustration of the
transformation woman works upon the man she has chosen to love.
The act of love leads to a new birth. Gwyon Bach, Tristan, Diarmaid

and Noise all dare, as Hippolytus does not, to fly in the face of every law and previous obligation, taking the fundamental step of loving the woman who is the image of their mother. At that moment, through the power of love, the "I" becomes another.

There is a legend about St John Chrysostom, a bad pupil at school, who, when he went to pray before a statue of the Virgin Mary, was told by her to kiss her lips, thereby acquiring immense wisdom and miraculous skills in the arts, and earning the name St John Golden Mouth. This anecdote affords us an opportunity to stress the transgression inherent in St John's gesture of love, kissing the lips of the Holy Virgin being as close to blasphemy as Tristan's taking the wife (or future wife) of his uncle. There is a shaking of the balance, an act of rebellion in defiance of society, which is the price to be paid for the man's transformation, the destruction of the existing society and its replacement with another. The heroes of the adventure of love are outlaws, exceptional people whose love for the goddess usually leads them to some tragic end. In popular tales, which express not only the unconscious anxieties of mankind, but also its hopes, the goddess's lover became an adventurer who had passed a test and was rewarded with the daughter of the king. It invariably turned out that the king had no son, so the adventurer who had dared to transgress the class taboo became the king's heir; all because the princess was supreme authority and transformed the man she loved, making a king out of a poor vagabond. But the wheel turned full circle when the new king was imprisoned by his role of defender of the order he fought against, and his victory became defeat.

It is recognised that the act of love is linked with death. Among certain species, such as the praying mantis, coitus is followed by a wedding breakfast at the expense of the male. Both medical studies and the observations of psychoanalysis concur that the male orgasm reduces the man to a state close to death. With a great wrench he is "detached from the real" for a fraction of a second, after which, biologically speaking, he has no further reason for existence, since he has transmitted the semem that brings new life. As Freud puts it, "The ejaculation of sexual products in the genital act corresponds more or less to the separation of the *soma* from the *germen* [the first a part of living matter not involved in reproduction, and dying with the individual, the other a part of living matter active in repro- duction, and therefore surviving the individual in the womb of the species], which is why total sexual satisfaction is like death."

But this *lesser* death is not a true one for man, because orgasm, however complete, never achieves total satisfaction; or, to put it rather crudely, you have to leave something for tomorrow. The very nature of desire is "never to be totally satisfied, which is the condition of its rebirth."[47] Life being a perpetual rush towards something, desire is its fundamental motivation. That is what Schopenhauer meant when he suggested that man would find rest and happiness in a kind of *nirvana*, once he had succeeded in abolishing the will and desire to live, and therefore all pure desire, which leads to perpetual rebirth.

These assertions must be applied to our study of the true working of the myth of Tristan and Iseult, in the first place to refute Denis de Rougemont's argument that "the lover's ardour . . . is a blaze which cannot survive the explosion of consummation. But the *burn* remains unforgettable and makes lovers wish to prolong and renew it for all eternity." This concept obviously stems from the kind of superficial romanticism found in Wagner. The burn is only a desire that has never been satisfied, and the paradigm of love enjoyed by Tristan and Iseult is indistinguishable from a desire that is never totally satisfied and therefore forces the lovers continually to start again. They have been near death and have experienced the lesser death, but never really died. Rising from the lethargy that follows orgasm more determined than ever to begin the same act over and over again, which they would never want to do had their desire been satisfied, they hold the permanence and perpetuity of love with a capital L. The tragic death that concludes the adventures of Tristan and Iseult, Diarmaid and Grainne, Noise and Deirdre, and many others besides, is not a consecration of their love by the total satisfaction of desire, but the vengeance of society, which cannot bear that they should be completely wrapped up in each other. The vine and the rose-tree that grow from the two graves of Tristan and Iseult and intertwine suggest that everthing continues after death and that the two lovers are still eternally seeking each other. The image expressing this is much more beautiful and poetic than the morbid *Liebestod*, to which we have become much too accustomed.

For, at the bottom of the philtre, as we can never say often enough, there are *devilishly interesting things*, which the lovers seek through their embraces. The *geis* has been powerful enough for them to acquire a knowledge that immediately dispels all other consider- ations of the world — society, laws, and family ties; powerful enough to create a new situation of continual instability but also of continual progress, enabling the lovers to envisage an ideal, para- disaical situation where all their dreams of childhood or intra-uterine life will come true. This is why Tristan and Iseult begin a new life after each orgasm. But Tristan could not have done without Iseult to show him what was at the bottom of the philtre.

For all life originates in death, and *vice-versa*. "If the grain die it bringeth forth much fruit." This psychological and biological rebirth takes place inside woman, and all attempts to present her as repellent and monstrous are only symbols of the fact that we are born of clay. But society instils such strange ideas into man that he becomes afraid of woman, just as the Celtic heroes we have been discussing initially spurn the woman's love. For all of them woman is the mysterious dispenser of life and death, the living manure that feeds the child it carries with its blood and its milk — and the child is but a projection of man himself. So Keridwen feeds on her lover to give birth to her child, though Taliesin is only Gwyon Bach reborn. She, however, remains the fearsome, tyrannical and dominating mistress whom man will naturally dread and shun. But why is she the mistress?

THE MISTRESS OF THE ORCHARD

When, scarcely out of the maternal world, Peredur crosses the bridge, which typifies the frontier between what he was and what he is about to be, the first person he meets is a *maiden*. He finds her in a tent in the middle of an orchard, and steals from her a kiss, a pie and a ring. But his theft binds him to her absolutely, and consequently to all the women who are to guide him during the course of his strange quest. The kiss represents the sentimental, emotional, psychological aspect of his journey: he is to promise his love to all the women he meets, all of whom are merely temporary faces of the same goddess, the Empress. The pie he eats so greedily represents the natural, animal, material aspect of his pilgrimage, the food that woman gives him and that she will give him again; for even when man is weaned he takes his nourishment from woman. The ring is the magical, supernatural, metaphysical aspect of the Quest, the prefiguration of what the Empress will give him, the *geis* that now affects his whole destiny. And the main object of his search is the Mistress of the Orchard.

When Owein enters the orchard to undergo the test known as the "Joy of the Court", he immediately sees in the middle of the orchard a maiden who is responsible for the magic spell affecting the country. The Mistress of the Orchard extends her sphere of influence over the whole universe of which the orchard is a microcosm. The poetic image of the mother goddess who holds life and death in her hands, she stands by an apple-tree, which is the axis of the world, the centre of life. Her orchard is like the Garden of the Hesperides or the paradise of Genesis.

When Jaufré enters the castle of Monbrun, he goes to sleep in a marvellous orchard where birds sing hidden in the branches of the trees. On waking, he sees leaning over him the figure of Brunissen, the Brown Goddess, who falls in love with him and binds him with a kind of *geis*. For Brunissen, in deep mourning and bewailing the fact that she has been abandoned, is waiting for the lover—son whom she will transform by her love and with whom she will reign over a universe where good and evil have been finally reconciled and no longer exist, a re-creation of man's state before the original sin.

When a woman from the land of the Fairies comes to find Bran, son of Febal, she boasts to him of the beauties of her country and persuades him to go there; she specifically says that there is "an old tree with flowers, on which the birds sing the hours". Mananaan mac Lir, to encourage Bran to continue his journey, adds that there is "a wood with flowers and fruits whose leaves are the colour of gold" to be found on the Isle of Emain, the Land of Women.

Invited by the fairy Fand to come and live with her in the Land of Promises, Cú Chulainn sends his driver Loeg as a scout. Loeg tells him that he has seen "At the eastern gate three trees of bright purple in which birds sing sweetly and long. . . . At the gate of the castle there is a tree of silver in which the sun shines, brilliant as gold. . . . There are three-score trees whose tops touch and then do not touch; three hundred men feed on each tree's many and single fruits. . . . There is a girl in the noble household unlike the women of Ireland; pretty and clever, with hair that floats. . . . She wounds the heart of every man with her love and affection" (*The Illness of Cú Chulainn*. G. Dottin, *L'Épopée irlandaise*, p. 133).

When Conn of the Hundred Battles leaves Ireland on board a little coracle at the mercy of the waves, he lands on a marvellous island, which had "lovely apple-trees, a number of beautiful fountains flowing with wine, a forest full of shining clusters of fruit, nut-trees around the fountains with magnificent nuts, yellow as gold, and little bees humming harmoniously over fruits that drip scented juices". There Conn is welcomed by a queen who has a "chamber of crystal", where the sun shines richly in a sweet and limpid atmosphere.

Vivienne and Merlin are in a magnificent orchard called the "Haunt of Merriment" when she persuades him to teach her how to put a man to sleep, a secret she afterwards uses to make him her prisoner; there also he reveals the three magic words that enable a woman to prevent a man possessing her carnally against her wishes.

When Tristan wants to meet Iseult without anyone's noticing, he alerts her by throwing shavings of wood into a stream. She then leaves the chamber of her husband, King Mark, and comes to an enclosed orchard where her lover is waiting for her. There, outside the world, Iseult is the sole, omnipotent queen, her hair shining like the rays of the sun in a friendly darkness.

There are further instances of this kind, all apparently happening in a place outside the earth where reigns a queen whose characteristics are *beauty*, *light* and *authority*. The mistress, knowingly tyrannical, always obeyed, never rejected, has at her feet the lover, who "is re-created in the rays from her eyes".

It is important to note the solar nature of the Mistress of the Orchard, whoever she is. Obviously ideas have changed since Max Müller's school of thought made it right and proper to find sun heroes everywhere and to regard mythology as a game of hide and seek with the planets, which in any case explained nothing. But that does not prevent the sun's being inseparable from the Mistress of the Orchard.

First of all, Iseult appears with hair as fair as gold, or as the sun; Grainne's name comes from the Irish *grein*, which means "sun". The Queen of the Isle of Fairies lives in a crystal palace, or has a crystal chamber or chamber of glass in which all the rays of the sun converge. When landing on the island, there is a striking impression of light, which seems to rise from the very landscape. So the orchard, which lies in the isle of apple-trees, must be a kind of temple to the sun, where the sun itself lives.

In the Celtic and Germanic languages, the word for sun is feminine, which suggests a female solar divinity whose image has thus survived the creation of the sun god Apollo. Japanese mythology also has a sun goddess, and the ancient divinity of the Scythians was Diana, who was equated with the sun and became the Artemis of the Greeks. Classical writers stressed the bloody and cruel aspects of her worship.

The fate of the sun goddess was inextricably bound up with the rebellion of man against woman, which led to power being vested in a male-dominated, rather than in a gynaecocratic, society. There was a total reversal of religious values, the originally feminine divinities being replaced by masculine divinities adapted to the new social structures, of whom the paradigm is Apollo.[48]

There is a strong possibility that the Celts, like the other Indo-Europeans, recognised a sun goddess, who was in fact represented in iconography and inscriptions as the goddess Sul, honoured in Bath (Aquae Sulis). There still remain visible traces of the mother goddess in the various myths in which women take the chief parts — for example, the story of Tristan and Iseult, and its archetypes and equivalents. So Iseult, like Grainne and Deirdre, could well be the new and most recent face of the ancient sun goddess, whose image has been perpetuated within a totally male-orientated society.

Once we are prepared to look at the story of Tristan and Iseult as the vestige of a feminine sun cult, it becomes quite straightforward. Iseult (Isolde or Essyllt – there is no way of knowing the original form of the name, nor of tracing its meaning) is the sun woman. Mark (or March, a name meaning "horse") is the literary development of the driver of that ritual object of the Bronze Age, the sun chariot; he leads the sun into darkness and delays its rebirth, the usual role of the horse god who is his source. In the popular Breton legend of King Marc'h he "had horse's ears", and the horse is a ceremonial animal in many traditions. Mark's role is also confirmed by the Welsh version of the legend, in which, when condemned to share Iseult with Tristan, he chooses the time of the year when nights are longest. Tristan, whose original Pictish (and Breton) name was

Drustanos, possibly "strength of fire", is the zealot of this sun religion and takes his strength from its fire. As worshipper of Iseult, the sun goddess, he therefore wishes to steal her from Mark, who is keeping her in darkness too long. This is reminiscent of the Oedipal situation, since Mark represents the father and Iseult the mother.

This quality of solar divinity gives Iseult and all the Celtic heroines the tyrannical aspect under which they so often appear and which empowers the *geis* they have at their command with unconditional authority. It also explains why the lover of Iseult (and of all other heroines), as her worshipper and zealot, bows in ecstasy before the face of the goddess, for she is the source to which he aspires, the divine mistress over life and death: her rays warm and feed him and finally bring him suffering and death. For, just as Apollo dispenses happiness, prosperity and good health, but also disease and death, Iseult contains within herself the two fundamental aspects of the same reality: she is the cross-roads where opposites meet.

She is tyrannical, as are all the "dames" of courtly love (from the Latin *domina*, "mistress"). Chrétien's Launcelot experiences this with Guinevere. Grainne provides perhaps the most perfect example of what a woman can make a man do: unlike the Greek heroine (Phaedra) who cannot make herself obeyed, the Celtic heroine is sure that the lover will follow her and finally make love to her, so cutting the two characters off from the social world through which they wander. In contrast to Racine's Greek heroines, such as Hermione, before whom Orestes literally crawls, becoming undignified and degraded in the process, the Celtic heroine will never tolerate self-abasement of self-contempt, as Grainne proves. She wants a man conscious of his responsibilities and worthy of her esteem and love, all because she is *tyrannical*, in the ancient sense of the word.

For, though the tyrant of history is a real despot, cruel and bloodthirsty, things may have been very different in prehistoric times, especially if tyranny was exercised by women rather than men. The mother goddess of the Etruscans was called Turan, a derivative of the Indo—European root *tur* ("to give"), which is still recognisable in the Greek δῶρον. Just as the Celtic king was originally a moral ruler whose task was to unite the members of the clan and give them food and prosperity, so the tyrant-queen of societies with gynaecocratic leanings must have had the task of *giving* life, food, drink, prosperity, happiness and also, naturally, death, since we begin to die as soon as we are born. It is surely significant that in the prehistoric caves of Petit-Morin or the dolmens and covered ways of Locmariaquer there are images of a goddess who is both the protector of harvests, the hunt, and fishing, and also the tutelary divinity of the dead.

The ambivalent "giving" of women is reflected in Irish epic in the the education of heroes by warrior women with magical powers. In

The Education of Cú Chulainn, the hero, who is already very skilled in the martial arts, is sent to Scotland to improve his talents with the help of women who are both witchlike and warlike, and who are fearful to look upon. First there is Dordmair, whose description virtually matches that of the Hideous Damsel of the Mule in Chrétien's *Perceval* and the Welsh *Peredur* or of her counterpart Kundry the Witch, the warlike virgin who guards the Grail in Wolfram von Eschenbach's version of the legend. Then there is Scatach, whose name means "the woman who strikes fear" and her daughter Uatach, "the very terrible". Dordmair falls in love with Cú Chulainn, but he rejects her. Scatach offers him "the friendship of her thighs" and Uatach becomes his concubine. Finally there is Aife, whom Cú Chulainn marries for a year and who gives him a child. It is clear that the women can provide their initiation into magic and warfare only when there are sexual relations between the pupil and the "mistress", in both senses of the word. (Cf. J. M., *L'Épopée celtique d'Irlande*, pp. 88—95.)

Another Irish tale, *The Childhood of Finn* (ibid., pp. 141—3) shows how Finn mac Cumail, King of the Fiana, was brought up by two warrior women who initiated him into warfare and the chase. He perfected his education and obtained his weapons in the house of a blacksmith, whose daughter he married for a year (the practice of limited concubinage). This theme also appears in the Welsh *Peredur*, when the hero receives his education from the nine witches of Kaerloyw, who teach him tricks of magic and warfare (J. Loth, *Mabinogion*, vol. 2, pp. 75—6). In addition there are traces of this custom in the education of Launcelot at the hands of Vivienne, the Lady of the Lake, and in the kind of sponsorship given him by Queen Guinevere. This reveals the real and ancient character of Guinevere—Gwenhwyfar, who initiates her lovers into valour and feats of warfare. The lady of courtly love, who keeps a watchful eye on her lover's behaviour during tourneys, arms her serving-knight herself and develops a sense of valour in him, is basically the heiress of those warlike Celtic women, whose existence is proved beyond doubt, but who obviously belong to the very distant past.

Iseult gives everything to Tristan on the night she gives herself to him, providing him with that second birth he needed to be genuinely himself. But, since he has received an inestimable gift from Iseult, the biological (later moral) law of exchange dictates that *he must give her everything also*. Now the implacability of the *geis* becomes clear: if woman gives everything in offering herself, man must also give everything, must not refuse. It is a subtle psychological game which rests on purely biological foundations (the constant exchanges between the organism and the external world), and which dates back to the dawn of time. It is also love, which is a total exchange between two people.

The maternal nature inherent in all women demands that it be so.

The mother gives everything to her child, by bringing it into the world, feeding it, teaching it to live an independent life, and enabling it to discover sexuality and emotion unconsciously and innocently. The child starts with no other horizon than the body of its mother, and, though he slowly grows away from it, an indelible memory of it remains; so that ever after, the daughter will identify herself with her mother and the son will wish to be swallowed up in his. The relations between two lovers have, of necessity, an incestuous ingredient, in which the man's attitude to the woman will be one of dependence on the mother. Though he has tried in vain to forget this fact and relieve his sense of inferiority in laws that either disable or suppress women, he will never be able to eliminate it from his most instinctive reactions. The reign of the mother goddess has not ended, for she still lives behind the features of the tyrannical mistress.

So the role of Celtic woman is clarified, not so much through the history of the Celts as through their mythological thinking, which is much more important since it deals with the ideal woman of peoples whose independent attitudes allowed them to preserve intact ideas that were thought to have disappeared.

There has been too much of a tendency to regard the Celts from a classically Cartesian, and later an over-romantic, point of view. The character of Iseult has suffered a great deal from the lukewarm sentimentality inherited from nineteenth-century middle-class puritanism. Her adulterous love with Tristan seems shocking because such things are not done, at least not openly. The unhappy lovers are pitied as victims of fate, which is a convenient way of overlooking the shortcomings of personal responsibility. For Tristan and Iseult were never more conscious of their responsibility than when they drank the contents of the goblet. Never did Diarmaid and Grainne assert their responsibility so forcefully as when they ran away. The same applies to Noise and Deirdre, Blodeuwedd and Gronw Pebyr, and many other besides.

But perhaps we have forgotten that the gift of self can only be voluntary and that there can be responsibility only if there is freedom. For we are not free, but victims of prejudice, caught up in restrictive routine, saturated with ready-made ideas. And, lacking clear-sightedness, we totally misunderstand the real problems confronting mankind.

Women, in particular, have become enslaved in our society of slaves, who do not even perceive their condition because they are carried along by their own words. The word "freedom", however eloquently varied, does not give the necessary freedom of action.

Unlike the Western woman of today, the Celtic woman (Iseult, Grainne or Deirdre) was free, because she acted in full consciousness of her responsibilities and so was able to find love, an emotion beyond all restraints and rational laws. That is perhaps the most important lesson to be learned from the story of Tristan and Iseult.

Part III

Theories

"Woman is the goal of man" (Novalis)

When Claude Lévi-Strauss reflected that women have never been "individuals in their own right along with men", but media of exchange like coins, many societies even applying the name of their currency to them,[1] he was referring to a state of affairs that is now world-wide. But our study of the Celtic myths has shown that ideas have not always conformed to this situation. Throughout the ages, individual men and women have believed that women are not just passive objects, that matters were reaching the limits of tolerability in a material, psychological and even logical sense; and that it was vitally necessary to amend them.

Celtic law gave women a position that they did not enjoy in the majority of contemporary societies. They were able to play some part in political and religious life; they could own property, even when married (though certain conditions were attached to ownership); they could govern; they could choose freely when it came to marriage; they could divorce; and, if they were deserted or molested, they had the right to claim considerable damages.

But we must not assume that Celtic women lived in an out-and-out paradise. The laws protecting them were made by men living in an androcratically structured society, i.e. a *patriarchal* one. The in-

247

tention of these laws was to confine women to a limited, though liberal, area where they would not be a nuisance to the mass of male individuals who between them shared the real power. It would appear that the Celts had been forced to keep some aspects of former social structures, because women's moral influence had remained strong. It is difficult to discard old customs, and the Celts very likely took longer than other peoples to rid themselves of social practices inherited from earlier gynaecocratic societies. Women did enjoy a *liberal* sphere of influence; it was conceived and drawn up by male legislators who had the greatest possible respect for their customs in theory, but organised affairs so as to diminish their practical importance. There are a number of historical examples within Celtic societies, Welsh, Breton and Irish, that show that the laws favourable to women were not automatically applied; under the influence of Christianity they were gradually abandoned completely.

The myths alone have come down to us. These divulge, as we have seen, the real intentions of the individuals who form a society. They show that the Celts tried to give women a harmoniously balanced position in relation to men. It is immaterial that this was often a question of attitude or intention; it was a kind of *message*, or ideal programme, which was carefully considered through the centuries and elaborated by intellects that recognised a very different system of logic from the repressive one of the classical Mediterranean. In short, it was in every way a rare conception of the role of women; but it was never really put into practice, since independent Celtic civilisation as such disappeared, and can be retrieved only in fragments from the different cultures of Western Europe.

The problems of women are now becoming urgent to a degree never before reached. It would therefore be of very great interest to examine Celtic ideas about women, their role in society, as well as marriage, sexuality and love. Our society is tired of centuries of running around in self-destructive circles. The feminine half is beginning to react with the extremism that such awareness demands, and everyone is throwing the whole question back into the melting pot. Why not include our knowledge about Celtic women in the discussion? To analyse myths, study legends, and compare them with historical facts is a fascinating work in itself; but it is completely useless and sterile unless we project the problems raised into the present historical setting, which concerns us so deeply. When nations unconsciously re-enact myths in modern life, it becomes an urgent matter to explain them clearly: then they can be used for positive ends, for active thought which may lead to a change, not of the social structures (these are secondary) but of mental attitudes or states of mind. Let us first change our outlook, our mental structures: the rest will quickly follow of its own accord, for material or judicial structures derive directly from conscious intelligence.

So far our discussion has been confined to as rigorous and far-reaching an analysis as possible, but, in the light of the above paragraphs, it would now be advisable to branch out into a speculative and theoretical treatment of the subjects covered. It will obviously be debatable but that is the purpose. If a work of this kind limits itself to analyses even though pushing them to the point of audacity or contradicting officially accepted teaching, it is still only another book to add to a collection written in order to describe, classify and preserve (preferably in formalin: then it does not perish). A purely analytic work can only be negative. Does a twentieth-century audience care whether second-century Breton women wore brassières, or fourth-century Irish women used make-up? There have been many books of this kind claiming to show truth and reality, refuting previous books, and themselves contested and refuted twenty years later. Their authors were careful to respect the established order, the university hierarchies, and the officially accepted, rational ideas.

The practical lessons of the past must be learned in every way possible. Interpretation is no insult to the past. How else can we act, since our entire past is judged from our present position? We must interpret, set out new hypotheses, launch new ideas, even if it may entail reviewing them in the light of fuller information. Ideas can bear fruit only if they reach fertile soil and take root.

Now let us set out these hypotheses.

Chapter 9

Women in Social Life

A woman reader wrote a series of rather bitter comments to a magazine with a large circulation. She was a student who, in her own words, did "not feel victimised, or not much". Here is one of her comments: "Why is nothing done to open more day nurseries? Because men want sole power in everything that really matters. By not encouraging the necessary facilities, they shut women up in the home."[1]

This comment should not be dismissed just because it has been said before or because women concentrate their demands on petty details. The statement contains the core of the problem: as long as women are held responsible for the *upbringing* of their children they will be kept in a state of inferiority, because they will inevitably be cut off from the world of adult activity. The argument that the *upbringing* (but not the education) of children is part of the biological province of woman is not valid, because men are perfectly capable of organising this function when they want to. Besides, there is a division of labour in the masculine sphere, and there is no reason why the children of several mothers should not be entrusted to one mother who would be responsible, at least during the daytime, for this purely animal *upbringing*. Such a system was developed in the U.S.S.R. and is currently in force in Maoist China, though for very different reasons; because there women are freed from enslavement to children in order that they may be enslaved in the work system.

But the Communist system — as it is called! — has invented nothing new. This practice derives from customs found in so-called "primitive" societies, where the children from an entire village are brought up together, in the care of a few chosen mothers or grandmothers. According to the ethnologists, the results are far from bad; there is a merriment and harmony in the community of children that one would seek in vain in our great "civilised" cities, where every time young people band together it is for a vacuous or demanding purpose.

The Celtic custom of fostering was in common use in historic times and even within Christian society. Responsibility for the upbringing and education of a child would be taken over by another father and mother. The results appear to have been beneficial; the foster-fraternity between children created emotional and moral ties that were a great help when the children reached adulthood. Emotional and affective bonds also grew between the adopted child and his foster-parents, which helped the child's psychological growth. Finally, it prevented the child from being enclosed in a confined social unit, developing in him a sense of human fellowship and introducing him to a world that had expanding boundaries. All families were linked together through mutual adoption, and themselves united by emotional ties that were more flexible and powerful than rigid rules and regulations.

Another argument will be raised: there is nothing lovelier than the sight of a mother taking care of her child. This is a sentimental trap. The repressive patriarchal society spreads it at the expense of true sensitivity. The idea is to replace the sexual instinct with a less dangerous, maternal sentimentality, with the added advantage of maintaining parents and children in a state of mutual dependence. So we are ensnared by a tuppence coloured sequence, pretty enough in itself to begin with, but dangerous because of its aesthetic appeal. It starts with the ideal couple, mother and child, borrowed from ancient religions, but emptied of all real substance because this was fundamentally revolutionary. The magnificent role of the mother is then stressed in speeches. Prizes are distributed to deserving and heroic mothers. Officials of the patriarchal society award mothers decorations and, what is worse, cynically confer medals on the mothers of children sent by those same officials, to their death, in the "Field of Honour", the usual result of aggression in this society.

Why should mothers have to sacrifice not only their lives, but also their own personalities, for the exclusive benefit of their children? Society replies, "We must safeguard the future of the race." Another idiotic argument, but wrapped up in packaging that, when one understands the hateful way it is fabricated, becomes intolerable. Until when do we safeguard the future of the race? Until the aggressive and repressive patriarchal society has found the means of destroying our whole planet? Everybody marches on, including the women to whom these words are addressed. Flattery is enough:

those who feel flattered start purring and stop thinking: another victory for the secret forces that control society, be it capitalist, liberal, democratic or socialist.

The main point is to restore women's *whole personality*. Patriarchal society has deprived them of it for centuries. The biological reasons invoked to justify this action are pure invention, but unfortunately they have been invoked continually for centuries, to vindicate the oppression of one class, one caste, one race above others. In a sense it is semi-fascist to believe in the weakness and biological inferiority of women: Hitler's doctrine of the supremacy of the Germanic race was based on such an argument. So women are in possession of their own personality. But what does this consist of?

Here women's liberation movements fall into a trap that, once more, men have laid for them. Some of these movements allow themselves to be patronised, directly and indirectly, by public figures who have come into prominence via the masculine path and who are merely products of the male-dominated society. Furthermore, the refusal to wear brassières, on the grounds that they are symbolic of male domination and the commercial exploitation of women, is a futile and ineffectual gesture. Men have other means of domination, and when the manufacturers of underwear see their customers stop using this particular garment, they will quickly adapt and start manufacturing other trappings — unisex pullovers, for example.

In fact, the main trap is denying one's sex. The most ardent feminists claim they achieve equality by functioning just like men. This is a way of shocking and creating a stir, in terms of propaganda and putting forward demands. But let us be realistic. If women are different from men, it is probably because their talents do not fit exactly the same functions; but this does not mean that they must automatically be barred from these functions. Since few women have held important posts in the world, there is at present no way of knowing exactly of what they are capable.

To discover this one must remain objective and not give in to absurd, yet widespread, notions like: "Women are capricious, they cannot be entrusted with positions of responsibility; physiological factors, like menstruation and the menopause, change their character; women often change their minds; women are not able to make decisions; etc. etc." For it is really a question of cultural and not biological or physiological factors. Girls are taught from their earliest years that they must not bother their minds with science and technology, but must interest themselves in human problems and interpersonal relationships.

However, in more primitive societies, where the division of labour, hence the division into social castes, is less rigid, women have held all manner of positions. There were even women warriors among the

Celts. There is a fine example of this in the Irish tale of *The Birth of Conchobar*. After the massacre of the guardians of Ness, the girl "went to war and took up arms and went with three times nine men". In other words, she became the leader of a band of warriors. She sowed terror everywhere and it was only when she met the Druid Cathbad that she renounced her life as a warrior in order to marry him, having first taken care to secure her own future. This marriage did not prevent her remaining involved in Ulster politics, as the mother of King Conchobar. Conchobar entrusted many missions to women, particularly to his female messenger Leborcham. It was often women who ruled their people. Queen Medb of Connaught was a formidable character who had an eye on everything and imposed her will everywhere. She also proved a skilful military chief of staff. There is the historical example of Boudicca, who supported the struggle of the Britons against the Roman legions. We should not forget that in the Indian Republic at present there is a female head of government, as there was in Israel until recently. (Both have nevertheless been anti-feminist.) These two governments have not been without influence in their domestic achievements, as well as in their foreign policy.

There is evidence, throughout the Celtic legends, of women taking an unrestricted part in public life. They are queens, princesses, priestesses, prophetesses, maids, servants, peasants, workers, educators, warriors, horsewomen. Women do not appear to be ostracised in these idealised mythical societies as they are in the present day. How have we reached this state? "Parents always induce a sense of subordination and submission in their daughters (the divine image of the passive woman, full of self-sacrifice and courage.) If you are not a good housewife, they are told, you will stay an old maid. They even use blackmail to stop them being too independent."[2] Perhaps we should reflect a little on what Engels said in 1884: "The emancipation of woman, her equality with man, is and will remain absolutely impossible while she continues to be barred from productive, social work and is confined to private domestic work." Engels may be out of date, but comments of this kind are still valid, as events unhappily show.

When women were given the right to vote in France (in 1945!), a number were elected to Parliament. But with each succeeding legislative assembly the number of women in all parties decreased. This shows that the problem is not one of partisan politics: it is a social one. The appalling habits of the past are too strong for recent new opportunities.

Given the present possibilities, and taking the lessons of the past into account, it is ultimately up to women themselves to put an end to their second-class citizenship. The French Civil Code has already been partly amended, and present legislation is giving an increasing number of rights to single and married women. But of what use are these rights if nobody claims them? Men obviously maintain a cautious silence. But why do women? Above all, why do they not act?

Action is in fact limited to supporting a new class struggle, which is senseless: one's sex has nothing to do with one's social class, whether it be by birth, education or profession. Men and women will always have to live together, and society must be the product of a total agreement between its members.

Hence the problem is not so much knowing what women can do in contemporary society: we know they can do anything, can occupy any position, provided they have the necessary qualifications, which they often have. The problem is finding a new balance between men and women; not to enable them to put up with each other, as they do in marriages that have failed, but so that they can work together towards something more exciting for them both. As they say in the American women's liberation movement, "There is a total liberation beyond and inherent in social liberation; it involves a dramatic overthrow of the basic relationship which has existed for thousands of years between men and women; it therefore involves a thorough reconsideration of the code of sexuality."

By blinding ourselves to the position of women in society we also forget the psychological factors peculiar to woman. These are conditioned by education, surroundings, culture, instincts, desires, and intellectual or practical potential; as well as by the judicial framework within which she is enclosed, like all human beings. At this point the problem of marriage confronts us; and marriage is and has been the essential basis of the patriarchal society for thousands of years. We also face the problem of sexuality, especially the liberation of repressed sexuality; and, finally, the problem of love, which is probably the most important. We tend to forget about love when talking about sex. It would be useful to recall Plato's words: "If by some magic a town or an army were composed only of those who loved and were loved, it would be impossible for this town or this army not to have found the surest guarantee of its prosperity. Such men would in fact refrain from all evil and would only wish each other good."

An essential element in the woman's role is the biological fact that she gives life. She is therefore a creator, even though the act of creation is relative. We have seen how, in the Celtic world, she was an initiator and transformer, a deliverer. We have seen how the perfect love of Tristan and Iseult united the two lovers; how there was always the desire to go further and discover the "devilishly interesting things" at the bottom of the vessel. We have also seen how the woman's transformation of the man was a kind of new birth, a new life: as if the creature were finally freed from all treacherous influences that prevented his seeing the point. Humanity needs this transformation and revelation to restore a new *raison d'être* after so many centuries of vagaries and wars. Masculine society is aggressive and must submit to a peaceful transformation by women and what they stand for. Then it will finally be able to free itself of the taboos besetting it. Woman, as an individual, can liberate herself only if there is general liberation. This is the price of her emancipation. A revolution in the structure of human thought is imperative, and therefore it is right to attack these structures first of all.

Chapter 10

Marriage

O f all the institutions that have a direct effect on women, marriage is the most discussed and the most open to question and doubt, because of its fundamental ambiguity. Women actually have an ambivalent attitude towards it. On the one hand, they denounce it for isolating them; on the other, there is not a single woman who does not want, even if subconsciously, to get married, and she will do everything to achieve this end. However, this contradiction, which no one would wish to attribute to women's instability and lack of logic, is easy to understand. When a woman marries, especially within the patriarchal legal framework, she has to suppress a large part of her personality. On the other hand, her social career is so dull and uncertain that she in the end comes to regard marriage as the lesser evil, a kind of emotional, material and, especially, sexual security. This contradiction would seem to negate the absolute value of marriage, allowing it only a relative one. Yet marriage is the very basis of our society. Society functions so badly because its basic institution, marriage, is discredited.

The utopian socialist Charles-Louis Fourier, who was exposed to the contempt and sarcasm of his contemporaries, was courageous enough to set out the problem succinctly in the nineteenth century. "Marriage, like all civilised customs, has led to the opposite of its original purpose: it has merely produced a secret and universal debauchery and the protection of the law for those who violate it the most openly."[1] Why? Because love is by definition free, and so runs slap bang against "marriage, the absolute principle on which collective morality is based." Free love, as an "element of natural life", is overwhelmed by the heavy social substance of marriage, "the immediate moral fact". This relates to what Hegel said of the family resulting directly from marriage: it is not a social institution *per se*, but an essential stage in law and moral conscience.

The relative nature of marriage is thus revealed. It is diametrically opposed to the Christian conception, which has passed into civil law: when a man and a woman marry, they have to swear to make it last as long as they live, for better and for worse, and whatever may happen. This ideal of stability has now been ousted by the new notion of instability and the temporary. For to say that the family is a *stage* demotes it — and with it marriage, which is the certificate of its existence — to a secondary, if necessary, role. The ambiguity of marriage is apparent from every angle.

Let us admit for the moment that marriage is on the one hand a consecration of love and the realisation of an emotional choice, and on the other hand an institution ensuring the permanence of society through the protection it offers the children, who are the hope of that society. The second definition is beyond dispute and is confirmed in every society without exception, whatever the detailed rules and conditions of different beliefs and cultures. The acknowledged aim of marriage is children: "Increase and multiply!" By this definition, we must look at marriage in a purely social perspective.

But why are childless families tolerated? It is true to say that they have always been regarded as monstrous exceptions. In some cases they have been annulled automatically and the man able to remarry; naturally, there was no question of the man's being sterile — it could only be the woman's fault. In other cases a repressive system of duties and taxes was instituted. On the religious level, a childless family has always been regarded as more or less accursed.

In fact, childless families are tolerated because marriage represents a general repression of sexuality. A man and a woman who make love officially are not outcasts; society can keep an eye on them, which is not the case with a clandestine pair of lovers. Society needs its basic units and one realises that the *upbringing* and education of children may not be the real, practical reason for the institution of marriage. Individuals find themselves dependent on one another, instead of being responsible for themselves. This is the framework the woman enters. There are two advantages: first, the man will never be alone again and will take responsibility for his wife and for any children he may have; secondly, the woman will be in the care of a guardian, apparently for her protection, but in fact to keep her under control. So, even though modern legislation is showing her greater respect, the married woman is still a second-class citizen. As Claude Lévi-Strauss comments, "The mutual bond at the basis of marriage is not set up between men and women but between men using women, who are merely the instigating, passive cause."[2] In fact, marriage is a means whereby a man asserts before other men *that he has a wife*. Through this he establishes links with another family (that of his in-laws). He sets up a chain of alliances between families, and this chain cements society together.

The legend that expresses this historical reality best is the rape of the Sabine women by the first inhabitants of Rome. They were outlaws of all kinds who had gathered in an area to which Romulus had accorded the right of asylum. To begin with it was an act of violence, the brutal seizure of their neighbours' daughters (probably their wives as well, though this was never mentioned). But it became the prelude to negotiations that led to a positive alliance between the Sabine and Roman peoples, who thereby became members of one, wider family. This was the dawn of Roman society, and civilisation. It is an excellent example of marriage creating a society and contributing to its development.

There is a similar instance among the Celts, in the Irish legend of the marriage of Ethne and Cian. The Tuatha Dé Danann landed in Ireland and came into conflict with its former occupants, the Fomors, a maritime people. After a few skirmishes, peace was established through the marriage of Ethne, the daughter of the Fomor Balor, and Cian, one of the Tuatha Dé Danann. United, the two peoples made war on a third, the Fir Bolgs, who were trying to gain a foothold in Ireland. They won. Marriage had consolidated the bonds between two peoples and created a new society. Lug, son of Ethne and Cian, became its hero; though later, after the Fomor Bress had abused his powers, Lug became an eager partisan of the Tuatha Dé Danann and re-established the balance in their favour.

Marriages have always been political or economic arrangements in royal and aristocratic circles. Kings married the heiresses of a dukedom, an earldom, or another kingdom; they could end a war by deciding to marry an enemy princess. This was the reason for the marriage of the Irish Iseult to King Mark of Cornwall. In France before the Revolution, the aristocracy married to hallow the union of lands or titles; a nobleman might marry a commoner to refloat the bankrupt treasury of the nobility. The phenomenon can still be observed today among the middle classes. Peasants too have "married" land rather than people.

The warmest defenders of marriage, apart from the clergy, who after all depend on it, were the noblemen and the rich. Marriage was the necessary condition of their economic prosperity and the inheritance of wealth. The wife still enjoyed a position of privilege in this kind of marriage: she possessed a fortune or a comfortable living, and such families could allow the mother's release from housework and child-rearing. The mother of the noble or wealthy family was not the one to bewail her lot. On the contrary, she was an ardent propagandist for marriage and the joys of maternity.

Charles-Louis Fourier claimed that the revolutionaries of 1789, who had thrown out all the old, outworn ideas, had continued to regard marriage as sacrosanct, and that was the cause of their defeat. It is true that Fourier had not realised that the revolution of 1789 was not a popular revolution, but an uprising of the rich middle class against an aristocracy that considered itself still in power, although it no longer had any economic basis. Even so, Fourier was right: to attack marriage is an act of revolution that may radically change the foundation of society. In his *Nouveau monde amoureux* he adds, "To suppress marriage is to destroy the mastery of men and the alienation of women."[3]

The problem is to be aware of marriage as a social and economic act, for the moment disregarding the emotional element and sexual instinct. This problem was debated in the seventeenth century by the *Précieuses*, who, having proved the incompatibility of love and marriage, were already recommending divorce and "trial marriages". But the *Précieuses* did not condemn marriage as such; it was not until the end of the nineteenth century that this happened. It was even applied in the U.S.S.R., where free marriage was given some encouragement. The Marxist theoreticians based their hopes on this, but it proved a complete failure, because it became an institution no longer called marriage, which was recognised by the law and so made official. This, of course, was to safeguard the interests of any children who might be born.

Nowadays we are continually hearing about the approaching disappearance of monogamous marriage. Hidden within this hope lies the undeclared desire of men (naturally, men speak of it most) to return to some kind of polygamy; because, biologically, a man cannot be satisfied by one woman. Without denying the truth of this, we can see that it is a very egoistical and completely anti-feminist attitude: while the man may be unfaithful, the woman may not; the practice of polygamy, which is commonplace, though masked in bland hypocrisy, should be made official. We must look at the evidence. Polygamy favours the man exclusively, debasing the woman to an object of current consumption. It is a luxury reserved for the privileged, as was the case (and still is in certain countries) among the Moslems. Moslem women can hardly be said to have enjoyed any great freedom in the course of history; neither have they been regarded as human beings in their own right.

Does this mean that monogamous marriage is indestructible? It would seem impossible to deny, for with what could we replace it? It is the foundation of our society. Even if it were to be suppressed, by a stroke of the pen, it would return, as happened in the U.S.S.R. We must first change the nature of our societies.

Unless monogamous marriage has become a caricature of marriage.

What, in fact, has become of the family, that direct result of marriage? It has become a ridiculously narrow and suffocating cell, turned in on itself, and seizing up completely. Since conditions of life have changed and the urge towards individualism grown, the family no longer revolves round a reduced axis symbolised by a bunch of certificates, official documents that really only concern the husband, the wife and, by proxy, the children. In a childless marriage, the wife is housekeeper. This is practical, convenient and costs less than employing a servant. It is impossible to find servants any more, so the wife is praised to the skies because she can run the house so well and make nice little meals for her husband. Has she not been told again and again that this is an excellent way of keeping husbands at home? Her voluntary role is stultifying, to say the least. If she does not want to stay at home, it becomes even worse: it is still her duty to do the housework when she comes home. She is caught in a trap and cannot escape.

Her position is even more degrading when she has children. She is now totally out of the running unless she reacts with an effort of will and intelligence. She is condemned to the kitchen and nursery. The household gadgets invented to make her work easier only chain her down all the more to her secondary, but terribly useful, role.

There is another, more serious, point to make. In a family of this kind, small as it is, the only hope she has of obtaining any help is by paying for it. Because of the nature of contemporary life, where everyone lives in enclosed and separate boxes, she cannot rely on other members of her own or her husband's family, except in special cases.

Finally there is the drama of the husband or wife disappearing through death or divorce. Then the family crumbles. If there are no children the family disappears altogether. In the case of divorce, any children are bitterly contested. They may be entrusted to other parents, whom they hardly know, forced to make a new life for themselves in circumstances that are not particularly favourable to their psychological or emotional development. This is not a systematic and negative criticism of divorce, but some established facts that everyone knows.

The modern family is not viable. It carries the seeds of its own destruction, which makes the marriage that led to it suspect. The family of today and the families of ancient societies, the Celtic among them, are worlds apart. In those times, the husband—wife couple were never isolated, never outside a group of which they might, but did not necessarily, form the pivot. There were parents, grandparents, cousins, brother, sisters around this couple; the family was spread out around the means of existence, which often demanded the presence of a number of people. Economic realities demanded this, and traditional practice had made it a hard and fast rule from the earliest times. Consequently the woman never had to bear the full burden of the housework, nor the burden of bringing up children on her own, for it was shared out among the various mothers, as well as among the grandparents. This considerable advantage for the woman was also a considerable advantage for the children, who were able to develop freely both among themselves and in contact with a great number of other people in an open environment. The egoism of the small, nuclear family was avoided, and the family had a far greater social importance.[4]

It is not claimed that a family of this ancestral type was a perfect institution, nor that the woman enjoyed a life of unalloyed happiness; but it fitted in with social conditions, economic realities, and a specific mental outlook. It led to a definite equilibrium, which people accepted in degree according to temperament. Our present small families no longer correspond with economic, social, cultural and psychological realities. The husband and wife are each working in their own spheres, sometimes in completely different circumstances, with different preoccupations and in an environment that is harmful to the unity of the couple.[5] The children participate in a compulsory, institutionalised education that emphasises the generation gap by bringing into the family a different culture, which is a constant subject of discussion. The unity of the small, reduced, modern family, which could still hold its own at the beginning of the century, is a snare and a delusion. Nobody believes in it any longer anyway.

We are now up a blind alley. It is not possible to go backwards to that dear old ancestral family, permeated though it was with patriarchal attitudes. But neither is it possible to preserve the nuclear family, which is already falling to pieces. Should we suppress the family? How? The family is a biological necessity because man is by definition a rational and *sociable* animal. A child cannot serve an apprenticeship in sociability except within the framework of the family, where his emotional instincts will be satisfied. The family has not disappeared and is nowhere near disappearing. But there has to be a thorough-going change in the outlook of the family and in marriage, which is its framework.

There was an extraordinary flexibility in the Irish and Welsh Celtic families. Celtic marriage was not very stable. It was a contract, but like all contracts it could be revised. The Celtic was unlike the Mediterranean mentality in this respect, the latter being soaked in Roman jurisprudence and severity. If the family is a stage in development, we should recognise that its structure can never be final; it should be regarded as a temporary institution, equipped to face particular circumstances. It is ridiculous to suppose that a man and a woman can commit themselves for good when nobody knows at the time of their commitment what the future holds, what new necessities will arise for the couple, for the individuals, and for the whole of society.

It is not true that divorce was instituted as a solution to these problems. In the opinion of specialists in law and the family, divorce is a necessary, *lesser* evil in the present state of affairs, making it possible to avoid the worst. It has an essentially negative role, because it condones failure and attempts to ensure that failure will not change into tragedy. Divorce is a medicine gulped down to cure a disease, but it gives rise to side-effects as serious as the disease itself. It is only a makeshift solution to relieve the conscience of our hypocritical society.

We have to start again from the foundations, namely with education. How can we still have the nerve to spout such nonsense about marriage to children? How can we still have the dishonesty to end fairy tales, novels and films with stereotyped images illustrating the phrase "They lived happily ever after and had lots of children"? How can we teach children that marriage is an *end* when it is only a *means*?

When everybody realises that marriage is a means intended to legalise a factual situation, to create deliberately chosen family ties to join two vital energies in a legally defined and freely accepted framework, to bring up and educate consciously wanted children in certain conditions, only then may it be possible for the sacrosanct institution of marriage to be given a new value by returning to its rightful position.

To achieve this, people must be taught *from childhood*, that marriage is not a consecration or a permit for sexual activity. The woman will then decide to marry not in order to give herself over to guilt-free sexuality, but because she has chosen the state of marriage with everything it entails. Celtic society was enlightened in this sense, tolerating any kind of sexual relationship outside marriage. There was, among the Celts, a profound serenity, as well as a kind of quiet, smiling amorality; good and evil were not defined in a formal, arbritrary fashion. In Celtic legends it is quite common for men and women to have sexual relations at a chance meeting without any sentimental romanticising or forced declarations.

The necessity for free sexual relationships entails another problem: contraception and voluntary birth control. When marriage is no longer the main outlet for sexual activity (it has often been the only one, especially among Christians, prostitution being the alternative), then free sexual activity as such will be totally different from the kind whose aim is procreation. Acknowledging the human being's right to sexual relationships outside marriage means defining a new morality; this new morality revolves around a prohibition on having children outside marriage (for the children's sake) and thus necessitates the teaching of contraceptive methods. Society would lose nothing, as procreation would be protected and encouraged within the exclusive framework of marriage. There would be two advantages. First, it would limit the number of births, which is important in present social conditions if we have any concern at all for the future of humanity. Secondly, it would place an entirely new value on marriage, as we could then look upon it as a firm and eminently practical basis for a child's upbringing. Women who choose to marry would do so fully aware of the situation, with the excellent and natural aim of having children.

There is yet another necessity. Maternity must be voluntary and consciously sought by the woman, with total responsibility accepted by the man. To achieve this, children would have to be prepared for the idea that they too may be parents one day, with all the obligations that involves. Women must know what to expect and what is possible for them. Voluntary motherhood has led many women to a total harmony of all their faculties. All this requires a complete revolution in the educational system and customs, for these questions are not normally discussed. Young people should be taught that it is possible for any idiot to produce a child if he/she meets another idiot, but that to educate a child requires intelligence, thought and devotion. If procreation is confined to married people (who are not forced to get married) this would be the surest way of achieving happiness for a couple and security for the children, whilst according marriage its deepest worth.

Everything depends on the choice we make. A socialist society attempting to return to a non-urbanised economy might bring their children up communally, and would conceive the problem differently. But is such a retreat possible in our industrialised societies? It seems more akin to a dream than to reality.[6] The only fruitful return to the past is in using precedents that can be put into practice today. It is not for their enlightened achievements in education and the liberation of women that we return to the Celts. They lived in a very different economic context from ours. Their civilisation was essentially agricultural, pastoral and warlike. Contemporary civilisation is diametrically opposed to that system and is developing away from it; our society is urban, industrial and peace-loving (in theory at least). But the fact that the Celts did not attach the same importance to marriage as did Christian society cannot fail to interest us. Remember that sexual relations between a married man and a concubine were *legally authorised*, and that a legal wife had the power to refuse the presence of a concubine she did not like. This may seem trivial, but it shows that the man did not have all the advantages, and proves that marriage, a social institution intended for the survival of the race, had nothing to do with sexual relationships, because it was not destroyed by an extra-marital affair. Celtic society, like a number of other primitive societies, was much more tolerant in this area of morality, and had different ideas about fidelity. A couple would never swear exclusive faithfulness to each

other. Celtic fidelity, as the stories of Cú Chulainn and of the quest
of Peredur prove, was simply an attachment to a chosen person, to
whom one always returns and for whom one has a special feeling.
This is not inconsistent with other adventures or even other feelings,
which do not in any way change the relationship of the two people
in question.

Every human being is intrinsically free. This the Celts understood.
Romano-Christian society made men and women each other's slaves,
to the women's greater disadvantage. Men believed they had the right
to own women, who believed that men possessed that right;
consequently, in sexual relationships the man owned the woman and,
what is sadder (though the result of centuries of habit), she was
happy to be owned. It is an insensitive and dogmatic argument to say
that this is biologically necessary for the woman to reach orgasm; for
it denies the psychic elements in orgasm. Women have for centuries
been subjected to the worst kind of slavery: that of their own
psychological make-up. Women dream of being possessed (some even
say of being raped) because men desire and achieve this result in
order to improve their standing and make believe they are stronger.
But consider the effect of such an orgasm on men and see who is the
stronger. *Animal triste est post coitum*, said the ancient Romans:
although "animal" is a neuter noun in Latin, it clearly refers to the
male. This wretched state of affairs has given rise to a number of
psychological reactions in men, culminating in the image of the
devouring and dangerous female.

Marriage is a social institution intended for the procreation and
preservation of the species. If we want it to be strong and durable,
the mentality of the contracting parties must change and the terms
of the contract be completely redefined. The husband and wife
should promise to be faithful to each other in the fulfilment of a
common achievement (the upbringing and education of children),
but should also promise each other *personal liberty* on levels that do
not affect the continuity of the marriage. Why should a man not
have a relationship outside marriage, provided it does not undermine
the material stability of the family nor the emotional situation
developing within it? And why should a woman not do as much? She
would have children with her husband; she could protect herself
against unwanted pregnancies by using contraceptives. This will
appear immoral and revolutionary to some. It is undoubtedly
revolutionary, for we must find a way out of the blind alley; but it is
not immoral, because the criteria of morality have to be brought up
to date.

There is another aspect, which is not social and is sometimes
wrongfully neglected; the emotional aspect. *Is marriage a realisation
of love?* Sweeping aside all the mumbo-jumbo associated with
romanticised marriage the basic truth is that marriage is a social,

legal and binding institution, whereas love is a feeling, a matter of individual emotion (this without regard to the sexual elements). So how can we make *marriage*, which is rigid and defined, coincide with *love*, which is fluctuating and elusive? When a Christian priest asks the bride and groom to promise to love each other, does he not realise that the heart has its reasons of which reason does not know? The response to the question is a temporary feeling of the moment, a feeling that cannot in any way foresee future events. One cannot force a human being to love or hate. The fact that marriage tries to force a man and a woman to love one another for the rest of their lives is a form of swindle. There is *deceit* from the beginning, and if the argument is followed through to the end, the bottom drops out and the marriage is therefore null and void.

The problem has been raised on many occasions and in different civilisations, the heart of the matter being clearly analysed during the courtly period and at the time of the *Précieuses*. On both occasions the discussion reached the same conclusion: *marriage is incompatible with love*.

Courtly love, as defined by the poetry of the troubadours and by courtly romances, was a vindication of free-love relationships. It was a code of behaviour for love confronted with a given situation, i.e. marriage. No courtly lady could love her husband. She married to start a family. She could certainly respect her husband, entertain affection and all kinds of feelings for him. *But not love*. Love she kept for her chosen knight. The ideal, almost mystical, element (of Platonic origins) was stressed. Scholarly theories have been founded on this, substantiated by the doctrine of "distant love", expounded so brilliantly by Jauffré Rudel. The purity and nobility of this courtly love, a triumph of the spirit over the flesh, has been set up as an example to be followed. It is true that mystical experiences were achieved, and that often the lady offered her lover only spiritual delights.[7] However, this should not blind us to the fact that courtly love was total, and therefore of the flesh as much as of the mind. It justified adultery well and truly.

The courtly romances support this. In outline, the love of Guinevere and Launcelot conformed to what was expected of courtly lovers and had nothing pure or ethereal about it. Neither had the love of Tristan and Iseult. Here we return to the actual source of that courtly love: though there was some Mediterranean (and no doubt Arab) influence on the poetic expression of love, the main directive came from the older and coarser Celtic model, represented by the legends of Tristan and Iseult, Diarmaid and Grainne, Blodeuwedd and Gronw Pebyr. These were about the rebellion of the married woman who no longer believed in the emotional validity of marriage and ruthlessly claimed the right to choose for herself whom she would love and by whom she wished to be loved. The *fine amor*, a far preferable description to that of "courtly love" , was a social reality as well as an emotional and carnal one. In a period of triumphant Christianity, it was a real rebellion against established ideas; but this rebellion hardly materialised except in literature, which was a way of stifling it.

The distinguished *Précieuses* of the seventeenth century had also been deeply disappointed by marriage and took up the same themes, twisting them to suit the fashion of the day. The *Carte du tendre* is very explicit, for alongside the river Inclination there are two opposite paths open to the patient progress of the lover. Passing through Obedience and Trusting Friendship, he can reach *Tendre sur reconnaissance*; this is very like marriage. But through Respect and Goodness he can reach *Tendre sur estime*, which is one step higher: it is love, which, according to the definition found in Corneille, can exist only if there is real respect for the person loved.

We have therefore reached the conclusion that marriage and love cannot co-exist, *at least in theory*.[8] It seems equally impossible to make marriage and sexuality co-exist, although the aim of marriage is procreation.

As a corollary to these conclusions, we reach a third: love is not identical with sexuality either. This should be repeated again and again, for it is the only way to overcome the misunderstandings lying in wait for everyone in our society, because society is silent about the true implications of its purpose. Women would not be slaves if they realised the true nature of their problems from childhood. Men too might find a way of regaining their balance; they cannot do so in our present circumstances because everything is based on misunderstandings. To liberate women is to liberate men as well. Giving women an awareness of their true responsibilities, restoring their whole personalities, will make men aware of their own responsibilities and their true role. A new harmony will grow between couples who do not need religious or secular benediction to love each other or to satisfy sexual needs. On the contrary, by giving birth to children, they become deeply integrated into the active life of the community. When this happens, marriage will be a "blessed state", protected by relevant laws; because this blessed state is the assurance of the present and future harmony of society.

Chapter 11

Sexual Liberation

Sexual liberation is the key to achieving an increasing balance and harmony between couples, and the liberation of the woman's personality, because it is essentially a question of liberation, and not revolution which implies a radical change with a return to the original source. Sexuality has never abandoned its well-springs, and has managed well enough without any imposed contrivances. All it suffers from is being put under lock and key. It is there in all its abundance, but is considered a shameful, diabolical function. We should be destroying barriers, and not aiming vaguely at some kind of revolution that encroaches on areas having little to do with our purpose.[1]

Sexual liberation is, however, linked with revolution, whether in social behaviour or in politics. But is does not necessarily result from a political revolution. Neither the French, the Russian, nor the Cultural Revolution in China have achieved anything new in this direction: they have even led to a certain amount of repression. But political revolution will come about *through sexual liberation* and therefore *through the liberation of women*. That is why contemporary societies, under pressure of public opinion, are only making a show of liberating woman and tolerating the kind of sexuality that is not much more than a safety-valve.

One preliminary point should be made: the sexual function is never an end in itself. Viewed as such it is a trap that can only gratify the egoism of down-at-heel hedonists. The sexual function is a *means*, which also implies a *method*. It could almost be said to be a *modus operandi*, just like mathematics or one of the basic sciences.

The sexual function could be regarded as the scientific fact posing a number of questions relating to the erotic, in the widest sense. A human being has to learn to use his eyes, ears, limbs, which serve his physical activity; he has to learn to use his brain in order to exercise his intelligence; similarly he has to learn (or rather ought to learn) to use his sexual function.

But for what purpose? Nostalgic moralists will reply that the only end is reproduction. But the concept of ultimate purpose is scientifically unacceptable, so this argument is not valid. Here we have what the argument is about: whether or not the sexual function has an ultimate purpose, and to define this. As it is impossible to establish this scientifically, it would be best for everyone to have total freedom to appreciate it in his own way, just as everyone can decide his religious or metaphysical attitudes for himself.

Sexual functions can be used for reproduction. But this is only one possibility. Sexual union is not necessary to conception, as artificial insemination shows. Complete sexual union, reached in the simultaneous orgasm of both partners, is essentially a psychosomatic manifestation qualitatively different from procreation. "A frigid or violated girl who has had no intimate relationship with the man who has possessed her can still become pregnant; and biology teaches us that penetration of the ovum by the spermatazoa can take place mechanically, long after a couple's orgasm."[2] When we reflect on the way we use our limbs, our sensory organs, our whole body, we find that it is impossible to say that any one part is connected to any one particular function. We breathe through and smell with the nose; we perform all kinds of actions with the foot or the hand. The mouth is used for eating, for taste, sometimes for breathing and for verbal communication.

Because of the sense of touch, the body is one of the sensory organs, all of which enable us to communicate with everything outside ourselves. These are the vital transmissions between the self and the non-self, between subject and object, what we are and what we are not, what we are now and what we shall be. They are the *means of knowledge*. Why should the sexual function not also be directed towards knowledge? The goblet from which Tristan and Iseult drank had *devilishly interesting things* at the bottom. It is with this mental perspective that lovers of all periods and civilisations have with noble words (and pain!) unconsciously directed their action. Blodeuwedd deceived Lleu Llaw Gyffes because he did not bring her the knowledge for which she had hoped. She expressed this unconsciously by commonplace sexual dissatisfaction.[3] Diarmaid agreed to follow Grainne because he realised in his heart that she had the power to give him a knowledge that he had never yet acquired. Here we come back to our former conclusions about the new birth that woman gives to man, lover-mother to lover-son. This is of such deep significance that it should never be left out of any discussion of the sexual function and its liberation. By repressing sexuality, though at the same time reserving it for a reliable, governing élite, society keeps people away from the complete knowledge to which they have a natural right: this knowledge is dangerous to a society based on repression, though officially it is dangerous to the people themselves. The same problem arises in education, which is supposed to be universally available, but is in reality kept for the privileged.

The Tantrist philosophers of the East, both Hindu and Buddhist, realised this: when wisely organised, sexual practices led the individual to a freedom that became increasingly more perceptible with each stage reached. The kinds of sexual relations advocated by the troubadours during the courtly period had similar elements. We can hardly postulate any direct influence, but in both schools of thought we find the same "adoration" of the woman, which did not necessarily entail a physical relationship. The idea appears in the legend of Diarmaid and Grainne, because Diarmaid waits a long time before touching Grainne, although he has run away with her and they live together. Perhaps he was living out his quest for the woman after all? The very nature of the quest is a point in common between Tantrism and Celtic love; but it is certainly the only one.

Many writers and philosophers nearer home, some of them "visionaries", have developed the same themes: a knowledge of the world through sex, a liberation of the mind through sexual relationships, the energising power of the orgasm, and so on. It is difficult to sort out from these various formulas which of them belong to the realms of magic, which to religion, which to science, or which quite simply to sexual obsessions. In his work *Metaphysique du sexe*, Julius Evola analyses a few, and these emerge as syntheses of various traditions all of which have the central theme that woman "is the *Janua Coeli* and the prerequisite instrument of liberation" (p. 358). But note the term "instrument", which here expresses the ideas of the fanatic Maria de Naglowska.[4] The ideas of Aleister Crowley are more interesting. He set up a secret, sexual organisation, the O.T.O. (*Ordo Templaris Orientalis*), whose ritual is recorded in a manuscript called *Agape-Liber C: The Book of the Sangraal*.[5] The title is significant because it refers to the famous Quest for the Grail, in other words the quest for woman of the Celtic legends.

Crowley maintained that love, or, more accurately, certain practices of sexual love, led to ecstatic union. As the control and practice of these ecstasies was acquired, one ascended the road to liberation. In other words, for him sex was the way to reach God. Performing the sexual act was not to obtain emotional comfort or for procreative ends, but to give birth to a new current, to renew strength. It was a sacred act of magic, a true sacrament, "an orgy prolonged in honour of the great god Pan", a "transmutation" in the alchemic sense of the word.[6] In simpler terms, this act is a breach, a way of splitting open or fracturing ordinary consciousness and entering into contact with higher realities.

However, confused and suspect these ideas may be, they nevertheless appear very close to our observations of Tristan and Iseult and the whole mythical web implicit in the story. If love is a breach, and sexual relations are part of this, it is a factor of progress. For one breaks away, sometimes violently, from a constituent part in order to achieve some sort of regeneration. Nature is well made and rejects the useless. The dead branch of a tree breaks and falls to the ground; the tree continues to live. The human body rejects the poisons that are formed inside it or the bacteria that harm it. Sexual relations facilitate a break with the paralysis of a dead social life: it is a well-known fact that lovers who have enough in each other reject the society that is no longer any use to them, *ipso facto*. This is also a kind of break with the past. The transformation a man undergoes with a woman is a rebirth after the "little death" in orgasm, a rediscovery of the world as seen through fresh eyes. Humanity has known this for a long time, as the myth of Circe re-created in the Celtic legends shows; but this myth has suffered the same fate as all others, interest being taken only in the story and not in its meaning.

As the sexual function is a means of knowledge and discovery, transformation and purification, it is particularly desirable that it should be freed of the whole context of shame and guilt with which it is burdened. As it is not essentially directed towards any given end, the realisation that it must have free range in all directions is of primary importance. In other words, there must be freedom not only of so-called normal sexual relations, but also of other manifestations of sexuality; whether or not the people who practise them realise it, auto-erotic or homosexual practices, regarded as "perversions", are only acts of rebellion against the repression of the sexual instinct.

Masturbation has always been anathema, surrounded with fire and brimstone. But, while society condemned it (medically, socially and for religious reasons), it also, hypocritically, encouraged it, by prohibiting "normal" sexual activity. These condemnations have no biological foundation: masturbation has never led to physical or moral decadence. Since the individual is free, there is no reason why he should not make whatever use of his body he wishes.[7] But the opposite attitude taken by some women in the feminist movement is another matter, and a serious one at that. As if to wreak vengeance on the men who have enslaved them and used them as sexual objects, they systematically extol solitary pleasure as the only way that female sexuality can function. The ghost of Lysistrata is prowling in the wings of feminist meetings. "No more relationships with men," say these women, "and if sexual tensions persist despite everything, masturbate."[8] Others go further: "Is anything more pleasant than auto-eroticism? With such strong arguments in favour of masturbation, like technical competence, convenience, egocentricity, why introduce a partner"?[8]

We could easily achieve a "mystique of auto-eroticism", which would do nothing to solve the social problem inherent in the inevitable relationship between the sexes. These extreme views, over and above their satirical or blasphemous aspects, grow from a medical and psychological discussion about the specific nature of the feminine orgasm. It relates to the real debate on the role of the clitoris and the vagina.

Two kinds of orgasm exist. One is set in motion by clitoral, the other by vaginal stimulation. Of course, "vaginal and clitoral orgasms are not separate biological functions",[9] but there is no doubt that two different feminine character types derive from them. Because the vagina is (in principle) stimulated by masculine action, it might be tempting to say that the "vaginal" woman is submissive to man, while the "clitoral" woman escapes this domination, especially since the vagina is the passage leading to conception.

Basically this would only be a quarrel about two kinds of sensuality. But there are other arguments: during coitus, "Direct stimulation of the vagina results in identical responses to those produced by the indirect stimulation of the Mons Veneris or the manipulation of the clitoris."[10] It follows from this that "the receiving and transforming organ, the clitoris, is the sensual focal point of the woman."[10] This role of the clitoris, demonstrated by modern science and anticipated by psychoanalysis, was taken for granted in all primitive societies and is implicitly acknowledged in so-called civilised societies. In fact, sexual morality stresses the sensual and social value of the vaginal orgasm: only when a woman has full contact with a man is she in possession of her personality; only vaginal sexual union is allowed because it is "natural" and enables procreation to take place (it is the *vas naturale* of the theologians); only a woman who has known "the joys of motherhood" is a fulfilled woman; and just as the male child's penis is accepted and acknowledged by his parents, his mother in particular, the vagina has to be accepted and acknowledged by the man, preferably the husband (hence the importance of virginity for a young bride). One might suppose from all this that there is a ban on the clitoris. In some primitive societies the clitoris is in fact surgically removed, so that young girls cannot reach orgasm alone or with other women; this is tantamount to ensuring their dependence on men.[11]

So, according to the theorists of the feminist movement, the clitoris is not there to serve the vagina during foreplay. Neither is it an "atrophied penis" inspiring "penis envy" in women. It is a totally separate organ, the focal point of stimulation, excitement and orgasm. It is *the female sexual organ*, and the woman who wishes to liberate herself must use it to the full, whether on her own or homosexually.

There is no question of rejecting homosexuality: when the sexual function is freed from the possibility of procreation, and given free rein, there is no biological or moral rule why female homosexuality should be regarded as unnatural and unhealthy. Female homosexuality can lead to physical and psychological flowering[12] just as much as heterosexual practices can. It is a question of temperament, preference and circumstances; it is a matter of freedom as well.

But the "mystique of the clitoris" is debatable and, in the final analysis, dángerous. "Homosexuals may have a useful function. But when they allow themselves to become obsessed by their standpoint, they risk alienating heterosexuals from the feminist movement. I find their mystique of the clitoris and all those sexual dogmas that they try to impose on us boring and irritating".[13] This is the heart of the problem: there is a great risk of going in the direction opposite to the one intended, with the result that, instead of liberating women, the imposed dogma may lead them into a new kind of slavery. The unreal aspect of these theories would be highly vulnerable to masculine opposition and exposure. So what would be gained?

The main point is to insist that women must achieve a sexual equilibrium. It does not matter much whether it is found alone or in homo- or heterosexual practices; whether it is found in vaginal or clitoral orgasm or any other sensations: a woman's body must belong to her alone, and she must discover what suits her best, decide how she will *know herself best*, and, hence, on her surroundings. She must have the opportunity of choosing between a sensuality directed towards conception, in which case she will be a mother, fully conscious of her responsibilities, with all the troubles and joys that entails; and one directed towards pure eroticism, in which case she will be a lover, or a virgin lover,[14] almost a priestess of love, the hierophant of a goddess, as in ancient religions.[15]

But this cannot happen unless there is total moral freedom. It will take time and patience before the collective mentality, accustomed over centuries to making sex clandestine and guilty, can allow free sexual relations from the age of puberty. This would be entirely natural. What is contrary to nature is to coerce young people of both sexes into continence, on the fallacious pretext that it would ruin their health or risk their starting a family, for which they could not take on the responsibility.

Here women have an essential part to play: first, as mothers educating their children, and teaching them, especially the girls, the whys and wherefores of sexuality; secondly, as lovers or as wives, who, as the Celtic myth snows us, must assert their personality. Woman is an *initiator*, or rather she should be one, if it were not for the fact that her deepest instincts and natural dispositions have been stifled. While at present it is usually the man who initiates, and then in a brutal, traumatic and violent fashion for both partners, it would be more normal if the woman did so, because she holds the secret of life within herself, and she is profoundly sensitive and intuitive. Here too the Celtic example teaches us that woman, the mistress of feeling and impulse, is the centre on which the rays of world activity converge. Strabo, the Greek geographer, tells of the women of the Namnetes, who lived on an island at the mouth of the Loire and were priestesses of a mysterious divinity. They would sometimes go to the mainland to initiate men into their secrets. Then there were the virgins of the Île de Sein, described in legends common to the whole Celtic world, who received visitors on their island and initiated them into the mysteries of love. The maidens scattered around the castles of Arthurian romances did the same. The queens of marvellous islands, like Morgan, and the fairies of Emain Ablach did so too: they made the traveller drink a potion that gave life, youth, beauty and knowledge. It was this drink that Iseult gave to Tristan.

When woman is no longer a shy creature who waits in a corner until the all-powerful male deigns to notice her, then there may possibly be a radical change in society. For not only will women be able to express their sexuality freely, but they will also be able to stand on equal terms with men in their social, emotional, and sexual life. Then there will be no more hypocrisy, no more holding to ransom; prostitution, which is another kind of slavery, will disappear of its own accord; sexual crimes will disappear,[16] and women will no longer be accosted in the streets by men in search, not of a kindred spirit, but of a quick fuck.

In the long run, sexual freedom leads to freedom in attitudes towards sexuality. Wilhelm Reich rightly concluded, from the observation that sexual problems spring from sexual repression, that "The revolutionary movement is unaware of the fact that the moral regulation of instinctive life creates precisely what it means to control: anti-social impulses." He added, "Only a regulation through sexual economy can eliminate the contradiction between nature and culture; with the elimination of sexual repression, perverted and antisocial impulses will also be eliminated."[17]

The purpose of sexual liberation is clear: to eliminate the restraints produced by the repressive patriarchal society; to eliminate sexual obsessions by a natural and open use of the sexual function. Because it is an integral part of the human personality, such liberation would also create a greater harmony in the human being and guarantee *his social behaviour*, which is extremely important. Nothing can be achieved without the agreement of society as a whole, because man is a social creature. If we want to integrate women into society, the complexes inherited from dead cultures must be eliminated. We may then find that the shadowy creatures dormant in our nostalgic dreams will come to life again; figures such as Iseult, Grainne, Blodeuwedd, Guinevere, Dahud the "Good Witch", Keridwen, Rhiannon — in short, the goddess, the princess submerged in cultural darkness.

Chapter 12

Love

If marriage is one thing and sexuality another, there is yet a further primordial element of life that affects women closely. That element is love: a superbly noble feeling, having nothing to do with reason or any of its consequences. Laws, rules and morality, whether religious or secular, are not its concern. The subject has to be raised because, in discussing sex, the element of love is often neglected, except in the totally inaccurate sense manifest in the expression "making love". It would obviously be incorrect to suppose that love plays any part in the price-scaled sexual relations of prostitution, or in the intimate exchanges practised at wife-swapping parties. Yet in our current vocabulary "making love" means exactly the same as "communicating genetic information", to use the strange jargon of some erudite biologists.

We have already seen that it is high time to analyse marriage, restoring its true worth, and to free sexuality of all constraint. Likewise, exposure of pseudo-love, along with a complete redefinition of love, is long overdue. The stultifying societies in which we live have succeeded in making us forget the power of love by means of their sentimental songs, in which artistic worthlessness vies with dishonesty; this dishonesty has been defended on the grounds that people need to forget their troubles. The more love is imprisoned in sentimental, rose-water romanticism, the less dangerous it becomes for patriarchal society, which has no need of two people loving one another truly for it to build the judicial superstructure that perpetuates it. On the contrary, the less people love each other, the easier it will be to turn their unrequited need for affection to utilitarian ends, thus channelling their psychic tension and playing upon it according to need with a whole complex of official moans and groans. Economic activity is based on the alienation of human emotions: the more a human being's emotional needs remain unsatisfied, the more isolated he feels; and, the more isolated he feels, the more he will tend to join the nearest social group for comfort. This is why people talk about work as a comfort, because it enables them to escape despair and puts the individual in a group, giving him a new sense of responsibility.

Since these lies are not all that obvious, patriarchal propaganda is usually quite successful in coming up with provisional alternative solutions. A seamstress will work all the better if she hopes to meet "Prince Charming" when she leaves the workshop in the evening. If she does not, she will go and see a film, which gives her a glimpse of "Prince Charming" in the shape of a fashionable actor. That night she will dream about him, and this will enable her to face another working day, starting the whole process again the following evening. This is the mainspring of economic activity in the modern city, and no amount of electoral speeches will effect any change. Love stories are as much in demand as pornography, and for the same reason; dissatisfaction is knowingly sustained for the greater benefit of those in control.

Even if the girl's dream comes true, the framework in which society contains her love will, for its own protection, contradict her dream; for the intention is to limit something that is inherently without limit. "Starting from the most powerful primordial aspirations of the individual," writes Benjamin Peret in his important work *Le Noyau de la comète*,[1] "sublime love offers them a path of transmutation which results in a harmony of flesh and spirit, and joins them in a higher unity in which the one may no longer be distinguished from the other. . . . Sublime love is therefore first and foremost a rebellion against religion and society in conjunction." Compelling the couple to obey rules, society introduces possibilities of transgression, which causes anxiety. In order to prevent their withdrawal, society pulls them into collective life by binding them with moral and material commands, creating duties, especially in the woman. She will therefore tend to limit her former, once unlimited aspirations, because she must have a sense of *reality*, because the family must live, because the home must be maintained. Just as the consumer society makes wage-earners dependent on it by offering credit for household appliances, houses and cars, the couple are held on a leash and will never be able to excape from their situation. It is on the family, and therefore the regulated and supervised couple, that society relies, for the family is peaceful, has woven the net that enmeshes it, and has set an exact limit on the aspirations of love.

"Man is a social being because, according to all the evidence, he has an innate feeling of his own inadequacy stemming from the human condition, as it is appropriately called. This is the source of his anxiety. He is thus led, from the beginning, to look outside himself for what he lacks, because the need for love reveals a disunity within us" (Benjamin Peret). Clearly this has little to do with sexuality; we are concerned with something quite different and beyond the sexual function. Love is, of course, a feeling that arises and grows from the sexual instinct; it is grafted onto a vague longing resembling the sense of melancholy that disturbs adolescents. When this longing meets an object that seems to respond to it, there is a transformation which is irreversible and incomprehensible. There is no question of sublimation, but quite simply of making a utopian state manifest and real. One begins to realise what a terrific force love is: it starts as blind instinct, and succeeds in crystallising a person's total energy towards a whole realisation not only of himself, but also of the other person, who will soon be one with him. "The West aspires to this harmony, though not in full consciousness. That is why sublime love remains asocial, even antisocial, in our world, which sustains the contradiction at fever pitch in order to feed its oppressive power; it is discernible in the most trivial details of everyday life" (Benjamin Peret).

This "sublime", "total", "liberated" love consists of thousands of different elements, sexuality among them. But it largely revolves around a feeling that essentially eludes all control and classification. Because of their intuition and sensitivity, women understand it unconsciously and naturally. Should their unlimited aspirations be disappointed, they carry their affection over to their children. Then the mother can think only of her son or daughter, who may be able to realise what she has only glimpsed. The affection parents have for their children, and the hopes they place in them, can be the result of their own frustration. When a woman is disappointed in human love and feels the need to transfer it to an ideal and perfect sphere, she becomes a mystic. Nuns' prayers are hymns of love, often very carnal and offered to a god who is *All Love, All Perfection, All Beauty.*

All this shows frustration and a lack of balance and satisfaction. Luckily there are legends that, like dreams, restore the fullness of love. They are in a sense the "utopias" of love, expressing the hopes of a humanity seeking to reconcile the need to exist within a society with the freedom to love. The Celtic myths are the most beautiful and significant. They show us sublime and total love, even though the heroes come to a sad end; they tried to shake off the yoke and went as far as they could. But their failure was not necessarily the failure of love.

When the mare-goddess Rhiannon prowled round the mound of Arberth in the hope of seeing King Pwyll, whom she had loved for a long time, and then ran away from him in order to be caught with even greater desire, she had the same aspirations as any little shopgirl, goddess though she was. She dreamed of sublime love, and it was realised. But when she abandoned her main function, which was purely erotic, and became a mother,[2] she lost all her power and rights. Patriarchal society could not forgive her for bringing happiness to the man in whom she realised herself, thus isolating him. But the situation sorted itself out: the son formed an alliance with the mother. An alliance of this kind is divine, as we can see in early Christianity; it is probably the·most natural and instinctive possible, in spite of what the psychoanalysts say.

Many difficulties can arise between two lovers, and always derive from social taboos and commands. Only one of the couple is free: the other is already the prisoner of a repressive system. This happened with Diarmaid and Grainne, because Grainne was already the wife — or fiancée — of Finn. It happened with Cú Chulainn and Fand: Cú Chulainn was already married to Emer. He had to choose between them and, bowing to patriarchal law, returned to Emer. Fand was the last manifestation of gynaecocratic law and suffered inconsolable sorrow.

The story of Cú Chulainn and Fand (related in *The Illness of Cú Chulainn*) poses an interesting problem. Is absolute love exclusive, or can it involve several people?

Celtic texts would seem to indicate that fidelity in love does not exist, at least not in the modern sense. Queen Medb had an official lover, Fergus mac Roig, as well as other suitors; but she still loved her husband, King Ailill, deeply. Queen Guinevere also had an official lover, Launcelot of the Lake; though she was terribly jealous of him (according to the texts, which are coloured by Christian influences) it seems that she still entertained a sincere love for her husband, King Arthur.[3] Gawain was always ready to perform the hardest feat to prove to his most recent maiden that he loved her more than all the others. The hero Cú Chulainn was faithful to his wife Emer, but he nevertheless had temporary and occasional relationships with other women.

The Celtic understanding of fidelity was essentially relative. It was primarily a matter of fidelity to a freely chosen person, who was loved unconditionally, so to speak. Temporary liaisons could be explained by sexual desire, or by an emotional quest totally different from the bond uniting the original couple. The notion of jealousy does not really arise in Celtic texts, at least not the possessive kind of jealousy found in Western literature. Possessive jealousy is the logical outcome of Christian marriage and an exclusive love in which two people "own" each other. This has left its mark on the vocabulary of love: "you belong to me", "you take me", "you are mine", and other such nonsense, which only demonstrates a fundamental egoism. This has had an effect on morality: it leads to crimes of passion. Luckily it has given us some beautiful writing by Racine, notably when he is speaking through the mouth of Hermione, Roxana or Phaedra.

Yet sublime and absolute love is completely altruistic, because it is concerned for the happiness of the partner. Love is not merely selfish satisfaction of the instincts, it is the replacement of one's own instincts by those of the other; there is a direct interpenetration not only of bodies, but also of the whole psyche, the whole network of emotions. Love reaches towards the other, or the others; when it does not, it is just an egoistical and possessive passion. Western love is warped by this narrow vision, which originally stemmed from social causes as much as magical ones. To avoid the kind of triangular relationships that threatened the stability of the basic unit of society was the first preoccupation of the patriarchal system, and manifested itself in the supervision and possession of women by men. It had the unforeseen result of women becoming psychologically possessive of men, as the practices of polygamy and legal concubinage demonstrate. To this first preoccupation can be added another, which, however out of date and stupid it may seem to us, should by no means be overlooked: the woman being the "receiving crucible", it was dangerous to risk its receiving the more or less magical inflows from a third person, not to mention the possibility of conception.

So love was undermined by society because it was an extremely powerful factor favouring emancipation. As such, it was poisoned with questionable ideas conducive to possessive ownership, egoism and jealousy. Fortunately some of the myths have preserved the free and pure nature of love.

Examples of altruism are rather few and far between; but they are based on the same idea as Charles-Louis Fourier's definition of what he calls "pivotal love". This contains "a transcendent fidelity, which is all the more noble because it conquers the jealousy that divides ordinary love".[4] Love that is neither exclusive nor jealous enables the person to reach beyond his own state and raise himself to the heights of the early Christian dream: to love the other, even if unknown; to love *all the others*. This is clearly in keeping with the basic law of Christianity. Fourier suggests that, until now, men have spoken only of "loves" and not of "Love". In the new world that he advocates, a divine state, in which harmony will completely disperse all the seeds of discord, war and hate, will be achieved. Undoubtedly a utopian vision, but it is also a conception of love as a cohesive factor in a society that would in fact no longer be repressive. "Pivotal" lovers have no farewells: there would only be changes in harmony with their nature at any given moment in their development.

Here we see the essential difference between love, a positive force that leads people beyond their own condition towards an expansion of their personality; and passion, a phenomenon provoked by social repression, a self-destructive force, a depressive state in which the person can no longer act freely and positively because he is acted upon (the word "passion" comes from the Latin *patior*, "to bear", "to submit"). The romantic view of passion as the creator of great works must be eradicated. Passion is nothing but destruction, as Racine showed so well in all his tragedies, and, with all respect to the dreamers who consider it a means of escape, can only make the human being's fate worse. Grainne's love for Diarmaid was never a passion: it was a perfectly conscious, lucid feeling; nor was its effect on the beloved destructive, because Diarmaid fulfilled himself through it. Finn could not forgive him for this achievement; hence the fury with which he tried to beat him. This also explains the tribulations of Tristan and Iseult: far from being necessary for the permanence of their love, as Denis de Rougemont would have us believe, these were *the vengeance of society on behalf of its outraged conventions*. "Love, the only love there is, carnal love, I adore you, I have never ceased to adore your poisonous, mortal shade. The day will come when man can recognise you for his only master and honour you even in the mysterious perversions with which you surround him" (André Breton, *L'Amour fou*, Paris 1966).

This certainly is an *amour fou*, a mad love. Love as seen by the Celts does not need to be rediscovered. It exists, but has been concealed. It needs only to be made a reality again, in the form it took in literary texts dating from a time when it was still known that "Mutual love . . . is a device of mirrors that faithfully reflect the image of the woman I love from the innumerable angles of the unknown. It is always a heightened divination of my own desire, intensified with golden life" (André Breton, *L'Amour Fou*).

As though by chance, it was women's voices that gently sang the most beautiful love songs in those times that now seem so distant. These mysterious, divine beings wove a fragile, tangible bridge between heaven and earth.

We start with conjugal love; for it did exist, *despite marriage*. In the Irish tale *The Madness of Suibhne*, the hero went mad after being cursed by Saint Ronan for desecrating the church.[5] Thereafter he led the life of a vagabond in the woods. His wife Eorann was forced to remarry for political and economic reasons, but she did not forget the unfortunate Suibhne, whom she still loved. When she met him in the forest she sang to him,

> "Welcome to you, dear, dear, splendid fool:
> Although sleep may be its lot,
> My body has been ravaged since the day
> When I learned you were no more. . . .
> Although the king's son leads me

Into the joyful halls of feasting,
I would prefer to sleep in a tree's small hollow,
With you, my mate, if only I could. . . .
If the choice had been left to me
By the men of Ireland and Britain,
I would prefer to live on cress and water,
With you, without sin. . . .
I am sad, O mad one, to see you blind and
  in distress,
It grieves me that your skin
Has changed colour,
That briars and thorns tear you. . . .
I wish that we be together
And feathers grow on our bodies,
In light and in darkness,
I would wish to wander with you, each night
  and day. . . ."

There is a connection between this touching litany and the
lamentations of Deirdre, the Irish national heroine. She loved the
young Noise deeply, though she was promised to King Conchobar.
The King avenged himself and Noise died. This is what Deirdre sang:

"The one for me the most beautiful under the sun,
Who for me was the most dear,
You have taken him from me, such a great shame,
I see him only in my death. . . .
Two deep red cheeks prettier than a meadow,
Red lips, eyelashes black as beetles,
Teeth the colour of pearls,
Like the noble hue of snow. . . .
Well-known to me was his clothing distinct
Among the warriors of Scotland,
His beautiful purple coat for the meeting,
With its red gold border. . . .
The dear blue eyes, loved by women
Struck terror in his enemies,
After the wandering in the forest, in the noble assembly,
Dear voice high across the darkness of woods. . . .
I sleep no more, my nails have lost their crimson,
Joy comes no more upon my waking,
Since the sons of Usnech no longer come. . . .
I do not sleep half the night
On my lonely couch,
My spirit flies to infinity,
I no longer eat nor laugh. . . .

Do not break my heart today,
Soon I will go to my approaching tomb,
Grief is stronger than the sea,
Do you know that, O Conchobar?"

This image of a grief "stronger than the sea" brings us to other lamentations, which are a kind of *credo* of absolute love. When Iseult was delayed by the storm, she arrived at Tristan's bedside too late: he had died for love of her. She sang,

"Friend Tristan, when I see you dead,
By reason I can live no more.
You are dead to my love,
And I die, friend, of tenderness,
For I could not come in time
To cure you of your illness. . . .
If I had come in time
I would have restored life to you
And spoken gently to you
Of the love that was between us . . .
But though I could not cure you,
Together we can die!
Seeing I could not come in time
Nor change the course of destiny
Since death arrived before me,
I will sup of the same drink.
For me you have given your life,
And I shall be a true friend,
In the same way I wish to die for you. . . ."[8]

Note that Thomas's text gives love unlimited powers, because Iseult, bemoaning the fact that she did not arrive in time, distinctly states that she could have changed the course of destiny (*e jo l'aventure ne soi*). Iseult was a witch, a *fairy*, a protective and creative divinity, and her words are magical. They give love the tragic power to reunite the lovers in death, so granting them that new life on another level, in another reality, that was denied to them on earth. This brings to mind another love song, from *The Courtship of Etaine*, one of the most beautiful love legends in the Irish epic literature: "My love is a thistle, it is a strength and violent desire, it is like the four quarters of the earth, it is infinite like the heavens: it is the breaking of the neck, it is a drowning in water, it is a battle against a ghost, it is a race towards the sky, it is an adventurous race under the sea, it is a love for a ghost."

The mysterious Sin, that disturbing heroine of another Irish tale, *The Death of Muichertach*, avenged the death of her father by

bewitching his killer King Muichertach, whose concubine she
became. She then caused his death by her magic spells. She was the
victim of a conflict between duty and love, and when she was asked
why she acted in this way, she said:

"I myself wll die of grief for him
The noble king of the western world,
For the burden of all misfortunes
I have heaped on the ruler of Ireland.
I, alas, made the poison
That vanquished the king of noble troops . . ."[9]

When Fand, the cursed and jilted fairy, had to leave Cú Chulainn
(who had decided to go back to his wife Emer), she expressed her
love in a few verses of great poetic beauty:

"It is I who will set out on a journey,
But it will be of necessity,
And even if it should prove glorious,
I would prefer to remain. . . .
What a disaster to give one's love to a man,
If he takes no notice!
It is better to go away
If one is not loved as one loves. . . .
Farewell to you, Handsome Dog,[10]
It is willingly that I go,
Although this is scarcely my wish,
But there is always the right to flee. . . ."[11]

The most moving poem, possibly the closest to the Celts' image of
women, is *Duanaire Finn*, about Diarmaid and Grainne. The two
lovers were fleeing, and stayed only one night in any place. They led
a painful, dangerous existence. Grainne, the eternal mother of her
lover—son, watched over him as he slept, singing a lullaby that
contained all the love in the world, its joys and sorrows, and the
triumphant strength that makes it inviolable by society.

"Sleep for a little, a very small while,
And fear nothing,
Man to whom I have given my love,
Diarmaid, son of O'Duibhne.
Sleep here, deeply, deeply,
Son of O'Duibhne, noble Diarmaid,
I will watch over your rest,
Charming son of O'Duibhne. . . .
My heart would break with grief

If I should ever lose sight of you.
To part us would be to wrench
The child from his mother,
Exile the body from the soul,
Warrior of beautiful lake Garman. . . .
The stag in the East does not sleep.
He does not cease to bellow
In the bushes of the black birds.
He does not want to sleep.
The hind without horns does not sleep.
She moans for her dappled child
And runs through the undergrowth.
Sleep for a little, a very small while,
And fear nothing,
Man to whom I have given my love . . ."[12]

This love poem, attributed to an anonymous poet of long ago, is surely the most perfect illustration of the woman's attitude. *She watches.* Like the doe who trembles for her fawn in the midst of a hostile universe, she is first and foremost a mother protecting the man *she has chosen*, whether he be her lover, husband, or the son she had wanted. It matters little which of these he is; they are one and the same. This is the great lesson woman teaches us: love is altruistic and makes a thousand sacrifices; love is creation, a continuous creation by which the woman *makes* the man, body and soul. With all his pretentions and inherent egoism, man knows he is inadequate on his own, and can find his fulfilment only through the woman, the chosen fellow-creature who has given him life and will give him life again. "The perfect self-sufficiency that the love between two people tends towards will then encounter no more obstacles" (André Breton, *L'Amour Fou*).

Until now, only poets have really understood woman. This is probably because woman, like poetry, is a continuous creation, a crucible in which scattered energies are melted down, and which embraces the unique act that resolves all contradictions, abolishes time, breaks the chains of loneliness, and leads back to a lost unity. What mystery surrounds this strange character!

"In the hollow of your breast has cried
A woman with blonde curls
And lovely eyes of smoke.
Of fox-glove are her dark red cheeks,
And the treasure of her teeth
Is a winter snow. . . ."[13]

This creature, who is beauty in its highest degree — a "convulsive" beauty, as André Breton puts it — will, in our imagination, "be withdrawn and erotic, fixed and exploding, contingent and magical, or not exist at all." She will always have this ambiguous character, this sweetness mixed with fear — but a fear like that of birds caught in the trap of life:

> "The girl of the sea, charming and treacherous,
> Half woman and half fish,
> Who sings to spellbind sailors
> And breaks their ships."[14]

But who can know the real face of the goddess who waits on the Marvellous Island? For the sailors are dazzled by the sun and lost in the spume of the sea.

Notes

INTRODUCTION

1. There is no proof at all of ignorance among primitive peoples about the male role in the begetting of life, but some legends stress this point, and we find it in the Christian myth of the Virgin Birth, also known as the child "conceived by the Holy Ghost". The mere fact that the problem has been raised to the mythical level shows that it corresponds to an actual concept and may for that reason be considered.
2. *Les Croyances primitives et leurs survivances*, Armand Colin, 1960, p. 59.
3. "In my opinion, however, the domination of the male can be traced back to the discovery of the idea of paternity, when primitive peoples linked the sexual act with procreation. This was a major discovery for humanity. It seems that as long as the idea of fatherhood had not been grasped, all agricultural societies felt such a respect for fecundity and the mother's ability to perpetuate the species that it was not possible to establish a true patriarchy; childbirth had too great a prestige magical power and religious worth. In my opinion, this is what happened, judging by the faint traces of pre-patriarchal communities in Neolithic times." (Kate Millett, an American of Irish-Catholic descent, and author of *Sexual Politics* (Hart Davis, 1971). This extract is quoted from an interview published in *Lectures pour tous*, no. 210, July 1971, p. 135.)
4. "It would appear that prehistoric, or at least Palaeolithic, man had a sexual life regulated like the animals, with monogamy, periods of coupling, the attaching of importance to female consent, and absolute devotion to very small children." (André Morali-Daninos, *Histoire de relations sexuelles*, Presses Universitaires de France, 1965, p. 11.)
5. This sexual promiscuity is recorded in a historical text. Describing the British, Caesar states: "Groups of ten or twelve men have wives in common, particularly brothers along with brothers and fathers with sons; but the

287

children born of the unions are reckoned to belong to that particular house to which the maiden was first conducted." (*De Bello Gallico*, V, 14.)

6. "It is therefore understandable that the first artistic representations of human beings were of women, and not couples, or even groups ... the oldest portrayal of coupling is in the cave at Laussel. Another, more recent, shows a man in the posture of imploring adoration before a woman taller than himself. It is possible therefore that a worship of women had been established at this time — a worship of nature more erotic than religious, perhaps with the therapeutic aim of calming man's doubts and anxieties about the fulfilment of his desires." (André Morali-Daninos, op. cit., pp. 11--12.)

7. "I do not believe we have enough knowledge in the matter to speak of a matriarchal system. I think there was a patriarchal tendency and a matriarchal tendency and I do not think we are in a position to state that everything preceding patriarchy was its exact opposite namely matriarchy." (Kate Millett, op. cit., p. 135.)

8. "My child, I have entered a religious order that is entirely dedicated to the adoration of the Virgin — a truly Marian idolatry. I felt the patriarchal and oppressive nature of religion, but the worship of the Virgin to which we had vowed ourselves brought some compensation; it was a reassurance." (Kate Millett, op. cit., p. 134.)

9. This is not a feminist book in the sense that some impassioned women occasionally understand the term. I am basically concerned that a truth wilfully hidden by masculine society should be restored, so as to make it possible to reconsider completely the relationship between the sexes, which, I repeat, is the foundation of the family unit and therefore of the whole of society.

10. "The few 'primitive' peoples surviving today possess a conception of the universe which we lost in the Iron Age. Their knowledge has become misrepresented, emphasis being placed on the tranquilising aspects, and not on the positive aspects that are so necessary to the present state of civilisation. It has deliberately been used to corroborate outdated dogma and there has been a conscious playing upon the corrupt and distorted hunger for myth in the West." (Vincent Bounoure, "Preface à un traité des matrices" in *Le Surréalisme même*, no. 4, 1958, pp. 18—19). This severe judgement should be remembered every time we are attracted to a legend handed on from any Western civilisation.

PART I

CHAPTER 1: THE HISTORICAL CONTEXT

1. Albert Dauzat, *La Toponymie française*, Payot, Paris 1960, p. 39.
2. There is a detailed study of this subject, especially on the interplay between legend and history, in Jean Markale (hereafter referred to as "J.M."), *Les Celtes*, Payot, Paris 1969, pp. 65—90 (the chapter on "Rome et l'épopée celtique").
3. These events are so strange that the border-line between history and fable is constantly moving. Cf. J.M., op. cit., pp. 91—119 (the chapter on "Delphes et l'aventure celtique").

4. In particular, animalist art and the decoration of horses' trappings; above all, the technique of metal engraving (the most famous example is the Gundestrup cauldron in Copenhagen).

5. Note that Gaul was divided into four main regions: Belgium between the Seine and the Rhine; Celtic Gaul between the Garonne and the Seine and extending east towards Switzerland and the Alps; Aquitaine, south of the Garonne (very limited Celtic population); and, lastly, what later became Narbonnaise, bordering on the Mediterranean, of mixed Celtic-Ligurian population. We may add Cisalpine Gaul, which is the plain of the Po (a Celtic name), whose population was both Celtic and Ligurian and where we find the very widespread Celtic name of Milan (Mediolanum — the place in the middle. Cf. Meslan, Meillan, Moliens, etc.)

6. For more details concerning the Cimbri and the Teutons, see J.M., op. cit., pp. 45—63 (the chapter specially devoted to them).

7. See J.M., op. cit., pp. 121—58, a critical account of these events.

8. For a detailed history of Britain, see J.M., op. cit., pp. 227-–83.

9. Cf. J.M., op. cit., pp. 203—26 (the chapter on "L'Eglise chrétienne celtique"; also the "classic" on this question, *Les Chrétientés celtiques*, by Dom Louis Gougaud (Paris 1911), and the recent work with the same title by Olivier Loyer (P.U.F., 1965).

10. For the history of the Gaels see J.M., op. cit., pp. 159—86 (chapter on this subject), and P. Rafroidi, J. Guiffan and J. Verriere, *L'Irlande* (Armand Colin, 1971).

11. It was the Scot James Macpherson who revived the Celtic tradition towards the end of the eighteenth century by composing Ossianic poems derived from songs of oral tradition. North-west Scotland and the Hebrides still preserve songs and very ancient music which help us to know the ancient Celtic music.

12. Eamon Kennedy, Irish Ambassador to Paris, in a radio interview with J.M. ("L'Impossible royaume d'Irlande", O.R.T.F., 1971).

13. As long as there is no all-out effort to kill off Breton language and culture — which has been the case up till now. Brittany's unique characteristics are entirely bound up with her bilingualism and her dual culture. There is freedom of thought in France provided one follows the Parisian model.

CHAPTER 2: THE JUDICIAL FRAMEWORK

1. The Irish laws were edited by O'Donovan (*Ancient Laws of Ireland*, 6 vols, Dublin 1865—1901). Consult W. Joyce, *Social History of Ancient Ireland* (2 vols. 1903), and Miles Dillon, *Early Irish Society* (Dublin, 1958). The Welsh laws were edited by Aneurin Owen in the nineteenth century (*Ancient Laws and Institution of Wales*). An English translation of these laws was published by Melville Richards (*The Laws of Hywel Dda*, Liverpool 1954). Breton law was studied by E. Durtelle de Saint-Saveur (*Histoire de Bretagne des origines à nos jours*, Rennes 1952—56). D'Arbois de Jubainville, in *Cours de littérature celtique*, vol. VII, brings the subject together in a way that is still valid.

2. There is an etymological similarity with the Irish *finn*, the Welsh *gwynn* and the Breton *guen* or *gwenn*, all meaning white or fair. The two derivations are not contradictory.

3. In royal families the right of succession disappeared at this point. It was only a *right* that was involved here, as kingship was acquired by election only.

4. Most heroes in Gaelic epics swore this oath: "By the god who judges my tribe!"

5. This statement is of basic importance for an understanding of the Celts' social system and hence their epic literature. See J.M., *L'Epopéc celtique d'Irlande*, Payot, Paris 1971, pp. 171—5.

6. This system has many points in common with the so-called "utopian" ideas of Babeuf, Proudhon and Charles Fourier. It is also comparable with the sharing of common property in France in 1792. But there is no more than a fleeting resemblance to the systems derived from Marxism-Leninism, based on both the division of labour and compulsory output.

7. Some contracts were made on solemn oath and thus guaranteed by divine powers. Those who did not fulfil the conditions of a contract were doomed to the vengeance of the gods.

8. "Women were by no means excluded from positions of authority." (Tacitus, *Agricola*, XVI.)

9. *Ancient Laws*, vol. 1, pp. 202—4. The text states "to give them to a husband" (*rod y wr*). The age at which boys became responsible for their actions, could own property, and were no longer subject to paternal correction was fourteen.

10. Expressions such as "hanging one's head", "lifting up one's head", and "holding one's head high" are interesting in this context. Apparently, Moslem women do not hesitate to lift up their skirts to cover their heads in the presence of a stranger, not caring about exposing their sexual parts. Shame is where society places it, and the example of *enebarz* shows that the Celts did not have the same idea of shame as Christian societies and those deriving from Christianity. A link with the symbolic emphasis placed on faces and names is also found in some traditions and in the old Celtic epics: knowing the face and name leads to mastery of a person, hence the use of masks and nicknames. In consummating a marriage, the bridegroom made himself master of his wife, therefore of her face, socially a much more important part of the body than the genitals, marriage being a social institution.

11. "Welsh law has escaped the influence of the Romans and the Church in the sphere of marriage more than in any other field." (J. Loth, *Mabinogion*, vol 2, p. 27.)

12. Especially in the case of adultery. Celtic laws were completely innocent of that masterpiece of the Romano-Napoleonic code which punished the unfaithful wife, while allowing the husband some diversion.

13. *De Bello Gallico*, V, 14. This polyandry is more in the nature of "collective marriage". Cf., Dio Cassius, LXII, 6; Strabo IV, 5; and St Jerome, *Adversus Jovianianum*, II, 7.

14. Quaintly enough, Philippe VI of Valois, King of France, supported the candidature of Charles de Blois, husband of Jeanne de Penthièvre, for the ducal throne, by invoking this Celtic principle. Jean de Montfort, who supported Breton independence, claimed this same throne by invoking the Salic law, which eliminated Jeanne de Penthièvre!

15. Matrilineal descent continued for a long time with some peoples, notably the Natchez of North America, who are famous thanks to Chateaubriand. The social structure of the Natchez "was based on a graduated caste system;

the aristocracy was divided into three classes, the Suns, the Nobles and the Honourables, while the people formed one undifferentiated class, called the Puants. Although the aristocrats had an obligation to marry into the people, their children inherited their mother' social class and forfeited their father's noble position". (Vincent Bounoure, *La Peinture américaine*, Editions Rencontre Lausanne 1967, p. 42.)

16. J.M., *Les Celtes*, pp. 215—17.
17. Cf. my study of St Bridget of Kildare in *Cahiers du pays de Baud*, no. 3, Baud (Morbihan) 1971.
18. J.M., *L'Épopée celtique d'Irlande*, pp. 88 and 141.
19. J.M., *L'Épopée celtique en Bretagne*, Payot, Paris 1971, p. 182. See also the education of the young Lancelot du Lac by the fairy Vivienne (the Lady of the Lake) in the *Romans de la Table Ronde*.
20. J.M., *L'Épopée celtique d'Irlande*, p. 110.
21. Some further details of Celtic laws relating to women. According to Irish Canon Law (chapter 17), daughters inherited as much from the father as sons did. If the father left only girls (chapter 20), they would inherit the lot, but when they died the father's brothers or other family would inherit and their own children had no rights. In accepting the inheritance (in fact it was merely a life-interest), they had to do military service, an obligation that was abolished at the end of the seventh century, when the inheritance was halved. According to the Civil Laws (Miles Dillon, *Relationship and the Law of Inheritance, Studies in Early Irish Laws*, Dublin- London 1936) a father who had sons lost his rights to the mother's inheritance, this being shared between the sons. A woman could transfer the ownership of land to her heirs only when this ownership had been acquired for services rendered, or as a gift. The son of the sister, adopted by the maternal (foster) uncle, was put on the same footing as the nephew, son of the brother (uncle). The sons of the sister were often considered the *glasfine* (grey or blue family); in fact, the father was considered a stranger arriving in Ireland by the grey or blue sea (*Ancient Laws of Ireland*, vol. 4, p. 284). This father therefore had no family in Ireland: he could not give a family to his son, who was considered part of the mother's family. Cartimandua, the daughter of a king of the Brigantes who had no sons, became queen by rights of paraphenalia. She married the great warrior Venutius, renounced him, and then married the knight Vellocatus and drew him into the royal circle. (Tacitus, *Histories*, III, 45; *Annals*, XII, 36- 40.)

PART II

CHAPTER 3: THE SUBMERGED PRINCESS

1. J. M., *Les Celtes*, pp. 19—43.
2. Esther Harding, *Woman's Mysteries*, Bantam, 1973.
3. The majority of modern sociologists, being men, are loth to admit the hypothesis, so brilliantly argued by Engels in *The Origin of the Family*, of predominantly female societies. Thus Lévi-Strauss, in *Elementary Structures of Kinship*, makes the peremptory and debatable assertion that "Authority, whether public or purely social, always belongs to men." It is, however, possible to envisage that some matriarchal-type societies were based on the moral authority of women, who would then have benefited from ideological power, if not the executive power held by men. But the

problem is far from being solved one way or the other, and will never be by arguments such as these.

4. Erich Neumann, *The Great Mother*, Routledge, 1955, pp. 39 and 42.
5. Cf. W. Lederer, *Gynophobia ou la Peur des Femmes*, Payot, Paris 1970, p. 39.
6. E. Harding, *Woman's Mysteries*, Bantam, 1973.
7. Otto Rank, *The Trauma of Birth*, Harper Row, 1973.
8. Ferenczi, *Thalassa, A Theory of Genitality*, Norton, 1968.
9. Ibid.
10. J. M., *L' Épopée celtique en Bretagne,* pp. 189—90.
11. Braunschweig-Fain, *Éros et Antéros*, Payot, Paris, p. 224.
12. Ferenczi, *Thalassa*.
13. Obviously Pomponius Mela just transposed an historical memory. The Druids had themselves buried on islands (a rite doubtless arising from the myth of the Island of Women), particularly the Île de Sein and the Isle of Mon (Anglesey), a well-known Druid sanctuary.
14. The monks of Glastonbury made this identification in the twelfth century to swell their coffers, partly because the rich then wanted to be buried there and partly because it attracted an influx of pilgrims. They even displayed King Arthur's tomb and spun a whole story about how it had been discovered.
15. J. M., *L'Épopée celtique d'Irlande*, pp. 43—55.

CHAPTER 4: OUR LADY OF THE NIGHT

1. J. Przyluski, *La Grande Déesse*, Payot, Paris, p. 24.
2. Translation in J. Loth, *Mabinogion*, vol. 1, pp. 81—171. Analysis in J. M., *L'Épopée celtique en Bretagne*, pp. 27—59.
3. In contrast to Jan de Vries' peremptory assertion in *La Religion des Celtes* (Payot, Paris, p. 133) rejecting the "infernal" quality of Epona without taking account of the role of Rhiannon, about whom he nevertheless says much that is relevant.
4. J. Zwicker, *Fontes, Historiae Religionis Celticae*, no. 64.
5. J. Gonda, *Les Religions de l'Inde*, Payot, Paris 1962, pp. 203—8.
6. J. M., *L'Épopée celtique d'Irlande*, Payot, Paris 1971, pp. 34—8.
7. J. Loth, *Mabinogion*, vol. 1, p. 179. The first term used in Welsh to denote the pig was *hob*, which has since disappeared and been replaced by *moch* (Breton *moc'h*, and Vannetese *moh*). One also finds *hwch*, "pig" (later "sow")(Breton *hoc'h*) and *twrch*, "wild boar", "wild sow" (Breton *tourc'h*, "boar", Vannetese *tourh*).
8. H. Zimmer, *Mythes et Symboles*, pp. 92 and 204. Published in English as *Myths and Symbols in Indian Art and Civilisation*, Oxford University Press, 1969.
9. H. Marcuse, *Eros and Civilisation*, Allen Lane, 1969, p. 154. My italics.
10. The cat was also used as a female animal of the Devil. Not only did it devour its own kittens, but it was also regarded as hypocritical and cunning, and its beauty and feline suppleness together with its supposed "cruelty" made it an ideal image of woman, both attractive and dangerous. The woman and the cat were always supposed to have been accomplices. The black cat is the pet animal of witches. Even female pubic hair is called "pussy"! The Egyptians had a cat goddess and there seem to be traces of a similar divinity among the

Celts, notably the cat Palu, born of Henwen and one of the three scourges of Britain. In *The Voyage of Maelduin*, the seamen reach a mysterious island on which stands a fortress where they find a display of riches and a meal prepared. The only living soul in the place is a cat, which leaps from one pillar to another. The seamen eat the food that seems to have been prepared especially for them, but when one of them tries to take a necklace, the cat hurls itself at him and reduces him to ashes before resuming its place on the pillar. This cat guarding a fortress of the Other World may be one aspect of the goddess of the Other World.

11. Roger-Henri Guerrand *La Libre maternité*, Casterman, 1971.
12. Drach, *De l'Harmonie de l'église et de la synagogue*, vol. 2, 1844, p. 48.
13. P.-M. Duval, *Les Dieux de la Gaule*, Paris 1957, p. 45.
14. W. Deonna, "Le Dieu galloromain à l'oreille animale", in *L'Antiquité classique*, vol. 25, 1956. Cf. *Gallia*, vol. 8, p. 95.
15. Cf. J. M., *L'Épopée celtique d'Irlande*, pp. 156–7.
16. Cf. Weisweiler, *Zeitschrift für celtische Philologie*, vol. 24, pp. 35–50, and *Heimat und Herrschaft*, p. 173.
17. Tamara Talbot Rice, *The Scythians*, Thames & Hudson, London 1958 (2nd edn), pp. 168 ff.
18. Leto was worshipped at Saint Gildas-de-Rhuys (Morbihan), which has been a sacred place since earliest antiquity. Cf. the *Catalogue of the Museum at Carnac*, pp. 88–9.
19. Cf. J. de Vries, *La Religion des Celtes*, pp. 181–2. It is difficult to say anything concrete about a goddess associated with the cow or bull. There are certainly traces of bull worship in the great epic of the *Tain Bo Cualnge*, and generally throughout the Ulster cycle, but such worship appears to be totally masculine and Indo-European. We can, however, point to the fact that the goddess Morrigane appears to Cú Chulainn in the form of a cow, and that many Irish and Welsh stories describe enchanted cows that have risen from the Other World and symbolise its wealth and fertility, though, like the *tarvos trigarannos* of the Cluny Museum, these cows are linked with bird-women. There is also, in Ireland, a fairy called Boyne ("White Cow"), who gave her name to the river Boyne.
20. *Revue Savoisienne*, 15th November 1867; *Revue Archéologique*, July 1868.
21. D'Arbois de Jubainville, *Tain Bo Cualnge*, pp. 126–7.
22. *Celticum*, vol. 7, p. 499. This is a fairly recent version of the legend from a sixteenth-century manuscript. In the twelth-century version from the Book of Leinster, all the author says is that, after the death of Cú Chulainn, "the birds came onto his shoulder" (G. Dottin, *L'Épopée irlandaise*, p. 156).
23. J. M., *L'Épopée celtique d'Irlande*, p. 54.

CHAPTER 5: THE GREAT QUEEN

1. J. M., *L'Épopée celtique d'Irlande*, p. 91.
2. B. Malinowski, *Sex and Repression in Savage Society*, Routledge, London 1927. My italics. What Malinowski is discussing is myth, rather than practical belief.
3. The name is sometimes wrongly spelt Llew Llaw Gyffes ("the lion with the sure hand"), which is not consistent with the old spelling. The name *Lleu* is an ancient word, comparable to the Irish *lu*, "small", which seems more

likely as the Irish *u* is always rendered as *eu* in Welsh (e.g. *cru*, "blood", becomes *creu*).

4. The character of Deirdre (who appears in Irish legend) corresponds, at least initially, with this definition. Conchobar, King of Ulster, reserved the young Deirdre exclusively for himself and had her brought up far away from men, under the care of devoted women. Cf. J. M., *L'Épopée celtique d'Irlande*, p. 65.

5. For everything concerning the *Vita Merlini* and the original legend of Merlin, cf. J. M., *L'Epopée celtique en Bretagne*, pp. 109—31.

6. The Gospel of the Egyptians, quoted by C. R. S. Mead in *Thrice Greatest Hermes*, vol. 1, p. 153.

7. Braunschweig-Fain, *Éros et Antéros*, p. 42. My italics.

8. Ibid., p. 104.

9. Ibid., p. 105.

10 Ibid., p. 105.

CHAPTER 6: THE REBELLION OF THE FLOWER-DAUGHTER

1. Herbert Marcuse, *Eros and Civilisation*, p. 154.

2. O. Rank, *The Trauma of Birth*, Harper Row, 1973.

3. Compare the poem attributed to Taliesin, *Cad Goddeu* ("Fight of the Trees"), a mixture of several original texts: "When I came to life my creator fashioned me through the fruit of fruits, the fruit of the primordial god, the primroses and the flowers of the hill, the flowers of the trees and bushes, the earth and the earthly course. I was fashioned through the flowers of the nettle, the water of the ninth wave. I bear the mark of Math, having to become immortal, I bear the mark of Gwyddyon, the great purifier of the Britons, of Eurwys and Euron, or Euron and Modron, of five times five masters of knowledge, of the wise children of Math." (J. M., *Les Celtes*, pp. 366—7.)

4. Gronw Pebyr can be translated as "strong young man". The character appears to be mentioned in the *Cad Goddeu* ("They were not yet born in the abyss, those who visited me, except Goronwy of the meadows of Edrywy"), though in an entirely different context.

5. There is an evocation of this legend in a chant entitled *Achau y Dylluan* ("Genealogy of the Owl") by Dafydd ab Gwilym, a fourteenth-century Welsh poet. When asked its name, the owl replies that it is called Blodeuwedd and was daughter of a Lord of Anglesey (i.e. Gwyddyon). And when the poet asks who transformed her into a bird, she replies, "It was Gwyddyon, son of Don, from the region of Conwy, who with his magic wand — there is none like it — made me leave my beauty for the sad state in which you see me, accusing me of having loved Goronwy, the blazing sun of a brilliant race, the sturdy young man, the Lord of Penllyn, the handsome, the great." (J. Loth, *Mabinogion*, vol. 1, p. 208.)

6. Braunschweig-Fain. *Éros et Antéros*, p. 107.

7. Ibid., pp. 107—8.

8. Ibid., p. 109.

9. Cf. J. M., *L'Épopée celtique en Bretagne*, pp. 111 and 117.

10. Cf. the commentary on *The Education of Cú Chulainn* in J. M., *L'Épopée celtique d'Irlande*, pp. 88—95.

11. Cf. *The Death of Fergus*, in J. M., *L'Épopée celtique d'Irlande*, pp. 73—4.
12. For a fuller description of the Phibionites and the Manichaean syllogism, cf. Fendt, *Die Gnostischen Mysterien*, Munich, 1922.

CHAPTER 7: THE GRAIL, OR THE QUEST FOR WOMAN

1. J. M., *L'Épopée celtique en Bretagne*, pp. 208—9.
2. *The Legend of Sir Gawain*, 1897; *The Legend of Sir Lancelot du Lac*, 1901; *The Legend of Sir Perceval*, 1906; *From Ritual to Romance*, 1915.
3. *The Battle of Mag Tuireadh*, trans. G. Dottin, in *L'Épopée irlandaise*, p. 37.
4. *The Death of the Children of Tuirenn. Ogam*, vol. 16, p. 244.
5. R. A. S. Macalister, *Book of Conquests*, poem 66.
6. Dottin, *L'Épopée irlandaise*, pp. 72—3.
7. *Ogam*, vol. 10 pp. 371—80.
8. J. Loth, *Mabinogion*, vol. 1, pp. 297—9. J. M., *L'Épopée celtique en Bretagne*, p. 144.
9. *Mabinogion*, vol. 2, p. 119.
10. Cf. everything concerning the tradition of severed heads in J. M., *Les Celtes*, pp. 91—119 (the chapter on "Delphes et l'aventure celtique") Here we refer only to details relevant to the Grail.
11. *Perlesvaux*, ed. Nitze, lines 6600 ff.
12. Ibid., lines 6685 ff.
13. An act dating from the fifteenth century and preserved in the Bibliothèque Nationale de Paris (fonds latin no 9093) concerns the supposed relations between St Patern and King Caradoc, *cognomento* Brech-Brass.
14. *The Birth of Conchobar. Ogam*, vol. 11, p. 61. Cf. a study of "The Bloody Branch of the king of Ulster" in *Ogam*, vol. 10, pp. 139 ff.
15. In the tale of *The Death of Cú Chulainn* in the Book of Leinster (see *Ogam*, vol. 18, p. 352) Conall avenges Cú Chulainn by killing his murderer Lugaid, places his head on a stone and forgets it. Coming back to look for it, he notices that "the head had melted the stone and passed through it". In the Edinburgh version of the same tale, Conall avoids this by lining up the heads he has cut off, including Lugaid's, on a branch.
16. Hence his nickname of Conall "the Cross-eyed". All the women who loved Conall began to squint, just as those who loved Cú Chulainn became one-eyed and those who loved Cuscraid started stammering. The "infirmities" of Conall and Cú Chulainn go back to some ancient legend, traces of which can be found in Greek, Celtic, Germanic and even Roman mythologies. So, Vulcan is lame like the Fisher-King, Nuada is one armed like Tyr, Wotan and Horatius Cocles are one-eyed like Cú Chulainn.
17. A practice confirmed by literature and archaeology. There have been finds, especially in Ireland and Scotland, of balls made out of carved, hard stone or dried clay and intended for slings.
18. J. Loth, *Mabinogion*, vol. 2, p. 92. Compare the following Ethiopian tradition described in Solinus (*Polyhistoria*, XXXI): "One can draw the stone called *dracontias* from the brain of a living dragon, for if the serpent knows it is dying the stone loses all its properties and consistency. . . . These serpents lie in wait for their prey in caves and holes. The boldest men, who ride there in speedy chariots, scatter soporific mixtures and cut off the head

of the sleeping dragon. Then, as a reward for their daring, they carry away the stone."

19. J. Loth, *Mabinogion*, vol. 2, pp. 94—5.
20. *The Prophetic Ecstasy of the Phantom*. Miles Dillon, *The Cycle of the Kings*, p. 12.
21. Per-Jakez Melias, *Le Pays Bigouden*, Brest 1971, p. 42. The original runs, "Il y avait une fois et une fois il n'y avait pas et cette fois là il y avait quand même. . . .".
22. "Le Graal dans l'ethnographie", in *Lumière de Graal*, a special edition of the *Cahiers du Sud*, 1951, pp. 13—36. ₁
23. "Pour lire les Troubadours", *Cahiers du Sud*, no. 372, pp. 163—94.
24. Ed. M. Thomson, 1931.

CHAPTER 8: ISEULT, OR THE LADY OF THE ORCHARD

1. J. Gracq, *Le Rivage des Syrtes*, Corti, 1951, pp. 55—6.
2. The first and best known version is that of Joseph Bedier (Piazza, 1922), but, though its beauty is incomparable, it makes too much use of the amorous casuistry found in the courtly version. Far better is the adaptation by André Mary (*Tristan*, Gallimard, 1941), which preserves a number of details from many different versions of the legend.

   Chief texts. So-called "common" version: fragment by the French author Béroul (middle of the legend), dating from 1165 (published by Muret, 1913); German adaptation by Eilhart von Oberg (including the beginning of the legend). So-called "courtly" version: fragment by Thomas of Erceldoune (end of legend), dating from 1170 (published by Bedier in 1902—5); German adaptation by Gottfried von Strassburg (beginning and middle of legend, breaking off more or less where Thomas begins); abridged Danish version (*Tristan Saga*) written by Brother Robert in 1226; English adaptation (*Sir Tristrem*) and Italian adaptation (*Tavola Ritonda*). Episodic poems of the twelfth century: the two *Folie Tristan*, and the *Lai du Chevrefeuille* by Marie de France. Later adaptations: *Tristan en prose* (thirteenth century), and the *Morte d'Arthur* by Thomas Malory (fifteenth century).
3. It has become common to assume that there is some Greek influence here, as this episode is so close to the legend of the Minotaur, who also claimed a tribute of young men and women. But there is a similar theme in Irish epic literature in *The Courtship of Emer*, where Cú Chulainn saves a king's daughter who has been promised as a tribute to one of the Fomors, a mythical marine race who supposedly invaded Ireland before being hounded out by the Tuatha Dé Danann, the builders of megaliths and introducers of Druidic magic. The Morholt and the Minotaur are probably both products of old Indo-European mythology, and are two aspects of the same theme (rivalry between a marine race and earthbound peoples).
4. A frequent theme in Celtic mythlogy: the hero lets himself be carried by the waves and the winds in a rudderless boat. King Conn of a Hundred Battles and then his son, Art, also entrust their fate to a boat sailing at random over the sea, and this takes them to an island ruled by a benevolent fairy. The "boat of Salomon", which takes heroes to the Grail, is also pilotless, and doubtless belongs to the same tradition as the mysterious voyage of souls

described in Procopius (*De Bello Gothico*). This voyage, in rudderless boats, ends in the "Island of Britons".

5. Obviously the swallow is Iseult, who, since she is in love with Tristan, comes to hover round him (the bird-woman being a common theme in Celtic mythology). The Queen of Ireland, who has taught Iseult her magic, is very likely a historical transposition of Morgan, Queen of the Isle of Fairies, who could also change herself into a bird. Tristan's recognition of Iseult's hair is evidence of his subconscious interest in her.

6. Brangwain may well be, as Joseph Loth suggests, the Welsh heroine Branwen, sister of Bran the Blessed. She would thus be a kind of love goddess, a role she clearly adopts in the legend of Tristan as trustee of the philtre.

7. This forest is equivalent to the orchard, and is a feminine, maternal symbol. In Gottfried von Strassburg's German version, the lovers take refuge, not in the forest, but in an underground cave the ceiling of which is made of precious stones and in the middle of which there stands a bed of crystal. This is obviously the *chamber of love*, and symbolically the essence of the female sex; in it Tristan and Iseult recapture the earlier state of paradise, actually re-creating the intra-uterine life. As Denis de Rougemont says in *Passion and Society* (p. 133), this cave of love, the *Minnegrotte*, "is pictured as a church. . . . But instead of an altar there is a bed. The bed is consecrated to the goddess Minne as the Catholic altar to Christ, and on the bed the courtly sacrament takes place: the two lovers 'communicate in passion'." We should perhaps qualify de Rougemont's interpretation by saying that the erotico-religious ritual performed by the lovers has less to do with courtly love than with the very intense and instinctive desire to rediscover the intra-uterine condition, for Diarmaid and Grainne also take refuge in a cave, and the Irish text is free of any courtly influence.

8. This exchange of swords seems proof in the French texts of Mark's affection for the two lovers, despite his fits of anger. But in the fragment of Welsh epic (*Revue celtique*, vol. 34, pp. 358 ff) that gives the original ending of the legend, the real and much more authentically Celtic and ancient reason for Mark's alleged forgiveness is that "whoever drew his [Tristan's] blood would die, and whomever he drew blood from would also die". So if Mark had struck the sleeping Tristan he would be bound to die himself. The exchange of swords is a recognition of his impotence and also an invitation to exchange the queen, for, weapons being personal to their owners, Tristan will wish to recover his sword and have to offer Iseult in exchange.

9. Here the various versions differ. For Béroul and the "common" tradition, the effect of the love potion has a limited life. Three years to the day after drinking it, Tristan and Iseult come to their senses and no longer love each other; so it is normal, rational and morally gratifying that the queen be returned to her husband. The "courtly" tradition makes the effect of the love potion unlimited, which is more consistent with the eternal obligation of the *geis* in the Irish archetype. In the Welsh version, King Mark, unable to act against Tristan himself, seeks the arbitration of King Arthur, who decides that Mark and Tristan should share Iseult, each having her for half the year. As Mark chooses the season when there are no leaves on the trees, Iseult joyfully declares that she will always belong to Tristan, because the "holly, ivy and cypress" keep their leaves throughout the year. Denis de Rougemont suggests that the original version is Béroul's, because the effect

of the love potion is limited. On the other hand "Thomas, a sensitive psychologist and highly suspicious of marvels, which he considers crude, minimises the importance of the love potion as far as possible and depicts the love of Tristan and Iseult as having occurred spontaneously. Its first signs he places as early as the episode of the bath" (when Iseult recognised Tristan as the murderer of the Morholt) (*Passion and Society*, p. 28). But de Rougemont believed that the Celtic legends were influenced by the epic element, and that the internal tragedy was most evident in courtly romances. In this, he mistakenly disregarded the theme of the love potion as a degenerate rationalisation of the *geis*. The original legend is better represented in Thomas, even if he mixes courtly considerations with the myth.

10. In the Welsh Triads there are two "Essyllts" (the Welsh version of Iseult, from which the French "Yseult" probably came). The first is Essyllt *Fyngwen* (a mutation of *Myngwen*), which means "with white or blonde tresses"; she is mistress of Drystan and must be Iseult the Fair. The second is Essyllt *Vinwen* (mutation of *Minwen*), which means "of the white lips" and was probably mistranslated as "white hands", since *min* was pronounced *main* (French "hand") and *wen* was usually rendered as "white". This would seem to suggest that the legend developed in Wales, if it did not originate there.

11. In Thomas's romance the way in which Kaherdin learns that his sister's marriage to Tristan has not been consummated is very similar to the episode in the Irish story of Diarmaid and Grainne. In both cases the woman is out walking with the man when mud splashes up on her thighs and she exclaims that the mud has been bolder than her lover.

12. The fact that Tristan's returns to Iseult the Fair become a vital necessity, for which he is prepared to brave the whole world, is not so much a sign of the nature of fate but of magic obligations. As Iseult represents the sun, Tristan needs her in order to recover his strength, because contact with her is essential for his life.

13. This episode, notable for its poetic beauty, exists only in *La Folie Tristan* (Oxford MSS), and indicates the solar symbolism of Iseult. The theme of the crystal chamber, where the mysterious fusion of beings takes place under the re-creative rays of the sun, is a Celtic one. So, in *The Courtship of Etaine* the heroine, who has been turned into an insect by a witch, is taken by the god Oengus into his "chamber of sun" to cheer and revive her. Art in *The Adventures of Art, Son of Conn* is received by the queen of the mysterious isle in "her crystal chamber so lovely to behold, with its crystal doors and inexhaustible vats, which, though never filled, were always full". Similarly, the archetype of Iseult tells how she fell in love with Diarmaid: "In my chamber with its lovely view, through my windows of blue glass, I saw and wondered at you. I turned the light of my eyes on you that day and since then I have never given my love to any other and I never shall."

   The fairy Vivienne shuts Merlin in a castle of air or glass, and, throughout the British tradition, the Other World is frequently referred to as Kaer Wydr (Castrum Vitreum). The crystal chamber to which Tristan wishes to take Iseult is clearly an image of paradise.

14. The castle is in Thomas's version; others have a grotto guarded by the giant Beliagog, whom Tristan has conquered in single combat and who has sworn loyalty to him. Unlike the heavenly, solar paradise of the crystal chamber,

the Hall or Grotto of Images, in which Tristan tries to create the original situation on his own, is a kind of transitory paradise, terrestial and imprisoned in matter. There is also a hall of images in the story of Launcelot. When imprisoned by Morgan, he paints on the wall of his room his memories of his affair with Guinevere (*La Mort le roi Artu*).

15. Here Thomas interpolates an interesting comment on sources of the legend, accusing certain authors of having invented the end of the story: "Here they leave *Breri*, who records the deeds and tales of all the kings and counts who lived in Brittany", though whether he meant Britain or Brittany we have no way of knowing. It seems certain that Breri, who is frequently referred to in the various texts, though under different names (for instance, Bleri, Bledri, Bledhri and Bledherious), was a real person. Giraldus Cambrensis calls him "ille famosus fabulator" and there is every reason to suppose that he passed on tales to French authors, showing that there existed a Welsh Arthurian tradition before that of Thomas and Chrétien.

16. The way in which the Dwarf had compelled him to go was typically Celtic: following a practice of which there are plenty of examples in Irish epics, he made a play on the hero's nickname, Tristan "the Man in Love". As such, Tristan should be ready to help all men in love, or else contradict his name and be dishonoured. It was a real Druidic *satire*, and Tristan had no alternative but to obey.

17. This was the third time Tristan was wounded during his life, and the number three is obviously symbolic. On all three occasions he killed whoever wounded him, and his injury was always venomous, in some way magical, and had to be cured by a fairy or magician. Returning home as best he could, he realised that the doctors could do nothing for him, as his wound was becoming increasingly infected.

18. The delays in Iseult's voyage are linked to the ancient myth of the sun, delayed by the night (possibly represented here by the black sail), which is consistent with the idea of Iseult as the sun.

19. This last detail appears only in the prose versions of Tristan, but it does occur in the old Irish text, *The Story of Baile of the Sweet Speech*, in which the lovers were also reunited in death and buried in two graves, from one growing a yew, from the other an apple-tree. Later both trees were cut down and made into two tables, which, when they touched, "joined together as the honeysuckle twines round a branch, and became inseparable" (Dottin, *L'Épopée irlandaise*, p. 186).

20. This legend has come down to us in its entirety only through oral versions collected in the eighteenth century. But the antiquity of the myth is confirmed by fragments that have been preserved in the oldest manuscripts. See G. Dottin, *L'Épopée irlandaise*, p. 160; *Revue celtique*, vol. 33, p. 52, and vol. 30, p. 168; and, for the complete oral version, Cross and Slover, *Ancient Irish Tales*, p. 370. In *L'Épopée celtique d'Irlande* (pp. 153—64), I have tried to make a summarised reconstruction of it from the whole collection of texts. It is an epic tale from the cycle of Finn, or of the Fiana, or of Leinster, which bears a deep imprint of Gaelic mythology and was soon adopted in Scotland, where local folklore retained many traces of it (it was used later by MacPherson in his Ossianic poems). But, apart from the mythological element, it contains historical traces referring to the existence of a warrior militia, the Fiana, in the second and third centuries A.D. The earliest forms of the epics in this cycle could, possibly, date from then, even

if they were later reintegrated into other traditions. In any case, this legend is certainly older than that of Tristan, and the authors of the early versions of the Tristan story (perhaps including Breri) were quite familiar with it.

21. Just as Tristan, Mark's nephew, goes to find Iseult in Ireland and succeeds in the challenge of the crested snake.

22. The eighteenth-century oral version places the beginning of the drama at the wedding feast, when the marriage of Finn and Grainne had not been consummated, thereby giving Grainne a kind of moral justification. But the oldest version, preserved in *The Yellow Book of Lecan*, places the feast a long time after the marriage, when Gráinne is already a prey to hatred and despair.

23. This provides the authors of Tristan with the theme of the magic potion, which here merely sends the guests to sleep; the maid and the cup become Brangwain and the silver goblet.

24 Diarmaid is distantly related to Finn, and foster-son of the famous Oengus mac On, one of the Tuatha Dé Danann. In some stories a fairy gives him a grain of beauty, which makes him irresistible to women.

25. Iseult loved Tristan from the time of his first visit to Ireland, when, under the name of Tantris, he was cured by her and taught her to sing and play the harp.

26. Similarly in Béroul's *Tristan*, God is continually protecting the lovers as if they were not guilty.

27. It can hardly be a coincidence that Thomas's *Tristan* has a similar anecdote, the sole difference being that Kaherdin is walking with his sister Iseult of the White Hands and so learns that her marriage with Tristan has not been consummated.

28. Another version has Diarmaid imprisoning Oisin in the grotto. Oisin then cut shavings of wood and threw them into the stream to show Finn where he was being held. The shavings or refuse in the water of the stream forms yet another theme in common between the legends of Diarmaid and Tristan, who throws shavings into the stream to summon Iseult.

29. There is a similar episode in Béroul's *Tristan*. When the lovers hid in the forest of Morois, Tristan's hound Husdent found his master's scent and made the woods echo to his howling. Tristan wondered whether to kill the animal that threatened to betray them, but, on Iseult's advice, trained Husdent to hunt without baying.

30 His death is similar to Tristan's. Diarmaid was compelled by the *geis* to join the hunt, against his wishes, and was the victim of a venomous wound. Tristan, too, was the victim of a venomous wound, received during the course of a war he had been compelled to join by a threat to his honour (therefore also a *geis*) from Tristan the Dwarf. For both Diarmaid and Tristan, healing arrives too late. Yet Finn, like Iseult, had the power to cure, and his ill-will is a counterpart to the storm and calm that delay Iseult's arrival until too late.

31. This obviously comes closest to the story of Tristan and is most consistent with the logic of the legend. For Grainne has clearly demonstrated her love for Diarmaid — to the extent of renouncing power, wealth and a quiet life for him — and therefore her hatred of Finn, with whom she could never have been reconciled.

32. For the impressive list of *geisa* imposed on Conaire, see J.M., *L'Épopée celtique d'Irlande*, p. 177. See also ibid., pp. 131—7 for *The Death of Cú Chulainn*.

33. J.M., *L'Épopée celtique d'Irlande*, p. 92.
34. Ibid., pp. 122—8.
35. Ibid., pp. 106—8.
36. J. Loth, *Mabinogion*, vol. 2, pp. 104—5.
37. Ibid., vol. 2, pp. 114—17.
38. Ibid., vol. 2, pp. 19—20.
39. P. Sébillot, *Le Paganisme contemporain chez les peuples celto-latins*, O. Doin, Paris 1908, p. 103.
40. Ibid., p. 95.
41. Ibid., p. 96.
42. Ibid., p. 97.
43. Ibid., p. 98.
44. Ibid., p. 99.
45. Ibid., pp. 108—9.
46. Braunschweig-Fain, *Éros et Antéros* Payot, Paris, pp. 103—4.
47. Ibid., p. 244.
48. Ibid., p. 241.

PART III

1. *Elementary Structures of Kinship*, Tavistock Publications, London 1970.

CHAPTER 9: WOMEN IN SOCIAL LIFE

1. *Lectures pour tous*, no. 210, July 1971, p. 159.
2. A woman reader of *Lectures pour tous*.

CHAPTER 10: MARRIAGE

1. *L'Attraction passionnée*, J.-J. Pauvert, Paris 1967.
2. *Elementary Structures of Kinship*.
3. Published by Simone Debout, edited: J. J. Pauvert.
4. This was the indo-European *gens*, which consisted of customers, allies, slaves and servants as well as the members of the family. This type persisted for a long time in agricultural districts where a large number of workers were needed around the family lands. Mechanisation and the transformation of agriclture into an industry have dealt the death blow to this institution. It does not work in present economic conditions. The laws of sociology are like the laws of nature: anything no longer useful, or perhaps even harmful, destroys itself. Present social and economic structures are such that each member of the family is forced to work elsewhere, sometimes in another country, his business taking him daily further from his original environment; his training may separate him from the group. This is one of the consequences of the division of labour and specialisation. Each member of the original group tries to reconstruct a new family unit on his own, but a unit based solely on the couple is necessarily limited, and, when it reaches a certain stage, the problems arise again and are solved by a further splitting up. There is a parallel in the situation of the Christian parish, which was originally a community based on the families of one village. Hence the decline in village life in some districts.

5. It is obvious that a couple stands a greater chance of breaking up when the husband and wife are each separately in contact with people with whom they may fall in love. But this is an emotional or sexual problem. More important is the cultural factor (taking the word "culture" in its widest sense); for the contacts a husband and wife have in their jobs may influence their own attitudes profoundly, and lead to intellectual, psychological, and even political divergence. This highlights the seriousness of the situation of the couple in a rapidly changing society that has not yet found its new norms. There has been too much emphasis on the moral break-up of the family and not enough account taken óf the basic problem. An ethic can be defined only on the basis of social and economic realities.

6. Experiments in this direction are not so much for women's benefit as for directing them into an economic system based on the repression of instincts. The kolkhozes, the Chinese communes, and the Israeli kibbutzim exist in temporary situations of supposed combat; hence no valid conclusions can be drawn.

7. Sometimes the lady granted kisses, caresses, and the sight of her naked body. So she did not overlook the carnal aspect of the bonds uniting her with her knight, even though she would not go beyond a certain point. "Indeed, this 'pure' love was sometimes more brazen, but it excluded the act, to which, in the Middle Ages, a certain importance was attached because of the hereditary transmission of vices and virtues. But the 'caresses and the kisses' had none of these dangers. That is why husbands as a rule allowed their wives to put themselves to the test" (René Nelli, "Sur l'amour provencal", *Cahiers du Sud*, no. 347, p. 37). At the time when Christianity was trying to subdue the knights and make them less bellicose, the Church adopted courtly love in order to "soften" them, making it extremely spiritual. "Make love not war" was not a twentieth-century invention.

8. We say "in theory" advisedly. For there are many married couples who love one another truly and sincerely. They have been able to go beyond the legal situation and achieve a personal growth. In such cases there is no incompatibility between marriage and love.

CHAPTER 11: SEXUAL LIBERATION

1. For example commercialised eroticism and pornography. This is a false revolution, and the element of guilt is strengthened.

2. Julius Evola, *Métaphysique du sexe*, Payot, Paris 1959, p. 372.

3. All knowledge comes from the interaction of the sensory organs with the outside world. Condillac and all the eighteenth-century philosophers maintained this, while, in Jean-Jacques Rousseau's *Émile*, the senses are used as the basis for all education. This is corroborated by the discoveries of modern science.

4. Author of a book entitled *La Lumière du sexe* (Paris 1932), a ritual of initiation into Satanism.

5. A manuscript that Julius Evola states he had no opportunity of consulting. Crowley died in 1947 and had had a fairly disturbed life. He deliberately posed as a "satanic" visionary, even believed in something called the "Great Beast 666". Was he sincere? Did he use men's credulity for his own ends? It does not matter, for his work demonstrates a trend.

6. Julius Evola, op. cit. p. 362.
7. In Britain in 1971, a sex education film supported by university and religious authorities dealt with masturbation. It contained a sequence in which a young and desirable teacher was seen masturbating while the commentary stated, "There is nothing shameful about the sexual instinct and nothing wrong with so-called solitary pleasure." In another sequence, two naked children were seen in the same situation. The film caused a scandal and the teacher was dismissed. But the important point is that the film was made, shown, and in the end won the approval not only of a wide public, but also of important civil and religious figures.
8. Roxanne Dunbar, founder of Cell 16 of Boston.
9. Ti-Grace Atkinson, member of the Radical Feminists.
10. Masters and Johnson, *Human Sexual Response*, Churchill, 1966.
11. One of the purposes of male circumcision was to prevent masturbation. In France and Britain, around the year 1900, religious and medical authorities preached clitorectomy on the grounds that the clitoris was the great disturber of women's balance of mind.
12. The social conditions in which Lesbian relationships are formed are guilt-ridden and secretive. Most cases that come to the attention of psychoanalysts and sexologists are therefore unbalanced, sometimes tragic. This is not because Lesbianism is a disease, but because it cannot be practised freely, away from any social or moral restraint. Thus there are bound to be traumas. When homosexuality is recognised as perfectly valid (not only by the law but also by society in general) there will be fewer Lesbians suffering from pathological problems.
13. Simone de Beauvoir, in *Le Nouvel observateur*, no. 379, 1972, p. 49.
14. Among the girls who take part in Tantrist practices, menstruation seems to disappear eventually. This tends to show that sexual activity can achieve a harmonious balance in pure eroticism, unrelated to procreation.
15. Among the Celts the concept of female divinity included the idea of power and sovereignty, and the royal woman, the "royal whore", is a kind of erotic priestess who, by sharing her sexuality with her lovers, brings riches and power, prosperity and happiness.
16. In Scandinavia, where commercial pornography is allowed (though at the back of this there is clearly a more liberal attitude to morals), sexual crimes have already decreased.
17. Wilhelm Reich, *The Sexual Revolution*, Vision Press, 1969.

CHAPTER 12: LOVE

1. Preface to the *Anthologie de l'amour sublime*, Albin Michel, 1956.
2. In fact this was not her fault. The subjects of Pwyll (who stand for the patriarchal society) demanded an heir for the king in order to ensure a stable future for their society which was threatened by the presence of Rhiannon (who represents the ancient gynaecocratic structure).
3. Greater than Iseult had for King Mark, for whom she felt a mere respect; and unlike Grainne, who hated Finn.
4. "Polygons have the virtue of creating one or several pivots of love. I use this word to mean an attachment that can survive the storms of inconstancy. A polygon, although he often changes mistresses, alternately loving several

women at once, then one exclusively, also retains an ardent passion for some pivotal woman to whom he returns from time to time. She is a lover of permanent attraction, whom he loves even during the fiercest of his passions. . . . This love is for him a bond of a higher order, a focal point related to the other loves as white is related to the seven colours of the rainbow" (Charles-Louis Fourier, *Le Nouveau monde amoureux*).

No man has ever stated the problem of fidelity in love more clearly. But our education gives us no preparation at all for this conception, which is extremely dangerous to existing social institutions: these serve the capitalist patriarchy, whose gain depends on sexual and emotional lack of satisfaction. Women's present unliberated position is obviously destroyed by this concept of absolute love centred on a chosen person, but nevertheless allowing the individual to enter fully into a variable chain of emotional or sexual ties. These would undermine a family structure based, at present, on anxiety, fear of tomorrow, the necessity to feed the children, and so on.

5. This detail reflects the struggle between Christianity and Druidism in the Ireland of the early Middle Ages. The legend of Suibhne, apart from its historical context, relates both to the theme of the *geis* and the theme of the madman of the woods, which was well known through the story of Merlin (cf. J.M., *L'Épopée celtique en Bretagne*, pp. 109—28).

6. *Baile Suibhne*, MSS. of the seventeenth century with English translation by O'Keeffe, in *Irish Texts Society*, vol. 12, 1910.

7. Book of Leinster, twelfth-century MSS. G. Dottin, *L'Épopée irlandaise*, pp. 81—2.

8. Thomas, *Tristan*, line 3112.

9. *The Yellow Book of Lecan. Revue celtique*, vol 23, p. 396.

10. *Cú Chulainn.*

11. *The Sickness of Cú Chulainn*. G. Dottin, *L'Épopée irlandaise*, pp. 142—3.

12. *Duanaire Finn*, edited and translated into English by Eoin MacNeill, 1908.

13. Prophesy by Cathbad concerning Deirdre in *The Exile of the Sons of Usnech*.

14. "Ar more-verc'h koant, hen draitourez, / hanter-besk hag hantervaouex, / a kana flour d'ar verdaidi, / da lakaat brevi o listri." Prosper Proux (1812—1873).

Index

Legends are shown in italics with the symbol (L) following the title.